MW00561133

George Merrick, Son of the South Wind

UNIVERSITY PRESS OF FLORIDA

Florida A&M University, Tallahassee
Florida Atlantic University, Boca Raton
Florida Gulf Coast University, Ft. Myers
Florida International University, Miami
Florida State University, Tallahassee
New College of Florida, Sarasota
University of Central Florida, Orlando
University of Florida, Gainesville
University of North Florida, Jacksonville
University of South Florida, Tampa
University of West Florida, Pensacola

Song of the Wind, painting by Denman Fink for George Merrick's book of poetry.

George Merrick,
Son of the South Wind

Visionary Creator of Coral Gables

 ARVA MOORE PARKS

University Press of Florida

Gainesville · Tallahassee · Tampa · Boca Raton

Pensacola · Orlando · Miami · Jacksonville · Ft. Myers · Sarasota

VIVA FLORIDA 500
1513-2013

A FLORIDA QUINCENTENNIAL BOOK

Copyright 2015 by Arva Moore Parks
All rights reserved
Printed in the United States of America. This book is printed on paper certified under the standards
of the Forestry Stewardship Council (FSC). It is a recycled stock that contains 30 percent post-
consumer waste and is acid free.

This book may be available in an electronic edition.

20 19 18 17 16 15   6 5 4 3 2 1

Library of Congress Control Number: 2015938077
ISBN 978-0-8130-6151-1

The University Press of Florida is the scholarly publishing agency for the State University System
of Florida, comprising Florida A&M University, Florida Atlantic University, Florida Gulf Coast
University, Florida International University, Florida State University, New College of Florida,
University of Central Florida, University of Florida, University of North Florida, University of South
Florida, and University of West Florida.

University Press of Florida
15 Northwest 15th Street
Gainesville, FL 32611-2079
http://www.upf.com

For Mildred Heath Merrick and Robert H. McCabe

George Edgar Merrick, 1925. Courtesy of Mildred Merrick.

What manner of man is this George E. Merrick? . . . Dreamer? Yes, and more—a dreamer with the faculty for surrounding himself with men to translate his dreams into practicality, into buildings and lakes and waterways, and beautiful landscapes, into flowers and shrubs and homes, and into churches and schools and institutions of learning, and beaches and playgrounds and cities! . . . Writer, poet, dreamer, philosopher, lover of all things beautiful, creator, thinker, kindly, courteous, good natured, gregarious human man—all of these can be applied to George Merrick.

Vernon Knowles, "An Impression of George E. Merrick," *Miami Daily Tribune*, June 3, 1925

CORAL GABLES
Miami Riviera
40 Miles of Water Front
GEORGE E. MERRICK

Charles S. Chapman

City of Coral Gables advertisement, *Forbes* magazine, 1926. Author's collection.

Contents

In 2006, the Coral Gables Garden Club commissioned a statue of George E. Merrick in front of Coral Gables City Hall. Author's collection.

Figures

Drawing of George and Eunice Merrick's home on South Greenway Drive, Coral Gables. Author's collection.

Preface

When I moved into a historic Coral Gables home in 1970, I never dreamed that someday I would write a biography of George Merrick, the city's founder. Many thought the purchase was a mistake. By this time, the city had lost much of its historic ambience and George Merrick was largely forgotten. The home, which I later learned was designed by Walter DeGarmo, one of Coral Gables' most vaunted architects, was a bargain because it was rundown and in what was then considered a declining neighborhood. The move opened my eyes to what was around me and marked the beginning of my study of and love for Coral Gables.

As a native Miamian, I have always considered Coral Gables a part of my life. Until I was nine, I lived in Riverside, now Little Havana. My parents belonged to the Coral Gables Country Club, where I attended many children's events. I went to day camp at Salvadore Park and learned to swim at Venetian Pool. Even as a child, the city's winding streets, lush landscaping, and romantic entrances and plazas fascinated me. (I was convinced Rapunzel lived in the Douglas Entrance.) After I moved into a Mediterranean-style Miami Shores home, I often went to Coral Gables to see friends, shop, and go to the movies.

My first career was teaching high school history. While working at Miami Edison Senior High, my alma mater, I participated in a summer school program for teachers at the University of Miami. As luck would have it, my professor was the preeminent Florida historian Dr. Charlton Tebeau. He encouraged me to go to graduate school full time and pursue the study of Miami history—an idea I had never considered. He not only inspired me and became my mentor but also introduced me to many members of Miami's pioneer families who shared their memories with me.

After I decided to write my master's thesis on Coconut Grove, Dr. Tebeau arranged for me to interview Eunice Peacock Merrick, granddaughter of Charles and Isabella Peacock, who built South Florida's first hotel in what today is called Peacock Park. Although we mostly talked about Coconut Grove, her late husband, George, often came into the conversation.

In 1974, Coral Gables Administrative Programs Director Don Lebrun, whom I had met at the Historical Association of Southern Florida, recruited me to lead the new City of Coral Gables Preservation Board. With no model to guide us, we forged ahead. Fortunately, the board included many who had known George and others who had grown up in Coral Gables. We learned fast and soon focused on the Merrick House, which was in serious disrepair. Our crusade to convince the city to buy it from the Merrick Manor Foundation put me back in touch with Eunice Merrick. She introduced me to George's brother Richard, who became our most valuable resource as we struggled to restore his boyhood home and open it to the public. Although considerably younger than George, they were very close. Through his eyes, we were almost able to reenter the past and get to know his remarkable family.

The preservation board next focused on saving the Biltmore Hotel. Although the city had acquired it in 1971, its future remained in doubt. Following a series of failed and controversial plans, the preservation board convinced the Coral Gables Commission to prepare a formal Request for Proposal (RFP), which they had never done. After the RFP was released nationally, six developers came up with formal proposals. The commission then appointed a selection committee and approved its choice of developers. Because Coral Gables did not yet have a preservation officer, I became the liaison among the developers, the city, and its preservation board. This provided me with the opportunity to witness the reemergence of George's Biltmore and study his role in its creation.

These early preservation efforts helped spur a growing appreciation of George Merrick. As a result, more people began to worry that Merrick's original ideals were being ignored and compromised. Under the leadership of Mayor Bill Chapman, the Coral Gables Commission appointed a new board that studied the problem and created what was called the "Mediterranean Ordinance." As a member of the board, I began a long study of George's unique Mediterranean style.

By this time, I was spending much of my time researching Coral Gables. My children had grown up there, attending the Methodist Church and Coral Gables public schools. They swam at Venetian Pool, played sports at the Youth Center, and rode their bikes down its tree-shaded streets. Their experience added to my passion for George's Coral Gables and for preserving his community-building ideals.

Everything came together after Richard Merrick's widow, Mildred, a former University of Miami research librarian who had helped me as a graduate student, offered me a great gift. She had become the caretaker of a cache of original Merrick papers. For more than two years, we met at least once a week, carefully organizing the material for donation to the University of Miami Libraries Special Collections. Even though I had been studying Coral Gables for many years, much of the material was new to me. Included was a series of unpublished short stories that George had written. Because of my knowledge of Miami history, I immediately realized the stories were autobiographical, not fiction. After further research, I was able to document the events he described, thus making the stories a unique primary source.

The more I learned, the more I wanted to share it with others. I realized that because of a lack of primary source research, misinformation had been inadvertently promulgated—even by me. Besides utilizing new primary sources, I knew I needed to follow noted historian David McCullough's admonition to "get him behind my eyes." Thus the long journey to write George's biography began.

My first order of business was to study George's family heritage and how it helped define him. For the next several years, I visited many places, including the Eastern Shore of Maryland, where the Merricks began their American experience. I followed his mother's family—the Finks—into Ohio and traveled the circuit of his Methodist preacher grandfather. With the help of local researchers, I poured through archives and newspaper and church records. Next I followed his mother's family to Pennsylvania and then brought his parents together at Lebanon Valley College in Annville, Pennsylvania, where a gold mine of material survived. In Gaines, New York, where his father, a Congregational Church minister, began his career, local newspapers and church records provided an in-depth understanding of his remarkable parents, as well as his own early development.

I also visited Duxbury, Massachusetts, where Solomon Merrick had his last church before moving the family to Florida.

With all of this knowledge behind my eyes, I became convinced that readers could not fully understand George's thinking without first understanding his family background. I discovered that many of his ancestors had pioneer experiences in untamed lands and, as a result, were not afraid to take chances or make change. I even found remarkable similarities between their stories and his. His parents and grandparents shared their past and taught him to be proud of his heritage and carry it forward in a positive way.

To understand George's thinking, I read literary works, religious documents, and planning books and studied the fertile writings of philosophers such as John Ruskin and Ebenezer Howard. I traveled to many of the planned communities he referenced, including Forest Hills Gardens in Queens, New York; Shaker Heights in Cleveland, Ohio; and Roland Heights in Baltimore, Maryland. After absorbing all of these people, places, and a plethora of new primary material, the task of pulling it all together began.

Mildred Merrick encouraged my research and continued as a valued collaborator. She read drafts and added her own perspective to the story. Sadly, she died before the book was published, but she knew that the manuscript had been completed. Without her, it could not have been written.

It is impossible to name all the people who helped along the way, but I have compiled a long list in the acknowledgments. Several members of the Fink and Merrick families, however, deserve special mention. Elaine Fink Schumacher, granddaughter of George's cousin George Fink, shared three incredible scrapbooks with me. They made it possible to put George Fink back into the story where he belonged. Her research in newspapers and libraries further documented his pivotal role. Likewise, artist Nancy Fink Giacci, granddaughter of George Merrick's artist uncle Denman Fink, who was George Merrick's most important collaborator, shared family lore and added to my understanding of the Fink family. George's nephew, the late Don Kuhn, also helped my understanding by recounting his personal relationship with his uncle George and sharing his letters.

I am the first to admit that my respect for George grew with each chapter. I hope the book will not only educate and document his position as a leading visionary city planner but also thrust the city he created onto the list of America's greatest and most enduring planned communities.

George Merrick, Son of the South Wind

Introduction

> Ever since the family had come to the Biscayne Bay country the boy had
> loved the south wind. To him it held promise, romance, and fulfillment.
> And, not as the north wind bringing down the cold waves; not as the
> west wind carrying the drowning rainy-season floods and the mosquito
> plagues; not as the east wind with its ten day drizzles in the fall and
> weeks of raw petulant rages in the spring; no, unlike these other, these
> jealous alien winds,—the south wind the boy knew as spirit of the land.
>
> George E. Merrick, "The South Wind and the Boy"

Much has been written about George Merrick, but his true character has
remained elusive. He moved to the wilderness of South Florida from Duxbury, Massachusetts, when he was thirteen years old. For him, it was love
at first sight. For the rest of his life, he would recall his first impression of
the green world he encountered. He never forgot what he called "cloud
mountains" and how the hopeful breeze of the south wind inspired him.

Although he dreamed of going to Harvard and becoming a writer, for
the next eight years, he worked in the fields, helping his father create the
Coral Gables Plantation. These years were difficult for him, but he continued to gain knowledge from the land and from his fellow workers—young
black men who had come to South Florida from the Bahamas.

At age twenty-one, after the groves began to bear, he went off to Rollins
College, where he received his first formal education since leaving Duxbury. It further awakened his intellectual spirit and strengthened his desire
to write.

After two years at Rollins, his father encouraged him to attend law
school in New York. Although he hated law school, he loved New York and

believed his dreams were coming true after he had a short story published in the *New York Herald Tribune*.

After a year in New York, his father's illness brought him home to help manage the groves. When his father died a short time later, George had no choice but to take over the groves and become head of the family.

He never planned to become a developer, but his creative mind saw an opportunity to turn the 1,200-acre grapefruit grove into a model suburb. Unlike other local developers, he would create a plan based on South Florida's history, geography, and tropical lifestyle. An avid reader, he studied the philosophies of John Ruskin, William Morris, and Ebenezer Howard and was converted to their ideals. He read Florida history and became enchanted by its long-forgotten Spanish past. He looked south to Cuba and the Caribbean—the birthplace of his beloved south wind. Slowly, Coral Gables' future began to form in his mind.

He knew how to dream, but he did not know how to develop, so for seven years he launched more than twenty subdivisions around Miami. Although working day and night, he still found time to write poetry, especially to his young wife, Eunice. His childhood dream came true in 1920 when Boston's Four Seas Publishing Company published a small book of his romantic poems, *Song of the Wind on a Southern Shore*.

A short time later, he launched Coral Gables, "Miami's Master Suburb." At the same time, he promised himself that once it was completed, he would go back to his writing. In the meantime, Coral Gables would become his most important work and what would later be called his "poetry in stone."

George Merrick, Son of the South Wind: Visionary Creator of Coral Gables traces the roots of both sides of his remarkable family and focuses on his life from birth to death and beyond. More than a biography, it is the story of Coral Gables. It is, as a *Miami Herald* editorial stated at the time of his death, "a life-story woven out of poetic idealism, practical vision and the hardiness of character that surmounts adversity and recognizes no personal defeat. . . . George Merrick was Coral Gables. The city will be forever his city, quiet and beautiful—a poet's dream in stone and steel and concrete, in murmuring fountains and lazy waterways, in striking archways, streets and parkways, in imposing mansions and charming homes."

~ 1

The Merricks of Maryland

The natives of this Eastern Shore, who though far removed
they may be from this genial presence, still softly sigh—
"this is my own, my native land."

Prentiss Ingraham, *Land of Legendary Lore*, 1898

In the summer, strong south winds stir the great Chesapeake Bay and
cool the serpentine creeks, rivers, and peaceful coves of Maryland's Eastern Shore. Here, more than three centuries ago, and one hundred years
before the British colonials fought for their independence, George Merrick's paternal ancestors sought a new life far from their Welsh homeland.
Although times and circumstances changed, the Merrick pioneering spirit
survived and pushed generations of Merricks—including George's father,
Solomon—toward unknown frontiers.

Like his English countrymen, the first Merrick to come to America left
familiar places, home, and family, boarded a ship with a group of strangers,
and spent months being tossed about by a fickle sea in the most horrible
and primitive of conditions. Those who survived, and many did not, faced
a strange wilderness, often alone. Many left England simply because they
wanted a better life. Others fled some sort of oppression—political or religious—that forced them to make this irreversible life change. Whatever the
reason, one thing was for sure. It was a terrible gamble and once they had
left home, there was no turning back.

By the time the Merricks came to the Eastern Shore in the 1660s, the
worst of the hardships experienced by the first settlers had been overcome.

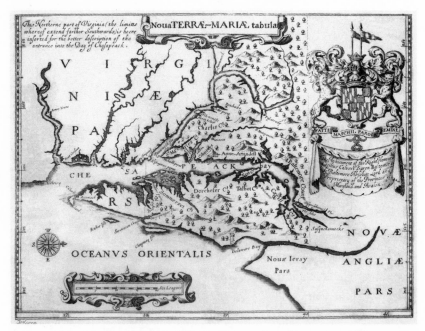

FIGURE 1. *Nova Virginiae Tabula*, by John Ogilby, 1671. Seven generations of George Merrick's ancestors called the Eastern Shore of Maryland home. The first landowner in Talbot County was John Merrick with his wife, Jane. Permission of Talbot County Free Library.

Most of the hostile Indians had departed and lack of food was not a day-to-day problem. Friendly Indians helped them plant corn and harvest the munificence of the bay—crab, clam, oyster, and fish. Game hunters rarely came home empty-handed because the skies and marshes were alive with waterfowl, and great numbers of deer roamed the forests.

Maryland was different from most of the other American colonies. In 1632, King Charles I gave Cecilius Calvert, Second Baron of Baltimore, a charter for ten to twelve million acres in what would become the "Free State." Unlike the Pilgrims in New England, the Roman Catholic Calvert family opened up their proprietary colony to all Christians, including Quakers.

The Calverts, eager to bring prosperity, as well as religious tolerance, to their land, enticed their aristocratic English peers to Maryland with large land grants requiring only token rents. Spurred by the success of the Virginia Colony's tobacco culture, the Calverts' chosen people sought out the flat and sandy, yet fertile, land arcing between the Chester and the Great Choptank Rivers on Maryland's Eastern Shore.

The intense demand for labor brought another group of people to the Eastern Shore. Yeoman farmers, craftsmen, and those without land or prospects soon joined the landed gentry. Following carefully proscribed rules, many men and women who could not afford to pay their own way to America became indentured servants. They agreed to a contracted period of servitude, usually between four and five years, in exchange for free passage. As an additional inducement to both planter and laborer, the planter received fifty acres of land for each "head" whose passage he paid. These "headrights" allowed the planters to acquire thousands of acres of land. Maryland law required planters to grant each indentured servant who worked out his or her term of labor "freedom dues." These dues included fifty acres of land in addition to tools, clothes, and a year's supply of corn.

This was the world John Merrick, the first Merrick born on the Eastern Shore, knew. From fragmentary records and family lore, it appears that his father was also named John and came from Wales as a young man with his father, Daniel. Some say Daniel was an indentured servant who may have first come to the Virginia Colony and then, when his servitude was completed, crossed the border into Maryland. Although the names of his parents may be shrouded in historical mist, family Bibles record John's birth in 1667 and the fact that he grew up in Talbot County.

Young Jane Walker, the third of Daniel and his wife, Alice's, seven children, caught the eye of John Merrick and the two eighteen-year-olds married in 1688. Although details of John's early life are obscure, he obviously was a young man of some charm and ability even though he could not read or write. In this era, men outnumbered women four to one so Jane could have had her pick of suitors. Although very young and of modest means, John, like many of the Merrick men, married for love and married well. The Walkers were a prosperous family and Jane brought much to the marriage, including seventy acres of land on the Miles River, where the young couple settled down to raise their family.[1]

Religion was an important part of Jane and John Merrick's life. This strong spiritual dimension was deep and long-lasting and would be passed on and define the Merricks for generations. The frequent comings and goings of Francis Asbury, the most prominent American Methodist preacher, influenced the Merricks. Methodist societies soon sprang up all over Talbot County. Asbury traveled the Eastern Shore on horseback, preaching in private homes and makeshift chapels to anyone who would listen. His piety and dedication cemented the Methodist tradition of "circuit-riding," positioning it at the forefront of religious experience in the expanding frontier.

John and Jane were also proudly prolific. Because children were wealth to the planter, they were especially blessed with the arrival of six sons. But the Merrick family also experienced great despair. For some reason, perhaps because he was sickly, John wrote his will although he was only thirty-six. "Being sick and weak, but of sound mind," he penned, "I leave my wife Jane full and sole executor for what goods and chattel, and creatures it has pleased God to endow me with. I leave all to her, to her discretion to the bringing up of my children."[2]

Three years later, and only months after the birth of his last son, John died, leaving his wife with six children, ranging in age from eight months to seventeen years. Sadly, future generations of Merrick men and their families would also suffer the tragic consequences of early death.

In 1726, John and Jane Merrick's third son, Daniel, born in 1695, married Mary Ferell, another Talbot County girl. Their oldest son, Solomon, who was born in 1729, continued the Merrick tradition by naming one of his three sons Solomon and another Daniel. Little is known of this Solomon, except that he also died young (at thirty-four), when his third son, Daniel, born in 1757, was only six years old.

Daniel grew up in Talbot County and in 1776, like many of his Merrick cousins, served in the Talbot County Militia during the Revolutionary War. At the end of the war, he returned to Talbot County just in time to witness the transformation of Talbot Court House into the bustling new town of Easton.

Following his marriage to the widow Underwood, he became the first in his family to leave the farm and the first to live in town. As a tailor, he elevated the family into the new town-centered middle class. Two years later, he and his wife welcomed their first child, Maria Christina; a son, Solomon, followed the next year.

But once again, untimely death impacted the Merrick family. A short time after his wife's death, Daniel died—leaving Solomon, age thirteen, and

Christina orphans. Within a year, Christina also died. Ten days short of his fifteenth birthday, desperate and alone, Solomon bound himself to Joseph Steingasser, a tanner, for eight years. While this seems cruel today, it was commonplace at the time and, under the circumstances, a way to care for orphaned or unwanted children. The arrangement turned out to benefit Solomon because he learned a trade.

Solomon was not a young man without prospects. He still owned his father's home and had four slaves. His joy was complete when, on June 9, 1825, he married Ann Kemp. The Kemps, who were also an early Eastern Shore family, had been strong Quakers. Ann and Solomon, however, became Methodists and were married by a Methodist preacher. Family lore recalls that Ann told Solomon she would not marry him as long as he owned slaves because both the Quakers and the Methodists strongly opposed slavery and profit-making from their sale. Whether for love, principle, or both, one month before the wedding, Solomon sold his slaves to a family member for a token five dollars. No member of Solomon's family would ever own a slave again.

Ann did not live out the year, leaving Solomon once again alone. A short time later, he married Elizabeth Hopkins, in a Methodist Church ceremony. Elizabeth was the daughter of Jonathan Hopkins, scion of another old and prominent Maryland family. Just nine months later, John Wesley Merrick was born, named in honor of Methodism's founder.

But despite happy events at home, the deepening depression cast a pall over the Merricks and the Eastern Shore. Solomon felt the pain. In one advertisement, he offered to exchange shoes for "County Produce—Such as Hides, Corn, Meal, Bacon, Lard, Rags, Feathers, etc." in order to provide for his family. Finally, after two long years of struggle, he made the difficult decision to move his young family to the new, promising town of Baltimore in hopes of finding a better market for his trade. To finance the trip, they sold most of their possessions—furniture, tables, chairs, stoneware, and even the baby's cradle—and mortgaged their home. Adding insult to injury, he was also forced to sign a deed of trust, a form of bankruptcy, to settle his debts. It was a bitter blow.

Baltimore, once the poor, wrong-side-of-the-bay cousin to the prosperous Eastern Shore, was no longer a sleepy, backwater town. It was booming.

Since the 1750s, it had grown from a mere crossroads with a smattering of houses to the current brick-and-mortar town of more than thirty thousand people.

Many newcomers moved to Baltimore in the early years of the nineteenth century. Unlike the Eastern Shore, where people were of predominately English ancestry, Baltimore attracted large numbers of German, Irish, and French immigrants. This gave it a different, cosmopolitan feel. After six generations of Eastern Shore living, the move must have been unsettling for the Merricks.

By 1834, even booming Baltimore was experiencing serious economic problems. It was time to take the family, which now included two more sons—George Washington, born in 1831, and newborn James Henry—back home to the Eastern Shore.

Solomon may have had some success in Baltimore because when he returned to Easton, he opened a new shop on Court Street, right in the center of town bordering the courthouse square. He placed an impressive advertisement in the Easton press, complete with a drawing of a boot and two shoes. It read:

Boot & Shoe making & repairing
DONE BY
SOLOMON MERRICK.
The subscriber begs leave to inform the citizens of Easton & the public generally that he has taken a shop on Court Street between the stores of Mr. John T. Goldsmith and the tailor shop of Mr. James L. Smith, where he at all times be found by those who may feel disposed to favor him with work, and assures the public that he will pay strict attention to his business and humbly hopes to meet with a share of their patronage. He flatters himself that from his own experience, and the assistance of good workmen, he will be able to give satisfaction to all who may please to give him a call.
The public's obedient servant,
SOLOMON MERRICK[3]

Unfortunately, the depression endured and the Merricks' financial situation deteriorated, forcing Solomon into yet another deed of trust.[4] But hard times did not stop the arrival of children. Between 1835 and 1840, the Merricks had three more sons, including Charles Fletcher, George Merrick's grandfather, born in 1837.[5]

Unable to make a living as a shoemaker, Solomon gave up his trade for the second time and took up farming in order to keep food on the table for his family of six active boys. This change of lifestyle must have been difficult. The older boys had grown up in town and had never done hard, physical work. Easton had a public school, which they surely attended. Now they gave up city living and were isolated in the country with little opportunity for formal education. They spent their days from dawn to dusk helping their father and had little time for recreation. Working together, the family improved its finances and in 1851, Solomon was able to purchase forty acres in the small community of Matthewstown.[6] Unfortunately, Solomon would not live to see the farm prosper or his children grown. He died the following year, leaving his wife with six sons between the ages of nine and twenty.

Charles Merrick was fifteen years old when his father died. Born soon after the family returned to Easton, he had lived his entire life in Talbot County and had learned how to farm. After his father's death, the close-knit family stayed together on the farm, older brothers helping younger. Tragedy struck again in 1855 when Ebenezer Solomon, who was three years younger than Charles, died.[7]

In April 1858, young Charles Merrick married the lovely Susan Frances Cloudsley of Baltimore.[8] Born to an old and prominent Baltimore family, she, too, had known death and dislocation. Her mother, also named Susan, died when she was only two years old, leaving her father, John, with five young children.[9] For some reason, John Cloudsley was not able to care for his large family, so Jacob and Louisa Greasley took the baby, Susan, and raised her like a daughter.

Jacob Greasley was an impressive man, many thought even larger than life. He arrived from Germany in 1831 at age eighteen with no money and no prospects. After being stranded in Philadelphia, he walked all the way to Baltimore. On his first Sunday there, he attended the Otterbein Church, affiliated with the United Brethren in Christ (UBC). During the worship service, as the story goes, he put his last few coins into the collection plate.

Impressed with the young man's spirit and faith, a church member took him home, taught him the meat business, and launched his career as a butcher.

Greasley, like the boys in the novels of Horatio Alger Jr., thrived in America and quickly became a well-known and prosperous butcher in Baltimore's famous Hanover Market. As soon as he had enough money, he brought his parents, brother, and sister to America. At twenty-four, he married Louisa Lenox, daughter of a well-known Baltimore family. Although Louisa had been raised an Episcopalian, they were married in the Otterbein Church.[10]

Charles and Susan were also married in the Otterbein Church. It was easy for Charles Merrick to join the United Brethren in Christ. Some called the UBC the "German Methodists" because their teachings, doctrines, and style of worship were so similar. In addition, Philip William Otterbein, the founder of the UBC, was very close to Francis Asbury, and Otterbein participated in Asbury's 1784 ordination and witnessed the birth of the Methodist Episcopal Church in America at Baltimore's Lovely Lane Meeting House. For many years, the UBC and the Methodists talked of merger. This effort failed principally because the Dutch, Swiss, and Germans wanted their church services in German and the Methodists had a strong English-language heritage.[11] (The two churches merged in 1968, creating the United Methodist Church.)

How or where Charles and Susan met and the details of their long-distance romance are unknown, but the outcome of their union is clear. It would change the course of Merrick family history.

After their marriage, Charles and Susan returned to the Merricks' Matthewstown farm. Their household included Charles' mother, Elisabeth, and his two younger brothers, Joseph and James.[12] Before the first year was out, Charles and Susan welcomed their first son, whom they named Solomon Greasley Merrick after each of his grandfathers.

In April 1860, Charles and Susan had Solomon baptized at the Otterbein Church in Baltimore. Undoubtedly, they made the eight-hour steamboat trip to Baltimore because proud Grandfather Greasley wanted him baptized in the church where he was a stalwart trustee.[13] Although the Greasleys never formally adopted Susan, to them she was their much-beloved daughter and they doted on her children.

By this time, the nation was seriously fractured as Northern and Southern members of Congress clashed over the hot issues of the day: the extension of slavery and states' rights.

Maryland, more than most other states, reflected the national division. Although many of the planters were committed to the South, an equal number of residents strongly favored the Union.

Although the war did not come directly to Talbot County, many Talbot Countians went to war, on both sides. For some reason, Charles Merrick was not among them. It could have been because he was the sole support of his mother, wife, young family, and two minor brothers. If he had gone, he would have most likely been a Union soldier. Susan's brother, Thomas, was a much-decorated Union lieutenant colonel and, later, family members spoke of great affection for Abraham Lincoln. In addition, although they were never practicing Quakers, the Quaker influence was a part of the Merrick family tradition, especially when it came to the issue of slavery.

Although the Greasleys' presence was a powerful tug toward Baltimore, as long as the fighting raged, Charles, Susan, and young Solomon stayed safely on the Eastern Shore. As soon as the war was over, they sold the farm, packed up their belongings, and moved to Baltimore. When they left, they took six generations of Eastern Shore history with them. They would never live there again, but the pulsating rhythm of the Chesapeake and their sense of pride in their Maryland heritage would stay with them and be passed on to future generations.

Young Solomon was seven years old when the family moved to Baltimore. Soon after his family's arrival, his baby brother Jacob was born and again named after Grandfather Greasley. For several years, the family lived close to the Otterbein Church, near today's Camden Yards. Charles worked as a huckster, or salesman, probably at Jacob Greasley's Hanover Market stall. Jacob Greasley took Charles under his wing and trained him as a butcher. When Charles was proficient, he took over his father-in-law's butcher business, which by this time had moved to the Richmond Market on Pennsylvania Avenue.

Besides being a hard worker and a good butcher, Jacob Greasley was a very good businessman. "With frugal living, hard work and wise investment," the Otterbein Church records reported, "he retired after only 20

FIGURE 2. Jacob Greasley, Solomon Merrick's beloved adopted grandfather, set an example by buying property and developing homes near Baltimore's Druid Hill Park. "Scenes in Druid Hill Park," *Picturesque America* (New York: Appleton, 1874).

years."[14] Actually, the only thing Greasley retired from was the market. After he turned his lucrative meat business over to Charles, he focused all of his energies on real estate development and the church.

As early as 1840, Greasley leased land on an old estate named "Newington" on the Reisterstown Road just north of the city limits. His tract extended from the busy turnpike almost to the grounds of the imposing Rogers-Buchanan Estate "Druid Hill." Even though the industrious butcher at one time had stalls in three of Baltimore's markets, he hardly fit into the landed gentry mold. But he was a visionary, way ahead of his time. His choice of land proved prophetic when in 1860, the City of Baltimore purchased Druid Hill and turned it into a magnificent 745-acre public park. If Jacob Greasley was there when the park opened on October 19, 1860, he must have been a very happy man.

Druid Hill Park was the third major urban park in America. It was financed by a tax on the new horse-drawn trolley that was spreading out in all directions from the downtown area. In 1866, two years after the trolley came to the park, Greasley bought nearby land for $5,000.[15] During the next ten years, he made a lot of money buying and selling real estate near the park. In one transaction, for instance, he made $25,000, which at the time would have been a small fortune.[16]

Besides buying and selling land, he also developed a subdivision near the park.[17] As development inched its way northward from downtown, Reisterstown was renamed Pennsylvania Avenue Extension. Camden Station was less than four miles away.

Greasley built a block of Baltimore-style row houses on both sides of his newly created Francis Street, named after daughter Susan Francis Merrick. In 1871, Charles, Susan, and their two boys moved into a three-story brick house in the middle of the block. At about the same time Greasley built the row houses, he built himself an imposing Second Empire–style brick mansion facing Druid Hill Avenue. It had three stories, a mansard roof with dormer windows, and a wide columned front porch. It equaled or surpassed the other mansions on the avenue. Besides its many elegant features, the fact that the Merricks' backyard was just a quick walk across the alley added to its charm, at least as far as Grandma and Grandpa Greasley were concerned.

Building houses was not Jacob Greasley's only interest. In 1871, his brother Carl, or Charles, who also lived in the neighborhood, leased some land to the Otterbein Church for a new mission. Among the twelve charter members were Jacob Greasley, Charles, Susan, and Charles' mother.[18]

The same year, church members participated in a community church-raising for the new Salem Mission Church. It took only seven and a half days and $467 to build the new building. During the planning and construction, Charles and Susan held services in their home across the street.

The following year, work began on a permanent church on leased land. The rather imposing stone edifice was completed in 1874. It had beautiful stained glass windows, impressive chandeliers, a pipe organ, and solid walnut appointments. Three years later, Jacob Greasley purchased the land and gave it to the church. He also was the church's largest donor and served as a church trustee and steward from the time it opened until his death. Charles Merrick shared his religious zeal and became the first lay superintendent of the Sunday school.[19]

Solomon grew up in this nurturing environment, centered on church and family. His family included both his grandmother Elisabeth Merrick,

FIGURE 3. Jacob Greasley financed the Salem United Brethren Church (now Gethsemane Baptist) that still stands on Francis Street in Baltimore across from the town house he built for his adopted daughter, Susan, and her husband, Charles Merrick. Donating land for a church would continue as a family value. Photo by author.

the Greasleys, and a host of Greasley and Merrick cousins. It was almost as if he had two sets of parents because Jacob and Louisa Greasley treated him more like a son than a grandson. As the oldest son, he was especially close to both his father and his grandfather. This special relationship intensified when his brother Jacob died soon after the family moved to Francis Street. Charles and Susan also lost several other infant children, including Charles Frances, who died soon after his birth in 1876. These tragic deaths left Solomon with a great sense of sadness and responsibility that belied his young years. The deaths put eight years between him and his nearest sibling, brother Harry, and twenty-three years between him and his youngest sister, Lucy. This age gap caused him to feel an extra obligation toward his little brother and three younger sisters, as well as to his parents and grandparents. Everyone looked up to Solomon and he lived up to everyone's expectations.

He was an outstanding student and an avid reader who took to the classics and, of course, the Bible. He attended the prestigious Baltimore City College, which was an all-male public high school that emphasized a classical education. He also excelled in elocution, winning many prizes for his oratory. He was thoughtful and serious; smiles did not always come easily.

His strength was in his intelligence, diligence, forthrightness, and high moral character.

Solomon's social life also revolved around the church. The yearly church picnic at Druid Hill Park was always a greatly anticipated affair. Undoubtedly he also visited the park for family outings. Visible from his grandfather's house, the park was a popular gathering place for not only the neighborhood but also the city.

Clearly, "Solly," as his grandfather liked to call him, took the church teachings to heart. He studied the scriptures and led an upright, exemplary life. When he announced that he wanted to become a preacher, no one who knew him was surprised. He was a natural. His proud heritage, with its strong spiritual underpinnings and the unrelenting encouragement of his family, set him on a straight path toward his future as a man of God. With great pride, Jacob Greasley, the uneducated butcher-turned-wealthy-developer, sent his beloved grandson to college, the first family member to seek higher education.

One can only imagine the mixed emotions his devoted, extended family felt as they put him on a train that August day in 1879. He was off to the United Brethren's Lebanon Valley College in Annville, Pennsylvania. There he would meet the love of his life, the spirited and talented Althea Corilla Fink. She would bring him joy, make him laugh, and share in his dreams for the future. He would not return to Maryland to live, but Maryland would live in him for the rest of his life.

~ 2

The Fink Family

The mountaineer who wanders from this land . . . may live
where rolls old oceans . . . he may prosper in the riches of the
world; he may attain fame and greatness and power but his
heart is in the romantic hills and enchanted valleys stretching
down from the Alleghenies toward the great river which flows
out to lose itself in roaring breakers and washing tides and
which so fitly typifies human life.

Wilma Dykeman and James Slokely, *The Border States*

On a hot, humid August day in 1737, the ship *Samuel*, with its human cargo "packed like herring," sailed up the Delaware River on the last leg of its seven-week transatlantic voyage from Rotterdam.[1] Among the more than two hundred weary Germans aboard was Johann Nickel Fink [Finck], the first of Althea Fink Merrick's ancestors to come to America. In the years to come, the Fink family would leave its mark on the American frontier and on Althea's son George Merrick. Their pioneer experiences built their confidence, honed their faith, fostered their creativity, and taught them forbearance laced with unabashed optimism. More than 150 years later, in the wilds of South Florida, this proud family's strong frontier values would serve Althea Fink Merrick well as she and her children added a new chapter to the Fink family saga.

The story begins with thirty-three-year-old Johann Nickel Fink, who quickly Americanized his name to Nicholas; his wife, Charlotta Gervinis; and their two-year-old son, Johann Philipp. The young Fink family, along with his sister, Maria Magdalena, and her husband, Ludwig Becker, began

FIGURE 4. Henry George Greatrake Fink, George Merrick's beloved grandfather, had a singular influence on him. University of Miami Special Collections. Courtesy of Mildred Merrick.

their hopeful journey from the small village of Kusel in the German Palatinate. The Finks and Beckers, like many of their fellow Palatines, were Protestant separatists.

William Penn, the wealthy proprietor of the British American province of Pennsylvania and the new town of Philadelphia, understood their fear and capitalized on it. As a persecuted Quaker, he promised a New World nirvana based on religious toleration, universal suffrage, and peaceful prosperity. Having traveled to the Palatinate, he remembered it as the perfect place to recruit residents for his "noble experiment." The Palatine Germans were known for their frugality, industriousness, and superior farming ability—an ideal combination to populate the Pennsylvania backcountry and transform the forests into profitable farms. To lure them to America, Penn translated his advertising tract, "Some Account of Pennsylvania in America," into German and distributed it throughout the Rhineland. His advertising paid off and by the early eighteenth century, Philadelphia had become the principal port of entry for the incoming tide of Palatine Germans.[2]

After such a long, difficult passage, Nicholas and Charlotta must have been thankful for having survived. Before them lay William Penn's Philadelphia, with its carefully planned grid of tree-lined streets and array of impressive new churches and public buildings. Its population neared ten thousand and already included a large number of Palatine Germans, whom the locals called "Newlanders" or "Strangers."

Just eight miles northwest of the port lay Germantown. Founded in 1683 by thirteen German families, the town thrived as the rising tide of Germans turned into a human flood. Talented artisans and enterprising merchants opened shops similar to those they had left behind and turned the new community into a lively market town. Nearby, William Rittenhouse brought German papermaking knowledge with him and built the nation's first paper mill. German Quakers, Lutherans, Mennonites, Baptists, and Reformed congregations flourished.

Like William Penn, Maryland's Lord Baltimore lured settlers into the backlands by offering religious freedom and cheap, plentiful land. The first takers were wealthy landowners like Benjamin Tasker, president of Maryland's Governing Council. Tasker later deeded what he named "Tasker's Chance" to his son-in-law Daniel Dulaney, who, in 1746, sold nineteen separate tracts to a group of Pennsylvania Germans. The list of buyers included Nicholas Fink.[3]

Western Maryland, with its picturesque mountain backdrop and its gentle rolling countryside cut by flowing streams, surely reminded Nicholas Fink of home. Here, in the foothills of the great Allegheny Mountains, the new settlers cleared the land, planted crops, and built neat, German-style homes and barns.

Farming and enterprise were not the only things on Nicholas Fink's mind. Deeply religious, a trait he would pass on to later generations, he, like many of his countrymen, abandoned the Lutheran and Reformed churches and joined the German Baptists (Church of the Brethren), who were commonly called Dunkers.

Dunker worship, in contrast to the liturgical Lutheran and Reformed services, included emotional meetings, hymn singing, and Bible study. Following what is known as the "Great Awakening" of the 1730s, this style of worship flourished on the American frontier and greatly influenced later generations of the Fink family.[4]

Maryland was good to Nicholas Fink and his family. He was a successful farmer, large landowner, and prominent Dunker. By 1772, he had been involved in more than two-dozen land transactions and had sired a large family, including a son named Henry, who would be George Merrick's third great-grandfather.[5]

Although more than 150 years had passed since the first English settlers arrived in the New World, few people, except trappers and explorers, had crossed the seemingly impassable Allegheny and Appalachian Mountains. In fact, following what Americans call the French and Indian War, the British actually forbade settlement there to avoid conflict with the American Indians. But once the returning soldiers and trappers told of the area's endless horizons, great rivers, flowing streams, fertile valleys, and abundant wildlife, it was only a matter of time until the more independent and adventuresome would disregard the edict and plunge into the wilderness.

Henry Fink and his son, also named Henry, were two of those individuals. In 1772, Henry Jr. followed explorer Samuel Pringle over the mountains and into a new land. His unbridled confidence, imbued by his frontier experiences, built his courage and heightened his lust for the unknown.[6] That year, Henry appeared as one of the earliest settlers on Horseshoe Bottoms on the Cheat River near today's Parsons, West Virginia. Within a year, he moved a short distance away to the new settlement of Buckhannon. Here, two generations of Henry Finks, along with Henry Fink Sr.'s sons, Daniel and Solomon, took on yet another frontier.

For the Finks, life on what was then the Virginia frontier would prove to be difficult, challenging, and dramatically tragic. Although the virgin land was beautiful, seductive, and free for the taking, it was also raw, dangerous, and highly contested. Several members of the Fink family claimed tracts near a small, meandering stream they named Fink's Run. As true West Virginia pioneers, Henry Fink and his family attained a large measure of immortality, enjoying references in most early West Virginia history books. "Fink was an industrious and progressive citizen," W. R. Cutright wrote in his 1907 *History of Upshur County*:

He worked with vigor and determination that accomplished much good to himself and his neighbors; his clearings were the largest and best in the settlement, consisting largely of improvements of the beautiful bottoms around his home. His crops were large, general, and various for a new settlement. Especially was this with his corn crops whose size both delighted him and interested his neighbors. To make the Indian corn of his own and his neighbors' farm more palatable, he built the first gristmill in the Buckhannon settlement.[7]

His stature in the community was further enhanced when, in 1787, the Virginia State Legislature appointed him to the board of trustees for the proposed Randolph Academy, the area's first educational institution.[8]

But the Fink family also experienced unspeakable tragedy after Henry Sr. and his son John were killed by the Indians. After Henry's death, the remaining family members abandoned their homes and gristmill in Buckhannon and moved away. But their presence is immortalized in the West Virginia hills. Two hundred years later, maps show Fink Run Road curving along Fink's Run, which still flows through the Buckhannon foothills where Henry Fink and his sons made history. A historic plaque stands next to the Upshur County Courthouse noting the site of John Fink's death at the hands of the Indians. A short distance away, at the historic Heavner Cemetery, the local Daughters of the American Revolution erected an imposing obelisk that reads:

John Fink
Revolutionary Soldier
Killed by the Indians,
February 15, 1782.

Not even great loss could kill Henry Fink Jr.'s pioneering spirit. A short time after his father's death, he moved his family, which included his wife and four children and his widowed mother, to Fayette County, Kentucky. This was a brave or, some would say, foolhardy, decision. Like West Virginia, Kentucky, "the dark and bloody ground," had also experienced years of Indian conflict. But despite the problems with Indians, Kentucky's promised land pulled Virginians like a magnet.

Henry Fink purchased his first Kentucky land in the thriving town of Lexington. It included 195 acres on Hickman Creek that he acquired in April 1792. Court documents also reveal that his mother, Hannah, granted him power of attorney over his father's estate, loaned him considerable sums of money, and guaranteed his notes. But business deals did not go well for Henry and by 1799, he was "seriously indebted" and put in debtor's prison. His mother helped pay off his creditors by selling his land and his personal property, with any excess funds going to her.[9]

At some point, the Finks moved to Georgetown, the county seat of Scott County just twelve miles north of Lexington. It was a growing frontier town with an impressive spring that powered several mills, including the first paper mill west of the Alleghenies.

Despite hard times, Henry and Maria Magdalena Fink had several more children after moving to Kentucky. The first was another Henry, George Merrick's great-grandfather, who was born in Scott County in 1795. The following year Henry Fink hired an agent to sell more than one thousand acres he still owned in Buckhannon and another five hundred owned by his wife in Hardy County, West Virginia. The residue of this sale was to go to his three daughters: Hannah, Coty, and Elizabeth. This may have been the act of a desperate father because, according to his son Valentine's biography, within a year both he and his wife were dead. In 1819, when his father-in-law, Valentine Powers, wrote his will, he bequeathed a sum of money to help support the "orphaned children of Henry and Magdalena Fink."[10]

With his parents gone, seventeen-year-old Henry Fink set out on his own to the new state of Ohio. His first stop was Chillicothe, then the state capital. His aunt, Catherine Fink Cozad, lived nearby at Hallsville with her Methodist circuit-riding husband, Job Cozad. It was here that Henry had his first encounter with the Methodist Church—an event that would greatly influence his future and that of his children.

Ohio offered abundant land and opportunity for a young man like Henry Fink, who was unafraid to take a chance. Chillicothe also had a paper mill known for its superior product.[11] But before Henry Fink could settle down in Ohio and take advantage of growing trades and cheap land, America's war for independence began. All able young men were drafted into the service, including Henry, who joined Daniel Musselman's Ohio volunteers.[12]

At war's end, Henry did not return to Ohio, although it never left his mind. Instead, he moved to Delaware. The most intriguing possibility for his move has to do with paper. Young Henry was familiar with the paper-making industry in Georgetown, Kentucky. Perhaps he even answered one of the many advertisements that sought young boys to work in Delaware's paper mill. The paper trail gets even hotter when, ten years later, he listed his occupation as papermaker[13] and named his third son and George Merrick's future grandfather, Henry George Greatrake Fink.

Clues to why Henry would give his infant son such an unusual name lie in Delaware. Laurence Greatrake, formerly of the Apsley Mill in Hemel Hempstead, England, was a Wilmington celebrity. In 1817, he, along with Thomas Gilpin, built the first papermaking machine in America on the Brandywine. Did Fink learn the papermaking trade from Laurence Greatrake and work at the Gilpin mill? Or was he friends with Laurence's son George, who was his contemporary and also a papermaker? Perhaps Eliza Davis, the Delaware girl he took for a wife, was related to the Greatrakes. The only thing known for sure is that for at least five years, he lived near the Gilpin mill at a time when the world was coming to marvel at Greatrake's "endless web."

On July 22, 1819, Henry married Eliza Davis at the Asbury Methodist Church in Wilmington.[14] This event, and Eliza's subsequent adult baptism at the same church the following year, once again put Henry in close contact with the Methodist Church. The often emotional and personal involvement of the Methodist service was not unlike his family's Dunker experience, and the possibility of layman participation likely stirred his soul. People noted his speaking ability at church meetings and encouraged him to become a licensed Methodist exhorter—the first step in the process of becoming a Methodist minister.

With a growing family that now included sons Elias and Isaiah, the frontier of new opportunity beckoned to Henry Fink. Sometime before the birth of his third son, Henry George Greatrake, in 1826, Henry moved his wife and young sons back to Ross County, Ohio. He also transferred his exhorter's license to the Ohio Methodist conference.[15] By 1833, Henry Fink had saved one hundred dollars—enough money to buy eighty acres in Goodhope Township, Hocking County, just east of Ross. The venture must have been profitable because he quickly added to his holdings and, by 1835, had acquired 320 more acres.[16]

Hocking County had timeless beauty, with primeval forests, the rush of flowing streams, waterfalls, deep gorges, and unusual sandstone outcroppings. The small community of Millville, later called Rockbridge after its natural bridge, lay a short distance away from Fink's farm. It sat on the newly opened Hocking Canal, which linked the area with Lancaster and the Ohio Erie Canal system. A group of Pennsylvania Germans founded Millville in 1815 and, by 1837, more than twenty-six German families lived in the area. Millville lived up to its name as the enterprising Germans, including Henry Fink, dammed up portions of the Hocking River and its branches to turn the machinery of a variety of mills. Henry may have used some Delaware papermaking skills because in 1850, he listed his occupation as papermaker and reported land valued at more than $3,000.[17] His mill or mills were on Buck Run, a picturesque meandering stream that took a southern course from the Hocking River. When he sold off a portion of his holdings on Buck Run in 1850, he listed a dwelling house and both a grist and a sawmill on his property.[18]

Young Henry, or H.G.G. as he was later called, grew up in the Hocking hills—a paradise for young, adventuresome boys. He and his brothers had caves to explore, trails to hike, and streams to ford. Schooling was minimal on the Ohio frontier, but Henry was an eager learner and an avid reader with a sharp, curious mind. The Finks were known to be a religious family and their social life revolved around the church. Although Henry and Eliza Fink deeded part of their land to the Salem Baptist Church and the Whippoorwill Cemetery,[19] it was the Methodist Church that had the greatest influence on their lives.

The Methodist Church perfected its philosophy and style of worship on the Ohio frontier. Their circuit-riding "saddlebag" preachers on horseback transformed the American religious experience as they rode from one wildwood settlement to the next. They preached in barns, fields, chapels, and log cabins. The isolated frontier families looked forward to their visits. They took them into their homes, fed them, and gave them a place to sleep.

The itinerant preacher's poverty, devotion, and evangelical, democratic gospel had great appeal. He treated the backcountry people as equals and spoke their language. The young, mostly single circuit riders became frontier icons. Most had no formal training, but the church had a well-regulated process leading to ordination and an almost militaristic hierarchy. The preacher-to-be usually began as a licensed exhorter—someone who spoke out or "exhorted" at services and helped the preacher bring in the converts. After several years as an exhorter, those who demonstrated special gifts could become ministers on trial. They "studied in the saddle" and learned to preach by preaching. At the annual conference, the elders and special committees quizzed and examined the provisional ministers as to their biblical knowledge and suitability for permanent status. After two or three years on trial, the best received "full connection." (In 1853, after two years as an exhorter, both H.G.G. and his brother Earl D. became Methodist ministers on trial.)

The Methodists were also known for their emotional camp meetings, which became a Methodist trademark and the highlight of the year for the lonely backwoodsmen. People traveled from miles around to participate in the four-day-long religious revivals, which were held in forest clearings and carefully scheduled between wheat and corn harvesting seasons.

Another important Methodist event was the annual conference, held each August or early September. Here the bishop would license exhorters and ministers and mete out the following year's assignment for his itinerant clergy. Although Earl left the ministry after only four years, H.G.G. spent the next twelve years serving the Ohio Conference in ten different circuits.

"He was a large, fine looking man, with a rich, deep voice; a natural orator," the *Ohio Annual Conference Yearbook* recorded at his death, "and a very good preacher; very profitable to the large congregations that, as a rule attended his ministry."[20] At more than six feet four inches tall, reed thin with piercing blue-gray eyes, H.G.G. had a commanding presence. When he was a young boy, George Merrick wrote that his beloved grandfather, prematurely gray with a long, flowing Old Testament beard, seemed like the personification of Moses and God when "his shouting Methodist voice would soar up and away into the rafters."[21]

H.G.G.'s first assignment was in Ohio's coal-mining district of Nelsonville, less than twenty miles from his Millville home. The following year, he was assigned to Etna, a small town on the National Road near Columbus. Here, he met the love of his life—sixteen-year-old Almeda "Medie" Wagy. The Wagys, who came from Switzerland via Virginia, were one of the oldest families in Licking County. Medie, the sixth of seven daughters, lived with her parents, Jacob and Katherine (Swisher), on the old Wagy homestead that was the legendary camping ground of the famous Indian Chief Logan.[22] Within sight of their home was a small church known as the Green Chapel, where H.G.G. Fink preached as part of his duties on the Etna Circuit. When the young preacher met the spirited Medie Wagy, it

FIGURE 5. George Merrick's grand-mother, Almeda "Medie" Wagy Fink, although small in stature, was known for her strength and determination. Courtesy of Donald Kuhn.

was love at first sight. The couple wanted to marry right away, but Medie's parents made them wait until she was eighteen. In the meantime, H.G.G. moved on to a new assignment on the Irville Circuit fifty miles away. On May 17, 1856—Medie's eighteenth birthday—the couple exchanged vows at the new Pataskala Methodist Church that had replaced the Green Chapel. They began their married life in Elizabethtown (now Perryville).

Medie was pretty and as petite as H.G.G. was tall. But, as George Merrick recalled, she was easily his grandfather's match. Strong, independent, tart-tongued, and outspoken, she reminded George of the girl on a can of Old Dutch Cleanser. She had to be strong and independent to survive frontier life as the wife of a circuit-riding preacher. Her husband kept a grueling pace and was usually away from home six days a week. His pay was less than $500 a year, so money was always a concern. Adding to the stress was the fact that the family had no roots, was always on the move, and had no home of its own.

The impending arrival of their first child, Eliza, called Katie, born in 1858, undoubtedly helped H.G.G. get a rare, two-year assignment on the Hebron Circuit. After that, new assignments and new children came like clockwork. They welcomed son William when H.G.G. served in Roseville, known as the pottery capital of the world. The following year, George Merrick's mother, Althea "Allie" Corilla, arrived in the small hamlet of Deavertown. The Finks remained there for two years and then in quick, one-year succession moved on to Pickerington, Maxville, and Baltimore, Ohio.

With the outbreak of the Civil War in 1861, the young Fink family's life became even more trying. Because inflation was rampant and money hard to come by, H.G.G. sold Bibles and religious tracts to supplement his meager income. Antislavery and pro-Lincoln, he was an outspoken abolitionist—a point of view not always popular, even in pro-Union Ohio.

Although H.G.G. did not serve in the army, the war was omnipresent. He worried about his brother Elias, who fought in several major battles. He ministered on the home front, collecting clothing and supplies for the troops and offering solace to the anxious and grieving. The stress of war and the family's impoverished, nomadic existence took its toll. In 1866, worn out and exhausted, H.G.G. Fink asked to be relieved from duty because of illness. He was "supernumerated," the term for a Methodist minister without a church.[23]

Back in Millville, now called Rockbridge, H.G.G.'s father's life had taken on a new dimension. Sometime between 1860 and 1870, when he was listed on the U.S. Census as a physician, Henry Fink had become Dr. Henry Fink, the proprietor of Fink's Magic Oil. In this era, one did not have to go to medical school to become a doctor. Henry Fink might have taken correspondence courses, but a more likely scenario was that his Magic Oil had become so popular that his friends and neighbors simply started calling him Dr. Fink.

With H.G.G. on leave from the ministry, his father convinced him to take over the manufacture of Fink's Magic Oil and market it nationally. This meant leaving small-town southeastern Ohio and moving two hundred miles away to Pittsburgh, the nation's emerging manufacturing center.

The overnight trip to Pittsburgh by train was a far cry from the arduous Atlantic journey taken by the first Finks to come to America, but the change in lifestyle was just as startling. Since their marriage, H.G.G. and

Medie had lived Spartan-like lives in eleven small rural communities. In addition, both had grown up in frontier settlements. Now they were embarking on a journey that would take them to a city with more than eighty thousand residents! But the move must have been more exciting than scary. "Here all is curious or wonderful—," James Parton wrote in an 1868 article on Pittsburgh in the *Atlantic Monthly*, "site, environs, history, geology, business, aspect, atmosphere, customs, everything."

Allie was nine years old when the family moved to Forty-eight Smithfield Street in the heart of the Triangle, the busy business and manufacturing district, where the tranquil Monongahela and the rushing Allegheny Rivers united to create the mighty Ohio. Smithfield Street was a major thoroughfare that ran toward the busy Monongahela wharf and the impressive bridge designed by the legendary John Roebling, who later designed the Brooklyn Bridge.

The city also had a variety of educational institutions, including a unique School of Design for Women that operated from the same building that H.G.G. rented for his Magic Oil production. Allie, who even as a young child demonstrated great artistic ability, may have had her first formal art training in the school's Saturday children's classes.

H.G.G.'s office was within walking distance of their home. Here, he concocted and bottled the bright red elixir that would quickly change the Fink family's fortunes. Fink's Magic Oil came in two sizes of clear, embossed aqua bottles. The small bottle sold for twenty-five cents and the large one for fifty cents. His secret formula was 67 percent alcohol, had a faint cinnamon odor, and was "composed of purely vegetable extracts compounded according to a private recipe."[24] It was packaged in a tan cardboard box with his patented trademark—a bottle with a floating ribbon inscribed "for pains and aches." The box also listed the product's promised cures for "Rheumatism, Neuralgia, Headache, Toothache, Earache, Sore Throat, Diarrhoea, Chills and Fever, Cholera, Cholera Morus, Colic, Burns, Scalds and all Aches and Pains." Enclosed "Directions for Use" included seventeen different instructions—one for each malady. It was clearly all-purpose medicine; the patient could drink it diluted in hot or cold water, rub it in "until it smarts lively," or use it to "bathe the seat of pain." All this plus a money-back guarantee!

Using his best sales techniques honed while saving souls, H.G.G. turned

FIGURE 6. H.G.G. Fink became a millionaire manufacturing Fink's Magic Oil. Author's collection.

the business into an amazingly profitable venture. Within the first twelve months, he reported a net worth of more than $18,000 (equivalent to $252,000 in 2015 dollars).[25] He achieved this remarkable success by hiring a group of salesmen and launching an aggressive and creative advertising campaign—a skill he would pass on to his grandson, George Merrick.

His best salesman was John Austin Hall, whom George Merrick described as a "nation-roaming agent." Hall was always traveling and hawking Magic Oil at county fairs. J. Austin Hall's sales acumen not only sold a prodigious amount of Fink's Magic Oil but would have a powerful impact on George Merrick's life. Years later, Hall would play a pivotal role in convincing the Merrick family to move to South Florida.

Although H.G.G. was hardly in the category of future Pittsburgh giants like Carnegie, Frick, Westinghouse, and Heinz, he knew them, especially H. F. Heinz, who began his horseradish and pickle business the same year Fink started manufacturing Magic Oil. Heinz was active in the Methodist Protestant Church, an offshoot of Methodism opposed to the authoritarian power of the Methodist Episcopal bishops. Their mother church was just blocks away from the Finks' Pittsburgh home. H.G.G. later transferred his preaching license to the Methodist Protestant denomination and served for eight years with H. J. Heinz on the board of the Methodist Protestant University in Kansas City.

As H.G.G.'s income skyrocketed, the family took on a new, more elegant lifestyle. In 1872, they moved away from the Pittsburgh smoke to the small borough of Springdale, sixteen miles up the Allegheny River. Following H. J. Heinz's example in Sharpsburg, just ten miles away, Fink also moved his Magic Oil production to Springdale, conveniently located on the Western Pennsylvania Railroad line. He built a laboratory next to his house and expanded his offerings to include a laxative called "Fink's Purely Vegetable Pills" and a cough powder called "People's Remedy." He also added a printing press to his operation where he printed boxes, flyers, and advertising documents. As the money rolled in, he purchased more than fifteen parcels of Springdale real estate, including both commercial and residential lots.

But despite his affluence and business success, H.G.G. never forgot his calling. He remained active in area camp meetings, both as a revivalist and as president of the association. In 1885, he reactivated his preacher's license in the Methodist Protestant Church and supplied local churches when needed. Three years later, he was the first person listed on the charter and served on the board of trustees of the new Springdale Methodist Protestant Church. He and his wife gave the land and helped fund the construction of

FIGURE 7. H.G.G. and Medie Fink built an impressive new home in Springdale, Pennsylvania, where both George Merrick and his uncle Denman Fink were born. It was featured in *History of Allegheny County Pennsylvania, with Illustrations, Description of its Scenery, Palatial Residences, etc., Plate XLIV* (Philadelphia: L. H. Everts, 1876).

a picturesque church located a short distance from their home. (His grand-son George would later follow his example.)

The Fink family's new, two-story frame house on Pittsburgh Street was quite a showplace and was featured in the 1876 *History of Allegheny County Pennsylvania with Illustrations, Description of its Scenery, Palatial Residences, etc.* One of the largest homes in Springdale, it sat on well-landscaped grounds on the main street. The house was filled with the laughter of a growing family that now, besides Katie, William, and Allie, included son Romulus "Romie" and baby daughter Daisey. But the laughter turned to sorrow two years later when Katie died at age eighteen. The distraught family sought solace by erecting a large granite obelisk-shaped monument in the Springdale cemetery to commemorate Katie's short life and untimely death.

Allie now had the added responsibility of being the oldest daughter. Close to her parents and adored by her siblings, she developed a strong sense of family that she would pass on to her children. She was also an outstanding student, accomplished musician, and gifted artist. Because of her many talents, her parents encouraged her to go to college—an unusual pursuit for young women of her generation. Instead of sending her to a girls' school, which was the normal path for college-bound women, her parents sent her to Lebanon Valley College, a rare co-educational institution located 225 miles away in Annville, Pennsylvania.

On August 26, 1879, nineteen-year-old Althea Fink boarded the train for Annville. Within a day of her arrival at Lebanon Valley College, she would meet another freshman, Solomon Greasley Merrick, who, six years later, would become her husband and change her life's direction.

~3

Solomon and Allie

The Discriminating Mind and the Understanding Heart

Lebanon Valley College Centennial

If it is true that opposites attract, Solomon Greasley Merrick, with his quiet eastern reserve, and Althea Corilla Fink, with her outgoing western exuberance, were destined to be together. Solomon was strikingly handsome, though "sober and unsmiling," according to his son, George. He had intense, blue-gray eyes and raven-black hair, carefully parted and brushed back from his forehead. "He was inordinately proud of his Roman nose and of his white, finely smooth skin," George wrote, "and of his unusually broad muscular hands, which so belied the frailness of his short but well-knit figure, so straight and English in manner and bearing!"[1] Intellectual, serious-minded, and pious, young Solomon dreamed of becoming a minister.

Allie was pretty, petite, and vivacious like her mother. She had a high forehead like her father and piled her mass of curly golden hair high on top of her head, leaving a few cascading curls to draw attention to the "joking or quizzical glow" of her brown eyes. She wore a perpetual smile that her teasing father said she kept to show off her dimples.[2] She was creative and wanted to be an artist.

Lebanon Valley College was 225 miles from Althea's hometown of Springdale and 98 miles from Solomon's Baltimore abode. It dominated the rural village of Annville, Pennsylvania—a picturesque, innocent sort of town that prided itself on having few distractions. Its population was predominately Pennsylvania Dutch—sober, industrious, and friendly.

A unique institution connected to the United Brethren Church, the college was "created by a body of devout but unlearned people"[3] who wanted their children to benefit from a fine liberal arts education. But the founders had to overcome two groups of objectors. The first opposed higher education because they believed it diluted spiritual faith. The second spoke passionately against coeducation. Despite these strong and widely held views, the fledgling institution opened its doors in May 1866 after the people of Annville gave the church two buildings of the former Annville Academy.

By the time Solomon, Allie, and the ten other freshmen arrived in Annville in August 1879, the small school had survived both financial and internal challenges plus a continuing effort to reverse the college's commitment to coeducation. It had a new, progressive young president named David Denman DeLong, who was also an ordained United Brethren minister. His college-educated wife, Emma, was a full partner and professor of Greek language and literature—the first woman in America to hold such a position. She also taught gymnastics and was known for insisting that both male and female students sew dresses for the African missions.[4]

The college campus was just a short distance from the Annville Railroad Station. It had a large park-like common flanked by two imposing brick buildings that served as both classroom and dormitory. Solomon lived in the North Hall and Allie in the South or "Ladies Hall," which was also home to the president and his wife.

Although Lebanon Valley College offered some scholarships, most of the students, like Solomon and Allie, came from families that could proudly afford the $180 tuition, which also covered room and board. Students choose between two courses of study leading to a bachelor's degree. The Classical Course emphasized Greek and Latin and focused on the ancient writings of Cicero, Virgil, Homer, Ovid, Plato, and Livy. Aspiring scholars also took four years of higher math, as well as other demanding courses, including astronomy, biology, history, philosophy, and "Evidences of Christianity." The Scientific Course, considered slightly less stringent, did not require Greek, offered fewer courses in ancient literature and more in science, English, history, and modern languages. For a small additional fee, students could add vocal music, piano and organ, chorus, art, and modern languages.[5]

In addition to classroom studies, the college required students—both male and female—to participate in Friday afternoon "oratoricals," at which

FIGURE 8. Solomon Merrick and Althea "Allie" Fink met in 1879 at Lebanon Valley College in Annville, Pennsylvania. Allie lived in the South or Ladies Hall (*foreground*) and Solomon across campus in the North Hall. Permission of Lebanon Valley College Archives.

they wrote essays and read them to the group. Once a month, several students gave an "oration" at the chapel on Saturday night, a popular event that was always "crowded to the doors."[6]

Solomon, a superior student, joined the Classical curriculum's freshman class, but Allie, not having the benefit of a good secondary education, had to attend preparatory classes. Although these classes usually added a year of study, Allie, who was bright, eager, and competitive, quickly advanced into the Scientific Course and leapfrogged into the sophomore class on schedule.

Although Solomon and Allie were strikingly different in both personality and outlook, they shared a love of music. They took voice classes together and Solomon sang in the college chorus. Allie, a piano and organ student, often accompanied the singers. The college catalogue listed both as German language students, an interest that must have pleased both of their grandfathers.[7]

Despite the challenging curriculum, students had time for fun. President DeLong was the first president to introduce "mixed socials," which included picnics and dinners for the entire student body. On special occasions, the Ladies Hall residents held a "sociable" in their parlor and entertained the gentlemen with games of charades. Students also looked forward to "chestnut picnics," when they went to the woods to picnic and collect chestnuts. The Quittapahilla Creek—or what the students called "The Quittie"—was another popular gathering spot for canoeing and other social activities.[8]

According to the college catalogues, student life revolved around the Literary Societies—Philokosmian and Kalozetean for men and Clionian for women. Similar to sororities and fraternities, they met every Friday night in their own decorated meeting rooms. The highlight of the year was the societies' gala anniversary parties and literary performances.

Allie was a popular student and a born leader. Elected secretary and then president of the Clionian Society, she was often called upon to represent members in faculty meetings. She was also a fearless orator and took pride in her writing. Most of her surviving essays reflect strong opinions, an optimistic point of view, and her emerging feminism. "Now that her barriers have been removed," she wrote in a paper entitled "Women in Literature," "she can, without restraint, give full scope to her intellect. What can she not achieve?" In another entitled "Woman," she wrote: "It is common thought among men, and which they freely express, that the mind of woman is inferior to man and that such and such is a woman's work as if she were a creature endowed with no high powers other than to be the servant of man. . . . They can bear no rival near the throne," she added, "and would rather keep woman a jeweled captive than see her elevated to her true position in society."[9]

Allie was an outstanding student, as well as a talented artist and musician. But while she focused on developing her artistic talent, she wrote that

FIGURE 9. Solomon Greasley Merrick and Althea Corilla Fink at the time of their marriage. Courtesy of Mildred Merrick.

she believed art was not as important to humanity as poetry and architecture—a point of view she would pass on to her son, George.[10]

Allie was happy at Lebanon Valley College but, being especially close to her family, she sometimes wrote of her longing to be at home. In one particularly poignant letter, written soon after her brother Denman was born in 1880, she described the family scene and wrote that she "could sit for hours and let my imagination carry me and place me in one of those vacant chairs." But, despite her melancholy, she added, "I will try and content myself as best I can knowing it is for my good we are separated."[11]

Her father would often jump on the train and surprise her with a visit. Always seeking ways to encourage her, he arrived on one of these excursions with a life-size bust of Minerva (Athena), the goddess of wisdom, and presented it to the Clionian Society at their Friday night meeting. The presentation was "a total surprise to nearly all the members of the society," the *Annville Gazette* reported, adding, "(the Dr. seems to be especially talented in surprising others)."[12]

During these visits, H.G.G. often would preach at Sunday services. On one such occasion, the *Gazette* reported, "his sermon will be long remembered as containing much of interest and wholesome counsel to young men contemplating the sacred office of the ministry."[13] In light of the fact that his beloved Allie was "keeping company" with prospective minister Solomon Merrick, this particular sermon might have been aimed directly at him.

Solomon was as popular and as much of a leader as Allie, but in a different way. His earnest demeanor and superior intelligence inspired respect and even awe. "We all know he is the wise one," Allie wrote.[14] Clearly the most outstanding male student in his class, his fellow members elected him president of the Philokosmian Society and the brothers and members of the YMCA followed suit. "Mr. Merrick is a young man of promise," the *Gazette* confirmed.[15]

Solomon's college experience had another dimension. When he was a senior, he began preaching in neighboring communities and led college Bible classes that, the *Gazette* noted, were particularly popular with the ladies.[16] Almost every week the *Gazette* listed where he was preaching and the topic of his sermon. "Mr. Merrick is favorably received wherever he goes," the *Gazette* reported, "and promises to be an energetic and useful man in the church. . . . His piety among us is salutary."[17]

As their four years at Lebanon Valley College drew to a close, the Class of 1883 selected Allie to write the class prophesies. One by one she predicted the future for each graduate, leaving Solomon to last. "Looking on his countenance," she wrote, "seeing the imprint of the soul within him on his face, we judge he is the pious one of our number. While the rest of our brothers may be toiling up the hill of earthly fame," she predicted, "he will be toiling as eagerly as a shepherd of mankind leading them to a better life beyond."[18]

For Solomon and Allie, their college years had been happy, profitable, and life changing. It was here that they fell deeply in love, became engaged, and planned their future together. Years later, Solomon wrote his wife a loving letter, reminding her of their days at Lebanon Valley College. "I found myself thinking," he wrote, "of old Annville days—our love story and song, the parlor, the music room, trailing arbors, tube roses [and] waltzes down by the mill."[19]

Although committed to each other, Solomon had been accepted to a three-year program at Yale Divinity School, so they had to part. Solomon moved to New Haven and Allie got a job at Lebanon Valley College as head of the art department. Even though they were both busy and productive, they missed each other terribly and had few opportunities to be together.

FIGURE 10. During their honeymoon in Perry, Maine, in 1885, Althea Merrick drew this romantic picture of "My Hubbie" in her sketchbook. Permission of City of Coral Gables Historical Resources Archives.

At the end of his first year at Yale, Solomon went to Hematite, Missouri, for a summer preaching assignment. A church member remembered him as a popular young minister who wrote to his fiancée every day and was deeply depressed if a day went by without a letter from her. He also confided that he did not think he could wait until he graduated to marry.[20]

A year later, at the end of his junior year at Yale, he and Allie exchanged vows at the DeLong residence in Annville. Following a popular Lebanon Valley College tradition, President DeLong, "the marrying president," officiated.

The young couple began their married life in Perry, Maine, where Solomon had another summer preaching assignment. Perry was a tiny hamlet on Passamaquoddy Bay, seven miles from the thriving town of Eastport. From the drawings in Allie's sketchbook, including one entitled "my Hubbie," the newlyweds spent a romantic summer amid Perry's picturesque coves and bays.

In the fall, Solomon was back at Yale and Allie returned to Lebanon Valley College, where the catalogue listed her as Mrs. S. G. Merrick. Before the school year ended, however, she was pregnant and returned to her parents' home in Springdale, where she gave birth to their first child, George Edgar, on June 2, 1886, in the same bedroom where her brother Denman had been born six years earlier. George's Grandfather Fink took one look at his lusty, curly-haired grandson and predicted that someday he would follow the family tradition and become a great preacher.

With a new son and a new degree from Yale Divinity School, Solomon was busy looking for a church of his own. When George was just a month old, he traveled to the small village of Gaines, New York, to meet with the elders of the Gaines Congregational Church, who were seeking a new minister. Gaines sat halfway between Rochester and Niagara Falls. It was founded in the early years of the nineteenth century as a way station on the legendary Ridge Road that had opened up New York's western frontier. Once a thriving town with great promise, it lost momentum in 1825 when the Erie Canal passed it by and development shifted to the nearby town of Albion. In the years that followed, Gaines settled into somnolent contentment as a quaint farming community noted for its apples.

The Congregational Church was the town's largest church and its lofty steeple verified its preeminence. Here, on July 3, the town gathered to hear what this highly educated young preacher had to offer. His sermon and pious demeanor obviously impressed the church elders, who soon offered him the $600-a-year position as "pastor and teacher."[21] "The church and congregation are very much united in him,"[22] the *Orleans Republican* noted. He was ordained on September 1, and a short time later, Allie and baby George moved into the two-story, gray-brick parsonage that sat nearby at the end of the lane just off Ridge Road.

The people of Gaines were proud of their first full-time minister and his thoughtful, energetic wife. The *Orleans Republican* confirmed their respect with almost weekly reviews. "If church members individually could exemplify the doctrines set forth by the pastor, Rev. S. G. Merrick," it opined, "sin and evil would stand rebuked if not put up a fight."[23]

The Merricks' life and young George's earliest memories revolved around the church, the close-knit Gaines community, and the surrounding countryside. Because almost everyone was a farmer, people measured their days by seasons—planting, harvesting, and picking. Church events, sermons, and holidays often had an agrarian theme. Although Solomon was one of the few who were not farmers, he was born on a farm and liked growing things—a love he passed on to his son. He always planted what George called an "orderly, thrifty, flourishing garden" and was well-known for getting a variety of vegetables days ahead of the full-time farmers in his church. Although many farmers grew vegetables and grains, apples were the cash crop, and even those who were not major apple growers had an orchard. George wrote that after living in Gaines, he spent the rest of his life trying to find another apple as good as the ones of his boyhood.[24]

George was precocious and inquisitive and never knew a stranger. His scholarly parents taught him to read before he entered school and after that he always had his nose in a book. He lapped up the stories from his father's sermons, routinely won the Bible verses memorization prize, and related people in his life to biblical and literary heroes.

Even though he spent hours reading, he was also active and energetic; nothing made him happier than running barefoot through the fields with his friends, catching frogs in the pond, gathering wild blackberries, or swimming in the "ole' swimming hole."[25]

As the preacher's son, he was expected to attend many church-related activities—Sunday school, two Sunday services, weekly prayer meetings, missionary society events, and church socials. He accepted these responsibilities as part of his life and thrived on the interaction with all kinds of people. He was known for being a particularly sensitive and caring little boy. He showed this side of his personality when his sister Ethel was born in July 1888, followed by his sister Almeda "Medie" a year later. Without coaching, he became a doting and watchful big brother.

The parsonage was not only filled with the growing Merrick family but both Solomon and Allie's parents and siblings were also regular visitors. When the Finks came, usually with their young son Denman, H.G.G. would insist that he be allowed to fill the pulpit on Sunday morning. George recalled how his conservative father would reluctantly agree and then squirm in his seat as the staid people of Gaines looked shocked when "his shouting Methodist voice would soar up and away into the rafters."[26]

George adored Grandpa Fink and the feeling was mutual. "His wondrous Biblical beard visualized God himself to me,"[27] George wrote. Solomon, on the other hand, could barely tolerate his larger-than-life father-in-law and thought he was a "long whiskered blowhard."[28] The two men were as different in temperament, style, and outlook as were Solomon and Allie. George recalled that whenever his father got angry with him or his mother, he would say that they were both like Grandpa Fink. It was not meant as a compliment.

Grandpa Fink was known for his surprises and enjoyed living up to his reputation. On one visit, the family returned home late in the evening to discover that Grandpa had hired someone to build a new wooden boardwalk from the lane to the front door and from the back door to the privy! As a man of means, thanks to Fink's Magic Oil, he was also generous. One summer he treated the entire family to a week at Lakeside on Lake Ontario—George's first experience on water.

At least once a year, the Merrick family traveled by train to both Springdale and Baltimore. Sometimes Allie and the children would enjoy an extended stay in Springdale without Solomon. During these visits, George loved to play with his uncle Denman, who was only six years his senior, and with his cousin George, who was just six years his junior. At the time, no one realized that the lives and fortunes of these three creative boys would someday be joined together.

George, with his usual literary references, remembered his boyhood in Gaines as a sort of utopian, Vicar of Wakefield–type experience colored by "the contented existence of my then idyllically happy father and mother."[29] But the years were not without strife. The family was, according to George, "as poor as church mice." Often, the elders could only pay part of Solomon's salary and kept an "arrears" column running in the church ledger. To help alleviate the financial strain and to show their love and respect for the family, the parishioners held a twice-a-year "Donation Social" at the parsonage. Members arrived bearing bags of flour, vegetables, preserves, and all kinds of supplies. Occasionally, someone would slip an envelope with a bill or so in it into the grateful pastor's hand. George, who had a sweet tooth, loved these socials because the ladies of the church also brought pies, cakes, cookies, and other delights that everyone enjoyed at the end of the evening.[30]

Illness, as frequently noted in the Albion press, also plagued the Merrick family. One of the most frightening incidents occurred during a prolonged diphtheria epidemic when three-year-old Medie contracted the often-fatal disease. Once discovered, the entire family was quarantined for several weeks. Luckily, Medie recovered, but many others—mostly young children—were not as fortunate. Solomon, who had to conduct frequent funerals, anguished over how to deal with such tragedy and struggled to find ways to offer solace to the grieving families.

Although it was not called depression at the time, Solomon suffered from what George described as "unusually gloomy spells"[31] that made him think of the biblical King Saul and his despairing periods. During these episodes, George sympathized with his steady, optimistic mother, who he said was kept very busy trying to counteract his father's despair.

In January 1892, Solomon's despondence became so severe that he abruptly resigned his position "because of illness" and went to be with his family in Baltimore. Returning in better spirits two weeks later, the church leadership convinced him to withdraw his resignation.

Sometimes when Solomon was ill, Allie would preach the Sunday sermon in his stead. "Owing to the illness of Rev. Mr. Merrick last Sunday," the Orleans American reported, "his amiable lady filled the pulpit to the satisfaction of all who were so fortunate to listen to her."[32]

Allie was Solomon's equal partner in all church activities. She served as president of the Missionary Society and the Women's Christian Temperance Union (WCTU). Although she supported her husband in every way, she also showed her independence by listing her name as Althea F. Merrick, instead of Mrs. S.G.—an unheard-of practice for a married woman of her era. She taught art lessons, listed her occupation as "artist" in the census records, and did some painting of her own, including a romanticized oil of the parsonage. But, despite her busy life, she always had time to nurture and encourage her young children, who lovingly called her "Mody." In March 1894, she gave birth to twins—Helen and Ruth—increasing the family to seven, with five children under the age of eight.

In January 1895, church elders enthusiastically signed Solomon up for his ninth year as pastor and voiced the desire to keep him in Gaines for the rest of his life. To meet his growing family's needs, they planned a donation to raise a subscription to increase his salary. "For all the labor lovingly given, for all the warm friendship and personal interest of a devoted pastor and his wife," the *Orleans Republican* implored, "let Gaines show its appreciation in the old fashioned but warmhearted way."[33]

By the time George celebrated his ninth birthday in June 1895, his happy days in Gaines were drawing to a close. The elders of the Pilgrim Church in Duxbury, Massachusetts, were looking for a new minister and thirty-six-year-old S. G. Merrick was on their list. The call to Duxbury came in early October, and soon thereafter Solomon told the stunned Gaines congregation that he had accepted an "unsought but providential opening to a larger field of labor"[34] that provided greater opportunities for his children and an increase in salary. "There was scarcely a dry eye in the house," the *Orleans American* wrote, "It will be some time before we get a Pastor that will please as well as Mr. Merrick. His amiable wife is also a worker in the Christian field and is entitled to a fair share of the honors with her husband."[35]

The plan was for Allie to take the children to Springdale while Solomon went ahead to Duxbury to make preparations for the family's arrival. Before she left, the women of the church presented her with a beautiful album quilt embroidered with more than five hundred names to show their "love and affection," as professed in a poem written for the occasion.

When Allie and the children boarded the train for Springdale, most of the town came down to the depot to tell them goodbye. The *Orleans American* echoed the entire community's sentiment with the line, "We have lost a near and very good friend in her removal."[36]

On November 10, Solomon preached his farewell sermon and left the next day for Duxbury. With a sad goodbye, the *Orleans American* summed up Solomon's tenure in Gaines: "It is not the privilege of many to be so deeply loved and respected by an entire community."[37]

Gaines and Duxbury were similar in size but as different as night and day. While Gaines exuded an egalitarian and welcoming frontier spirit, Duxbury was a more insular, old-family enclave proud of its Mayflower pedigree. Dominating the Duxbury landscape was a towering 130-foot monument to Miles Standish, who, with six other signers of the Mayflower Compact, had founded the town in 1632.[38] Although the oversize column may have looked strangely out of place in the picturesque village tucked on the shores of its namesake bay, its message was clear. The people of Duxbury revered their Pilgrim heritage.

Just six miles north of Plymouth and twenty-seven miles southeast of Boston, Duxbury had a romantic maritime heritage as a shipbuilding center and busy port. It also honored Massachusetts' recent intellectual flowering—those heady years that today's scholars call the "New England Renaissance." It had a free public library with more than five hundred books, an impressive collection for such a small town. The town had strong grammar schools and was inordinately proud of its esteemed Partridge Academy, a public/private secondary school housed in an impressive Greek-temple-style building.

When the Merricks arrived in November 1895, the glorious New England fall had just finished washing the landscape in crimson and gold and the colorful leaves were blowing about. Washington Street, the town's main thoroughfare, looked much as it had a half-century earlier. The predominant Colonial- and Georgian-style homes, with their distinctive white picket fences, gave the town a quaint, yet formal, atmosphere. The two-story parsonage, which was to be the Merricks' home for the next four years, looked like it belonged in the picture. It sat right in the heart of town on a swatch of land between Washington Street and Duxbury Bay.

Solomon had only a short walk down Washington Street to reach the front door of the stately Pilgrim Congregational Church, which looked like a New England church was supposed to look. Despite its name, by Duxbury standards the church was quite new, though it had impressive historical connections. It claimed kinship to the Pilgrims and to Elder Brewster, who brought Duxbury's first residents together for worship in the early 1600s. Brewster's original church remained Congregational until the early 1800s, when the majority of its members embraced the Unitarian faith and the rest left to become Methodist Episcopalians. In 1843, long before the outbreak of the Civil War, the Methodists split over the slavery issue and abolitionist Seth Sprague founded a new independent Wesleyan Methodist Church, giving land and funds for the present building, which was completed in 1844. The circle connected in 1870 when members of Wesleyan Methodist voted to rejoin the Congregational Church. Three years later, to honor the 250th anniversary of the arrival of the Mayflower, the church changed its name from Wesleyan Congregational to Pilgrim Congregational Church.[39]

Besides being an important religious institution, the Pilgrim Church also served as a cultural, political, and social center. Each year, the town council held its town meetings in the church's spacious assembly hall. The church also sponsored concerts and other forms of entertainment, such as lawn parties and the popular annual Sunday school picnic and ice cream social that brought the whole town together.

As minister of such an important church, Solomon quickly became a part of the Duxbury scene. Besides preaching two sermons each Sunday, leading prayer meetings, and attending a plethora of church events, he often addressed civic organizations like the Odd Fellows and the Grand Army of the Republic (GAR). He participated in town-wide celebrations, including the long-awaited dedication of the Miles Standish memorial. He also instituted a series of guest lecturers at the church, including a young black man from the Tuskegee Institute.

Allie continued her leadership in the WCTU and headed the Home-workers Society, which met for weekly sewing bees and raised money by selling their wares at the annual church bazaar. Even the Merrick children joined in. The newspaper listed the girls as participants in a community-sponsored "doll drill" and young George as part of "the managing commit-tee" of the Junior Endeavor Society's invitational lawn party.[40]

Although George was only nine years old when the family moved to Duxbury, he was emotionally and intellectually mature for his age. Within a short time, his teachers recognized his many talents, especially his gift for writing. Even before he moved to Duxbury, he had devoured every book in the family library—classics, religious texts, and magazines. Once he got to Duxbury, he found an exciting new world in the public library. Here, in addition to the familiar classics that he loved, he discovered more con-temporary writers such as Ralph Waldo Emerson, Henry David Thoreau, George Washington Cabel, and William Dean Howells. Their sometimes-controversial points of view piqued his nascent concern for social and racial justice.

His teacher, Miss Florence Chaffin, took a special interest in her bright young charge and encouraged him to continue his unusually mature read-ing and writing habits. Besides great literature, she also introduced him to the works of famous New England poets such as Henry Wadsworth Long-fellow, William Cullen Bryant, and Emily Dickinson. George was stunned by the power of their words and the descriptive and visual images they could elicit from familiar scenes or in his imaginative mind.

Miss Chaffin was not the only one who encouraged his writing. His mother, who shared his love of poetry, treasured every word he wrote and carefully preserved his schoolboy strivings. His essays and poems, written between the ages of nine and twelve, prove that he had inherited his fair share of the prodigious Fink creativity. They also show his romantic outlook on life, another Fink family trait. "The best part of life may be found in the country," he wrote in a story about a knight named Sir Roger who loved country folk best. He also found inspiration in his surroundings and from well-known New England poets. He wrote a Ralph Waldo Emerson–inspired poem about "The Battle of Lexington" and a Longfellow-style rhyme entitled "The Pilgrims."

Grandfather Fink, who thought everything George said and did was extraordinary and often told him so, found a unique way to encourage his writing. When George was ten, Grandpa arrived in Duxbury with another of his legendary surprises. To George's delight, he presented him with a printed version of his poem "The Pilgrims," which he had run on the printing press he used to create his Magic Oil labels. The title page said it all.

A POEM ENTITLED THE PILGRIMS.
COMPOSED AND WRITTEN BY
MASTER GEORGE EDGAR MERRICK

The author of this poem is only 10 years old, the eldest son of Rev. S. G. Merrick, Pastor of the Congregational Church at Duxbury, Mass.

Published by the Grandfather of this juvenile author, Rev. H.G.G. Fink, at

SPRINGDALE, ALLEGHENY COUNTY, PA

In the year 1896

Years later, George remembered how proud he felt when his adoring grandfather stated: "My grandson George's poem is more excellent than anything Longfellow wrote up to thirty years of age."[41] He also recalled the feeling in his stomach when his disparaging father laughed scornfully at the whole episode and thought George's writing was nothing more than childhood prattle.

George was not only known as a budding poet and scholar but also appreciated for his thoughtfulness. "Right here in Duxbury," he wrote when he was ten, "we can do mission work for Jesus by doing what we are told to do if it is right and by having a cheerful word for everybody."[42] When he was twelve, a member of the church sent him some money toward the purchase of a bicycle because of his caring concern and "pleasant, gentlemanly and respectful manners."[43]

Although George blossomed in Duxbury, his father's life took a different turn. Financial pressures continued to press and became more critical after son Charles was born in 1897. The punishing New England weather added to his depression. The parsonage had no modern conveniences, and the family had to burn wood and coal in a variety of stoves to keep the cold at bay. The unusually frigid air was hard on everyone and the family suffered from a variety of winter-borne ailments. The situation worsened during the winter of 1898–99, when New England experienced a series of blizzards called "The Storm of the Century," which is still used as a benchmark for severe weather. Weeks of high winds and below-zero temperature brought an unprecedented increase in infectious disease. In February 1899, at the height of the storm, George, who was usually the healthiest member of the family, contracted pneumonia and, according to his mother, was "lying at death's door." As George struggled to survive, his almost five-year-old baby sister, Ruth, contracted diphtheria and within three days was gone.[44]

The family was inconsolable. The tragedy was compounded by the fact that the snow was so deep that for three days, they could not remove Ruth's body for burial. The situation thrust Solomon into total despair and again Allie had to be the strong one. Despite her own unspeakable grief, she found the inner strength to preach at several Sunday sermons in order to protect her prostrate husband.

H.G.G. and Medie Fink came to Duxbury to give the family emotional support. With them came Grandpa's latest surprise in the form of J. Austin

Hall, his close friend and leading Magic Oil salesman. Fink, with what George called his "prescient inspiration," arrived with a plan for the Merrick family's future that would take them away from dreary New England winters and the unyielding pressures of the ministry. Hall was his salesman—his biblical Paul—the man who had traveled the world spreading the gospel of Fink's magic elixir. If "Brother" Hall could sell Magic Oil to the masses, he certainly should be able to sell Solomon Merrick on his plan.

As the snow continued to swirl outside the sad household, George wrote that he sat entranced, listening to Hall weave what he described as "tales of a wonderful new fairyland of enchantment around a newly planted town called Miami on Biscayne Bay. No greater contrast could be imagined," he added, "than that between those tales of enchanted sunshine in the South and the frigid scene of ice, desolation and death around us."[45]

George, with his romantic view of life, pictured Hall as a veritable Marco Polo, fresh from the unknown with magnificent stories of future possibilities in a place that seemed as remote and mysterious as Marco Polo's Cathay. Despite the fact that his father said he was as impulsive as his mother and grandfather, George was ready to try this Swiss Family Robinson adventure that Hall described.[46]

At first, Solomon, with his practical and pessimistic view of life, thought the Fink-Hall proposition was just another of his "all-knowing" father-in-law's romantic visions. The very idea that he should give "Brother" Hall the family's life savings to invest in South Florida real estate was beyond ludicrous. But as Hall's stories continued night after night and Allie and George joined in the sell, Solomon began to pay attention.

Grandpa Fink insisted that his son-in-law should buy lots in the new town of Miami and build houses for tourists like Hall planned to do. Solomon, remembering his own grandfather's success in the outskirts of Baltimore, was more interested in the backcountry. Hall told of a small community called Cocoanut Grove (changing to Coconut Grove after 1919). It even had a small Congregational Church. Behind it were vast pinelands where farmers were starting to raise citrus trees. As Hall's stories continued, George realized that his father had totally disregarded his grandfather's statements that life was too hard in the backcountry for a man and woman of his and Allie's temperament and education. Solomon was talking about the possibility of buying land where he could grow citrus like the people of

Gaines grew apples. Perhaps he was even thinking that he could someday subdivide the land like his grandfather had done in Baltimore.

George wrote about the rising tension between the two strong-willed men as they continued to argue about what was best for the Merrick family. At first, George and his mother sided with Grandpa Fink. But Solomon was adamant and George knew that once his father's mind was made up, he would not yield. It was clear, George wrote, that "his prophet grandfather had lost the ten days' siege to his practical determined father."[47] But he had planted a seed.

Solomon decided to write to the Coconut Grove minister, whose name—James Bolton—he found in his *Congregational Church Yearbook*. He would ask if he knew of any land for sale in the Coconut Grove area that might be suitable for growing citrus. Once his father had posted the letter, George realized that his family's future was now in the "distant hands" of an unknown South Florida minister.

When the return letter from Reverend Bolton arrived, Solomon called the family together and began reading with uncharacteristic excitement:

There is a 160-acre homestead that a South Carolinian is now proving up. It is about three and a half miles back of Cocoanut Grove Village, which is on the Bay. There is no road, but a comptie trail. (Comptie is the root which many of the settlers make into arrow root starch, for shipment by weekly mail to Key West, where it finds ready sale from $11–$18 per pound.) This homestead has 50 acres of inside glade, (detached from the great glade). This is rich brown marl soil, suitable for all kinds of vegetable growing. Here you can immediately plant your first money crop and home vegetable garden, without any expense of clearing the ground, other than simply plowing it. There are about 110 acres of the Coral-rocky pineland. This is high and seldom overflows except during our four-month rainy season. . . . And then only in the low sinks or flats between the Coral reefs. . . . Here on this rocky Coral pineland you can plant, after clearing off the pine trees and palmettos that cover the rocky soil, your groves of oranges, grapefruit or alligator pears. Gregory's price is $1100 because he is homesick for his old home in Carolina. These cracker homesteaders seldom make permanent settlers. The Yankees and the native Conchs seem to be making the permanent quality of this new land though South and North are about evenly united so far. . . . The opening of the Royal Palm Hotel will provide a need for local market gardening. I would advise that your first year's crops be devoted to that purpose. It will involve little outlay. You can have your son George peddle the vegetables, and a boy of that age can readily do it. This will leave you free to work and to prepare the green goods for market. You can lay enough beyond the family's subsistence for the following year to clear and plant 10 acres in grove in the high land within the first year. Too, there is a bearing grove of 150 large, well-fruiting guavas (about an acre and a half). These can be sold for one dollar a pound at Captain Simmons jelly factory on the bayfront south of the Cocoanut Grove Village. These should produce at least $400 worth this coming summer and more the next year. I earnestly advise you Brother Solomon, to conclude the purchase of this Gregory homestead at once. As I believe he will be able to sell it within a few months. There is not another such homestead as all-round suited to your family's needs as you have so fully and frankly advised me.[48]

That night, George overheard his father telling his mother that he had come to a decision. The next day he would go to Plymouth and withdraw $1,100 from their $1,500 life savings and send a draft to Reverend Bolton to buy the Gregory homestead. "We will rely on him," he added, "and know that God—and not Grandfather Fink—is leading us."[49]

In late July, a deed signed by William Gregory arrived in the mail. The Merricks were the official new owners of a sight-unseen, 160-acre homestead in the backcountry of Coconut Grove. George, who, along with his mother, usually had a positive attitude, felt mixed emotions. He had just completed the eighth grade and had passed the competitive test for full admission into the prestigious Partridge Academy, which could lead to Harvard and a writing career. Now, he would be leaving Duxbury and the Partridge Academy and moving to an unknown world of swamp and alligators that he knew only through Kirk Munroe's adventure novels. But the move to Florida would remain a family secret until the church was properly notified. Solomon worried about the future and found it difficult to continue preaching, so his wife and a group of visiting preachers had to fill the pulpit.

FIGURE 11. Shortly before they moved to Florida, the Merrick family lined up for a final photograph in front of their home in Duxbury, Massachusetts. *Left to right*: Solomon Merrick, friends Howard and Myra Anderson, Ethel Merrick, Helen Merrick, Althea Merrick holding Charles Merrick, and George Merrick. University of Miami Special Collections. Courtesy of Mildred Merrick.

At the close of the service on September 16, 1899, Mr. Crowell, one of the many supply ministers, read Rev. S. G. Merrick's simple resignation "on account of ill health" and announced that the family would go to Florida for the winter.

A short time later, Solomon preached his final sermon at Pilgrim Church. "Many good wishes go with them from the whole community," the *Old Colony Memorial* stated in a final send-off that was quite unlike the one he had received in Gaines. The following day, a subdued family boarded the train for Baltimore. With them went a small casket bearing Ruth's remains. Her parents, unwilling to leave her alone in the cold New England soil, planned to reinter her in the Greasley-Merrick family plot in Baltimore.

After a simple ceremony at Green Mount Cemetery in Baltimore, Ruth's body was laid to rest with her Merrick relatives. Sadly, Allie and the younger children left for Springdale and Solomon and George boarded the train for Florida. As the train pulled out of the terminal, George thought about his father's courage and vision for undertaking such a risky venture. It was a lesson George would never forget.

~4

"When the Groves Begin to Bear"

There's a phrase we heard so often
In the days not long ago;
And the word—as always—soften;—
Bring the ache such mem'ries know;
I can hear my father's saying
"When the groves begin to bear."

George E. Merrick, "When the Groves Begin to Bear"

The train trip from Baltimore to South Florida took two days and was te-
dious. But despite the incessant stops and frequent change of trains, George
could not help but see the journey as a *Swiss Family Robinson* adventure.
His romantic mind imagined South Florida to be like the Robinson's tropic
isle. Surely, the Massachusetts Family Merrick's adventure would end as
happily. His father, on the other hand, viewed the move like he viewed
life. It was neither romantic nor exciting but simply necessary. He stoically
faced the future with clenched teeth and his usual no-nonsense resolve.

George was thirteen and just beginning the tumultuous rush to manhood. He relished the opportunity to spend time alone, man-to-man, with
his usually distant father. But even George would have felt despair had he
known what awaited him in Florida. His childhood was whizzing by as
fast as the strange scenery he saw from the open window. Within days, he
would take on the work of a man and face adult responsibilities beyond
those experienced by his favorite Dickens characters.

If Solomon, who, unlike George, always saw the glass half empty, had known what lay ahead, he would have been more depressed than usual. At some point during the trip, he heard the shocking news that yellow fever had broken out in Miami and the young city was quarantined. Now, with no way to turn back, they faced not only an unknown place but also a deadly tropical scourge that was worse than anything they had experienced in the frozen north. Because of the quarantine, George later wrote, the train could not continue on to Miami, so a sympathetic minister who lived near Florida's Loxahatchee River offered him and his father a place to stay. Their sojourn was brief; by early November, just two months after they left Baltimore, *The Miami Metropolis* recorded the Merricks among the newcomers.[1] George and his father had skirted the city's quarantine by sailing into Coconut Grove, which was actually closer to their final destination than the Miami depot was.

When George and Solomon arrived in Coconut Grove they felt encouraged. It was a small but thriving sailing community with large bayfront homes, lush landscaping, and an air of quiet sophistication. As they walked down the wooden wharf that jutted out into the bay from the foot of today's MacFarlane Road, they could see the rather imposing Peacock Inn, South Florida's first hotel, sitting proudly on the ridge to their left. It was owned and operated by Englishman Charles Peacock and his wife, Isabella. On the right, across the narrow roadway of glaring-white crushed rock, stood the Peacock and Son General Store and the newly completed, picturesque Union Congregational Church. The Coconut Grove schoolhouse and the Housekeepers Club—South Florida's first woman's club—were visible behind the church. In many ways, smaller but older Coconut Grove was far ahead of Miami. Besides a school, church, and woman's club, it had a library and yacht club and an impressive group of regular winter visitors and permanent residents. Kirk Munroe, a nationally known author of boys' adventure books, had a home there. George, of course, had read every one of Munroe's books, including several with Florida themes.

Down the bayfront on the road to Miami was a row of large, Key West–style homes. One belonged to the Albury family, whose daughter Sarah Louise married William Gregory. She, according to the old-timers, was the reason Gregory sold Merrick the homestead. Before long, Charles Peacock's son Alfred, who ran the general store, would own this house. There,

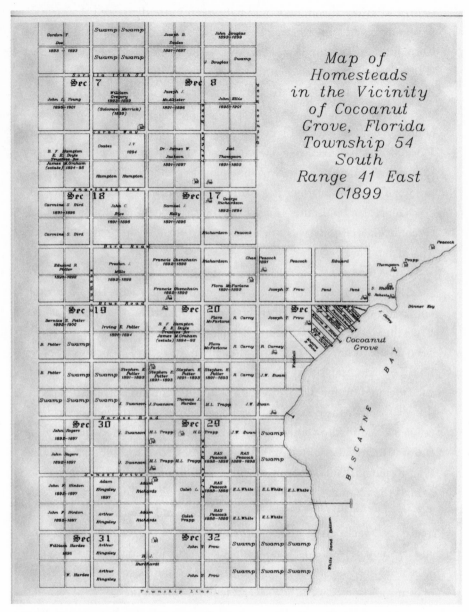

Figure 12. Under the Homestead Act of 1862, the U.S. government offered free land in mostly uninhabited South Florida. This map notes the original homesteaders in what would later become parts of Coconut Grove, Coral Gables, and South Miami. Coral Gables street names were added for reference. Courtesy of Eunice Peacock Merrick.

Eunice, his four-year-old daughter, would grow up and one day marry George Merrick.

Rev. James Bolton, the red-haired preacher who arranged for Merrick's purchase of the Gregory homestead, met Solomon and George at the boat. Bolton offered them a place to stay until they had the homestead ready for the family. Bolton was English and his young wife, Eva, who suffered from consumption, came from an aristocratic Kentucky family. A Methodist minister by training, he had served a number of Florida churches, including the one in Key West. The Boltons were true pioneers, having arrived in Miami in 1896. He preached in the fledgling settlement's first tent-church and witnessed the birth of the new city. The following year, he moved to Coconut Grove and became the first permanent minister of the established Union Chapel, which had recently officially connected to the Congregational Church.

The Boltons lived on a ten-acre tract on the southwest corner of the intersection of today's Grand Avenue and Douglas Road. Called "Minnewanda Lodge," locals considered it one of the prettiest homes back of the bayfront. The popular couple was famous for their beautiful roses, tropical trees, and luxuriant vines that spilled over a crude rock wall. "The scene," *The Miami Metropolis* opined, "had a New England air."[2] Here, George met the tropics and tasted his first exotic fruits—mangoes, avocados or alligator pears, rose apples, sapodillas, and guavas.

Just to the north was Eva's good friend Flora MacFarlane's homestead. Flora was a woman of many firsts—first woman homesteader, founder and first president of the Housekeepers Club, and one of the first Coconut Grove schoolteachers. Slightly southeast, early resident Joseph Frow had "proved up" another homestead. After he gained title, he moved to the bayfront, platted his homestead, and sold lots to many of the new black Bahamian residents who created a thriving community called Kebo. His daughter Lillian married Alfred Peacock and was the mother of baby Eunice.

George and his father spent their first Miami night in the Boltons' small attic room where, George wrote, they "became acquainted with the night agony of red-bugs, gnats, mosquitoes and jiggers."[3] Unfortunately, this sleepless night was but a prelude to a recurrent bedtime nightmare.

The final lap of their journey from New England to a new life began on what was then called Bolton's Road, now Grand Avenue. As they walked west, perhaps Solomon was looking forward to finding what his daughter Ethel later said he expected—"a tropical retreat where a family of culture might retire and live a life of more or less leisure as growers of fruits and trees."[4] These delusions quickly disappeared. Soon after they passed Bolton and MacFarlane's small clearings, they entered a wild and virgin pine forest. "Deep ruddy holes, barricading palmettos and sandy sinks were the gauntlets,"[5] George wrote.

What was called the Coconut Grove backcountry began just west of today's Douglas Road. This twenty-square-mile western portion of Township 54S/41E was considered so remote that the government did not get around to surveying it until 1891. Three weeks after it was opened to homesteaders, however, 142 would-be pioneers caught what *The Tropical Sun* called "Miami Fever" and filed claims.[6] The homesteaders, who were mostly young, male, Southern, and single, found the government's offer irresistible. If a person lived on the land for five years, built a house, and raised some crops, he or she could acquire a 160-acre square for only a small filing fee of about fourteen dollars. After fulfilling their obligation and receiving a patent or deed, many homesteaders, like William Gregory, sold the land and returned to their former homes with cash in hand.

Because the land available for homesteading had to be high and dry, it included vast expanses of rocky, palmetto-choked pineland. The locals called these high rocky ridges "reefs" and the intermittent sandy and sometimes seasonally soggy areas "glades" or "sinks." Homesteaders wanted some glade or prairie land in their tract because it did not require clearing. The glades' soil was good for raising vegetables—especially winter vegetables that grew to maturity before the summer rains. The rocky pinewood, although looking rather hopeless for raising anything, proved to be good for citrus—if someone was willing to put in the sweat and tears necessary to clear it.

When George and his father reached what is today's LeJeune Road, they turned right and passed by five more one-quarter-mile-square homesteads—Obenchain, Richardson, Kelly, Thompson, and Jackson—before turning left on Jackson Road, now Coral Way. To the north of what was hardly a road and barely a trail, "Red" McAllister's log cabin and clearing marked another homestead. (One day, George would own them all.)

The weary newcomers finally reached a stake at the intersection of what

Figure 13. Solomon Merrick was shocked when he saw the 160-acre site he had purchased sight unseen from homesteader William Gregory. The dirt road in the foreground would later become Coral Way. University of Miami Special Collections. Courtesy of Mildred Merrick.

is now Anderson Road and Coral Way. It marked the eastern line of the Gregory homestead and the Merricks' new life.

A short distance away—near today's Coral Way and Toledo Street—sat a crude, unpainted, two-room twenty-by-thirty-eight-foot board-and-batten shack with what George called a "blow way" or open section in the middle. Other structures included two small log cabins, a barn built out of barrel staves, and a makeshift packinghouse. After some investigation they found the two promised wells and about an acre and a half of guava trees.[7] Besides the so-called improvements listed on the deed, the sale also included a crude homemade wagon and an old mule named Maude.

At first sight, Solomon was beside himself. What had he done? How could he tell Allie? What would she say? Was his hated father-in-law right when he said they should buy land in town and not in the backcountry? His first impulse was to flee and return north, but George, the optimist, took on his mother's role and tried to soothe his distraught father. In reality, with their life's savings invested in this inhospitable, rocky piece of real estate, they were stuck. There was no turning back. He and George simply had to go to work and get the homestead ready for the rest of the family. At that moment, George stopped being a student and became a hired hand.

For the next month, George and his father awoke before dawn and made their way to the homestead, a two-mile march. Each evening, after a day of hard labor and insect bites, the exhausted father and son returned to the Boltons, where Eva had supper waiting. Almost immediately, the Boltons became their closest friends and, as George recalled, the ones who "translated a strange tropical country to our eagerly receptive ears."[8] But it was Eva who captivated young George the most. Back in Massachusetts, he had taken his mother's and teacher's nurturing for granted. Now with no teachers, no mother, and his father talking about rocks and fertilizer, she was the one bright spot in his suddenly dreary life. College educated in both Europe and America, Eva Bolton had many talents. She was a writer and book reviewer for national magazines, played the piano, sang, painted, and regularly won first prize at the county fair for her jams and jellies. She took an intense interest in the introspective young man and encouraged his intellectual curiosity. They discussed poetry and great books. They shared a love of the writings of John Ruskin and, as George recalled, talked for hours about how his description of the sky over the Roman Campagna matched the pastel-colored splendor of South Florida winter sunsets. Eva encouraged George's natural optimism, opened his eyes to the new world around him, and helped him keep at bay thoughts of what might have been at Duxbury and the Partridge Academy. He later wrote that she was the most brilliant and cultured woman he had ever met and called their conversations a "pointed up shining experience."[9]

At night, father and son were often kept awake by Eva's deep, tubercular cough and her husband's gentle, caring murmuring. During these wakeful moments, Solomon, despondent and with no Allie to cheer him, confided in George and shared his fears, miseries, premonitions, and dreams.

At the homestead, father and son found a helpful neighbor—if you can call someone who lived a half a mile away a neighbor. He was thirty-one-year-old John Lawrence Young and, like most of the homesteaders, he was a "Cracker"—a proud acknowledgment of his rural Georgia southernness. Young's homestead, with its simple two-story wooden cabin, bordered the

Merricks' on the west, extending from today's Columbus Boulevard to Red Road. Other nearby homesteaders—Dalkins, McAllister, "One-eyed Harris," "Old Dilks," Dr. Jackson, Montgomery, and the Ludlums—came by to meet the new "Yankee" preacher, the one they heard had a fancy education. They probably thought he wouldn't last long like some of the other city folks who came to the backcountry. But they didn't know Solomon Greasley Merrick and his iron will, his unyielding determination, and his overly demanding expectations of himself and those around him.

Unlike his father, whom he described as being "impassive to all but the discomforts of this strange land,"[10] George took every opportunity to meet his fellow backcountrymen and explore the strange new surroundings. He found the Crackers and their lifestyle totally different from anything he had ever experienced, although he remembered the Pilgrim Church Mission Board once collecting money for poor white southerners. He ate their food—corn bread, sowbelly, fried okra, collard greens, and grits—and declared it "strangely good."[11] He went to their gatherings and learned to tap his foot in time with the fiddle.

The Crackers, at home in the pinelands, taught him about what he called "a fierce, cruel kind of romance"[12] that included dogs, coons, snakes, lizards, and wild birds. They took him to see the Everglades, which at the time began a little more than a mile west of his new home. They shared stories about the people they called the "Bayfronters," who lived on the Coconut Grove ridge and hung out with their visiting friends, the "Swells." They ridiculed the bay-hugging "Conchs," who they said were "all mixed up . . . with many strange people strained into their kin."[13] For the first time in his life, George met racial prejudice face-to-face.

George called Cracker Young "their daily guide."[14] He taught them how to dig a well and plant winter vegetables in the glade, now the Granada Golf Course. It was the beginning of a friendship and working relationship that would last the rest of Young's life. When he married Edna Lee Ludlum on Christmas Eve, Solomon performed the ceremony.

With the quarantine still in effect, George and his father could not go to Miami for supplies and had to make do with what was available in Coconut Grove. Adding to their problems, the family's furniture and household items had been unloaded at Fort Lauderdale. Fortunately, the backcountry people, in typical frontier style, looked after each other. C. J. Rose, whose homestead was five homesteads east of the Merricks,' offered his mule team and wagon for assistance.[15]

Four days into the new century, word spread that the quarantine had been relaxed for local residents only. For the first time since mid-October, those living outside the city limits could enter Miami during daylight hours. Tragically, early the next day, the young city experienced its second major fire in as many months. In November, the Tuttle family's Miami Hotel had suspiciously caught fire after a yellow-fever victim died there. This time, another questionable fire broke out in F. T. Budge's Hardware Store and quickly spread to other buildings.

The affected stores were clustered around the northeast corner of Twelfth (Flagler) Street and Avenue "D" (Miami Avenue), considered the town's most important intersection. Imagine how George and Solomon felt when they got their first glimpse of the so-called Magic City and found it half burned down. Adding to the gloom, Henry Flagler's grand, bright-yellow Royal Palm Hotel—the city's reason for being—was still dark and shuttered because of the quarantine. They did not even have time to look around before joining the effort to help salvage stock from the burned-out stores.[16]

In the midst of a pall of disappointment and difficulty, George and Solomon received some good news. Despite the quarantine, Allie and the children, accompanied by family friend Rev. William Phipps, were leaving Springdale, Pennsylvania, for Miami. The plan was for the family to come to Lemon City, located five miles north of Miami, thus avoiding the quarantine. Because the train came in late at night, George and Solomon would meet them and spend the night in Lemon City. The following day they would sail to Coconut Grove where mule and wagon awaited to take them to their new home. *The Miami Metropolis* noted their impending arrival and added that father and son "no doubt are impatient to show these travelers from the frozen north all the wonders of their new tropical home."[17]

Wonders indeed. It was midnight and pouring down rain when the train pulled into the Lemon City station. The station, located at Northeast Fifty-Ninth Street, was a simple yellow wooden structure, identical to most of Flagler's other small depots. Lemon City, like Coconut Grove, was older than Miami. But unlike Coconut Grove, it began to decline when the railroad reached Miami. In fact, the owners of the one decent Lemon City hotel had recently barged the entire hotel down the bay to Miami where business was better.

When the Merricks arrived, Lemon City had only one small hotel called the Carey House, located a block from the bay between Northeast Fifty-Ninth and Sixtieth Streets. The exhausted, half-awake family, with Solomon and George carrying the small children, had to walk a quarter mile down a slippery sand road through a forest of pine and palmettos to get there.[18] The so-called hotel was really just a large house with small rooms, no indoor plumbing, and no electricity. The train usually arrived late at night, so Mother Carey, as she was fondly called, greeted guests at the door with a candle to lead them to their room. Because of the quarantine, the hotel was packed with guests and most had to double up with strangers to find a place to sleep.[19] The Merricks, all seven of them, had one room with one large bed that they extended with several chairs.

After a mostly sleepless night, the children were up early to get their first daylight glimpse of the region that was to be their home. Unlike the children, who were excited, Allie remembered having a "sinking heart."[20] At breakfast, she and the children were introduced to canned milk—the homesteaders' staple. It was something she and the children had never tasted or even knew existed. The milk, however, was nothing compared to the series of "never befores" coming their way.

Allie and the children met their first Conchs in Lemon City, although George and Solomon were already well acquainted with Coconut Grove's large Conch population. The Careys, like most Conchs, came from the Bahamas via Key West. They were part of the large white Bahamian community that had migrated to South Florida along with an equal number of their black countrymen. These seafaring Bahamians could proudly lay claim to being South Florida's first permanent, non-Indian residents.

Lawrence Young captained the sailboat that took the family from Lemon City to Coconut Grove. There they boarded the old work wagon that Solomon had fitted up with three kitchen chairs. The going was slow and bumpy and the chairs slid from side to side. Maude, who knew the way, zigzagged around the stumps and rocks and kept the wagon wheels deep in the well-worn ruts.

The raw, unfamiliar landscape was shocking enough, but when Allie saw the cabin, she wrote that she almost fainted. She discovered that she could

Figure 14. Richard Merrick was born in the original cabin in 1903. His drawing shows remarkable details of the 1903 addition, which remains as part of the Merrick House today. University of Miami Special Collections. Courtesy of Mildred Merrick.

stick her thumbs through cracks in the walls that had become doorways for a variety of creatures she had never before encountered. "How could we have any peace with such a place to sleep in?" she wrote.[21]

But Allie, who saw the best in everything and everyone, had promised her father that she would not complain. She agreed to stick it out for at least five years without returning north. Knowing that she could not leave, and being a natural optimist like her father, she wrote that she never let Solomon know her true feelings. Instead, she went to work, cleaning and patching.

The house, then considered part of Coconut Grove, was crudely built, like most of the other homestead cabins. But when Allie added her special touch, its interior was startlingly different. With her usual artistic style, she hung muslin on the walls to cover the cracks and then painted designs on the cloth to simulate wallpaper and brighten the room. She hung her pictures, put rugs on the floor, arranged the family's large collection of books, and put her pride and joy—the piano—in a place of honor. Son Richard, who was born in the cabin three years later, recalled that their house was the only one he knew that had pictures on the wall.

The first year was very difficult for the Merrick family. Solomon dreamed of planting citrus trees, especially grapefruit and other tropical fruits. He did not have to go far to be inspired. The famous John Douglas and Potter Brothers' groves were just a few homesteads away. Each was a grapefruit pioneer who made undreamed-of profits from what was then considered an exotic fruit.

Solomon had some knowledge of planting vegetables, having been known for his growing prowess during his days in Gaines, New York. But he knew nothing about growing grapefruit. Always the scholar, George remembered that every night when the family was in bed, his father was up reading horticulture books and magazines. But lack of citrus-growing experience was not the Merricks' greatest problem. They had no money to plant citrus trees and barely enough to survive. Until money was made and saved, the lowly guava became what George called their "manna from heaven."[22]

The Merricks had never seen a guava tree before they arrived in Florida, yet they had more than an acre of the spindly, spotted trees growing almost wild on their property. Although not native, guava trees seemed so because the Conchs had brought them from the Bahamas decades earlier. By early summer, the Merricks' trees were loaded with the sickeningly sweet-smelling fruit.

The chief local guava man was Captain A. F. Simmons, veteran of the Grand Army of the Republic. He and his wife, Dr. Eleanor Gault Simmons, South Florida's first woman doctor, lived in Coconut Grove at the site of the Kampong—the future home of plant explorer David Fairchild. Here, Simmons manufactured all things guava—jelly, marmalade, wine, syrup, vinegar, cider, and cheese. With a "Sweets for the Sweet" label, he sold his unusual products all over the United States and as far away as England, France, and Germany.[23]

The Merrick family's guava man was George. Almost every day during the fruiting season, George would climb the trees and shake the limbs until the ripe fruit fell to the ground. It was not as easy as it seemed. The mosquitoes were so thick around the trees that he had to wear a heavy long-sleeved shirt, long pants, and gloves even in the summer. He also had to cover his face with a mosquito net, which he draped over his straw hat and tucked into his shirt. He packed the fruit in wooden boxes retrieved from Peacock's store and used the plentiful beggarweed as packing material. He also

Figure 15. Thanks to Althea Merrick, the Guavonia School, with Winifred Cobb as teacher, opened in January 1901 in an outbuilding on the Merrick property. The students included (*right*) Medie, Helen, and Ethel Merrick. University of Miami Special Collections. Courtesy of Mildred Merrick.

filled the wagon with several layers of the weed's velvety leaves to protect the rather fragile guavas during the bumpy, one-and-one-half-hour ride to Simmons.'

Simmons' loading platform and scale sat just inside his rock wall, which flanked today's Main Highway. Here the guava sellers lined up to weigh in. George liked Simmons because as long as the guavas were firm, he paid one cent a pound and always rounded off even a quarter pound to the next highest number. That first summer, George sold him six hundred bushels of yellow jelly guavas, netting almost $300.[24]

With this unexpected windfall, it is no wonder that when Allie finally succeeded in getting the school board to open a school in the area, she named it Guavonia. When the family arrived in Florida, four of the children, counting George, were school age, but there was no school in the backcountry; the nearest was in Coconut Grove. Even though the Merricks offered the school board one of their log cabins for a school building, the board demurred, insisting there must be ten students before they would open a new school. Desperate, Allie scoured the surrounding homesteads to find the required number of students. She even offered to let some of the children stay with her family during the week. She made the same offer to the teacher.

Early in 1901, the Guavonia School opened with twelve students and teacher Winnifred Cobb. When the first term ended in June, *The Miami Metropolis* noted, "the work of the children done during the term would far excel work done in many a more pretentious building."[25] Not surprisingly, the student who received the highest award during the closing ceremonies was thirteen-year-old Ethel Merrick.[26]

George, although only fourteen, was not one of the Guavonia students. In fact, he did not attend school from the time he arrived in 1899 to the time he left for college in 1907. This was very hard on a gifted, literary-minded young man who had been at the top of his class in Duxbury. But despite lack of schooling, with the help of his encouraging parents, he educated himself. He went to the Coconut Grove Library every Saturday and borrowed books. Often, after dinner, he discussed his reading with Guavonia teacher Miss Cobb, who lived with the family. Mostly he read. At night and during his wagon trips to Coconut Grove, he read books by authors like Charles Dickens and Washington Irving. After years of reading several hours a day, George had a better literary education than most.

Solomon, like George, was a reader but had none of George's romantic notions. He was intense, no-nonsense, and hard-driving, and he liked to win. He proved his mettle as early as March 1901, when he won first prize for onions and beans at Miami's Henry Flagler–sponsored Mid-Winter Fair.[27] This was quite an accomplishment for a man who previously had tilled only a small kitchen garden.

In addition to beans, onions, and tomatoes, the Merricks also planted eggplant and peppers—vegetables that could tolerate the summer sun and extend the growing season. Besides helping plant and harvest the vegetables, George had full responsibility for selling them. Every day between November and May, he awoke at 2 a.m. and loaded the wagon. Then he and what he called his "vegetable-peddling mule partner," Maude, set out for Miami. Leaving the barn, he followed the narrow trail across the sink (now the site of the Granada Golf Course) to the backcountry's first north-south road (LeJeune). He traveled north on LeJeune to Eighth Street, then called Orange Glade Road, and followed Orange Glade through the thick pinewoods to the Miami Avenue Bridge, which crossed the Miami River. As he drove through the darkness, unable to read, he remembered sometimes "musing dreamingly" about someday building a community on the family's land. His daily Miami trips also gave his imaginative, poetic mind a glorious morning sunrise to write about.[28]

Although known as a dreamer, his dreams never got in the way of his strong work ethic and sense of responsibility. The first year, he sold tomatoes door-to-door. Then, as the crops improved and expanded, he regularly supplied vegetables to the Royal Palm Hotel and sold to brokers who operated from both the dock and the depot. He was well-known and respected by the close Miami community, and people were not surprised by his future success. Pat Railey, who worked at Budge's, remembered that every morning when he opened his door, George was sitting on the wagon reading a book while he waited. The wagon had a sign that read: "S. G. Merrick & Son Vegetable Wagon #1"[29] but everyone knew that there was no vegetable wagon #2.

In early 1901, Solomon raised capital by selling twenty-six acres of the homestead to Rev. William Phipps for $260. Phipps was a Methodist minister and close friend of Grandpa Fink. Phipps benefited from his close connection to his brother Henry, Andrew Carnegie's partner in Pittsburgh Steel, where both his son and son-in-law were company executives. He often stayed with his daughter and son-in-law, James Hunter, who built a fine house on today's Biscayne Boulevard and Fourth Street. Perhaps it was Phipps' purchase that gave Solomon the idea of selling plots of land to fellow ministers—an idea that George spoke about in later years.

With proceeds from the sale and profit from their vegetables and guavas, George and Solomon planted grapefruit trees—three acres by July 1901. But planting grapefruit was nothing like planting vegetables. The grapefruit needed high ground and that meant that the unyielding pinelands had to be cleared. This was no easy task. For the first time, Solomon had to hire help. George later wrote how "One-eyed" Harris and his crew chopped down the great, thick pines, rolled them into a pile, and burned them. Sometimes, George would drag especially good logs over the trail to Coconut Grove, where they could be cut into lumber at the Pickford sawmill.

With the pines cut, the next job of hand-grubbing the palmetto, comptie plants, and other stubborn flora fell to him and his black Bahamian helper and soon friend, Tim Gibson. Gibson taught George how to hand-grub rock and palmetto while staying alert to the sound of the rattlesnake—one of the pinewoods' most common and deadliest inhabitants.

Palmettos, the bane of the pioneer, were almost impossible to extricate. George wrote that they had "alligator seeming roots [that] run on top of the ground or near the surface and grip the ground tenaciously with its thousand corded centipede legs."[30] Even the best grubber could only clear a forty-by-forty-foot square in a day. The roots usually came out in ten-inch-long chunks that, when piled together and ignited, made an impressive blaze.

Then there was the rock. It, too, had to be hand-grubbed, loaded, and hauled away. George remembered feeling that nature had somehow cursed their land by putting so much rock in the way of planting. His father, in a rare moment of optimism, had admonished George, telling him that it was a blessing from God that they would someday use to build a home and a future.[31]

A few years later, George got another lesson in the value of what natives called "coral rock"—the lacey, oolitic limestone that lay just below the surface and often on top of the thin soil. He spent three weeks with the road crew paving what is now Coral Way. Most of the labor involved hand-grubbing the rock necessary to do what they called "rocking and rolling" a new road. Sixteen-year-old George received one dollar a day for his road building. His job was to help the crew hand-grub the rock with a pick and mattock, then load it on a dump cart. Next, he would help push the cart to the ten-foot-wide and two-foot-deep roadbed. After spreading out the load, the crew went back to grubbing. Meanwhile, the big hissing, wood-fueled steamroller rumbled down the new road crushing piles of rock in its wake. George remembered that when the workmen finished the road, the family was so happy to have the dirt trail paved that they joined hands and walked together down the middle of the new road as far as Montgomery's Corner (today's Red Road).[32]

It is hard to fathom the contrast between George's life on the South Florida frontier and what it might have been if the family had stayed in New

England. Instead of being educated by the dons of Duxbury's Partridge Academy, George's real-world education came from the Crackers and the "Saws," the local name for black Bahamians. He had his first drink in the pinewoods with One-eyed Harris and found his manhood in a nearby homestead cabin, where a willing Cracker wife took in paying customers. On Saturday night, he often went into town with the Cracker boys. One of their favorite hangouts was "North Miami," the wild pool hall and saloon district just north of today's Fourteenth Street, then the city limits.

North Miami also claimed the infamous "Styx," the town's red light district. George listened to the Cracker boys' exploits and eventually added a few of his own. He even witnessed a murder on the Miami docks and was shocked when the shooter was acquitted. He watched a hanging and instantly became a lifelong opponent of capital punishment. It was quite an education for a romantic, idealistic preacher's son.

The Saws had a more positive and lasting influence on his life. They taught him about the tropics, told romantic tales of the islands they had left behind, and opened what George called "a sesame world of romance."[33] They were what George called the "way-showers" and the most important influence on his understanding of how South Florida should develop.[34] They taught him to identify all the native trees and the many tropical fruits their fellow countrymen brought with them. Sometimes George would return from town through the Brickell Hammock, the thick hardwood forest that dominated the landscape between Miami and Coconut Grove. He would often stop along the way to collect leaves for the Saws to identify. It was the Saws who taught him to appreciate the south wind that brought the cool summer breezes from the Caribbean. For George, it also brought hope and romance. Through the Saws, he later wrote, he "saw, felt, smelled and knew much of the south wind's knowledge and of its fruitful peculiar contentment."[35]

The same summer that George and Solomon planted the first grapefruit trees, Solomon's life took another unexpected turn. Although he called himself a farmer, he remained connected to his religious life. Every Sunday, the family would pile in the wagon and make the trek to the Union Church in Coconut Grove. Richard Merrick recalled that old Maude would turn toward the Grove without being nudged when the whole family was dressed

up and in the wagon.[36] Occasionally, Solomon would preach and participate in baptisms, weddings, and funerals, but he vowed to never again be
a regular minister. When Bolton resigned in early 1901, the church fathers
tried to convince Solomon to take over the pulpit on a permanent basis.
After resisting for several months he was finally persuaded and, in July 1901,
became Union Congregational Church's second minister.[37]

Apparently, the Grove church had the same admiration for their new
minister as had the people of Gaines. "Rev. Merrick," *The Miami Metropolis*
reported, "is winning golden opinions for his work as pastor of the Congregational Church. As a speaker, he is bright and attractive; as a pastor sympathetic and devoted to his work. As a citizen, a splendid example of Christian gentleman."[38] One of Solomon's most difficult assignments came in the
fall when he had to preside at Eva Bolton's funeral. George was devastated.

Allie, as she had previously, also became a church leader. Two months after Solomon became minister, she initiated and led the church's Ladies' Aid
Society. Within a year, four dedicated members had raised enough money
through suppers and bazaars to pay off the church's $300 debt.[39] She was
elected clerk and occasionally took Solomon's place in the pulpit—especially when he was having one of his recurring bouts of depression.

If life on the frontier was difficult for Solomon and George, imagine what
it was like for Allie, who was more gregarious than her husband was. Her
nearest woman neighbor was two miles away. She joined the Housekeepers
Club in July 1900 and it became her only respite from work and loneliness.
For the first few years, she had no one to help around the house except her
young daughters—quite a change from her earlier life. She cooked, cleaned,
and did the washing in a big pot over an open fire. She also oversaw her
children's education and the Guavonia School, sometimes helped in the
fields, supported her husband's church work, and, most of all, encouraged
him when he was down. Years later, George recognized her pivotal role
in the family's survival when he wrote her biography for a book honoring
pioneer women. "It could not have been done but for her constant inspiration through freezes, floods, drought, etc., bad markets, sickness and all the
vicissitudes of an unknown land and unfamiliar conditions,"[40] he wrote.

The Merricks suffered through each of the trying events George listed.
But perhaps most traumatic was the record-breaking rains of the summer

of 1901. George vividly recalled the event in a story entitled "The Rainy Season." In an era before Everglades' drainage, what George called a biblical forty-day and forty-night downpour could cause problems unimagined today. After a crop-damaging drought that lasted six months, the clouds exploded in May and before the deluge ended in October, almost sixty-seven inches of rain fell.[41] "We were living with Noah," George wrote. All the land between the "reefs," including most of the homesteaders' cabins, flooded. Roads became impassible and the water was so deep on the low roads that some wagons floated away. The floods turned the usual three-mile trip to Coconut Grove into a ten-mile reef-hugging and sink-fording ordeal.

No matter how bad the conditions were outside, they were worse inside their "Ark," as George called it. First the glade disappeared, along with their vegetables, under as much as six feet of water. The overflowing water then began moving toward their cabin. As the water rose, the family removed boards from the barn and nailed them to the cabin floor to raise the level against the flood.

Then there were the roaches. They, plus a myriad of other insects, sought refuge inside the house. George wrote that the more they killed, the more the roaches seemed to reappear, as if raining from the skies.

The frogs were no less disconcerting. "There was something horrifying in the clamor that unceasingly enveloped the cabin," George wrote. "The din was as if every rain drop, as ceaselessly they fell, gave birth to a new voice; a new croak, gurgle, gurk, grackle and shriek." Adding to the noise was the loud bellowing of the alligators that swam in from the Everglades to devour stranded rabbits and snakes.

The barn sat on a high reef, but to get there from the cabin one had to almost swim. The plague of roaches in the barn was even worse than in the house. When George opened the bin to get feed for the animals, countless roaches scurried out. George and his father floated the wood for the cook stove on a makeshift raft to keep it dry.

But worse than the roaches and the frogs and even the water was what George called the "hypnosis of will and hope." His father had given up. Family prayer stopped and he no longer asked George to fight the hopeless battle against rust, fungus, and mildew. Adding to Solomon's despondency was the overflowing manure pit and the subsequent ground itch he contracted. It took over his feet and made walking difficult. Every day Allie opened the worm-like red eruptions and poured iodine into the open wounds.

Besides cooking, cleaning, fighting mildew, and tending to ground itch, Allie's most difficult job, according to George, was "her steady spirited endeavor to counteract [his] father's gloom and despair." As usual, when his father was in "his unusually gloomy spells," he would lash out at Allie, George wrote. The more she talked and tried to soothe him, the more he brought up Grandfather Fink. "Allie," he would yell, "you are just a female version of old grandfather Fink! Just him all over again. And now you are trying to make black white! You know just as well as I do those grapefruit trees are gone."

If George tried to intervene, or add encouragement, he received the same scornful comparison to Grandfather Fink. "You're Grandpa Fink all over again," his father would cry. "Not a bit of my family in you. Miracles and visions—trying always to make black white! You and your mother always banded against me."[42]

If truth were told, George and his mother indeed were very much like Grandpa Fink. Both were optimistic and cheerful and had a way of attracting people. From his earliest childhood, George was popular with both his peers and adults, especially women. In short, George, like his mother, had a full measure of Grandpa's charisma and salesmanship, and he and Allie did stick together.

When the rains finally ended, George wrote that it was like seeing sunshine for the first time. The water receded, the frogs vanished, and the house was finally free of roaches. Miraculously, the young grapefruit trees survived, each root encircled by the protective rock of the pinelands.

Although winter vegetable planting was a little late, the end of the drought helped the farmers more than the rain hurt them. In March, Solomon won seven prizes at the county fair for his beans and peas—more awards than most of the other entrants. Besides five dollars in cash, he also took home a pair of ladies' shoes for Allie, ten pounds of lard, one half barrel of flour, and some fertilizer.[43]

The arrival of Grandpa and Grandma Fink a few weeks later was the last thing Solomon needed, but it made George, his brother, sisters, and especially Allie very happy. It was the Finks' first trip to Miami and for Grandpa, it was love at first sight. "Mr. Fink is very enthusiastic over possibilities of this country," *The Miami Metropolis* reported soon after his arrival.[44]

Grandpa, with his usual ebullience and bigger-than-life personality, gave Allie and George a new dose of his famous optimism—or what Solomon derisively called "Finkism." His zeal was obviously flamed by his reconnection with his old Fink's Magic Oil salesman, J. Austin Hall, who had first lured the Merricks to Miami. Following his own advice, Hall, too, had moved to "The Magic City" and become a successful real estate entrepreneur. Grandpa's friend, Reverend Phipps, with Hall's prodding, had purchased a large tract of land on the north bank of the Miami River west of Twenty-Seventh Avenue. Phipps' improvements at what he called "Everglades Edge" included the extension of an old narrow gauge railroad. For ten cents, tourists could ride its circular route into the Everglades with a stop at a two-story observation deck.[45]

The Merricks were well acquainted with Everglades Edge and every winter when Phipps arrived, *The Metropolis* told of the Merricks' Everglades Edge excursion—a rare escape from their daily drudgery. In April 1902, *The Metropolis* reported that Allie, her parents, Reverend Bolton, and J. Austin Hall celebrated Reverend Phipps' seventieth birthday there.[46]

A short time later, obviously encouraged by Phipps and Hall, Grandpa Fink began buying downtown Miami real estate. As he had done previously, he put most of it in Solomon and Allie's name. Apparently, this was his way of helping the family without actually giving them money. During the Finks' visit, Solomon and Allie also added "the Coats 80" to their homestead. George later wrote that he had to talk his father into borrowing money—probably from Grandpa—to buy the eighty-acre tract from J. Vaughn Coats. The new purchase was contiguous to the original homestead on the south and matched up with its eastern and western borders. It had a sizeable "sink" that the family quickly dubbed "The Okra Sink" because okra was the first crop they planted there.[47]

Grandpa was still visiting when George and Bahamians Gibson, Delancy, Sweeting, and Rolle prepared the Coats 80 for planting. George's job was to create a straight line of white stakes exactly twenty feet apart to mark where the holes should be dug for the 317 grapefruit trees they planned to plant. Just before planting began, Grandpa showed up and pointed out some crooked rows that weaved a little to avoid the pine stumps. George recalled that his usually exacting father stood up for him, probably because he hated to agree with any of Grandpa's "domineering ideas and know-it-all attitudes."[48]

Grandpa, who was known for his surprises, once again lived up to his reputation. First, he had a porch built onto the front of the cabin and planted vines to give it a quaint cottage look. Next, to Solomon's dismay, he had the mass of tangled guava trees trimmed to give the grove a more orderly appearance. They may have looked better but, unfortunately, the trees never produced a bumper crop again. George was glad because he no longer had to deal with the guavas.

When Grandpa returned to Springdale in June, he was said to have written and published a book about South Florida entitled *A Million in Ten Years*. "He pictured it as it would be someday," Allie told a reporter in 1926. "He spoke of homes, stores, serpentine meandering roads, schools—everything that has come to pass."[49]

Although no copies of the book have been found, the story is plausible for several reasons. First, Grandpa owned a printing press to print labels and brochures for his Magic Oil. He also used it for private printing. Second, he authored an article for the *East Coast Florida Homeseeker* that included the same thesis. The article, published in May 1902, presented a glowing description of the area and its possibilities. "But, remember," he wrote, "after all our admiration of this grand country is not so much for what it is now as for what it can be made, for it is as yet just in the incipient stages of transformation." Then he added that he would provide the facts and figures to demonstrate, beyond a reasonable doubt, that "any man of ordinary business ability and moderate means can become a millionaire in ten years." Finally, the editor of the *Homeseeker*, after writing a flattering biographical sketch of Fink's success as a preacher and entrepreneur, added that Fink had become so fascinated with the area that he would happily answer any questions of those writing him in Springdale. "I feel that I owe this much to humanity to tell of this Eden land that I found on the South East Coast of Florida," he was quoted as saying.[50]

Richard Merrick remembered his grandfather pontificating to his father who, as usual, ignored what he considered "long-whiskered blowhard prattle." "I see the Indian trails and a great city here. You have a gold mine here," Grandpa would say while telling Solomon how to plant grapefruit, how to truck farm between the rows, how to sell the vegetables locally, how to ship the fruit north, and then how to subdivide the land. "Sadly, all my father saw was just work, mosquitoes, rock, and desolation," Richard remembered, "but grandfather said, 'I see great things here. You should build your house here.'"[51]

Within months of the Finks' return to Springdale, sixteen-year-old George wrote to tell his adoring grandparents what had occurred since their departure. He began the letter with an original short story and a quip: "As I did not have anything to write about I stuffed it up with a bear story, so please bear with it."[52] The story was about three men who, while walking the beach searching for turtle eggs, encountered a bear. It was quite descriptive and, for a sixteen-year-old, promising. At least Grandpa thought so.

"Grandpa's porch is still in place," George wrote as the letter continued. "The load of vines covering it is probably the reason it has not run away." He wrote how he had been busy grubbing and clearing three more acres for planting, as well as helping build six rock roads through the groves. He added that he planned to set out five hundred more trees if the family did not run out of "chink" first. He noted that they had not sold any more land and had not yet disposed of the downtown lots so they would probably have to stop planting soon. On the positive side, he reported that surveyors were out planning the route for the railroad and it looked like it would pass close to their farm.[53]

Despite George's hard work as a farmer and vegetable salesman, he still found time to write poems and short stories. His youthful desire to become a writer had not wavered. When an attractive woman evangelist spoke at the Union Church, a smitten George wrote her a poem. Grandpa Fink, who happened to be visiting at the time, read the poem aloud to an appreciative audience and added his usual far-reaching accolades. "Yes, George," he exuded, "you will be a great poet like Longfellow, Whittier, and like Lord Tennyson."[54] Years later, George wrote a short story about the event. "I was rewarded and stood through the good-byes in a warm satisfying glow,"[55] he remembered.

Although George and his father planted more than a thousand grapefruit and orange trees, and the vegetable crops improved every year, the

Merricks still faced difficult times. A severe hurricane hit in 1904 and another one came ashore in 1906, causing great damage to the trees and vegetables. Recurrent drought, storms, floods, and occasional frosts contributed to the unease. Just when it seemed like nothing else could go wrong, the Fort Dallas Bank, which held their first profits, went under, taking their savings with it. George saw himself as a sort of biblical Joseph in captivity enduring seven lean years of unimagined hardship before "the famine of spirit" ended. He later wrote a poem about the difficult years and his father's often repeated promise that life would be better "when the groves begin to bear."

Besides tending the groves—fertilizing, hoeing, spraying—George, his father, and their Bahamian workers continued improving and expanding the vegetables that grew not only in the glades but also between the rows of grapefruit trees. Their hard work paid off. At the March 1903 Dade County Fair, Solomon won the coveted Henry Flagler Prize. It honored the best display of vegetables grown by one person and came with a seventy-five-dollar gold piece and Flagler's personal blessing. He also won a ton of fertilizer for the best general display of vegetables and $12.50 for the best crate of eggplants.[56] After the fair, George wrote, Henry Flagler actually visited the farm to see their work firsthand.[57]

By the summer of 1903, the groves were beginning to bear, though they were not yet ready for a major harvest. The July 1903 *Homeseeker* published a "Letter to the Editor" from Solomon in which he described having twenty acres planted in citrus—three grapefruit to one orange. "My trees," he added, "especially the older ones, are looking finely (many tell me the best of their age anywhere around.)" He also told of the "Frenchman" (Charles LeJeune) who had purchased the Jackson property and now had more than eighty acres in citrus. "Things in this neighborhood are looking up as much as in any district that I know of," he concluded.

The editor commented on the remarkable growth of the Merricks' citrus despite being cultivated on one of the rockiest pieces of land he had ever seen. He also lauded him as one of the most successful vegetable growers in the county. "Through careful and intelligent cultivation," he added, "he has made the 'wilderness blossom like a rose.'"

Sometime in 1903, after their finances began to improve, Solomon sent George to Miami to buy lumber for an addition to their cabin. On the way home in the early evening, and with the wagon loaded down with lumber, the rear wheel hit a stump, breaking the coupling pole. "There I was, a timid kid alone in the pitch black woods peopled to my excited mind with panthers, wild cats and all kinds of ferocious animals thirsting for my blood," George wrote. Shaken and scared, he unloaded the lumber and tried but failed to fix the broken piece. When he was about to give up hope, he saw a bobbing lantern coming down the dark road. It was his father, who had walked more than seven miles searching for him. "I'll always remember," George recalled, "the great throb of happy relief and deep affection I experienced that night."[58] He often told this story as testimony to his father's love and how, during difficult times, the memory of the bobbing lantern became his symbol of hope.

Besides better financial circumstances, there was another reason to add on to the cabin. Allie was pregnant and gave birth to Richard Lionel—the Merricks' only child born in Florida—on November 29, 1903. Allie was a happy, involved, and rather indulgent mother. She taught her daughters to play the piano and Richard, who showed great artistic talent at an early age, to draw.

Despite better times, the family was still isolated and the younger Merrick children had no one to play with except each other. Because Richard was five years younger than Charlie, his closest sibling, and seventeen years younger than George, Althea took it upon herself to entertain him. He remembered her games and how she would scare him and then make him laugh by pretending to be a ghost in the woods. Sometimes, Richard recalled, his serious-minded father would shout: "Allie, why don't you let someone else make a fool of themselves once in a while?"[59]

As the Merrick enterprise grew, more Bahamian workers joined the workforce. They received $1.25 for a ten-hour day, personally paid by Solomon each Saturday afternoon. During the week, the single men slept in the barn and cooked over an open fire. Sometimes George joined them. Many went back to their Coconut Grove homes for the weekend. A few married couples, including several united by Solomon, lived nearby in small log cabins.

George became very close to his coworkers. Although the family lived in the midst of the Cracker homesteaders and felt compelled to follow local custom, they were not like them. Once when Grandpa was visiting, Solomon, worried about the Crackers' reaction, told Allie to go get her father, who was calling the workers "brother" and clearly enjoying their company. Many years later, George would honor these black Bahamians in a series of stories he wrote entitled "Men of the Magical Isles."

George was nineteen years old in early 1906 when the groves began to bear with such abundance that the family shipped two carloads of grapefruit out of South Florida. Although family lore held that they were the first to ship a whole carload, the *Homeseeker* gave that honor to someone else. First or not, one thing was clear—S. G. Merrick & Son had become one of the most successful truck and fruit growers in Dade County.

"Nothing Succeeds Like Success," the headline blared in a September 1907 *Homeseeker* profile of the family enterprise. After describing the hard years and subsequent financial success, the article reported that Reverend Merrick had money in the bank and could now take life easy and pursue his favorite pastime: reading books. "His son George," it noted, "had been his 'right hand man' through these pioneer years, working early and late to make the farm a great success."

For many years, Allie had been waiting for the groves to bear so the family could build a new house. Even when the old Gregory cabin had been expanded and the house and outbuildings encircled by an impressive rock wall with three rather monumental entry features, her dream house continued to percolate in her artist-mind's eye. Now, with funds in place, she put dreams on paper. Her drawings were not regular architectural plans, son Richard recalled, but rather a series of sketches. Of course everyone knew that her lovingly designed, two-story gabled home with its imposing colonnade would be built of coral rock.

Solomon hired Coconut Grove resident stonemason William deGuiselle, a former Belgian monk, and contractor Towsen to build the house from Allie's sketches. During construction, the family continued living in the wooden cabin. Then, when the new, two-story rock house was partially finished, the original board-and-batten cabin was separated from the clapboard rear addition and rolled down Coral Way to a new site near today's Granada Boulevard as an office for the growing Coral Gables Plantation.[60] The remaining rear portion was then attached to the new rock house.

In July 1907, before the house was completed, Solomon and Allie gave a party to celebrate George's twenty-first birthday and his coming of age. "There were numerous recitations, pathetic and humorous, good music and delightful refreshments," *The Metropolis* reported.

As part of the festivities, Solomon presented George with a gift from George Anderson, who had known and admired him when he was a little boy in Gaines, New York. When the family left Gaines for Duxbury, Anderson had given Solomon five dollars to place in an interest-bearing account for George until he was twenty-one. George graciously accepted the $9.60—which was meant to be a lesson in thrift, as well as a token of affection—and noted the lesson learned in a long thank-you note to Anderson.[61]

George expected his father to name him a full partner that night, like his mother and grandfather had been urging. Instead, to George's disappointment, there was no mention of a partnership. Instead, his father proudly presented him a $1,000 check as payment for his years of hard work. George accepted the check but later wrote of his discountenance and despair for what he described as a hollow gesture for "eight lifetime years of the boy's Heart's labor."[62]

At twenty-one, George was almost six feet tall and had a muscular build honed by hard work. Most thought him handsome with thick sandy hair brushed back from his broad high brow. His tanned face highlighted his piercing gray eyes, finely chiseled nose, strong lower jaw, and full lips. His distinctive "rock-leathered hands" were testament to the seven years of hard labor, or what he sometimes described as slavery, that "grew harder, narrower and steadily more shut in and without meaning."[63] But his life was about to take another dramatic turn. In the fall, he would travel to Winter Park, Florida, and enter Rollins College. It would be his first formal schooling since he was thirteen years old.

Although George sometimes wrote of the "dreary dark-to-dark tedium and drudgery" of the pioneer years, they left an indelible mark on his soul. He never forgot the lessons learned—the beauty of nature, the loyalty of friends, and the inspiration of the south wind. Years later, when his memories became more positive and selective, he lovingly recorded his keen observations in a series of short stories. His writing spoke of his sense of history, as well as his understanding of the frontier people and places that shaped him. Who knows what he might have been if the family had not moved to South Florida? But it was the South Florida frontier that turned a bright, introspective child into a strong, yet romantic, idealist who believed he could make the world a better place.

⁓ 5

Finding Self

Then felt I like some watcher of the skies
When a new planet swims into his ken

John Keats, "On First Looking into Chapman's Homer"

As the train left the Miami station, George felt like he had been released from an eight-year sentence of hard labor. During those disheartening years, his father promised that when the groves began to bear he would be free to return to school. Now, that day had come. George was twenty-one years old and mature beyond his years. Yet a piece of him remained child-like. He had not been in school since he was thirteen, and his father still controlled his daily life. "I felt like a green, untried boy," he wrote, "raw from the pines and rocks and fuller of inferiority complexes than any freshman who had ever entered Rollins."[1]

A small college in Winter Park, Florida, Rollins was a logical choice for George's reentry into the academic world. Founded by New England Congregational Church members in 1885, it was the first institution of higher education in Florida. Like Solomon Greasley Merrick, Rollins president William Freemont Blackman, PhD, had a Yale divinity degree and had been a Congregational minister. Later, he received a PhD in sociology from Cornell and was a Yale professor when the fledgling college recruited him.[2] His brother, E. V. Blackman, was the well-known Miami minister, promoter, and editor of Henry Flagler's *East Coast Florida Homeseeker* who had published articles by both Solomon and Grandpa Fink. William Blackman, like his brother E. V., also owned a grove in Miami, so it is likely that he

Figure 16. George Merrick, age twenty-one. University of Miami Special Collections. Courtesy of Mildred Merrick.

and Solomon knew each other. Two years earlier, Ethel and Medie had attended Rollins' Preparatory Academy. Watching his younger sisters go off to school while he continued to work in the fields was a bittersweet pill for George to swallow.

Winter Park was Florida's first planned community, founded by Loring A. Chase of Chicago and his friend Oliver E. Chapman. In 1881, they created their "town with a plan" as a winter resort for people of means. Nestled amid citrus trees and the elegant Seminole Hotel, the town, incorporated in 1887, boasted a ten-acre landscaped central park, meandering tree-lined streets, two major boulevards, strict architectural controls, and a separate Negro community named Hannibal Square. Advertising brochures spoke of "a necklace of opal lakes . . . shaded by live oaks and camphor trees that spread out blooming like a tropical garden in the sun."[3]

Figure 17. George (*third from right in front row*) looks more like a professor than a student in this 1907 photo of the Rollins College students and faculty. Permission of Department of College Archives and Special Collections, Olin Library, Rollins College, Winter Park, Florida.

Rollins' student body came from both the immediate area and from out of state. The school prided itself on its large number of Cuban students, who gave the school a unique, international flavor. Prospective students had to submit proof of graduation from a secondary school whose graduation requirements were equal to those of the Rollins Academy. Students without a high school diploma could qualify after passing a test on a daunting list of subjects that included English, history, algebra, solid geometry, biology, and physics.[4]

George neither met the enrollment criteria nor took the examination. He was simply admitted as a special student because of his family connection to the Blackmans and his local reputation. As a provisional student, he had to prove he could do college work before joining the freshman class. In the meantime, he enrolled in a stenographic course that included typing, shorthand, commercial arithmetic, commercial English, and business law. This course of study may have proved useful to him in later years, but it was hardly what he wanted. Still, it was his ticket back to traditional schooling—something he had dreamed of ever since he left Duxbury's Partridge Academy and moved to Florida.

When George arrived, Rollins encompassed twenty-five acres on picturesque Lake Virginia. It had eight wooden buildings constructed in the popular Arts and Crafts style. Six of the buildings faced Horseshoe Drive with its expansive central park. The campus was so heavily wooded that one visitor reported he almost missed it. Rollins, despite its connection to the Congregational Church, proudly advertised that it was "distinctively Christian in character but wholly unsectarian, both in spirit and control."[5] Students had to attend chapel or church services but the choice of denomination was theirs.

A surviving picture of the entire faculty and student body shows a mature-looking George, dressed in suit and tie, with his hand awkwardly stuck in his coat pocket. Surrounded by much younger men and women, he looked more like a professor than a student.

Responsible and self-directed, he found the strict rules of dormitory living ludicrous, at best. Each day the matron checked rooms for cleanliness and neatness and any infraction brought a demerit. Students also had to be in their rooms with their doors open from seven thirty to ten each evening so the dormitory matron could make sure they were studying. George, who had an unquenchable desire to learn, hardly needed supervision. One of his classmates later recalled that he devoured information that others might think dull and uninteresting.[6]

At first, George had a hard time adjusting to college. He was older than his fellow classmates and had different life experiences. He had bouts of homesickness—especially for his mother. When her birthday came in November, he wrote a long poem dedicated to her that included the lines:

How sweet the thought of Home Sweet Home,
When far its gentle cover,
But words their cords so sweet intone,
Were it not for thoughts of Mother.[7]

George never wrote about having any girlfriends at Rollins. This was probably because he was focused on learning and lacked social skills. He felt awkward around girls his age but was always comfortable with bright, older women. At Rollins, he connected with Susan A. Longwell, a sixty-year-old spinster, who taught English, philosophy, and Bible study. He shared Miss Longwell's passion for English literature—the only area in which he felt equal or even superior to the other students. She also encouraged his writing. He later recalled how Miss Longwell introduced him to John Keats, a romantic poet he strove to emulate. He especially remembered the day she read him Keats' poem, "On First Looking into Chapman's Homer." He understood and shared Keats' awe at discovering something new.

Years later, he wrote a story about his Rollins experience. He fondly recalled his dorm mate, James Madison Longmire, who was five years his junior. The irresponsible Longmire was somewhat of a laughingstock and always on the verge of dismissal. Despite their glaring differences, Longmire became George's closest friend and supporter.

As usual, when George felt insecure, he salved his unease with literary or biblical references. At Rollins, he remembered thinking of himself "as a lonely young David who had not yet met his Goliath."[8] He never told Longmire his feelings, he later wrote, but Longmire, like David's devoted friend Jonathan, seemed to understand.

Not surprisingly, it took George only one semester to gain admittance to the freshman class in both the School of Business and the School of Expression. One of the highlights of the 1908 spring semester was the annual competition for the James Ronan medal for oratory—one of the school's highest honors. Even though George was what he called a "four week" freshman, he had a secret desire to enter the contest. Longmire sensed this and encouraged him, even though no freshman had ever dared to participate. His competition was three upperclassmen, including Worthington Blackman, the president's son.

George wrote a speech that stood up for "the underdog." After years of working with the uneducated and often exploited Crackers and Saws, he developed an enduring empathy with them. His firsthand experience, coupled with fiery words from Elizabeth Barrett Browning's poem, "The Cry of the Children," which exposed child labor, became his thesis. When George read his completed speech, entitled "A Plea for the Weak," Longmire predicted victory because of George's sincerity and the fact that, unlike the others, he had already "felt life." Miss Longwell concurred.

On March 28, students and community leaders packed the lakefront gymnasium for the big event. Each contestant would have thirty minutes and would be judged on thought, literary style, and delivery. George was the fourth speaker, which meant he had to wait almost two hours before they called his name. "I wondered," he wrote, "if my mouth would actually open up there! And, if I did, could I make any noise at all! I had to hold hard inside to keep my trembling legs from running off."[9]

When his time came, he recalled walking up like a "little back woods golem." He had never made a speech. He looked out on what he described as a gray and white blur and his insecurities enveloped him. His words spilled out rote-like. He perked up when Longmire, his arms waving, popped up from the audience. With great flourish, he pulled out an imaginary stone, placed it into an imaginary slingshot, and fired away. "Something inside me grabbed that sling," George wrote, "and the fervor of Browning's words wrapped around me. I stood back myself, from a new someone that I had never known before—someone who was pouring out expression, something I had not before realized was in my oration. In glorious awe, and pride in that strong someone, I gave way, full way. I was feeling a purpose—that was succeeding in an important destiny. Something vital was fulfilling an irresistible urge. I was satisfied with that strange someone."[10]

No one was surprised when the judges named George the winner. "The auditorium rang with applause," the college magazine *Sandspur* reported, "and President Blackman called the winner to the stage and presented the beautiful gold medal in the midst of great enthusiasm."[11] The exuberant freshmen carried George over their heads, singing triumphantly and celebrating. In this moment, a new George emerged. "I knew I had won," he recalled, "but it didn't matter then. I had glimpsed something else. A satisfaction that didn't come as a medal."[12]

A week later, *The Miami Metropolis* covered the event, praising George for being as successful in college as he had been on the farm. "Dade County is proud of her young men," the article continued, "especially those who by diligent work and study attain high honors."[13]

After the May 28 commencement, at which George graduated from the Stenographic Course, he returned home for the summer to face the same old routine of working in the fields by day and writing poetry at night. It was not a happy time. His father's health continued to decline and his depression deepened. Although work had been under way on the family's new rock home, the failure of the Bank of Fort Dallas had wiped out their savings, so construction stopped. As a result, they still lived in the old, run-down wooden cabin.

Even Allie was not her usual cheery self. When George went to college, she lost her closest ally—a void no other could fill. Soon thereafter, her husband traveled to New Jersey for several weeks to close a land sale so the family could complete the house. Sad and lonely, she questioned her South Florida life and even her marriage. In a poignant letter, Solomon sought for-giveness for his "melancholy moments" and his "great heart that was never satisfied." "You are the dearest object to me on earth," he wrote, adding that he was willing to do anything to make her happy again. He even suggested selling the grove and moving away if that was what she wanted.[14]

With George assuming some of the responsibility for the grove, Solo-mon checked himself in to Walter's Park Sanitarium for Invalids in Wal-ter's Park, Pennsylvania, in a desperate attempt to restore his mental and physical health. Like many health resorts of the era, Walter's Park was well-known for its healthful granite spring waters, massage, electricity, and oxy-gen treatments, as well as its promise to treat "incurable heart disease" and other ailments.[15] Although *The Metropolis* reported that he was improving, Solomon's heart condition worsened. From Pennsylvania, he traveled to Baltimore for treatment at Johns Hopkins, where he hovered near death for several weeks.[16]

When his father arrived home slightly improved, George was able to return to Rollins. After winning the Ronan prize, he became a more con-fident, involved student and participated in many campus activities. He joined the local fraternity, Phi Alpha. He later wrote that he played sec-ond-string guard on Rollins' football team and became friends with Jack Baldwin, the team's center. Fifteen years later, Baldwin would become a pivotal player in Coral Gables' success. Another future connection came with the arrival of William Jennings Bryan, the Democratic candidate for president, who spoke to the student body from the back of a train. George never would have dreamed that someday he would hire the "Great Com-moner" to help him sell Coral Gables.

As sports editor of the college magazine *The Sandspur*, George reported the college's many athletic victories, which included the state football cham-pionship. He also made *Sandspur's* list of outstanding students, complete with a nickname—"Topsy." Because of his bold speech for the underdog, the editors predicted that someday he would become a politician with a socialist point of view. But to him, his greatest achievement, next to the Ronan prize, was the publication of his short story "The Unattainable" in *The Sandspur*.

Although the plot revolved around an artist, it exposed his own deep fears and insecurities. "Of what use is a continued struggle with his fate?" he wrote. "Hope gone, what does life hold for him? Drearily, his mind roams back over the years of struggle with bitter poverty, years that have tested his manhood and proved his worth. And now, when his days of struggle seem to be in the past, when he has thought himself so near to the dreamed of happiness, this hope that has become a part of his life is ruthlessly snatched away."[17]

George had reasons to worry. His father wanted him to become a lawyer and George's oratorical success only fueled that wish. As a dutiful son, George applied to and was accepted into Manhattan's New York Law School, although he wrote that he was more interested in literature than law. His Rollins days ended after only two years, but he remained a proud and loyal alumnus for the rest of his life. Likewise, Winter Park, and its emphasis on planning, architectural controls, and garden-like ambience, gave George his first inkling of the value of a planned community. It was another lesson he would not forget.

Near the end of September 1909, after another summer of hard work in the groves, George was set to leave for New York City to attend law school. He was not enthusiastic about studying law, but the thought of being in Manhattan was both exhilarating and scary. It was not that he had never been to a large city. When the family lived in Duxbury, he often went to Boston. He also visited Pittsburgh and Baltimore to see his grandparents. But for the last ten years, he had not left Florida. Despite two successful years in college, he still felt like a backcountry bumpkin.

His father picked New York Law School because it had open admissions and a two-year degree. George was already twenty-three, so the accelerated program had great appeal. Founded in 1891 by a group of dissident Columbia University Law School professors, by 1909 it had become the second largest law school in the United States.

At six o'clock in the evening on Friday, September 24, 1909, George kissed his family goodbye and boarded the evening train to Jacksonville.

There, he would transfer to a Clyde Line steamer for New York. George was booked on the *Arapahoe*, one of the company's newer ships. It was a rather imposing vessel, especially to George, who had never been on such a ship. Three hundred and fifty feet long, the *Arapahoe* had "cozy" staterooms, social halls, smoking and reading rooms, and a large dining salon that advertised "gastronomic luxuries."[18] Although the ship touted its luxurious accommodations, it also advertised that its fare of between thirty-five and fifty-five dollars was 40 percent cheaper than rail.

Late in the afternoon of September 28, after a rather stormy and uncomfortable trip, the *Arapahoe* neared New York Harbor. The welcoming Statue of Liberty, with Emma Lazarus' poem celebrating the "huddled masses, yearning to breathe free," resonated with George's life perspective and his own newfound freedom. He also felt kinship with the thousands of immigrants being processed each day under the vast domes and minarets of Ellis Island, now in view. Coming from the backcountry of South Florida, he understood and even shared their sense of bewilderment and alienation in what to him seemed like a foreign land. But the skyline—aglow in the late afternoon sun—turned fear into awe as the living panorama of the modern world pushing skyward consumed him.

Although the city beckoned, George's face-to-face encounter had to wait. The plan was to continue on to Haworth, New Jersey, a newly incorporated commuter suburb, where he would stay with his uncle Denman Fink. Five months earlier, Denman, his wife Zillah, whom the family called Betsy, their five-year-old daughter Enna and four-year-old son Bob, moved into a new Dutch Colonial house on West View Terrace that backed up to a golf course. Although Haworth was proud of its early Dutch heritage, it took a different turn when the Franklin Society subdivided many of the old farms and began an extensive advertising campaign to lure New Yorkers to its newly planned suburb. The society imposed many building restrictions—generous setbacks, a minimum price, and wide sidewalks. Its advertising campaign and careful planning quickly attracted an impressive group of residents, including artists, publishers, professors, and teachers. The community was proud of its new Congregational Church, golf and country club, and the Haworth Beautiful Committee, which was busy planting trees and shrubbery.[19]

Figure 18. When George attended law school in New York, he lived with his uncle Denman Fink and his uncle's wife, Zillah "Betsy," in Haworth, New Jersey. During this time, he and Denman began to talk about the future of Coral Gables. Courtesy of Nancy Fink Giacci.

At twenty-nine, Denman was already a well-known magazine and book illustrator. Showing artistic talent at a young age, he began his training under the watchful eye of his artist-sister Althea. At age sixteen, he lived with the Merricks in Duxbury while attending the School of the Museum of Fine Arts in Boston. When the Merricks moved to Florida, he transferred to the Art Students League of New York in New York City, where he studied with many well-known artists, including the illustrator Walter Appleton Clark. Clark encouraged him to submit a drawing to *Scribner's*, one of America's leading book and magazine publishers. *Scribner's* published his first illustration in October 1901. He was only twenty-one.[20]

Soon, his drawings appeared in most of America's leading magazines—*Century, McClure's, Harper's, Woman's Home Companion, The Saturday Evening Post,* and *Collier's.* Known for their artistic illustrations, these magazines were extremely popular in an era that has been characterized as the "Golden Age of American Illustration." Denman's work appeared with the drawings of Howard Pyle and James Montgomery Flagg, to name a few. Writers such as Willa Cather, Ida M. Tarbell, Sherwood Anderson, Henry Van Dyke, and Edith Wharton were frequent contributors to the magazines.

George was no stranger to the Denman Fink family. As children, they spent time together during the Merrick family's visits to Springdale, Pennsylvania, where Denman grew up. Denman also visited the Merricks in Florida, both before and after his marriage in 1903.

Denman and his wife were an especially attractive couple. Betsy had a fashionable, hourglass figure and piled her dark hair high on her head Gibson-girl style. Denman was strikingly handsome, with deep blue eyes and a full head of prematurely graying hair—a Fink family trait. With magazine work as his mainstay, in 1903 he also began illustrating books. One early commission was *The Barrier* by popular novelist Rex Beach. Two decades later, George would hire Beach to write a book about Coral Gables.

When law school classes started on October 1, George commenced his weekday, one-hour commute to Manhattan. It included a train trip to Weehaugen and then a ferry to the city, where he caught the Ninth Avenue to Courtland Street and then walked two blocks to 174 Fulton Street, just west of Broadway. The law school had its own twelve-story building with lecture rooms on the eighth, tenth, and eleventh floors and a law library on the ninth. Tuition was $100 per year, payable in advance.

Because it was a two-year school, George and the 197 other first-year students became members of the "junior class." Most were from New York and New Jersey; George was the only student from south of the Mason-Dixon Line. First-year classes included torts, criminal law, personal property, contracts, and a variety of real property courses that highlighted transactions such as sales, leases, and mortgages.[21] George hated law school but gained a lot of useful knowledge. The city, however, taught him more than any book.

The law school's location put George at the heart of Manhattan's financial and commercial district, south of Forty Second Street. Breathtaking Beaux-Arts masterpieces by legendary architects Carrere and Hastings, McKim, Mead and White, Cass Gilbert, and George B. Post had already left their mark and continued to rise skyward. New towers vied to become the next world's tallest building. The current champion was the Napoleon Le Brun and Sons Metropolitan Life Building with its illuminated Italian-style campanile. It had just surpassed Ernest Flagg's Singer Building, located a block from the law school. Although no longer the tallest building in the world, the Singer Building, which George described as "star-stretching,"[22] retained a commanding presence in the skyline and in his thoughts.

St. Paul's Chapel, completed in 1766, was directly across from the law school. It reminded George of Duxbury's Pilgrim Church and other buildings he had known during his Massachusetts years.

George often wrote that New York's "sky-climbing" towers inspired him. None left more of an impact than the spire atop McKim, Mead, and White's Madison Square Garden, which was patterned after La Giralda in Seville, Spain. Fifteen years later, he would build his own Giralda tower in Coral Gables.

George spent his weekends with the Finks. Together, they attended the Congregational Church at which Denman was a deacon. As the oldest in a large family, George had a special way with children, and Bob and Enna were no exception. Following his pattern of bonding with older women, he developed a close relationship with Betsy, although she, like Denman, was only six years older than he. Many members of the Fink and Merrick families were not particularly fond of Denman's strong-willed and flirtatious wife. They blamed her for encouraging Denman to abandon his dream of becoming a fine artist so he could bring home a steady income as an illustrator. But George, whom she nicknamed "Gorgeous," saw her differently. She listened to and appreciated his deepest thoughts and dreams.

Denman was equally supportive. He, too, encouraged George's writing and his close connection to the publishing world was a promising fact. But they also talked about other things. While in Haworth, and possibly in response to witnessing Haworth's emergence from farmland, he and Denman had their first discussions about the future of the Merrick groves. With new forms of transportation—subways, trains, and automobiles—

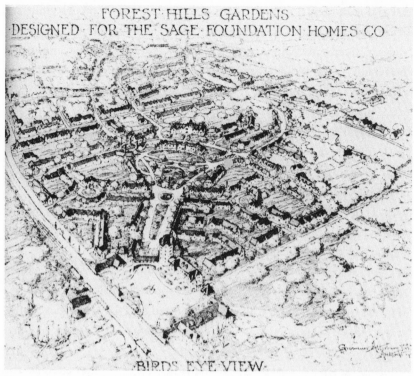

FOREST·HILLS·GARDENS
DESIGNED·FOR·THE·SAGE·FOUNDATION·HOMES·CO

·BIRDS·EYE·VIEW·

Figure 19. George and Denman visited Forest Hills Gardens in Queens, New York. Developed by the Sage Foundation, it had a singular influence on George's future plans for Coral Gables. (*Arts and Decoration* I, No. 3, January 1911.)

spurring suburban growth in New York, they began to imagine a future for the Miami backcountry as well. Together, they visited nearby planned suburban communities such as Tuxedo Park and Forest Hills Gardens, an early "Garden City" designed by Frederick Law Olmsted Jr.[23]

If the idea for Coral Gables was already planted in George's fertile brain, it was barely germinating. Even though he was a full-time law student and might have seen an exciting future for the family groves, he remained focused on one thing—his writing. He devoured the literary works in Denman's magazines and continued to read classic and contemporary writers. But most of all, he wrote. One unpublished poem, "A Floridian in Manhattan on Christmas Eve," was reminiscent of Walt Whitman's description of Manhattan in his legendary *Leaves of Grass*. It provides insight into his mixed feelings about New York City. He was clearly impressed by what he described as the city's "dazzling, night-knowledgeless Broadway," with its "surge-rushing, life-throbbing current." Yet he also felt the pain of the tenements, "where the outcast, the waif and the newsboy, the drunkard and worker each by their various fates are living . . . the embryo man of the nation." He wrote of the new subways, "where dark-loving dragon-like monsters rush wild and distraught," and his own daily ferry experience, "where the trampling, home-rushing armies in the march of a might embarking resistlessly pour to the barges." His newfound melodic and vivid imagery reflected both his broadening worldview and his emerging writing talent.

The long-anticipated breakthrough came in early 1910, when he entered and won the *New York Evening Telegram*'s short story contest. His prize-winning piece, "The Sponger's Delilah," had a Florida Keys setting. The plot was simple. A white Bahamian sponger forsook his loving childhood sweetheart for the "sensuous, voluptuous" Maria Guiterrez. When he discovered gold in a wrecked ship, he found out that Maria loved someone else and was only using him to find the bullion. Hurt and broken, he realized that his first love was the real treasure. The story ended with their reconciliation and his discovery of two more treasure-laden sunken ships.[24]

While hardly the best story George ever wrote, it was the first published in a major newspaper—a New York newspaper, no less. Encouraged, he wrote his father asking permission to drop out of law school at the end of the term to pursue writing full time.[25] But like the artist in his story "The Unattainable," "just when he . . . thought himself so near to the dreamed of happiness, this hope . . . [was] ruthlessly snatched away." His father, taking another turn for the worse, called him home. Although heartbroken at the prospect of having to leave New York, he knew he had no choice.

Before he left, he wrote a letter to Betsy, whom he nicknamed "Chaquita," possibly after the Bret Harte poem that appeared in a volume that Denman had illustrated. George included an original, humorous poem entitled "The Song of the Babies," with some thoughts that suggest he and Betsy may have been more than just friends. "I am thinking as much of Haworth as when I left. . . . Here is a throbbing melody born of a full heart—a heart overflowing with fervent emotion," he wrote. "I will be with you for the short stay before I leave (which being but brief, I am hoping you may endure without serious trouble) sometime Friday. With love to all, George."[26]

"Like the beaten prodigal son," George wrote, he came home. "But, un-like him," he added, "he felt bitter, unyieldingly bitter, yet hypocritically humble; accepting the pro-offered place of hired hand to his father.... There was no fattened calf save only in his mother's eyes. There were no rings for his fingers, save the bright welcome of Delancey and of the Sweetings, and of the Rolles and of Mackey."[27]

With his dream snatched away, he wrote of a "bitter truce" that often flared into his father's "raging recrimination and morose denouncement" of both Grandfather Fink's inheritance and his writing. His father's scorn took its toll on the "pithy, wilted stalks" of George's dreams, which now, he wrote, "seemed silly, futile, empty, hopeless."[28]

But he kept writing poetry, even after his father denounced it and he received a rejection slip from both *McClure's* and *Everybody's Magazine*. The editor of *Everybody's*, however, sent a letter stating that although the poem was too long for the magazine's use, "it is good verse of real poetic feel-ing.... You have a rare appreciation of the tropical."[29] He recalled reading the letter over and over again. It was one faint glow in a very dark night.

Despite his father's black moods, the family had a reason to be happy. By the time George came home, they had moved into their new coral rock home, which Allie called "Among the Pines."

During construction, the contractor had disconnected the original board-and-batten Gregory cabin from the clapboard addition and rolled it down the road to become a guesthouse. Then he attached the rear addition to the new rock structure.

The finished product looked more like a bayfront mansion than a back-country dwelling. The rock portion had six bedrooms, an upstairs study, and a bathroom. The wooden section, now remodeled, included a large liv-ing and dining room with French doors that opened to a porch. Behind the dining room was a small office in which Solomon kept the books and paid his workers each Saturday afternoon through an open window. The newly remodeled kitchen, in the same location as before, had a separate pantry and a small bedroom and bath for the domestic help.

The home's most dramatic feature was the wide, columned, U-shaped veranda that wrapped around three sides of the house. It was the family gathering place, and its wide overhang provided shade and protected the open windows from rain. Two long flower boxes, which Allie filled with ferns collected in the hammock, and a pair of concrete urns enhanced the entryway. A *porte-cochere* to house the family's first car—a Maxwell coup—jutted out from the veranda's west side. The sloping gabled roof, covered with Ludovici tile, complemented the golden glow of the coral rock.

Solomon and Allie shared the east, downstairs bedroom near the front door. Across the wide entry hall was the guest room. Sons Charles and Richard occupied the bedroom behind the guest room and daughter Helen had the one behind her parent's. George claimed the large upstairs bedroom on the west with the window seat and dormer windows with eyebrows that kept out the sun and rain. Across the hall was Medie's and Ethel's room. On the front of the house, between the two upstairs bedrooms, was a narrow study with a Palladian window. It served as both Solomon's library and Allie's studio.[30] A large bathroom and a walk-in attic completed the second floor.

The family was busy finishing the final details in order to get the house ready for Ethel's upcoming marriage to George Sydney Amsden, a wealthy Coconut Grove yachtsman and landowner. Twenty-four years older than Ethel, he was an officer in the prestigious Biscayne Bay Yacht Club and his yacht, the *Hesperus*, was described as "one of the most comfortable and hospitable yachts on the Bay."[31] He lived in a notable rock home on the "Boulevard," now South Bayshore Drive.

At 3:30 p.m. on September 23, to the melody of Wagner's *Lohengrin*, Medie, as maid of honor, and Ethel, on her father's arm, descended the long staircase and entered the living room, where the groom and George, as best man, waited. The next day *The Metropolis* reported that it was "one of the prettiest weddings ever held," adding, "the exceeding beauty of the large country house was further enhanced by the décor of roses and potted plants."

Two weeks later, Allie showed off her new home to her friends in the Ladies Aid Society of the Union Congregational Church. Once again, *The Metropolis* gushed with accolades for both the new home and the surrounding grove laden with grapefruit ready for harvest.[32]

With her oldest daughter married, her home completed, her husband's health slightly improved, and her eldest son home, Allie felt a renewed sense of well-being. Her contentment ended abruptly on October 15, when one of her nephews biked from Miami to tell her that her brother Romie had just received word that their father was dead. Allie was devastated, as was George, who had always felt especially close to his grandfather. Even though Solomon derided both Allie and George for their similarity to each other and to Grandpa Fink, he recognized, albeit begrudgingly, that their unceasing optimism came from him. Allie often called upon this Fink spirit when coping with her husband's depression. It was her positive attitude that held the family together with a bond of unconditional love. George proudly acknowledged that he inherited a full measure of what his father angrily called "Finkism." George considered Finkism a cherished gift.

That winter, the family adopted a permanent name for their new home. Allie's choice, Among the Pines, had already appeared in the local press and on the cover of a multipaged, photographic Christmas card that she created. Solomon, on the other hand, favored the name "Coral Gables" because he admired Grover Cleveland and his home, "Gray Gables," near Duxbury. After some discussion, the family chose the name "Coral Gables" for their home and called the surrounding acreage the "Coral Gables Plantation."

Although the Coral Gables Plantation continued to thrive and prosper, George was beginning to see new opportunities in Miami's burgeoning real estate scene. The young city was booming and its population now exceeded five thousand people. Riverside and Highland Park, Miami's first suburbs, were under construction to the west and north of the original city limits. In Coconut Grove, architect Walter DeGarmo subdivided what he called "Coconut Grove Park," another first for the area. Each day *The Metropolis* printed multiple advertisements for soon-to-be drained Everglades land. Many in the backcountry pushed to expand the Twelfth Street Extension (today's Flagler Street) between Seventeenth and Twenty-Seventh Avenues westward to the Glades. George counted the days until the new rock road and increasing number of automobiles would make the plantation accessible to Miami's rapidly expanding population.

As development pushed westward, George prodded his father to join him in purchasing land that was not contiguous to the original homestead. This fit into George's newly hatched plan to sell ten-acre tracts for citrus growing, along with an offer to manage the grove if the new owner desired. On January 16, 1911, he took the bold step toward his destiny when he placed his first-ever personally written advertisement in *The Miami Metropolis*.

"Citrus Grove Seekers Start Right," the two-column, half-page advertisement headlined. "Some people KNOW grove lands," it continued, "others merely sell them." Touting the money his family made growing grapefruit, he proudly added, "not one foot of these groves are for sale." He concluded with the promise that others could be just as successful and invited skeptics to see for themselves by writing or visiting "the Coral Gables Plantation, six miles west of the city." The advertisement ended with the large, centered, bold letters: Geo. E. Merrick, Miami, Florida. Grandpa Fink would have been proud.

Besides what George described as his father's semi-invalid condition, his mother also had a troubling problem. Although only fifty-one, Allie had developed cataracts, a Fink family tendency. As an artist, her deteriorating eyesight was particularly upsetting. In early summer, Solomon accompanied her to Nashville, Tennessee, where a well-known ophthalmologist removed them. While they were there, Solomon's condition worsened and Ethel and her husband went to help them travel to Althea's mother's house in Springdale, Pennsylvania, to recuperate. On June 16, just a day after their arrival, Solomon died at age fifty-two. When the news of his death reached Miami, *The Metropolis* put his obituary on the front page and described him as "one of Dade County's most highly respected citizens."[33]

Two days later, after his remains arrived from Pennsylvania, a large crowd gathered at Union Congregational Church in Coconut Grove to show their respect. In his eulogy, Rev. James Bolton, who twelve years earlier had helped him buy the Gregory homestead, spoke of his "indomitable energy" and "iron will" that had created the Coral Gables Plantation and brought new value to the backcountry. "While at times he was inclined to look on the gloomy side of things," Bolton acknowledged, "at other times he was bright, cheerful and hopeful." Bolton saved his highest praise for his six-year ministry at the Union Church, "where he was greatly beloved," and for providing a happy home for his family. Following the service, the funeral cortege, including a horse-drawn hearse, slowly made its way to the City Cemetery, where Solomon was laid to rest.

One can only imagine the void left by Solomon's death. Despite his stern, demanding personality, his family loved and respected him and longed for his praise. Now that he was gone, Althea looked to twenty-five-year-old George to head the family. Within a month, the court named him the legal guardian of the minor Merrick children—brothers Richard and Charles and sister Helen. He also took full charge of the plantation. Although he had been working in the fields for more than ten years, his father, to George's dismay, never relinquished control and continued to make most of the decisions.

New responsibility, George later wrote, brought out his natural, yet unknown, executive ability. Now that he was no longer his father's "hired hand," he made rapid decisions that streamlined the grove's operation. Still, his father's shadow loomed large and he recalled that he constantly asked himself if his father would approve of what he was doing.

No one who watched him in action was surprised when, just four months after his father's death, a front-page story in *The Metropolis* announced that the first carload of grapefruit out of South Florida would come from the Coral Gables Plantation.[34] Predicted to "fetch fancy prices," the first three hundred boxes set a new record at four dollars and forty-five cents a box, the paper reported.

With the grapefruit picked and on its way north, George could again focus on selling land. Following his grandfather's belief in the value of advertising, he placed an ad in *The Metropolis* every week. In addition to the ten-acre groves, he also promoted tracts for "high-land" trucking—a direct response to aggressive Everglades land salesmen who were in full force now that drainage had begun. The advertisement also gave him the opportunity to tout Coral Gables Plantation's pepper, eggplant, tomato, and bean crop as among the largest in the county.

The increasing profits from the vegetables and grapefruit, and some success selling land, made it possible for George to buy more land, sometimes in partnership with his mother and sometimes on his own. Although he continued to manage the groves, he began turning over the day-to-day operations to others, including his uncle Worth St. Clair, the husband of his father's sister, Emma. The St. Clairs moved to South Florida in 1910 to help Solomon when George was away. They built a large rock house on the street that George had convinced the county to name Coral Way.[35]

As the Coral Gables Plantation grew, George employed a larger labor force. At least six black families—the Johnsons, Roberts, Bethels, Delancys, Flowers, and Gibsons—lived in a group of cabins just north of the Merricks' home. Day workers came from Coconut Grove or nearby farms. George was popular with all of his workers because many had grown up with him in the fields. He respected and treated them as equals. In return, they were loyal, hardworking, and eager to please.

In May 1912, George assumed the role of father-of-the-bride at his sister Medie's wedding to her longtime beau, Bob McLendon. The Merrick and McLendon families were especially close. They had moved to Miami at about the same time and both were well-known and highly respected. Bob's sisters Lula, Popie, and Katie Miller often spent weekends with Ethel and Medie, and Ethel and Medie were frequent visitors at the McLendons' house. George and Bob were also good friends. In the fall of 1913, they became business partners and opened Merrick and McLendon Realty in the new Townley Building in downtown Miami. George, of course, immediately wrote an ad that appeared in *The Miami Metropolis*.

> *Merrick-McLendon Realty Company*
> *Best Things of Dade*
> *The Grove and Trucking Lands Specialists*
> *Here's Ours!*
> *Compare to all Others.*[36]

With Bob McLendon's assistance, it was now possible for George to become more consumed with real estate. Fortunately, the most active sales period occurred during the December to March tourist season, after the grapefruit had been harvested. George remained mindful that the real money still came from the expanding groves. In early 1913, *The Metropolis* reported that he had already shipped five thousand boxes of grapefruit at four to five dollars a crate and expected to ship seven thousand more. In addition, 150 crates of Coral Gables Plantation peppers had already been harvested and another forty acres of peppers and eggplants were ready to pick. Another crew of workers was busy planting one hundred acres of tomatoes and Irish potatoes. To move the fruit and produce to the station more efficiently, George had purchased a big Reo truck, with the words Coral Gables Plantation emblazoned on its side, and ordered a second one.[37] He also had an interest in the Coconut Grove co-operative packinghouse.

His real estate activities expanded as well. Less than a week after the city agreed to move the city docks from the river to the bayfront, George placed his first advertisement for nongrove land. The three-column, quarter-page ad, with a detailed map, featured a ten-lot parcel plus riparian rights next to

Figure 20. Realty Securities executives and employees line up for a group portrait. George, clearly their youngest vice president, can be seen on the right end of the back row. University of Miami Special Collections. Courtesy of Mildred Merrick.

the proposed new dock. Many years earlier, his father had acquired what at the time Solomon considered worthless property from his father-in-law. George, however, was not surprised by the land's sudden value because he viewed his grandfather as a larger-than-life prophet.

George's new downtown presence, frequent advertisements, and charismatic style attracted the attention of another growing real estate company—Realty Securities Corporation. Located across the street from the Merrick-McLendon Realty offices, Realty Securities was relatively new on the real estate scene. Their first project was developing Woodlawn Park Cemetery for whites and Evergreen Cemetery for blacks. Now, they were buying up land and were about to launch several outlying residential subdivisions. The company acquired some of the Merrick land, including the property near the city docks and another near the Coconut Grove railroad station. At first, George accepted partial payment in Realty Securities stock, thus becoming a stockholder in the corporation. Shortly thereafter, the two companies merged, with George becoming second vice president of Realty Securities and Bob McLendon, secretary. The merger made Realty Securities Corporation the largest real estate and development company in Dade County.

Under the new arrangement, George would be in charge of all development work and have oversight over the seven subdivisions the company had just placed on the market. "The corporation," *The Metropolis* added, "has planned a wide publicity campaign which it is believed will benefit Miami as well as its own business."[38]

George's partnering with the Realty Securities Corporation was part of a carefully calculated plan. As he watched Miami expand its borders, he realized that in the near future Coral Gables Plantation would be ready for development. But before he touched what he considered hallowed ground, he needed to learn how to successfully turn raw land into a livable community. For the next few years, he would be content to remain an understudy waiting for the big time. Even though he read the works of John Ruskin, Ebenezer Howard, and Daniel Burnham and studied the Garden City and City Beautiful movements, he understood that not even great books could take the place of firsthand experience. When the time was right, his years of reading, learning, and doing would prepare him to thoughtfully create what he dreamed would be an ideal, almost utopian community on his family's land.

His life changed direction when he joined the Realty Securities Corporation. But another event was about to have a far greater impact on his future. He fell deeply in love with beautiful, willful Eunice Isabella Peacock. Once Eunice entered his life, nothing would ever be the same.

Eunice

Brown eyes of fair Hispania;
Black hair of Indie Isle;
Inheriting of old Britannia
—Not your languorous Latin smile—
But your stubborn willful spirit,—
Your spunky saucy style.

George E. Merrick, "Valentine to an Island Love,"
February 14, 1918

From the moment of her birth on April 3, 1895, Eunice Isabella Peacock was adored. Born at Coconut Grove's Peacock Inn, she was the first grandchild of owners Charles and Isabella Peacock. Her father, thirty-one-year-old Robert Alfred Sanders Peacock, known as Alf, was Charles and Isabella's son. He, his parents, and his two brothers, Charles John and Harry, came to South Florida from England in 1875. Charles' brother, Jack, persuaded him to bring his family to what he called a "tropical paradise." At the time, Jack lived a lonely existence in a spartan shack on a piece of not-yet-named Coconut Grove real estate that had been homesteaded by South Carolinian J. W. Ewan. Because the shoreline curved into a natural cove, or bight, people called the entire area "Jack's Bight." (It is now the site of the Kampong National Tropical Botanical Garden.)

When Charles and Isabella saw the raw, isolated wilderness of Jack's Bight, they were horrified. The few residents lived on barely improved, 160-acre homesteads and had little contact with each other. There were no roads, hardly any trails, and only a few primitive docks jutting out from the mangrove-fringed coast. How could they live in such a place with no neighbors or even rudimentary signs of civilization? As they prepared to return to England, Ewan offered them an alternative. If they would help him run an Indian trading post on land he managed on the north bank of the Miami River for a group called the "Biscayne Bay Company," he would offer them a place to live nearby.

The north bank was hardly a settlement but had the most improvements. It was partially cleared and had a small cluster of buildings left over from former occupants and Fort Dallas, constructed by the army during the Seminole Wars. It was here, in 1880, that the Peacocks met Staten Island visitors Ralph M. Munroe and his wife, Eva. The Munroes came to South Florida hoping the winter warmth would help cure Eva's tuberculosis. At first, the Munroes rented Ewan's homestead dwelling, but they also found it too primitive and isolated, so they pitched a tent on the north bank a short distance from where the Peacocks lived. Isabella Peacock befriended the young couple, but despite her nurturing care, Eva Munroe did not survive the early spring and was buried nearby. Her distraught husband returned to Staten Island only to discover that their infant daughter had also died.

With little to keep him in Staten Island, Munroe returned to South Florida the following year with an idea. If the Peacocks would open a lodging house near Jack's Bight, he would bring in his northern friends for a winter sojourn. Their friendship and Munroe's proposition spawned the birth of Coconut Grove, the area's first real community.

Following Munroe's advice, the Peacocks purchased thirty-one acres from John Frow, who traced his South Florida roots to the 1840s. His father, Simeon, came to Key West from the island of Majorca and married Bahamian Sara Anne Thrift. An early keeper of the Cape Florida Lighthouse, located on Key Biscayne, Simeon Frow, and later his sons, John, Joseph, and Charles, all tended the light. When the U.S. government built the Fowey Rock Lighthouse on the reef and prepared to close Cape Florida, the Frows moved to the mainland. In 1877, John Frow purchased a 160-acre homestead in what would become the heart of Coconut Grove.

Besides selling land to the Peacocks, John Frow also sold a narrow strip to his brother, Joseph, for one hundred dollars. Joseph built a two-story wooden house on the ridge just south of the Peacocks' rustic, new hostelry they called the "Bay View House." There, with his wife, Euphemia Newbold, a native of Spanish Wells, Bahamas, they raised their five children—Lillian, Grace, Frank, Joseph B., and Charles. Joseph Frow led the effort to establish Coconut Grove's first school so his children could get an education. (Four of the first ten children enrolled were Frows.)[1]

Lillian Frow, Euphemia and Joseph's oldest child, grew into a beautiful young woman with shiny, knee-length wavy hair and a happy disposition. In early May 1894, when Lillian was in her late teens, she and next-door neighbor Alf Peacock, ten years her senior, eloped to Key West.

The newlyweds moved into the Bay View House where Alf was his father's partner in managing the popular establishment. Father and son also operated a general store—Charles Peacock & Son—located in a two-story building across the narrow street that became MacFarlane Road.

By this time, an increasingly sophisticated group of northern visitors and settlers had discovered Coconut Grove.[2] With the Bay View House as the springboard and Isabella Peacock as the acknowledged "Mother" of the nascent community, Coconut Grove became South Florida's largest and most influential settlement.

The Bay View House grew along with the community. By 1895, a year before the birth of the City of Miami, the Peacocks had added two impressive two-story buildings on the ridge and a large bathing casino and hall on the bayfront. They christened this new, enlarged complex the Peacock Inn.

Eunice Peacock spent her first seven years at the Peacock Inn. A beautiful, precocious child with dark, curly hair, she became a kind of mascot to the regular customers, including J. W. Ewan, who now made the Inn his home. Ewan, who was especially close to young Eunice, frequently wrote a column for Miami's fledgling newspaper, *The Miami Metropolis*. He often included quips about his "li'l darling." In one, he told a fanciful story about one-year-old Eunice entertaining guests with a solo on the French horn.[3] Six months later, he noted how she drummed on the piano and sang for guests. In a more serious tone, he added: "Grandma and Grandpa Peacock are certainly very proud of Miss Eunice and they may well be for she is an extremely bright child for her age."[4]

As her grandparents' only granddaughter and her parents' only child, Eunice grew into a loving and confident, if spoiled, child. Guests at the Inn, including Alfred Munroe (Ralph Munroe's uncle) and famous actor Joseph

Jefferson, also doted on her and gave her gifts. No one, however, influenced her more than Flora MacFarlane.

Flora came to South Florida from New Jersey in 1886 as a companion to Ralph Munroe's mother. Tall, with sharp features, she was educated, unmarried, and from an established New Jersey family. She soon moved to the Grove and became one of the area's first schoolteachers and its first woman homesteader. In 1891, promoting what she called "community uplift," she organized South Florida's first woman's club—The Housekeepers Club—which brought together women with varying backgrounds. In later years, she ran a sort of private school at the Inn, where she tutored Eunice and some of her cousins. Both Eunice and her mother became very close to "Miss Flora" and frequently visited her and her family in her northern home in Rocky Hill, New Jersey.

Another early visitor who would influence Eunice's life was Bostonian Jessie Moore. In 1895, Jessie purchased a plot of nearby bayfront land she named the "Moorings." After recovering from a serious illness, she embraced Christian Science and brought her newfound faith to the frontier. Beginning with services at the Peacock Inn, Isabella Peacock and Euphemia Frow became two of her earliest converts. With this strong influence from both her grandmothers and her mother, who also became a devotee, Eunice became a practicing member of the Christian Science Church and remained a follower her entire life.

When Alfred Peacock experienced serious health problems, he and Lillian left Coconut Grove for four months as he sought treatment in a Maryland Seventh-Day Adventist sanitarium that was similar in philosophy to Christian Science. While they were gone, seven-year-old Eunice lived with her grandmother Peacock and wrote sad but newsy letters to her parents, begging them to hurry home. Fortunately, Alfred's health improved, but when he and Lillian returned, the Peacocks decided to sell the Inn because Alf was still frail and Charles and Isabella were aging.

After the Inn was sold in late 1902, Alf, Lillian, and Eunice moved to the former William D. Albury house, the largest and most pretentious home on the bayfront. (Interestingly, three years earlier, Solomon and Althea Merrick had bought their land from the Alburys' daughter and son-in-law.)

Eunice's new home was a step up from the family quarters in the Inn. The

Figure 21. Young Eunice stands next to her father, R.A.S "Alf" Peacock, on the upstairs porch of their South Bayshore Drive home. University of Miami Special Collections. Courtesy of Mildred Merrick.

imposing, two-story Key West–style residence, built in 1892, had a front porch on each floor and a two-story bay window on the south overlooking the new Housekeepers Club. It stood high on the ridge overlooking Biscayne Bay with a front yard that reached the water. A long wharf extended far into the bay where the family sailboat *Widow* was tied up.

Although Eunice experienced a more enriched environment than did many of the other pioneer children, including her cousins, she still grew up in a frontier setting. While limiting in many ways, the frontier had a strong influence on her character. She developed an enduring love of tropical plants and animals, and even had a pet deer. As the oldest and only girl of the six Peacock grandchildren, she learned to stand up for herself with stubborn determination and refused to yield to her male cousins' bullying. But she also had a soft, feminine side. As school photographs attest,

Eunice stood out in a starched white dress and a large white bow in her hair while others appeared barefoot and in simple, homemade clothing. *The Miami Metropolis* frequently noted her achievements as an honor student, although her mother once confided to Flora MacFarlane, "Eunice is still very fond of play. We have to keep after her about her studies. I wish you were here with your patience."[5]

Although more Peacock than Frow, Eunice was a true daughter of Coconut Grove. Her mother's family included the original settlers—Bahamian seamen, lighthouse keepers, and fishermen. Through her mother, she was related to almost all the early families, including the Newbolds, Thompsons, Roberts, Saunders, and Careys. Both of her father's brothers married Bahamian women, giving her, in some cases, double first cousins.

Her father's side represented the settlers who came from England, Europe, and the northeastern United States. They included families like the Munroes, Hines, Nugents, and D'Hedouvilles. These individuals, some with European titles, interacted with Charles, Isabella, and Alfred Peacock at the Inn. When Ralph Munroe and author Kirk Munroe founded the Biscayne Bay Yacht Club in 1887, they asked both Charles and Alfred to join. The Frow men and Alfred's brothers, however, did not get an invitation because many Biscayne Bay Yacht Club members looked down on the "Conchs"—residents with Bahamian backgrounds who had less education and fewer social skills. This exclusion caused a rift between the Peacocks and Ralph Munroe, the club's first president, and, as a result, Alfred resigned in protest. Eunice grew up knowing of the incident and never forgot or forgave the slight.

By her early teens, Eunice was strikingly beautiful. Petite, with thick, waist-length dark, wavy hair and searing dark eyes, she drew attention wherever she went. Her parents, influenced by Flora MacFarlane, wanted more for her than Coconut Grove or even the young City of Miami could offer. When she was fifteen, Flora convinced them to enroll her in the State Normal and Model School in Trenton, New Jersey, just eighteen miles from the MacFarlanes' home in Rocky Hill. As the capital and largest city in New Jersey, Trenton's streets were lined with grand, classical buildings like the State House, Mercer County Courthouse, Library, and City Hall. The Model School was equally impressive with its cluster of domed classical buildings and landscaped lawns. Eunice, who had spent eight years in a two-room wooden schoolhouse, must have been in awe of her new surroundings.

From the beginning, Eunice thrived in this environment, although at first, her overly protective mother remained in Trenton to watch over her. "My Dear Wife," Alf Peacock wrote, "I can't express my pleasure at Eunice doing so well with her studies." "I am," he added, "putting my shoulder to the wheel so as to be in a position to give her all the education necessary."[6]

As the only Florida student in the school, "Peacock," as her friends called her, was engaging and popular. As a tenth grader, she took literature, history, algebra, zoology, singing, and English, as well as physical training. The Model School, known for its progressive educational programs and teacher training, allowed students to move to the next level whenever they were ready. Eunice advanced rapidly.

Eunice attended the Model School for two years and stayed with the MacFarlanes or visited school friends during holidays. She excelled in her studies, made lifelong friends, and was especially popular with the boys. Although fiercely independent and of strong spirit, she also exuded a kind of appealing, vulnerable femininity. Many young men clamored to protect what they called "a dear little girl."

Some of her many suitors included young men from Princeton University, located nearby. "You are a stubborn little bunch of sweetness," one wrote. "You have so many fellows and always thinking of just a good time."[7] Another hoped he would "have better luck than your friend the young doctor."[8] As she prepared to return to Miami, a flurry of notes arrived from young men begging to see her before she "headed south." Carefully preserved letters reveal that she left behind a trail of broken hearts and one special boyfriend named Joe Ryan.

Seventeen-year-old Eunice moved back to Miami in late 1912. She returned confident, poised, sophisticated, and prepared to enter Miami's social scene. She quickly became part of the crowd of socially active young people, including the sons and daughters of Miami's professionals and merchants. Although especially popular with the young men, it bothered her that she was never totally accepted by those who considered themselves the Miami elite.

George Merrick was not an active member of this crowd, although his family pedigree gave him access. He was not very comfortable in social settings and preferred intellectual discussions with older women. His sisters, however, were always trying to interest him in their friends, and he occasionally complied and had a date or two but no serious girlfriend.

George did not have much time for a social life. While still managing the largest grapefruit and truck-farming operation in South Florida, he sold acreage in what he called the "Coral Gables Extension." After he joined the Realty Securities Company, he became even more involved in Miami life. Its founders, T. O. Wilson, Clifton Benson, and J. E. Junkin, were older, established leaders who were active in church and civic affairs. Wilson came to Miami from Illinois, and Baltimore native Clifton Benson was an attorney who, after a brief time in private practice, joined Wilson as vice president. The third principal, Junkin, was a former Kansas newspaper owner.[9] The older partners became close friends and mentors to young George, who was only twenty-seven when he joined the group. George's unique talents, however, had a huge impact on the firm and its fortunes.

When George took over Realty Securities' development arm, it had already platted or was in the process of platting six subdivisions outside the Miami city limits. They included Kirkland Heights, Grapeland, and North Cocoanut Grove in the near southwest, Riverside Farms adjacent to the South Fork of the Miami River, and Aqua Vista and Acadia on the bay north of Lemon City. Like many other subdividers of the era, Realty Securities sold blocks, not lots, with the idea that a person could build a house on a block of land in the backcountry, turn the remaining acreage into a profitable grove, and wait for the city to reach its borders. When that happened, which everyone predicted would be soon, the owners could subdivide their blocks and reap greater financial rewards.

Once George joined Realty Securities, the company's modus operandi changed, along with its advertising. Ads became larger and included new sales gimmicks and the slogan: "Investments That Pay." One headlined a large brick wall in the shape of one hundred dollars and boasted "a hundred dollars given to each of our customers for lots, Blocks and Tracks in any of our Subdivisions where the amount exceeds $500."[10] The advertising paid off. By mid-January 1914, Realty Securities touted the fact that they had sold more than fifty pieces of property since the beginning of the new year.[11]

George's influence on both marketing and development was particularly apparent in the January relaunching of Grapeland, a close-in subdivision near Coconut Grove. For the first time in Realty Securities' history, it sold lots by auction. The company's chief rival, the Tatum Brothers, who were busy developing Riverside Heights, had initiated the practice in 1908 and had used it to their advantage. Three years later, another set of developers brought in a showman-auctioneer named Edward W. "Doc" Dammers to put on a colorful auction at Highland Park in direct competition with the Tatums. The following year, the Lummus Brothers also hired Dammers for the initial sales at Ocean Beach. Doc Dammers was destined to become the greatest auctioneer in Miami's history and ultimately to work for George, but in 1914, George chose the Boston firm of Lancaster & Mills for Realty Securities' first auction.

Advertisements for Grapeland promised free auto transportation to and from the development, with its new rock pillars. They promised to give away $1,000 worth of presents, including a cabinet Victrola "fine enough for a King's house."[12] Just as George had predicted, the crowds responded with both their presence and their pocketbooks. Clearly, George was learning how to sell real estate. His partners thought he was a natural.

A month later, Realty Securities relaunched the former North Cocoanut Grove as Cocoanut Grove Depot. In a full-page advertisement enhanced with a romantic, hand-illustrated open gateway, Realty Securities announced the introduction of a complete, well-landscaped townsite with a street named Merrick (Thirty-eighth Court). It included businesses, packing houses, and industrial sites near the railroad tracks and home sites and a "commodious clubhouse" north of Bird Road. The most innovative feature, however, was a free train ride from downtown Miami to the Cocoanut Grove Depot that sat on the corner of Twenty-Seventh Avenue and Dixie Highway. Lancaster & Mills again would auction land, and free lunch would be served before the special train returned to Miami.[13]

A month after the big splash at Cocoanut Grove Depot, Realty Securities advertised that Riverside Farms—rechristened Heights of Riverside—had adopted some "new schemes" and ideas to develop their property. These included a ten-acre park and community clubhouse for exclusive use of the residents, who also had riparian rights to the bordering South Fork of the Miami River. The main entrance had what was described as "massive stone gateways built with bubbling drinking fountains, artistically curved seats and provisions for rest and shelter."[14]

Lancaster & Mills sold an unheard-of 104 lots in Riverside Farms in a matter of days, inspiring Realty Securities to publish a large "Thank You" in the newspapers that touted the remarkable sales of their first season. "May Your Days Be All Sunshine and Your Investments Profitable," it concluded. "See Us First."[15]

A ray of sunshine was definitely shining on George; at least he thought so. In late 1913, he began keeping company with the girl he had been waiting for—eighteen-year-old Eunice Isabella Peacock, who had become one of the most, if not the most, sought-after young women in Miami. Clearly, she liked the attention and relished playing one suitor against the other. The competition only increased George's interest.

Although Eunice had a whole crop of admirers, most of Miami's unmarried young women also had their sights set on George. Not only was he handsome, smart, and charismatic, he was rich. Like the rest of the Merrick family, he never showed off his wealth, but a 1914 financial statement indicated he and his mother had a net worth of a whopping $312,172.92 ($7.3 million in 2014 dollars).

By 1914, the family owned 560 acres of real estate in what would become Coral Gables. It included 120 acres of grapefruit, sixteen acres of peppers, ten acres of eggplant, and one and one-half acres of onion.[16] (They reported $70,000 in gross sales from produce and citrus.) All of their agricultural land was irrigated with an expensive modern system, and they owned two trucks and a 1914 Hudson open touring car. They also listed almost $40,000 in Realty Securities stock.[17]

George's one weakness was luxury cars, which obviously impressed Eunice. During the early days of their courtship, George would take her on a drive every Sunday, Wednesday, and Saturday nights. Sometimes they went to parties, although this was not something he liked to do. Apparently, everyone knew this. In February 1914, when Katie Miller McLendon, Medie's sister-in-law, invited them to a party, she wrote, "I know, George doesn't dance and isn't crazy about cards but I think we can manage to entertain him."[18]

When Eunice was around, George was easy to entertain. By this time, he was clearly smitten. If Eunice felt the same way, she kept it to herself and continued to date others, much to George's dismay. In June, when she left Miami, as she did each summer, George sent his first telegram just as the train pulled out of the station. "I am wishing you a pleasant trip," he wrote in a wire to be delivered on the train as it headed toward Jacksonville. "All the way thinking you are getting farther away. Wishing so much I were along."[19] The first telegram was immediately followed by another sent to the connecting train from Jacksonville to Washington, D.C. "You see," he wrote, "I am still chasing after you—Habit is hard to break. . . . Never saw Miami so empty and lonesome."[20]

When Eunice had not replied in four days, George sent another telegram to Stewartstown, Pennsylvania, where she was visiting. He reminded her that she had not written and was so upset he went by her home to talk to her parents to make sure she was all right. "I have driven 3 mail clerks crazy inquiring for a letter from you," he wired. "Fourth one threatens to shoot me if I again ask. . . . Write immediately if only to save my life!"[21]

When word got to Eunice that George had been seen with another woman, he sent several letters of explanation, saying that the alleged date was only one of his sister's friends. "I have been with Mary only once," he wrote, "but only with folks." He then told her he had been going to bed early and that he had refused parties for work, adding that his sister Medie said he was getting to be an "old old grouch and sore head" because he missed her so much.[22]

In another, he told her how he had visited her father and found a whole contingency of her admirers there, trying to get her address. One of the most persistent was Bazille Brossier, the son of wealthy F. C. Brossier, another major Miami real estate developer. Bazille also wrote Eunice long letters that summer. In one he told her how George had refused to give him her address and warned him not be too attentive. "His warnings only encouraged me," Bazille wrote. "I realize he is a very large and manly personage, but I have one consolation, Napoleon was one half inch shorter than myself."[23]

Eunice did not write as often as George did, and when she did, she let him know about letters from other admirers and the fact that she had reconnected with some of her Northern friends. This only fueled his passion. He wrote that he worried one of her suitors would get a new roadster before he did, adding that he had ordered one because it did not have a back seat and he could be alone with her. "I am getting more greedy every day for Eunice," he concluded.[24]

Figure 22. Beautiful Eunice Peacock in her 1915 engagement photograph. University of Miami Special Collections. Courtesy of Mildred Merrick.

George continued his pursuit after Eunice returned to Miami in late September. By this time, his family knew that he was in love with her even though his protective sisters were not thrilled with his choice. Apparently, word got to Eunice that Ethel had told someone she did not think Eunice was the best person for her beloved brother. When Eunice told George what she had heard, George confronted Ethel, prompting her to write to Eunice denying the allegation.

Ethel admitted trying to match George up with her friends but denied saying that she preferred another or that Eunice was chasing him. "I love my brother far too much to hurt him," Ethel wrote, "and of course anything hurting you would necessarily hurt him. I am too loyal to George to say unkind things about you, even if I thought them which I do not."[25]

After a year of unrelenting pursuit, George won what he considered the prize of his life. In March 1915, he and Eunice became engaged. *The Inner Court*, Miami's society magazine, published her picture, which showed off her beauty and her large diamond engagement ring.[26]

When word of Eunice's betrothal reached her Northern friends, she received a stack of letters asking about her fiancé. One came from Joe Ryan, who signed himself "your once upon a time Joe." "You were always such a happy, cheerful and independent girl that I didn't think this would happen so soon," he lamented, but added, "[the] lucky man must sure be a fine fellow."[27]

Zillah "Betsy" Fink was also unhappy when she received the news in Haworth, New Jersey. "My darling Gorgeous," she began in her six-page letter. She scolded him for not writing or confiding in her like he used to and then asked directly, "Are you sure this is the true love, dear boy? Do you love her more than you ever loved a woman before? Please be sure before you go too far."[28]

With the engagement announced and plans for a February wedding under way, George and Eunice began planning their new home. They chose a large lot with a spreading, mature Royal Poinciana tree located just west of the Merrick family home, Coral Gables. (George had recently talked the Dade County Commission into naming the rural road that ran in front of the Merrick home Coral Way.) What the family called "the bride's house" would be built of "coral rock," and the architect would be H. H. Mundy, who had an office near George's in downtown Miami and had just designed the Christian Science Church in Coconut Grove.

Although Eunice had become George's highest priority, he remained devoted to overseeing the Coral Gables Plantation and pursuing his real estate career. As usual, Eunice went north for the summer to visit Flora MacFarlane and her Model School friends. This gave George extra time to focus on his business and agricultural interests. By this time, Realty Securities had branched out to other parts of Dade County. They platted the Townsite of Larkins (South Miami), as well as the Realty Securities Corporation addition to Goulds. Both were near the Florida East Coast Railway, which had opened South Dade to agriculture. These additions, like the Cocoanut Grove Depot townsite, combined George's knowledge of agriculture with his growing knowledge of real estate development.

Realty Securities' most newsworthy new subdivision, however, was called the "Railroad Shops Colored Addition." Although there were some black settlements in Coconut Grove, Lemon City, and on the south side of the Miami River, what was then called "Colored Town," later "Overtown," just north and west of downtown Miami, was the most populated. It was overcrowded and needed to expand. This caused conflict between white and black neighborhoods as white residents demanded that the city maintain the "color line." George and Realty Securities Corporation had a better idea. They would build a new community for Miami's black population that included not only home sites but also a ten-acre park and a site for an industrial school. It was located just north of the then city limits between today's Northwest Forty-sixth and Fiftieth Streets and Twelfth and Fourteenth Avenues. By fall, Realty Securities announced that it had sold 491 lots.[29]

Besides his many business activities, George was also becoming more involved in the community. He was elected secretary of the Dixie Highway Council, created to promote the new Dixie Highway that had just reached Miami from Chicago. He was also part of a group of what *The Miami Herald* described as "leading citizens" who planned a new men's athletic and welfare organization called the "Fort Dallas Club."[30] Amid these efforts that helped him as a developer, he never forgot his roots. He joined the board of advisors for the proposed new Dade County Agricultural High School and

Figure 23. A beaming George and Eunice Merrick on their 1916 honeymoon trip around Florida. University of Miami Special Collections. Courtesy of Mildred Merrick.

was elected chairman of the board of trustees of Coconut Grove's Union Congregational Church, where his father once preached.

Adding to his responsibilities, Florida Governor Park Trammel appointed him to the Dade County Commission for the new district number one. It included the area between today's Southwest Eighth Street and South Miami, continuing due west across the Everglades to the Lee County line. (Collier County had not yet been created.)[31]

When the popular new commissioner took his seat at the table in the County Courthouse, *The Miami Metropolis* penned an editorial entitled "Hope Much From George Merrick." It pointed out the sad condition of the roads in his district: "And he stands in a position to win everlasting appreciation if he will turn his attention to these particular places."[32]

None of these honors, however, could compare to the joy he felt on February 5, 1916, when he wed Eunice at her parents' home on what was called the "Fifth Street Extension." Rev. James Bolton performed the ceremony, which was attended only by close family. "Mrs. Merrick," *The Miami Metropolis* reported, "is a beautiful young woman of much charm . . . [and] George Merrick is a young man of forceful character." The article also included a long description of each of their family's accomplishments—Eunice's connection with the Peacock Inn and George's with his father Solomon Merrick and the Coral Gables Plantation. It also recorded George's work with the Realty Securities Corporation and his recent appointment to the Dade County Commission.[33]

The newlyweds left in George's new White touring car for a ten-day honeymoon through Central Florida. One of their stops was at the St. Charles Hotel in Orlando, where they stayed for several days. Years later, another guest told how had he met the young couple and they had shared their dreams about the future of Coral Gables.[34]

When Mr. and Mrs. Merrick returned from their honeymoon, they moved into their new home, which Eunice named "Poinciana Place." It was here, with Eunice as his closest confidant, that the secret plans for Coral Gables began to materialize.

To George's dismay, just four months after their wedding, Eunice insisted on going north for the summer like she did before their marriage. The couple got together in New York in July, after which George wrote via telegram: "I feel like boarding train straight back to you . . . surely miss you every minute . . . Bushels of love, George."[35] When he returned to Miami alone and lonely for his bride, he sent almost daily telegrams as again he despaired at her lack of response. He sent a telegram to the Misses MacFarlane in Rocky Hill, where she was visiting, asking them to "wire collect if Eunice there . . . have not heard . . . worried." Three days later, he sent yet another telegram. "Am extremely worried about you," he wrote. "If you are sick or anything demand knowing immediately by wire cannot otherwise understand such treatment have sent four wires . . . am exceedingly disappointed. . . . George."[36]

Following Eunice's belated response, George apologized for his impatience, reminding her how worried he was and how much he missed her. He also wrote about arranging for new furniture for their home and that he had planted a rose garden as a surprise when she returned.

Besides worrying about his absent wife, another project consumed his attention. In August, the company broke ground for the new Negro Indus-

Figure 24. Newlywed Eunice Merrick sits on the porch of her new Coral Way home, "Poinciana Place." Courtesy of Gael Stanley.

trial and Normal School in Railroad Shops Colored Addition. Six years earlier, Nellie Powers, an educated black woman, had opened her private Industrial School in Colored Town to provide a better educational experience for black children than the public grammar school. Impressed with her work, an unprecedented biracial committee came together to help fund a new school in Railroad Shops Colored Addition. White architect A. E. Lewis donated architectural drawings for a horseshoe-shaped school similar to the recently constructed white school at Silver Palm. A who's who of both black and white donors, including George, contributed funds to build the school on land donated by Realty Securities Corporation. When the groundbreaking occurred in August, Realty Securities President T. O. Wilson spoke along with *Miami Herald* editor Frank Stoneman and black entrepreneur D. A. Dorsey.[37] Never before had Miami seen such an interracial effort.

George also wanted to do something to relieve the overcrowding in Coconut Grove's black community. He had remained close to many of the families of the young men he worked with during his early hardscrabble years and some remained in his employ. Together with Rev. James Bolton, who lived on the edge of the black neighborhood and shared George's concern for its well-being, George planned a new subdivision to be called "St. Alban's Park," after the nearby Episcopal industrial school. Ever since thirteen-year-old George and his father had spent their first night in Miami at the Boltons' home, the Merricks considered Reverend Bolton almost like family, especially after his wife, Eva, died and he was alone.

Sadly, the plan for St. Alban's Park was put on hold after Reverend Bolton was brutally murdered on December 12, 1916, at his home on today's Grand Avenue. Making the situation even more tragic was the fact that his murderer was Clarence McKinney, the estranged husband of St. Alban's teacher Anna McKinney, who lived nearby and also did housework for Bolton. Apparently, Reverend Bolton angered McKinney when he helped Anna file for divorce and obtain a restraining order against him. When the constable arrived to arrest McKinney for violating the order, McKinney slipped through the back door and shot Bolton from behind as he dismounted his horse. A posse, made up of men from both the black and white Grove, apprehended McKinney and stopped a mob from lynching him.

George, who had been looking after Bolton's affairs and knew him better than anyone, spoke at his funeral at the Union Church and was named executor of his estate. He arranged for his burial at Woodlawn Park and had his wife's body removed from her grave next to the church and reinterred beside him.[38]

Within a month of the murder, McKinney was tried, convicted, and sentenced to death by hanging. George represented the family at the trial and attended the execution.

George did not seek reelection to the Dade County Commission when his term expired on December 31, 1916. Minutes of the meetings during his fourteen-month tenure reveal that he was a conscientious member who attended every meeting except when he was on his honeymoon or visiting Eunice out of town. He voted for all road improvements, as promised, and supported funding the initial work on the Tamiami Trail and the new County Causeway to Miami Beach. He spoke out for the poor and indigent just as he had at Rollins College a decade earlier. He also voted in the affirmative, although he was not a teetotaler, to accept the local referendum on which citizens voted to make Dade County dry.[39]

Despite George's many distractions, Coral Gables Plantation continued to prosper under his stewardship. In late 1916, the newspaper headlined that he refused $1,200 cash for the first carload of winter vegetables, knowing he could get a better price.[40] His real estate business also thrived. Realty Securities increased its office staff and sales force and purchased a building across the street from their former office on Avenue C (Northeast First Avenue). The company sold not only its own townsites, suburbs, farms, and groves but also other property on commission. At year's end, Realty Securities reported their largest volume of sales and the most profitable year in their short history.[41]

George's development skills increased along with his bank account. His burgeoning profits made it possible for him to expand his family's Coral Gables Plantation. Now all he needed was for the City of Miami to inch closer to what many still considered the backcountry. Thanks to George's continuing efforts, it would not be long.

The Dress Rehearsal

Before attempting to start Coral Gables, I served an
apprenticeship of a number of years in developing other tracts
of land. . . . I did this because I felt that when I once began
with the project that is now Coral Gables, I wanted to bring
to its development fullness of experience that would enable
me to translate into accomplishment the idea which had been
taking shape in my mind for many years.

George E. Merrick, *The Miami Herald,* July 28, 1929

By all standards, Miami was booming. In only twenty years, the young city
had grown from less than a hundred permanent residents to more than
thirty thousand, with an additional ten thousand during the winter. After
Dixie Highway opened between Chicago and Miami in 1915, and the chamber of commerce launched its first national advertising campaign a year
later, more than one hundred thousand tourists poured into town. New
trolley lines to Buena Vista on the north and Tatum Field (site of the former Orange Bowl Stadium) on the south spurred suburban development.

Miami's metamorphosis was particularly evident downtown. The eight-
story Ralston Building next to Realty Securities' new office was hailed as
the city's first skyscraper. On the bayfront, Matthew Elser's fairy-tale-in-
spired, three-story, two-towered pier building neared completion. It would
house retail stores, an aquarium, an auditorium, a dance hall, and a photo
studio complete with a stuffed alligator. Just across the street, the skeleton
of the ten-story McAllister Hotel rose skyward.

During the season, which lasted from December to March, the chamber
of commerce brought in Arthur Pryor's Band to play for the tourists each

afternoon at Royal Palm Park. The park also became the forum for William Jennings Bryan, the famous orator, former United States secretary of state, and three-time presidential candidate. He attracted thousands to his weekly open-air Sunday school class. He had recently built a winter home on Brickell Avenue and proposed a Pan American University for the area. A decade later, he would become a Coral Gables attraction and a University of Miami promoter.

Although George profited from Miami's rapid development, he viewed money only as a means to an end. Every dollar, every new project, and every additional acre of land added to Coral Gables Plantation moved him one step closer to realizing his dream. George also acquired less-tangible assets that he called Beauty and Inspiration—words he always capitalized. He found Beauty and Inspiration in James Deering's Vizcaya, completed in 1916. He was not the only one. Architect Walter DeGarmo, whose talent George would later tap for Coral Gables, wrote that the "Deering estate opened the eyes of the people to the beauty and satisfaction to be had from architectural design."[1] Within a few years, two of Vizcaya's creators, architect Phineas Paist and designer Paul Chalfin, would become important members of George's design team.

Soon after the completion of Vizcaya, Pittsburgh millionaire John Bindley built El Jardin, a beautiful Mediterranean-style mansion designed by architects Kiehnel & Elliott on the Coconut Grove bayfront. In the future, like DeGarmo, Paist, and Chalfin, Richard Kiehnel would also leave his mark on Coral Gables.

Although these magnificent homes and their architects influenced George's growing interest in the architectural style that would define Coral Gables, his most important inspiration came from his direct involvement in the construction of what would become Plymouth Congregational Church.

Union Congregational Church, where Solomon Merrick was once the pastor, began as a community Sunday school in 1887. It sat on Church Street, now MacFarlane Road, next to the library. When the Reverend George B. Spaulding took over the pastorate in 1915, he, with George's help as chairman of the board of trustees, vowed to create a beautiful new structure for the growing congregation and community. The church acquired a large tract of land on today's Main Highway from industrialist William

Figure 25. In 1917, George Merrick, chairman of the board, stands with friends at the new Plymouth Church. Its beauty increased his love for South Florida native "coral rock." Spanish stonemason Felix Rabon would later build homes in Coral Gables. University of Miami Special Collections. Courtesy of Mildred Merrick.

Matheson, who had a large home on the bayfront. Matheson paid for the services of famous New York architect and city planner Clinton MacKenzie to design a building that respected Coconut Grove's tropical environment. MacKenzie came up with a beautiful Spanish Colonial–style structure built of "coral rock." This design, especially the use of coral rock as a building product, had special meaning to George.

To raise funds for construction, George and Irving J. Thomas, another well-known real estate man, came up with the idea of subdividing some of the land around the church into an area they called Plymouth Court. Thomas' partner, Fin Pierce, donated the rock for the church building and the Mathesons brought in Spaniard Felix Rebon as the stonemason. George, with his background in development, was the hands-on overseer. He worked closely with Harriet James, wife of railroad magnate Arthur Curtiss James, who also had a large estate in Coconut Grove. George credited her with providing not only most of the funds for the new church but also most of the inspiration. "She herself," George wrote, "was the great inspiration for the planning and the working out of the plans. She herself was most largely responsible for the beauty of the building, grounds, patio and ensemble that was here brought into being."[2]

George, who always enjoyed the company of intelligent older women, frequently joined Harriet James as she worked with Felix Rebon to select the desired yellow shade of rock to create the color harmony she wanted. He found her search for perfection and beauty inspiring and later wrote that her work had a lasting effect on him and what he created in Coral Gables.[3]

By 1917, Miami was expanding in all directions. But its heady growth came to an abrupt halt in April 1917, when the United States entered what was then called "The Great War" that had been raging in Europe since 1914. Development slowed and in many cases stopped completely. The barely begun Tamiami Trail and the new causeway to Miami Beach were two of the first casualties. Contractors suspended work on the McAllister Hotel and the half-finished Negro Industrial School in Railroad Shops Colored Addition. Young Miamians, including George, registered for the draft and his brother Charles went off to war.

Like other real estate companies, Realty Securities' business suffered during the war and its full-page advertisements ceased. The company, however, continued to sell its existing subdivision and even introduced two new ones in early 1917. The first was Harwood, which had been carved out of Riverside Farms, and the second was called Swastika Park, located south of today's Seventh Street between Northwest Twenty-third and Twenty-fourth Avenues. (The term "Swastika" did not have the same connotation in 1917 that it would later have as a Nazi symbol. In fact, it was considered a good luck symbol. The name "Swastika Park" was probably selected because William Matheson had chosen it for his Coconut Grove estate.[4])

The outbreak of the war did not stop Eunice from embarking on her summer trip north. This time, however, it had a new twist. On May 24, what was described as an "auto party" left Miami in George's White touring car for a sixteen-day Florida adventure. The party included George and Eunice, Althea and her mother, Medie Fink, T. O. Wilson, and Mr. and Mrs. Clifton Benson. Benson kept a detailed and humorous journal that included notes about Florida cities, roads, groves, subdivisions, restaurants, hotels, and ice cream parlors, George's favorite stop. Eunice was with the group for eleven

Figure 26. St. Augustine's Spanish past influenced George's selection of the original Spanish-style architecture in Coral Gables. He and Eunice (*right*) stand by the historic city gates as Clifton Benson snaps their picture. University of Miami Special Collections. Courtesy of Mildred Merrick.

days until they arrived in Jacksonville and she boarded a train for her usual summer escape.

It was a remarkable journey. The journal provided insight into the "state of the state," the difficulties of automobile travel in that era, and the interests and personalities of the travelers. Clearly, they enjoyed each other's company and had a good time together.

The intrepid adventurers, with George as the only driver, traveled more than 1,100 miles crisscrossing the state—Miami, Daytona, St. Augustine, Winter Park, Tampa (with a stop at the new planned town of Oldsmar), Ocala, and Jacksonville—and then back to Miami via the East Coast. Benson recorded every detail, noting that they bridged or paralleled twenty-four named bodies of water and visited twenty counties. Averaging twenty miles an hour, the White consumed 180 gallons of gas and blew out three tires. (In one humorous aside, Benson noted that the ruts offered a new method of spinal adjustment.)

Benson concluded his four-page, legal-size, typed epic with a thank-you to George for being "at home at the wheel" and a "past master at the art" of driving. "It was a real vacation," he wrote, "as well as an education, as we saw at first hand the great 'STATE OF FLORIDA,' with its varied possibilities." He concluded, "It is indeed a 'land of opportunity,,' but we all returned more than satisfied with Miami and Dade County as the best of all."[5]

As usual, George kept the telegraph wires humming between Miami and Stewartstown, Pennsylvania, where Eunice was again visiting her friends. "Hello Sweetheart," he wrote. "Hope arrived safely. Am terribly lonesome already. Love, George."[6]

Former beau and now Army Captain Joe Ryan, who signed himself "your old pal," also wrote to Eunice in Stewartstown, hoping to see her again before he left for France, adding, "give a little remembrance once in a while to one who thinks a great deal of you."[7]

The big news in Miami was that the U.S. Navy would open a naval air station at Dinner Key. Although the people who lived in Coconut Grove were not pleased with the idea, they suffered quietly because they wanted to support the war effort. Soon after it began operation, Eunice's Uncle John Frow, the man who sold the Peacocks the land for the Peacock Inn, was killed when a seaplane landed on his fishing boat in Biscayne Bay.[8]

Everyone in the Merrick family supported the war effort. Althea and her daughters often entertained naval air station personnel at their Coral Gables home. *The Miami Herald* wrote a vivid account of one evening that included vocalists, dancers, and elocutionists, including Helen Merrick, performing on the east porch.[9] George was also involved as one of the leaders of the Liberty Bond Drive and chairman of several fundraising events.

Even with all of his activities, George found time to continue to write poetry, especially when Eunice was away. In fact, his youngest brother, Richard, recalled that George always had a pen and paper in his hand. He penned a poem to Eunice on Valentine's Day that lovingly described her "stubborn willful spirit" and her "spunky saucy style."[10] Another of his poems was published in the newspaper. He was disappointed, however, when he sent a query letter to Bobbs-Merrill Company and received a discouraging reply with the excuse that the company was publishing fewer books because of the war.[11]

In late 1918, George decided to leave Realty Securities Company. *The Miami Metropolis* carried a long story announcing his "retirement" in order to devote more time to his groves. It included several paragraphs about Solomon Merrick and the history of Coral Gables Plantation and how, under George's leadership, it had grown to twelve hundred acres—more than doubling in the last three years. The article included great detail about its current status, giving a rare glimpse into what had become a major, well-organized operation completely owned by George and his mother.

Coral Gables Plantation now had more than 100 acres in grapefruit that yielded 180 carloads of the prized fruit in one year. Besides expansive fields planted with vegetables, one hundred acres in avocado added to the mix. It employed more than forty men, owned three one-ton trucks, and operated three modern irrigation systems.

The most important part of the article, however, came at the end, when, for probably the first time, the press announced George's future plans for the Coral Gables Plantation. After noting its favorable location and how the demand for residences was growing, the article concluded: "Indeed, the plan is ultimately to incorporate the entire plantation as the 'Village of Coral Gables' (as the settlement group is already known). . . . All plantings and developments are being done according to a carefully mapped out program and plan, looking toward a final unique 'village beautiful' embracing the entire plantation."[12]

Although everyone now knew his future plans, George was not ready to begin until the war was over and he had more money in the bank. From experience, he knew the fastest way to make money was to continue in real estate. His first subdivision as George E. Merrick Company was Fernway Park, previously part of Riverside Farms. The park was a narrow, ten-acre swath of hammock land (Northwest Eleventh Street) with a roadway snaking through it. In an early advertisement, he compared its beauty to the new Royal Palm State Park in the Everglades.

Besides amassing capital, George also tried out a variety of marketing ideas. Fernway Park's promotion included an announcement that George Merrick "will entertain" five hundred people in the park and have them

Figure 27. Honing his marketing and development skills, George hired Edward L. "Doc" Dammers in 1919 as auctioneer for the development of Fernway Park. Two years later, Dammers would help launch Coral Gables. Permission of HistoryMiami.

transported from downtown Miami in one hundred automobiles! "One hour each day," the ad continued, "will be spent in the selling of these lots and one happy hour in the giving away of hundreds of very valuable souvenirs (no trash or cheap presents)."[13]

The most important addition to George's marketing plan, however, was the hiring of Doc Dammers and his company, Dammers & Gillette, as his auctioneers. Dammers was already well-known. His ebullient personality and showmanship drew people to his auctions just to watch him in action. George knew this and believed that by hiring Dammers he would turn his land sales into a popular tourist attraction.

At about the same time George launched Fernway Park, he became involved in a very public controversy with many of his Coconut Grove friends. The issue was whether or not Dinner Key Naval Air Station should be retained when the war ended. Arguing economic development, the Miami Chamber of Commerce and many of the business owners and developers, including George, were in favor of making it a permanent facility. Coconut Grove residents, including luminaries such as William Matheson, James Deering, and Ralph and Kirk Munroe, were strongly opposed. Even the local newspapers took sides, with *The Metropolis* being for closure and *The Miami Herald* against.

To make his point, George wrote a twelve-hundred-word letter to the editor of *The Miami Herald*, giving his reasons for being in favor of the station. He called Coconut Grove a "hermit town," comparing it to the hermit crab that takes over old shells and appears to walk in two directions at the same time.[14] Needless to say, the letter angered the opponents, who followed with a half-page ad blasting the proponents—especially George Merrick.[15]

The angry rhetoric continued to swirl after *The Herald* did an editorial entitled "Be a Man or a Mouse." It praised George for his "illuminating communication" and for being "outspoken and fearless." "Mr. Merrick," it concluded, "is a man and talks like a man."[16] Ultimately, Coconut Grove residents won the fight, and by summer the navy announced that the Dinner Key Naval Air Station would be closed. Despite losing the Dinner Key fight, George demonstrated with his surprising point of view that inside his idealistic, romantic soul there lurked the makings of a pragmatic businessman. (The site would later become the Pan American Flying Clipper terminal and later a Coast Guard station.)

For Eunice, summer meant that it was time to head north. Once again, her journey began with members of the Merrick family on a nineteen-hundred-mile odyssey to Haworth, New Jersey, where George dropped off his mother and grandmother to visit Denman Fink. After spending a day and night with Eunice in New York City, George put her on the train to Stewartstown, Pennsylvania, and drove back to Miami alone.

Soon after he returned home, and still feeling the glow of their time together in New York, George, whom Eunice called "Iggie," sent her a funny letter written on bank stationery. It notified her, "she has an overdraft on matter of letters . . . will not be tolerated by Bank of George E. Merrick lover and sole proprietor of Eunice I. Peacock Merrick Love Account. Deficiency must be taken care of in 5 days or proper proceedings will be initiated." George concluded, "I send you my deep all love of my heart, and I am missing you lots and lots all ready. Good night my dear, dear wifeie girl, Your old Iggie."[17]

Most of George's letters, however, had the same old refrain. "It appears absence does not make your heart grow any fonder," he lamented. "I am just about utterly disheartened waiting vainly for kind of letters I need so badly."[18] He wrote about "piles of worries over one darn thing after another all the time" and apologized for writing such a short letter because he was very busy.[19] Near the end of August he sent her a long telegram to Rocky Hill, where she was visiting Flora MacFarlane. "No good letter yet. Each day seems like month. Busy time begins Sept. 5–8. Don't you desire a little time together before my every moment occupied? Love, George."[20]

Despite his busy summer, George spent his lonely evenings writing poetry. Sometime he sent Eunice a copy of his latest work. Many of his poems spoke about his love for her. In "Love Afar," he sent her a "plaintive croon":

Far so Far—those dear eyes are—
Moon and Star!—to
Her a-far
Take now my heart's one tune.

"Returning Alone," which he dedicated to her, recalled their time together in Manhattan. It ended with these telling lines:

This only is true—
I cannot dream, even,
Dear, without you.

By the time Armistice Day came in November 1919, George was again busy with grapefruit, winter vegetables, land sales, and subdivisions. In late summer, he finally platted St. Alban's Park on Reverend Bolton's former homesite. Besides streets named Washington and Lincoln, he also named one Brooker, after Bolton's beloved horse, Johnny Brooker. A short time later, he and Clifton Benson purchased Flora MacFarlane's homestead and platted it as an addition to St. Alban's Park, thus expanding Coconut Grove's black community even more.

George's next big push came for what he called South Bay Estates, located off Grapeland Boulevard (Twenty-Seventh Avenue) just north of the new City of Coconut Grove, which incorporated in September 1919 in order to have more power against the growing City of Miami. In this advertisement, he pushed the fact that it was "almost adjoining" Coconut Grove's "Millionaire's Row." Once again, Dammers & Gillette were the auctioneers.[21]

At almost the same time, George also platted North Miami Estates. It was located north of Buena Vista Road (Northwest Thirty-Sixth Street) and south of Railroad Shops Colored Addition. The North Miami Estates ad was similar in style to that of South Bay Estates, and Dammers & Gillette were the auctioneers. The Herald reported that more than eleven full blocks and twenty individual lots were sold the first day.[22]

George ended the 1919-1920 season with Twelfth Street Manors, a 120-acre former grapefruit grove on Twelfth Street (Flagler) west of Thirty-First Avenue and north to Northwest Seventh Street. It was launched in March 1920 with partners A. H. Hazeltine and T. J. Hannan, and Dammers & Gillette ran a blitzkrieg-style, one-week auction. "Every lot in TWELFTH STREET MANORS is a FRUIT-FUL plot," George wrote, adding his hyperbolic rhetoric: "DOUBLE-PARKED, FRUIT-ARCHED PARKWAYS."[23]

Besides launching new subdivisions, George was also busy marketing the "grove estates" to the tourist crowd. The ads were pure George, filled with a little Dickens, Shakespeare, and history interspersed with some fairy tales. Running almost daily in January 1920, the ads ended with a play on GEM (George Edgar Merrick). The "G" had GROVE above and GEORGE below. The "E" turned into ESTATE and the "M" became MONEY-MAKERS AND MERRICK. One even included a poem:

ELEVEN famous Grove Estates
    I've "bragged on" now and then—
New Yorkers put some money down
    NOW there's only ten!

TEN profit-sharing Grove Estates
   All near the City's line
You'll say—if you will take a look,
   Less Mine, There's only Nine.[24]

It is hard to imagine when George had time to write serious poetry, but he did. In early 1920, the Four Seas Publishing Company of Boston accepted his manuscript for a volume of Florida-themed poems George entitled: *Song of the Wind on a Southern Shore*. The Four Seas Publishing Company was well-known for publishing new writers, especially poets. George was in heavy company. About the same time his book came out, Four Seas also published the early works of future legends William Carlos Williams, Gertrude Stein, Conrad Aiken, and William Faulkner. The company set the bar high but required a publishing subsidy that George, like the others, happily supplied.

During two summer visits to South Florida, George's uncle Denman Fink created six oil paintings to illustrate the poems. They included an example of Spanish architecture in St. Augustine, the Tamiami Trail, a cypress swamp, a grave in the Everglades, a seascape, and George's favorite "cloud mountains" of South Florida. Color plates of the paintings were interspersed throughout the thin volume. "Those who have seen the work of Mr. Fink," *The Miami Metropolis* reported, "say that he has finely interpreted the moods of Mr. Merrick's poems."[25]

When the book came out in late 1920, E. B. Douglas' downtown department store highlighted Denman's paintings and George's book in a special window display. *The Herald* published a positive review of both the paintings and the poetry, noting, "Merrick knows well his Florida in all her varying moods."[26]

George sent copies of his book to friends and colleagues and preserved many of the thank-you notes he received in return. "We are very proud to know we have a fellow townsman who can write such excellent verse," Emma Wilson wrote, "and shall look forward to your next book with much pleasure."[27] Coconut Grove pioneer Florence Haden recalled, "Perhaps you do not know how much Captain Haden and I admired you as a lad when you first came here. I think of all the boys we ever saw we liked you best and had the highest opinion of you."[28]

One of the most interesting letters, however, was not written to George but by George. In September 1920, he wrote to Marjory Stoneman Douglas, who was then the editor of a *Herald* column called "The Galley." From the letter, it was clear that he had not yet met her but admired her work. "I always turn to your page with lively anticipation," he wrote, along with a list of his favorite of her poems.

Remarking that he had asked Four Seas to send her a copy of his book, he added that he had worked "very modestly in the same field" and hoped she would find it of interest. "Again thanking you and assuring you," he concluded, "that none of your good ones will get by this *one* reader without being fully appreciated, I am, Yours respectfully, Geo. E. Merrick."[29]

This letter began a long and enduring friendship between George and Marjory Stoneman Douglas. A few years later, he hired her to write descriptive prose for some of his advertising publications.

December 1920 was a particularly busy month for George. On December 17, he and Eunice, with their friends John and Anna Graham, took a trip to Cuba via Key West. This was both his and Eunice's first trip to the island country and was also the closest he would ever come to viewing the type of architecture he envisioned for Coral Gables. He had now seen the real thing, and his ideas no longer grew simply from pictures in books. He absorbed Cuba's rustic, often decaying colonial buildings, with their interior patios, painted tiles, and ancient red-clay, barrel-tile roofs. He walked through town gates to the central plazas with their picturesque wells and heard the ringing of the bells in the myriad bell towers. He marveled at the tropical plants and the riot of bright colors calmed by the tropical sun. For George, the beauty of Cuban architecture transformed what sometimes seemed like his impossible dream into concrete future possibilities.

Shortly before he departed for Cuba, *The Miami Metropolis* ran a long news article concerning his buy-out of his Twelfth Street Manors partners. It would be his last subdivision before he launched Coral Gables. The others had been merely an audition for the big time.

Sales for the 1920–1921 season began with the December 10 advertisement in *The Miami Metropolis* announcing the "Most Stupendous Auction in Miami's History." Although the heavy text extolled Twelfth Street Manors, it also focused on the importance of Miami's westward expansion. "WESTWARD THE COURSE OF MIAMI'S EMPIRE TAKES

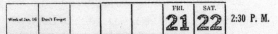

TO BUY RIGHT, BUY AT AUCTION

TWELFTH STREET MANORS
AUCTION
---Today and Tomorrow---

Week of Jan. 16	Don't Forget				FRI. 21	SAT. 22	2:30 P. M.

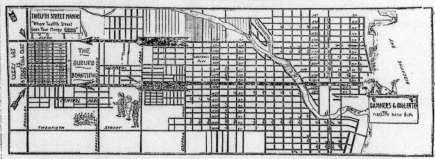

THE RECORD SELLING DEVELOPMENT
OVER 600 LOTS SOLD IN 50 DAYS

YOU REMEMBER LINCOLN'S SAYING: "YOU CAN FOOL SOME OF THE PEOPLE," ETC.
THINK THIS OVER!

WE MIGHT FOOL YOU, if you came from Keokuk or Wichita or Hoboken, and didn't yet know Miami's values, or of the Unparalleled Western Building Campaign, or the other vitally important factors which have put TWELFTH STREET MANORS in the investment lime light.

WE MIGHT FOOL YOU, BUT DO YOU THINK IT POSSIBLE TO FOOL MIAMI "OLD TIMERS" BY THE SCORE. level-headed business and professional men who have followed Miami investments from every angle, for from five to thirty years.

OVER HALF OF THE BUYERS OF THE 400 LOTS SOLD IN TWELFTH STREET MANORS DURING THE PAST 30 DAYS ARE MIAMI "OLD TIMERS."

For example, H. S. and B. S. Potter, pioneer residents of Coconut Grove, vitally interested from the beginnings of Dade county in its upbuilding—keen hard-headed investors. These Potter brothers, who have made themselves independent by their unerring ability to pick R E A L REALTY BUYS, have purchased six lots at their own price at our TWELFTH STREET MANORS AUCTION

COME OUT TOMORROW

Ask to see the List of MIAMI BUYERS at TWELFTH STREET MANORS, then "Ask the Man Who Owns One."

EXTRA
ADDED
ATTRACTIONS

Every day we shall give away, absolutely free, hundreds of dollars worth of valuable presents, including ELEGANT TEA SETS, BEAUTIFUL COFFEE SETS, ARTISTIC CHINA, RARE VASES, and many other articles too numerous to mention. You don't have to buy to receive a present.

We shall serve during the Sale every day Free refreshments. The famous, delicious Coral Gables Fruit Punch will be served.

FREE
SIGHTSEEING
TRIP

TAKE OUR FREE MOTOR CARS AT CORNER TWELFTH STREET AND AVENUE B. IN FRONT OF PUBLIC LIBRARY AND WOMAN'S CLUB, OPPOSITE THE HIPPODROME BUILDING. COME EVERY DAY, WHETHER YOU BUY OR NOT. EVERYONE WELCOME. CARS LEAVE FROM 1:30 P. M. UNTIL 2:15 P. M.

No charge to go in our Automobile to the Sales. Automobiles Free both ways.

IF YOU PREFER TO DRIVE OUT YOURSELF—GO STRAIGHT OUT TWELFTH STREET.

COME OUT TODAY

DAMMERS & GILLETTE and HARRY A. BURNES
SELLING AGENTS

157 Twelfth Street   Telephone 2140

Figure 28. To promote Twelfth Street Manors, George placed a series of full-page advertisements in both *The Miami Metropolis* and *The Miami Herald*. It would be his last subdivision before he launched Coral Gables. *The Miami Herald*, January 21, 1921.

ITS WAY," he wrote. The almost full-page advertisement even mentioned the Manors' close proximity to Coral Gables Plantation and the fact that George was negotiating with a company to build an electric railroad to the area.[30]

George also introduced some other elements that would follow him to Coral Gables. Twelfth Street Manors had an English Manor theme and two major one-hundred-foot-wide boulevards, Livingstone and Victoria. It also had what the newspapers described as the most extensive landscaping yet seen in any Miami subdivision. Special buses for would-be buyers replaced automobiles. Doc Dammers' unique style of auctioneering also provided entertainment, and those who came were reminded that they did not have to buy. The crowds arrived in huge numbers, drank Coral Gables Punch (aka grapefruit juice), collected gifts, and bought land. Sales were remarkable. It was not unusual for Dammers, perched on his old, red, mule-driven wagon, to sell more than one hundred lots a day. Sales were so brisk that George quickly added two new sections. "Where Twelfth Street Goes," he wrote, "Your Money Grows."[31]

George also appreciated the value of a little showmanship—a talent, his family said, he inherited from Grandfather Fink. In late March 1921, as the curtain fell on the 1920–1921 season, George added a draw like no other. He invited everyone to come to Twelfth Street Manors to witness a sort of Super Bowl of aviation: Mabel Cody's Flying Circus. The famous aviators took off from a makeshift landing field on barely cleared LeJeune Road and Flagler Street. Mabel Cody herself would perform the famous "whirl of death" and "Daredevil Lieutenant McGowan," assisted by "Flying Farmer McMullen," would perform a daring exchange from automobile to airplane. To top off the once-in-a-lifetime show, Pathé News would be on hand to film the event. "Those attending the flying exhibition," the article concluded, "will have an opportunity to buy at auction lots in Third Section Twelfth Street Manors. Presents will be liberally distributed and the delicious Coral Gables fruit punch will be served."[32]

Before Mabel Cody's famous aviators left town, *The Miami Herald* reported that George had taken the opportunity to climb aboard one of their planes and fly over Coral Gables to get what he called "an intimate bird's-eye view" of the development in progress. The plane crisscrossed the area, sometimes diving almost to the ground. With this unique perspective,

George reported that after the flight he had decided to "add embellishing little touches to it here and there."[33]

As March ended, George was able to focus full time on Coral Gables. Although he had been plotting Coral Gables' future in his fertile mind for more than a decade, at last the time was right to pull together a team of other creative souls who would help him turn his dream into reality.

From Dream to Reality

I know now that magic space
Where my grandfather's past, my father's knowledge and
My own new intuitions
Arose alive and moved on together.

George E. Merrick, "My Mighty Century Lost"

Two weeks after auctions ended at Twelfth Street Manors, *The Miami Metropolis,* in a front-page story, reported George's formal announcement that he would launch Coral Gables at the beginning of the next season.[1] It came as no surprise. Even though he discussed his plans with only a few confidants, everyone knew he dreamed of transforming the Coral Gables Plantation into a planned subdivision. Admitting he was an intellectual and a romantic, with a large dose of what his father called "Finkism," George had spent the last decade developing his practical side. "I never allowed a dream to put me on the run before I knew where I was going,"[2] he recalled. Each new subdivision expanded and honed his business, development, and marketing skills, as well as adding to his bank account. As a result, according to *The Miami Metropolis,* he had become "one of the most successful developers in the state."[3]

Despite his success, George did not see himself as a developer. He was an idealist and a visionary. His growing wealth did not diminish his optimistic personality, something he once described as his most cherished gift. He had learned how to make money but never lost his singular reason for doing so. His growing assets would allow him to develop Coral Gables his way, with profit as the least of his motives. For the past ten years, he had devoured the writings of such English visionaries as John Ruskin, William Morris, and Ebenezer Howard. He also studied the City Beautiful movement and the works of Frederick Law Olmsted and Daniel Burnham.

Those who knew him expected him to focus on philosophy and talk about ideals. His core values had not changed since his days at Rollins College, when he won the oratory prize for defending the underdog. He internalized Ruskin's views that everyone deserved beauty and that town planning and urban design were true art forms. He found a kindred spirit in Howard and Morris, who, like Ruskin, preached that homes built from local stone by local craftspeople had the greatest value. His parents' and his own home had proved Morris and Ruskin's theories correct. His direct involvement in building Plymouth Congregational Church further reinforced his passion for Miami's own "coral rock."

Ebenezer Howard's suburban English village, called Lechworth, designed by architects Raymond Unwin and Barry Parker, inspired him. Inspiration turned to conviction once he and his uncle Denman Fink saw Howard's Garden City views come to life in Forest Hills Gardens, New York. With the support of the Sage Foundation, which owned the entire project, and the talents of architect Grosvenor Atterbury and landscape architect Frederick Law Olmsted Jr., Forest Hills proved the value of thoughtful planning, place-making landscape design, artistic entry features, and strict zoning and architectural controls. What set Forest Hills apart from other developments was the developer-mandated Arts and Crafts–style architectural theme melded with some of the formalism of the City Beautiful philosophy. Samuel Howe, in a 1914 *House Beautiful* article, described Forest Hills Gardens as a painting.[4]

The architects of Forest Hills Gardens referenced an earlier subdivision named Roland Park, located eight miles from downtown Baltimore and only three miles from George's father's boyhood home. It, too, was an early Frederick Law Olmsted Jr.–planned suburb that was strongly influenced by the senior Olmsted's 1860 plan for Riverside, just outside Chicago. Roland Park did not mandate an architectural style but was known for its park-like setting and architectural features, including a distinctive Italianate-style water tower. Unlike Forest Hills Gardens, Roland Park was created for people of means.[5] George clearly adopted some of Roland Park's best features, including its artistic water tower, but stuck to his original plan to create a beautiful suburb for the middle class.

Although Forest Hills Gardens left an indelible picture in George's mind, he later said that it was Shaker Heights, a planned suburb eight miles east of Cleveland, Ohio, that influenced him the most.[6] Purchased in 1905 by brothers Oris Paxton and Mantis James Van Sweringen, their six-and-one-third-square-mile planned development started with mostly vacant land. It had no overriding architectural theme but instead strongly suggested that all homes follow one of three styles: Colonial, French, or English. This was not as open as it sounded, because through deed restrictions, or what the Van Sweringens called the "Shaker Heights Standards," nothing could be built without a professional architect whose plans had to be approved by the developers. The same was true for landscaping, lighting, and even paint color. The village also had strict zoning requirements that included setbacks, driveways, and location of garages, among other things.[7] George was also impressed by the fact that it attracted people from different income levels. The Vans, as they were commonly called, also had a marketing and advertising campaign that was unprecedented in its aggressiveness. In many ways, George saw Shaker Heights as almost a beginning blueprint, or at least an outline, for what he envisioned for Coral Gables.

His last step was to incorporate all he had learned into a plan that reflected South Florida's subtropical ambience. He considered what he called the area's "cloud mountains" and uplifting south winds that inspired his poetry. He remembered his first trip to Cuba and the Bahamas and how the first Europeans to come to the tropics had adapted their homeland styles to "the beauty and color of tropical skies, sea and foliage."[8] A trip to the "Ancient City" of St. Augustine gave him a renewed appreciation of the history and architectural remnants of Spanish Florida. In Flagler's Ponce de Leon Hotel, designed by renowned New York architects Carre and Hastings, he experienced Florida's first modern interpretation of Spanish and Mediterranean-style architecture.

Everything he studied and saw, combined with memories of his own life experience and Washington Irving's romantic stories in his *Tales of the Alhambra*, swirled around in his fertile brain until slowly his vision for Coral Gables emerged. After years of reading, planning, and dreaming, George

Figure 29. Even though Denman Fink still lived in Haworth, New Jersey, he was George's most important collaborator, working closely with him on every aspect of the original plan. Courtesy of Nancy Fink Giacci, artist.

came to the conclusion that in Coral Gables he could make his own "Castles in Spain" real. Now all he needed was to bring his handpicked experts together to help him turn his dreams into reality.

The first and most important member of his team was his uncle, Denman Fink. Although they had been talking about the future of the Coral Gables Plantation for years, in February 1920, Denman completed the first Coral Gables concept drawings during an extended South Florida sojourn.[9] By this time, Denman had a national reputation as an artist/illustrator. His work was featured in magazines and in New York galleries. During World War I, he had been chosen has one of the U.S. government's twenty-two artists to create posters in support of the allies and the Liberty Bond drives. His painting of a Portugal scene was purchased by the Portuguese government. He also was one of the artists selected to help the public support wounded soldiers.[10]

"When Mr. Merrick laid before me his plans for the development of Coral Gables," Denman later wrote, "and asked me to join him in carrying out his visualization of the scheme along purely Spanish lines, of the real old type . . . with a purely coral rock construction . . . I welcomed the invitation with open arms."[11] "Once the theme was decided," Denman's son Bob later recalled, "they sort of fed each other, one mind flamed the other."[12]

As an artist, Denman began by painting a series of oils that depicted South Florida's natural beauty. These paintings would help set the scene and would also be used as illustrations in George's book of poetry. At the same time, he, George, and their wives made an automobile trip to Palm Beach to view the work of Addison Mizner, the new talk of the architectural world, for his romantic Spanish-style buildings.[13]

Mizner came to Palm Beach in January 1918 at the behest of Paris Singer, heir to the Singer Sewing Machine fortune. Singer hired him to design a convalescent hospital for veterans of World War I. When the Everglades Club opened a year later, the war was over and the would-be hospital had been transformed into a private enclave for members of Palm Beach's wealthy resort society who had been lured to the area by Henry Flagler and his luxury hotels.

By the time the Merrick party arrived, Mizner had also been commissioned to build several Spanish-style waterfront mansions and had become identified as "the" Palm Beach society architect.[14] Although the beauty of Mizner's design impressed the visitors and reinforced George's decision to build Coral Gables with a Spanish theme, building mansions for the wealthy was the furthest thing from his mind.

One other project came to his attention. In July 1920, the newly created Town of Coconut Grove hired Philadelphia architect John Irwin Bright to create a town plan. Several of Coconut Grove's most influential residents, including Hugh Matheson, Dr. Charles DeGarmo, and realtor Irving J. Thomas, sat on the Coconut Grove Council. They wanted Coconut Grove to stand out from the rest of Miami with a formal City Beautiful–type ambience. If followed, Bright's Plan would have changed Coconut Grove from its legendary live-and-let-live, lush, tropical ambience into a formal Spanish-style enclave. MacFarlane Road would become a mirror-lake mimicking the formality of Chicago's Columbian Exposition. Grandiose Spanish-style buildings, including a city hall and hotel, would overlook the newly created water feature.

Bright also suggested that the entire black community be moved north of today's Dixie Highway into a new planned community that included schools, a library, and a day care center. The historic Kebo community would be turned into a golf course.[15] This element of the plan, of course, impacted the two new subdivisions George had just completed for his friends in the black community.

With great fanfare, the city council adopted the Bright Plan, including the preliminary drawings, which were widely published. The overly ambitious plan was never implemented, but at the time George was preparing his final plans for Coral Gables, it was very much in the news and may have influenced him.

Although George and Denman had no trouble envisioning Coral Gables' future, George realized he needed more than an artist to translate his vision into a formal plan. As fate would have it, Frank M. Button, the first registered landscape architect in Florida, entered the picture quite by accident.

Button came to Florida from Chicago in 1912 to oversee the planning and landscaping of Charles Deering's twenty-acre Buena Vista estate, now the Bay Point subdivision.[16] Deering, chairman of the board of the Deering Tractor Company, which became International Harvester, was the son of founder William Deering and brother of James Deering, who later built Vizcaya. Button was a partner of Ossian Cole Simonds, whose firm was highly respected in the Chicago area. Button's job was to plan the extensive landscaping, which, in addition to tropical plants and fruits, included canals and habitats for exotic birds, monkeys, and other subtropical wildlife. Simonds and Button's belief in respecting the natural environment was evident in the original plans for the site, which were left incomplete after Charles purchased property in Cutler and shifted his interest there.

Button, a native of Vermont, trained as a civil engineer at the University of Vermont and joined the U.S. Army Corps of Engineers upon graduation. He met Simonds when both worked with Frederick Law Olmsted on Chicago's 1893 Columbian Exposition. For the next twenty-three years, Simonds and Button worked together, first as collaborators and then as

Figure 30. It was fortuitous that Frank Button came on the scene just in time to put George's original plan onto paper. Much of his original layout can be seen today. Courtesy of Nancy Fink Giacci, artist.

partners. Their work included Fort Sheridan in Highland Park, Illinois, the extension of Chicago's Lincoln Park, and the planning and landscaping of parks, cemeteries, and private estates east of the Mississippi.[17]

Shortly after Frederick Law Olmsted founded the American Society of Landscape Architects, Button became its fourteenth member and was elected to Fellowship in 1910. In 1920, following his wife's death, he left the Simonds firm and, a short time later, moved to Miami with his daughter.

In early 1921, a close friend named Charles B. Stearns recognized Button walking down Flagler Street. Prior to public offerings, Stearns, a wealthy Chicagoan, had paid $38,000 for four blocks of soon-to-be Coral Gables. As one of the largest landowners, he had become close to Merrick and was involved in the early planning.[18] When Stearns saw Button, Button's daughter later recalled, he raced to Button, saying, "Hey Frank, you are just the man we want!"[19] Stearns immediately took Button to meet George in his Flagler Street office, and before the meeting concluded, George hired him.

The same month he hired Button, George paid $50,000 to John Burdine for what was called the Mackinac Building at 158 East Flagler Street. *The Miami Metropolis* reported that it was the highest price ever paid for a Flagler Street property. It was to be the headquarters for the new Coral Gables development that was totally owned by George Merrick.[20]

Button prepared a letter to Merrick dated April 18, 1921, that outlined his services to create the plans for a twelve-hundred-acre subdivision known as Coral Gables. Following the completion of a survey, Button would prepare a preliminary study, after which he would complete "the general plan of such scale as may be desired and detail plan of blocks or parkways and parks and other detail as may seem necessary."[21] The fee would be one dollar an acre, with $400 paid at completion of the study plan, $400 at the acceptance of the general plan, and $400 hundred when all plans were complete. In conclusion, he promised that all plans would be finished in two months!

The first thing George did after he signed the contract was to take his new colleague on one of his famous bumpy tours through the grapefruit groves and forest trails in his open Pierce Arrow. Impressed with the scale and landscape possibilities of the new subdivision, Button soon followed up with an undated preliminary study that clearly showed his enthusiasm for the project.

After describing the boundaries, which went two miles north to south from Southwest Eighth Street (Tamiami Trail) to Bird Road and one-and-one-half miles east to west from LeJeune Road to Red Road, Button praised the gentle and rolling land filled with grapefruit and avocado pears and more than forty acres of virgin pine forest. He wrote of the two glades that would offer vistas for homeowners and make perfect golf courses—one with nine holes and one with eighteen. He noted the live oaks and native palms, figs, and ferns that would appeal to any nature lover. He referenced what the locals called "the reef," or the high rocky ridge that served as home to the native Florida pines and ensured cool breezes.

After describing the land, which he said gave the planner great freedom, he explained his theories for roads, which followed a careful study of "the natural conditions and beauties of the property and care taken to preserve all trees and to take advantage of the hills and hollows."[22] He described the streets as broad, from fifty to one hundred feet wide, with some diagonal roads to highlight various points of interest. He proposed that the entire tract be encircled with a grand boulevard. He recommended that all streets have wide parkways planted with tropical trees and shrubs, adding, "Southern Florida has a greater flora than any other part of the United States." In addition to the park-like streets, numerous small parks and playgrounds would add to the scene, along with large ornamental plazas heretofore unknown in small subdivisions.

The business section would comprise three-and-one-half acres with a broad plaza "making a place for rest amid pleasing surroundings." "All in all," he concluded, "Coral Gables offers a location unsurpassed for ideal living conditions."[23]

George Merrick was obviously pleased with Button's preliminary work because the final plan followed Button's description almost word for word. At last, George had found a professional who shared his love of the land and his appreciation for all things native and tropical and had captured his vision on paper.

It was an exciting time for George and all the Merrick family. Just as he was signing the Button contract, his brother-in-law and former real estate partner, thirty-one-year-old Bob McLendon, became the youngest bank president in Florida at the Fidelity Bank and Trust Company. The euphoria did not last. Within a month, State Comptroller Ernest Amos closed the bank and took charge of its operation. It was a blow to the bank's depositors, including George. With fears of losing all of their deposits, a group of well-known Miamians came together and formed a committee to stall the closure in order to avoid a run on the bank. They came up with several alternatives, including a plan to offer interest-bearing term deposit certificates in lieu of withdrawal. Adding to the controversy, Miami was in the midst of an election in which, ironically, five bank presidents were running as a group for the city council. Rallies, attended by thousands of people worried about the Fidelity Bank failure and heated by barbs tossed by the other presidents running for office, filled the news. Finally, the election ended, the bank presidents were elected, and Fidelity worked out a plan to sell the wounded bank to the Banker's Financing Corporation of Jacksonville, securing the depositors' money.[24]

The situation with the Fidelity Bank reminded George of what happened to his father when the Bank of Fort Dallas closed in 1907 and the family had to stop construction of their new home. Fortunately, George, unlike his father, was able to recoup his money, but the situation seriously slowed his momentum and gave him many sleepless nights. In a long letter to his mother, written in July, he bemoaned the fact that he was so far behind due to the "Fidelity business." He wrote from New York's Hotel Woodstock, where he was busy trying to get new investors. He apologized for not writing but explained that he had little time for anything but business letters and hoped she understood "the load of business and worry and the great burden of planning and scheming and financing I have on me."

He also told of visiting Denman in Haworth, New Jersey, to talk over work he was doing on Coral Gables, including posters and a magnificent entrance design. Eunice, on her usual summer trip to Rocky Hill, New Jersey, joined him in Haworth for one day.

From Haworth George traveled to Bridgeport, Connecticut, where he met with Doc Dammers and Harry A. Burnes, whom he described as his most valuable assets. The men and their wives treated him royally, held club gatherings in his honor, and introduced him to many politicians, industrialists, and bank presidents. Even though he wrote that he was way behind in his Coral Gables work, his visit with Dammers and Burnes made him feel even more encouraged about Coral Gables' future. "He [Burnes] has single handedly put more cash in my way than any other person. I am building up a great organization and if no further catastrophe like Fidelity happens, I'll have Coral Gables a wonderful place someday."[25]

When George returned to Coral Gables, Frank Button was waiting with his first comprehensive map of the development, dated July 1921. Although there would be some changes before the final map appeared in November, the basic plan was set. At this point, however, it included only a few named streets, principally Granada and Coral Way.

Now all George needed was an architect to turn Denman Fink's drawings for the artistic entrances and plazas into architectural documents and to design the first homes. H. H. Mundy, who had designed George and Eunice's home and the Briggs' home across the street, was a natural choice. Another man, however, with close family connections, rose to the forefront and became the lead architect.

Henry George Fink, a practicing Miami architect, was George Merrick's first cousin. He had moved to Miami from Springdale, Pennsylvania, in 1904 and graduated from Miami High School in 1907. His father, Romie,

Figure 31. George Fink, George Merrick's first cousin, was another talented member of the Fink family. He designed most of the early homes. Courtesy of Nancy Fink Giacci, artist.

was Althea Merrick's brother. George, as he was called, married Josie Hinton, his high school sweetheart, in 1910 and became a Miami postman to support his growing family. But, like most of the Finks, he was a talented artist and designer and dreamed of becoming an architect. While serving as a postman in what is now Overtown, he took a correspondence course in drafting and in 1913 got his postman duties transferred to Philadelphia so he could attend night classes at the Drexel Institute. After three years at Drexel, he received a degree in Constructive Drawing and returned to Miami to work as a draftsman for well-known architect August Geiger. During his two years with Geiger, he designed many of the projects of Miami Beach developer Carl Fisher, including Fisher's private home. After leaving Geiger, he spent six months with H. H. Mundy, before opening his own office in 1919. It was about this time, Fink later recalled, that Merrick approached him to see if he was interested in being his lead Coral Gables architect but asked him to keep his plans for the new subdivision secret until he had acquired more property and was ready to begin.[26]

When the time came to make his position official, Fink was a well-known and honored architect who had designed many notable South Florida buildings. His most important was the original Miami Beach Public School (now Fisher-Fienberg), which *The Miami Metropolis* described as "true Spanish architecture" with patios, a stone fountain, and a red-tile roof.[27] When it was completed in September 1920, *The Miami Herald Record* called it "the handsomest building in the south."[28] Other commissions soon followed, including Miami's Mission-style First Christian Church, the Del Rio Apartments, and Miami Beach's First National Bank. In August 1921, the American Institute of Architects acknowledged his talent and professionalism and accepted him as its youngest Florida member.

With the addition of Fink, Merrick's artistic and intellectual dream team was now in place. But other, more practical issues, like marketing and sales, needed to be finalized. After several years of working together, Edward "Doc" Dammers was a natural choice for head of sales. In anticipation of the opening of Coral Gables, his Dammers & Gillette firm added Harry A. Burnes, the Connecticut real estate developer who had impressed George and had already sold blocks of land to his affluent fiends. The expanded firm moved into Merrick's new Flagler Street building, which soon sported a large blinking electrical sign beaming, "Coral Gables: Miami's Master Suburb." A short time later, George Fink moved his offices there as well.

Now all that was left to do was to create a marketing plan. For George, this was the easiest decision. He would create the plan, write the copy, and plan the advertisements himself. He had spent almost a decade writing advertisements for his other subdivisions and already had a reputation as a master salesman, just like Grandfather Fink. South Floridians did not know it yet, but they were about to witness the beginning of what would prove to be the greatest and most expensive advertising campaign for a real estate development in history.

To help promote Coral Gables and to document its development, George hired W. A. Fishbaugh, a commercial photographer who had already made a name for himself doing work for Carl Fisher and the Miami Chamber of Commerce. He began his career as a soldier-photographer in southern Africa's Boer War, then, following the Spanish-American War, moved on to document the Philippines. His international wanderlust took him next to Panama to capture the building of the Panama Canal. He then moved to Tampa for a decade before arriving in Miami in 1920. He was famous for his "Cirkut" photographs—large panoramas that captured scenes and crowds with a moving camera. Even before the first lots were sold, Fishbaugh took shots of new roads through the grapefruit groves and the first homes under construction on Coral Way. It was just the beginning of his Coral Gables work; ultimately, hundreds of his photographs would be used to promote sales.

By the time everything was in place, the summer of 1921 was turning into fall. With the first sales planned for late November, time was running out. Workers frantically slashed through the groves to turn the paper plan into real streets and boulevards, plazas, and parkways. Many of the black Bahamians who worked with George during the Coral Gables Plantation years continued as his construction workers. Their loyalty was unprecedented to the man who, as a boy and young man, had worked side by side with them in the fields and later built a new subdivision for their families.

Although working day and night on the final plans for Coral Gables, George missed Eunice, who had been away all summer. "Getting very anxious for you," he wrote in an August 27 telegram to her at Rocky Hill, where she was visiting friends. "Do you intend remaining beyond Sept.15? Love, George." Her yearly absences, especially during this important summer, became a growing problem.

She did return in September, just in time to participate in the naming of Coral Gables streets. She later recalled how she and George spread the Button map out on their dining room table, opened Washington Irving's *Tales of the Alhambra*, and named the streets after the old Spanish cities he described.

Denman Fink arrived from Haworth, New Jersey, in mid-October to work with George on the final plans and complete his designs for the entrances, plazas, and advertising posters that reflected the beauty of Old Spain. George, while overseeing development, approving plans, and keeping control over all the important details, spent evenings writing advertising copy in preparation of the media blitz planned for mid-November.

Figure 32. Frank Button completed his plan for Coral Gables in July 1921. By October, when it was first published, it had already undergone some changes. Following the first sale, the plan continued to evolve while holding true to the original concept. Permission of HistoryMiami.

The first articles announcing the impending public sale appeared during Denman's visit. On October 25, *The Miami Metropolis* included an article commending the "Subdivision Deluxe Just West of the City." It referenced those responsible for the plan, its artistic Spanish theme and distinctive architecture, and the miles of paved roads and tinted concrete sidewalks. The same issue included a full-page advertisement touting Coral Gables as "the most masterly achievement in Southern Florida since the construction of the Royal Palm Hotel."[29] It stated that the new planned suburb would take ten years to complete and that what was being offered was only the beginning of a much larger scheme.

At about the same time, Button completed the first map with street names, but it was not released to the public. Titled "Coral Gables 'Miami's Master Suburb,'" it listed George E. Merrick as owner and developer, Dammers & Gillette and Harry A. Burnes as selling agents, W. C. Bliss as civil engineer, and F. M. Button as landscape architect. The new subdivision's boundaries extended from just north of Avenue Sorolla (the original northern boundary of the 1899 purchase) south to Bird Road, west to Red Road, and east to Anderson Road, with a small section to LeJeune north of Coral Way. On this first plan, what would become the Granada Golf Course ended at Granada Boulevard and extended south of Coral Way for two blocks on what was described as "leased land." The original plan also included a business district facing today's Country Club Prado and Coral Way. It was called St. Augustine Plaza, with a block to the east reserved for public purposes, including a school, church, and library. The northern section of Granada Boulevard was only a strip of land from the street north of Sorolla, then called Coral Valley Road, to the Tamiami Trail, where the first entrance was to be constructed. A row of narrow lots flanked both sides of the street.[30]

The final countdown began on November 15, when the first of an almost daily barrage of full-page advertisements debuted in both *The Miami Herald* and *The Miami Metropolis*. The first, not surprisingly, was entitled: "The Realization of an Ideal." It was pure George, full of adjectives, hyperbole, idealism, and prophesies. The bulk of the three-column, seventeen-hundred-word essay honored his father and his farsighted vision that foresaw a great future for their 160-acre backcountry purchase that, in little more than twenty years, was now to become a sixteen-hundred-acre "Master Suburb." He promised that Coral Gables would unite Ruskinesque beauty and utility in a way unknown in South Florida. Using his habit of creating new words, he predicted that Miami's future was "Coral Gablesward." To seal the deal, he touted the million dollars already spent, along with another million being poured into new construction (the equivalent of more than $40 million in 2015 dollars). In summation, he ended with a touch of romance and poetic imagery—an enduring description of the Coral Gables he promised to create: "Not a thing of the moment, of the year or even of the passing period, but a wonderful monument to the achievement of worthwhile perseverance in the creation of beauty and the bringing true of dreams that will solidly endure and as beautifully and bountifully age as does the everlasting coral upon which this master development is founded."

Miamians expected new real estate developments to occur as regularly as the rainy season. This November, newspapers bulged with ads for the new subdivisions of Hollywood-by-the-Sea, Hialeah, Shenandoah, and Biscayne Park, as well as older areas like Grove Park and the relatively new town of Miami Beach. Some highlighted their proximity to downtown Miami and wrote thinly veiled negative comments about those that were more distant. Many people held that point of view. "They all were convinced beyond a shadow of a doubt," one contemporary later recalled, "that George Merrick was stupid, that he had a hole in his head . . . to go out in the country, out in the Everglades with the crocodiles and the sand flies and mosquitoes—but George Merrick believed in it."[31]

Two days later, both newspapers carried another full-page ad entitled "The Suburb Beautiful." It was signed by Frank M. Button and followed the same style as the first. Although none was completed, Button told of the planned entrances and plazas, including the "imposing" entrance at Southwest Eighth Street (Tamiami Trail) and the two-mile-long Granada Boulevard that commenced there. Only part of Granada Boulevard and little more than a mile of Alhambra Circle, which he wrote would encircle the entire development with a wide parkway in the center, were completed. Their raw newness stood out in stark contrast to the tall native pines and rows of grapefruit trees that dominated the scene.[32]

Following the every-other-day schedule, Denman Fink's essay, "'Castles in Spain' Made Real," was next. He, with the assistance of his nephew, George Merrick, wrote eloquently about "beauty and consistency" and their "faithful rendering of Spanish atmosphere, quaintness and charm." He added to the overarching promise that nothing would be done without careful forethought. "It is, in fact, a settling that is in every sense a real inspiration . . . silent testimonials to the great principles of harmony."[33]

Although George truly believed that people desired beauty and had a need to understand the depth of the process he had undertaken, he also knew that they had to be sold on the soundness of their investment. So after three days of serious essays, he unleashed Doc Dammers to push the other side of the equation and introduce a new slogan: "Where Coral Gables Lies, Your Money Multiplies."[34]

Two days later, H. George Fink, with George's help, returned to philosophy with the final essay, "A Coral Gables Home." Fink highlighted the fact that most developers sold only lots and blocks and how Coral Gables was different—it, for example, already had twenty-five homes and another twenty-five under construction. He added, "a suburb without homes is a library without books." He promised that the "coral rock" homes, plus a business district that would be just as beautiful and architecturally harmonious, would make Coral Gables a suburb like no other.[35]

Now that the philosophy and overall plan were more than explained, the rest of the almost daily ads were pure sales. In "An Invitation to Realtors" and "The Sugar Bowl," which appeared over the next two days, Doc Dammers stressed the investment opportunity of buying early before prices rose and Coral Gables became the highest-priced property in Greater Miami. He referenced his experience as an auctioneer in Miami Beach and expressed certainty that Coral Gables lots would make early purchasers "independently rich." He predicted that Coral Gables would be the best-advertised development in Miami's history and that it would soon have an office in New York City and Chicago. Up to this point, the ads had been more like teasers to raise interest and curiosity. Now, on November 24, just four days before the big event, realtors were encouraged to show up and "be prepared to buy."[36]

After two days of Dammers' heavy sales pitch, the next ad was simple and specific, listing the date and time of Monday, November 28, at two thirty in the afternoon, with additional news of the opening promised in the next day's paper. The same paper included another full-page ad listing twenty-seven people who had already purchased homes and lots in Coral Gables. Of those, six were members of the Merrick family and several of their homes were more than a decade old.[37]

The following day, a two-page spread appeared. It had banner headlines and promised that the opening auction would be "The Most Remarkable Event of the Year!" It also included the first publication of the Frank Button map dated November 1921 and the first Fishbaugh Cirkut photograph of Coral Way, which stretched across the two pages. George's super-salesman hyperbole, honed by almost a decade of real estate development, came to life full-blown, with the lead sentence repeating the slogan "Where Coral Gables Lies, Your Money Multiplies" and reminding readers that it was "the chance of a lifetime—the Opportunity of Opportunities to invest and make money." In an attempt to debunk those who thought Coral Gables was too far west and deep in the Everglades, he predicted that soon it would become part of the City of Miami and that Coral Way, which at the time ran only between LeJeune and Red Roads, would be cut all the way through to Biscayne Bay.

Despite George's seeming confidence, he took nothing for granted. To ensure crowds and not to be outdone by other developers, he followed the longtime custom of holding auctions and giving away presents for "fun and amusement." He also offered free transportation on new buses that would leave "every few minutes" from the Miami Women's Club on Flagler Street on opening day and every afternoon that week as the auctions continued.[38]

As a further inducement, as if anyone needed more, *The Miami Herald* printed a perfectly timed news story about George Merrick filing for incorporation of the South Florida Transit Corporation, which anticipated building a trolley line from North Palm Beach to Homestead, with a loop from Miami to Coral Gables and Coconut Grove. He, of course, would be president of the new company, which was backed by northern investors.[39]

At last, the long-anticipated birth was imminent. It appropriately would take place on the front lawn of George and Eunice's Coral Way home, "Poinciana Place," where the first serious plans were conceived. Auctioneer Doc Dammers and his famous mule cart would be there to herald the event and sell the lots.

Leaving nothing to chance, Denman Fink designed signs—"Follow the Golden Galleon"—that appeared every few blocks along Flagler Street from downtown to LeJeune Road. Caballeros dressed in Spanish costumes would direct the cars south to Eighth Street and west to two huge billboards adorned with Denman drawings of the new entrance-to-be. The signs provided the temporary entrance feature to newly landscaped Granada Boulevard and welcomed the curious, prospective buyer to Coral Gables and the future.

The day had come, after years of dreaming, planning, and building. George was a hopeful believer yet confident that the years of hard work and struggle would make his Spanish castles real. Coral Gables would, at last, become the realization of his and his father's ideal.

With Broad Vision and High Ideals

George E. Merrick, the owner and developer of Coral Gables,
has broad vision and high ideals in the building of
Coral Gables.

"Pointing the Way to Better Things," *The Miami Metropolis*,
December 21, 1921

George awoke early on November 28, eager to celebrate the birth of his child, Coral Gables. He had conceived it, named it, nurtured it, and financed it. He had set high standards and monitored every aspect of its development to make sure it lived up to his ideals. Nothing occurred in Coral Gables without his blessing. He had gathered a group of talented individuals to help him, but they accepted the fact that he was the one who made the decisions. He alone carried all the plans around in his head, wrote most of the advertising copy, did the hiring and firing, and approved or disapproved all architectural drawings and house plans. As George Fink later recalled, "When George did not like a plan, he frowned and said: 'I don't like it . . . do it over. I just don't like it.'"[1] The only time he was not involved was when he slept his usual four or five hours a night. But even confident, optimistic thirty-five-year-old George did not envision what was about to occur.

The auction was to begin at two thirty, but hours earlier, people started to arrive. By one o'clock the colorful guides, dressed in scarlet jackets, cocked plush hats, and red stockings, had directed more than a thousand automobiles to the big event. In addition to the automobiles, George's new fleet of buses left downtown Miami every few minutes, packed with locals and tourists eager to see what had been so widely promoted.

In truth, Coral Gables still existed mostly on paper. Only Coral Way, from LeJeune Road to Red Road, and Granada Boulevard, from the Tamiami Trail to Coral Way, had been completed. Workmen were busy constructing Alhambra Circle, commencing at LeJeune Road, and preparing what was called a "parked" median for the proposed trolley. Ponce de Leon Plaza, at Granada Boulevard and Coral Way, was under construction, along with a few new rock homes on Coral Way. Also visible were miles of coral-colored sidewalks that snaked through the pinewoods and groves. Despite the rawness of the suburb-to-be, rows of seemingly endless trees bearing grapefruit, orange, and avocado improved the scene and reminded everyone how George Merrick and his father had transformed a wilderness into a profitable enterprise.

Because of the swelling crowd, the auction started a half-hour early. Promptly at two o'clock, Doc Dammers, dressed in white and following his usual routine, stood up on his old, mule-driven wagon and began with his standard and well-known, "Ladies and gentlemen! Standing here on this paradisal spot, this sun-drenched haven where Mother Nature herself makes her annual escape from Old Devil Winter, it is my privilege and your opportunity to be present at the very first offering."[2] But unlike previous auctions, the crowd of five thousand was more interested in the large, full-color map of "Miami's Master Suburb" and Denman Fink's renderings of the proposed entrances and plazas than the stack of gifts spread out on a table.

The surrounding frenzy of activity heightened the crowd's enthusiasm. Armies of men were at work on newly cleared Coral Way. Another crew was busy transforming the family's former vegetable field into a golf course. In the distance, the sound of dynamite blasts resonated as workers removed stubborn palmetto roots from rocky pineland and created holes for new planting. Adding to the cacophony was the roar of the steam-driven bulldozers as they clawed their way through the woods to create new streets.[3]

Even though the map showed a new suburb of fifteen hundred acres, the only part of Coral Gables for sale that day was seventy-five-acre "Section A." It extended four blocks south of Coral Way to Sevilla, east to Anderson Road, and west to Columbus Boulevard. In addition to a rather ordinary grid of fifty-foot lots per block, Section A also included Ponce de Leon, Columbus, and Desoto Plazas, as well as the impressive, diagonal DeSoto Boulevard. It also noted an outdoor lagoon called "Grotto Park"—landscape architect Frank Button's original plan for turning an old rock pit into a community amenity.[4]

The plan also marked a proposed 18-hole, 143-acre golf course west of Granada Boulevard. George had been working on an agreement with the officers of the planned but unbuilt Coconut Grove Golf Course. He would give the corporation forty acres for a clubhouse complex and lease another hundred acres for a golf course for ten dollars a year for ten years. In turn, the Coconut Grove group, which included some of Coconut Grove's and Miami's most prominent people, would build a $30,000 clubhouse, pool, and palm garden and run the enterprise. At the end of the lease, the club could purchase the golf course for $50,000, plus the cost of construction. In addition, George would build a lake, a waterway, and a $10,000 plaza at Bird Road and Granada, then the southern boundary of Coral Gables, called the Coconut Grove entrance.[5] Of course on November 28, none of these plans and projects had been completed and few had been started.

Doc Dammers, with his theatrical flair and flamboyant promises, auctioned off lot after lot as the crowd followed behind his wagon. When a lot sold, he passed out a free piece of China to the buyer and sent his partner, Harry Burnes, to complete the deal. Every now and then, he would stop the auction and invite people to dip into a barrel of Coral Gables Punch that sat in the rear of the wagon.[6]

Throughout the week, Miami newspapers commented on the ambitious plan and sales activity, noting that Miami had never seen anything like it. When the auction closed after six days, three hundred lots had been sold for more than a half-a-million 1920 dollars. Although the auction had ended, news stories and Coral Gables' advertising continued unabated.

Buoyed by the public's response, within weeks George returned to his visionary idealism and pledged $10,000 from sales to create a permanent library in Miami. A few days later, he came up with a more grandiose and far-reaching announcement when he promised to provide free land and set aside $100,000 from sales to create a University of Miami in Coral Gables.[7] He credited his friend, the Reverend J. Delman Kuykendall, minister of Plymouth Congregational Church, for suggesting the idea.[8] From that day forward, George became one of Miami's earliest, strongest, and most constant advocates for the future University of Miami.

Following the initial auction, and before there was an office in Coral Gables, the growing sales force lured downtown visitors into the Flagler Street office. George Fink was at work planning the transformation of the front elevation of the nondescript Merrick Building into a small, but elegant, Spanish confection. It would showcase the Spanish theme with a sculpted plaster entrance, wrought-iron grilles and lanterns, orange-striped awnings, and a red-tile roof. The interior would be even more impressive, with a patio, twisted Moorish columns, beautiful Spanish tile floors, wainscoting, and genuine Spanish antiques. The rough-stucco walls would exhibit Spanish tapestries, Denman Fink renderings, George Fink architectural drawings, and Fishbaugh photographs. "In this new manner," a newspaper article opined when it opened, "Mr. Merrick has brought Coral Gables to Flagler Street, and in so doing has set a new vision upon that otherwise prosaic way."[9]

In addition to the visual collage, Doc Dammers lectured, musicians played, and Coral Gables Punch flowed. Once enticed, prospective buyers were whisked to Coral Gables in one of George's fleet of forty private cars. Not overlooking any opportunity to get people to come to Coral Gables, George also launched a regular bus service from downtown to his proposed business district.

While workmen continued the frantic pace of construction, George Fink was equally busy completing plans for the first business block on eighty-acre St. Augustine Plaza. In addition to becoming a business center, George hoped it also would become a semitropical art colony, like Elbert Hubbard's Roycrafters in East Aurora, New York.[10] A short time later, *The Metropolis* published a rendering of Fink's style-setting design for the first section, which was already staked out. It would include a dry goods store, garage, and filling station and would be completed within six months. In the Spanish style, it was replete with a terracotta roof, arches, a landscaped arbor, and striped awnings.[11]

The six hundred lots in Section B went on sale two days after Christmas following another flurry of newspaper advertisements. The second auction would have more free gifts (including boxes of grapefruit) and an orchestra for entertainment, as well as a ride in a German biplane for those who

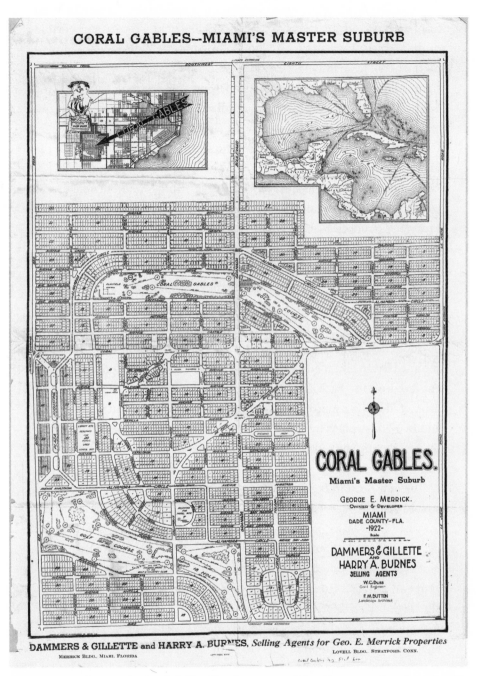

Figure 33. In early 1922, the Coral Gables Plan demonstrated that George continued to refine his original concept while sticking to its overarching ideals. Permission of HistoryMiami.

bought. The plane, with "Coral Gables" emblazoned on its body, took off from what was advertised as Miami's first flying field—the eastern portion of the nascent Granada Golf Course. In addition, newspapers reported on the new Denman Fink–designed, twelve-by-twenty-foot-high wooden signs painted in golden yellow, deep blue, green, and orange. Each depicted a romanticized "Golden Galleon" in full sail topped by a waving flag emblazoned with "Westward Ho." The news story was followed by another George-style full-page advertisement prompting readers to "Watch for the Golden Galleons and follow them. They will point the way to a really fair new land: a place where Beauty rests, Health abides and Fortune grasps you by the hand."[12] In another advertisement, Doc Dammers encouraged everyone "to go west young man."

By this time, it was clear that George Merrick's marketing genius was as impressive as his visionary idealism. In addition to a plethora of newspaper advertisements and signboards, the first promotional brochure—the twenty-four-page "Coral Gables, Miami's Master Suburb"—came off the press. Following the recurrent theme, the name "Coral Gables" was styled in "coral rock" and the cover included the drawing of a home and plaza surrounded by an abundance of landscaping. Denman Fink's golden galleon appeared on the back. The interior copy highlighted the same promises promoted in the newspaper advertisements, including the offer of free rock and free house plans by either H. George Fink or H. H. Mundy for all lot buyers. Pictures included the four homes that preceded the development, along with drawings of several new rock bungalows.

The new Section B, however, was different from Section A and demonstrated that George's vision had already started to evolve. In addition to lots for small bungalows, an ideal he would never abandon, Section B added larger lots that required higher-priced homes. It included more than thirty blocks and six hundred lots north of Coral Way, between Granada Boulevard and LeJeune Road and north to an L-shaped configuration that included Sorolla to Cortez and then south to Majorca and east to LeJeune.[13] Although the Coral Gables (Granada) Golf Course was still undergoing changes in its configuration, lots facing the golf course attracted special attention. At the same time, George was busy trying to buy more land to fill in the missing parcels in Section B between Granada Boulevard and

LeJeune Road. He also focused on acquiring additional acreage to expand the suburb's November 1921 borders.

In addition to the usual sales gimmicks, George, remembering the success of special events at Twelfth Street Manors, once again brought in Mabel Cody, described in the press as "the wing-walking, loop-looping, parachute devil," and her Flying Circus to perform from his flying field on two Sunday afternoons. Photographer William Fishbaugh was on hand to memorialize the event with one of his Cirkut photographs that not only showed the crowd, estimated at more than ten thousand, but also featured George and his closest advisors in the center of the view.[14] Pathé News covered the event, giving Coral Gables its first national exposure in theaters across America.

As the auctions and special events continued, sales soared and prices rose. By this time, buses brought in prospects not only from downtown Miami but also from Coconut Grove, Miami Beach, and Buena Vista. Before the season ended on April 1, two more auctions occurred. The first was a month-long sale between February 13 and March 13 and the second "The Grand Finale," which commenced on March 27. Three days later, The Miami Herald Record published a photograph of a smiling George and Eunice preparing to embark via seaplane for a celebratory, albeit brief, trip to Nassau.[15]

Within days, George was back at work. Newspapers touted his success, and Coral Gables ads trumpeted record sales of more than a million dollars in only four months. Besides sales, he had built thirty-one miles of road, twenty-one miles of sidewalk, and six miles of water main, and was installing the first "White Way" electric streetlights. He also created a ten-acre nursery on Columbus Boulevard near Indian Mound Trail, where Frank Button supervised the propagation of trees and shrubs that were rapidly turning Coral Gables into a garden. He employed a huge workforce to plant trees, clear land, and build streets, sidewalks, plazas, and entrances. In addition, he had more than one hundred salesmen and several executives and ran an advertising campaign like no other. It was not a time to sit back but to keep the momentum going.

"There will be no letup in Coral Gables activities this summer," an April 8 advertisement in The Miami Herald Record proclaimed. Two weeks later, George announced a 140-acre addition east of LeJeune to Douglas Road.

This purchase prompted a work stoppage on the St. Augustine Business District as plans emerged to move the Business Section east of LeJeune. In July, Denman Fink arrived to oversee the Alhambra Plaza Business District and a proposed new rock entrance on Douglas Road and Alhambra. The new plaza would include a fifty-foot-wide parkway between two thirty-five-foot-wide streets flanked by ten-foot-wide sidewalks.[16]

As plans for the new business district moved forward, home building increased. Under what George called the Coral Gables Home Building Plan, designed to attract local residents, buyers could choose from a variety of plans and lots. Prices began at $5,785 and went up to more than $10,000. After a $500 down payment, George financed the remainder at sixty dollars a month.[17]

Most of the homes were still rock, but the first concrete block stucco homes with rock detailing began to appear. Newspapers included detailed descriptions of more than fifty new Spanish-style homes, mostly designed by George Fink. All the homes—large and small—had fireplaces, sleeping porches, tile roofs, and a mandated garage. Most had a loggia or sunroom and a service porch, and many, an interior patio. To give Coral Gables a feeling of age, all the roofs were covered in terracotta—antique, hand-made tiles purchased from old Havana buildings and shipped to Miami by boat.

A few new, larger homes on the still-unfinished golf course were under construction. The first to be completed—a two-story rock edifice on the corner of North Greenway Drive and Madrid—received praise as one of the "most artistic."[18] Nearby, the first apartment building, also constructed of rock, rose on the corner of North Greenway and Granada across from the proposed country club.

To the outsider, it appeared that things could not be going better for George Merrick and Coral Gables. In reality, however, as George prepared for the next season, which began in November, he was running out of money. The Tamiami Trail Entrance was under construction but still not completed and the golf course remained little more than a cleared field. The new business district was laid out but awaited its first building. Seeking additional funds, George went to local banks for help. But despite what he had already proven he could do, they turned him down. "They called me a visionary and sometimes they were not so complimentary," he later recalled. "I begged them for aid but they rejected my plea, laughing. Then, after many sleepless nights, when often I was tempted to junk the entire project, a ray of hope came out of the darkness."[19]

Hope came via an accidental meeting with Charles S. (Jack) Baldwin, whom he had not seen since his days at Rollins College when they played together on the football team. Jack, a native of Melrose, Florida, joined the U.S. Army after college and served as a lieutenant in the Corps of Engineers during World War I. Following the war, he moved to Miami and worked briefly as a reporter for *The Miami Metropolis* before opening Baldwin Insurance Company.

After catching up on their lives since college days, George told Baldwin about his dreams for Coral Gables and his growing financial problems. To George's amazement, Baldwin had a solution; he would help George seek funds from the national insurance company he represented. Within days, the two men boarded a train for New York to meet with executives at the insurance company's home office. Because of Baldwin's strong support and George's track record, the insurance company came up with a major loan and, as a result, George was back in business.[20] For the rest of his life, he would credit his friend Jack Baldwin with saving Coral Gables.

With new money in hand, building not only resumed but accelerated. George Fink could not keep up with the demand for new homes, even though he was reportedly completing more than thirty plans a month. H. H. Mundy, who designed many of the early homes but never rivaled Fink's record, was busy with projects outside Coral Gables. Clearly, the time had come to bring in more architects. By this time, Coral Gables' stature had risen to the point where many notable architects were eager to work with George. Before the summer ended, Walter Charles DeGarmo and Martin Luther Hampton had come on board.

DeGarmo was well-known in Miami. He moved to Miami in 1904 and became South Florida's first registered architect and member of the American Institute of Architects. Born in Illinois, he had a degree in civil engineering from Swarthmore, where his father had been president, and an architectural degree from Cornell University, where he trained in the Beaux-Arts style. Following graduation, he worked briefly in Philadelphia and then for New York architect John Russell Pope, who later became famous for his classical designs, including Washington's National Archives and the Jefferson Monument.

Figure 34. The unprecedented popularity of Coral Gables caused George to add new architects to his team. They included Walter DeGarmo, the first registered architect in Florida. DeGarmo was already well recognized for his work in Miami and Miami Beach and added an important new dimension to Coral Gables. Courtesy of Kenneth DeGarmo.

DeGarmo learned about South Florida from his father and naturalist John Gifford, who had been a professor at Cornell with the senior De-Garmo. Gifford and the elder DeGarmo, both of whom lived part time in Coconut Grove, encouraged Walter to stake his future with the new City of Miami.

It did not take long for Walter DeGarmo to become one of Miami's most prolific and influential architects. As a Coconut Grove resident, he embraced South Florida's semitropical ambience and sought to develop an architectural style that took advantage of its unique environment. A decade before James Deering's Vizcaya transformed Miami's architectural taste, DeGarmo was designing Spanish Mission–style buildings that he believed suited Miami best. He was one of the first architects to include arcades, loggias, courtyards, and interior patios in his plans. His talent did not go unrecognized. In 1907, the Miami City Commission hired him to design Miami's new city hall, jail, and fire station. Next, the Dade County School Board selected him to design four Mission-style, look-alike schools—Southside, Northside, Riverside, and Sunset. As his reputation grew, Emma McAllister commissioned him to create Miami's first major skyscraper—the McAllister Hotel.[21]

He also dabbled in development. In 1911, he was secretary/treasurer of the Cocoanut Grove Development Company, which platted the Grove's first subdivision: Cocoanut Grove Park (as it was known then). When Coconut Grove's Housekeeper's Club needed a new clubhouse, they chose him to design the native-rock building that still stands on South Bayshore Drive. Following the Bright Plan for Coconut Grove, he also conceived other important Spanish-style buildings, including the original Bank of Coconut Grove, the new Coconut Grove High School, and the Clifford Cole residence, now the Coral Reef Yacht Club. Although he had lived and traveled abroad, in 1918 his passport application noted that he wanted to travel to Cuba to select decorative objects for his architectural work.

DeGarmo was also active in Miami Beach, designing both residential and civic buildings. One of his most notable was the Spanish-Colonial–style Miami Beach Congregational Church, which *The Miami Herald Record* called "One of the State's Prettiest Churches."[22]

Like DeGarmo, Martin Luther Hampton was a great fit for Coral Gables. A native of Laurens, South Carolina, he arrived in Miami in 1914, following classes at Columbia University and practical experience as a draftsman for several New York architects. After briefly working with Miami architect A. E. Lewis, he traveled to Cuba, where he studied art and grew to appreciate Spanish-Colonial buildings. When he returned to Miami, he joined August Geiger, another early architect and Spanish-style pioneer. One of his first projects was to help design the new Spanish Mission–style City Hospital and a look-alike school in Redland. He, like George Fink, also worked with Geiger on many Miami Beach projects for Carl Fisher, including the Miami Beach Golf Club.[23]

Hampton was also recognized for his art. His bird's-eye view of Miami, painted in the summer of 1916 when he was working with Geiger, became the chamber of commerce's most important early promotional piece. It depicted the growing skylines of Miami and Miami Beach with an artistic, romantic aura.[24]

Figure 35. Another major early architect was Martin Luther Hampton, who designed the Country Club of Coral Gables and the first hotel, the Coral Gables Inn. In 1923, he traveled to the Mediterranean for the specific purpose of bringing ideas back to Coral Gables. Author's collection.

Soon after the United States entered World War I, Hampton joined the Army Corps of Engineers. Following the war, he opened his own firm in Miami with associate Robert Reimert Jr. One of their first major commissions was the new Miami Country Club, built by the Florida East Coast Hotel Corp.[25] The club's Spanish-style architecture, complete with multiple towers and a central open courtyard surrounded by loggias, arches, and colonnades, impressed George. He hired Hampton & Reimert to design the new Country Club of Coral Gables—Hampton's first Gables project.

Just before the beginning of the new season, George kicked off another push for local residents to purchase homes. At the same time, he announced a thirty-two-page promotional brochure, entitled "Coral Gables Homes," that highlighted the work of George Fink. Adding to the news was the announcement that George and Eunice had sold Poinciana Place, their home on Coral Way, and engaged Fink to design a new, larger home for them on a walled South Greenway Drive block that once was the site of the Merrick packinghouse.

Even though Coral Gables was rapidly expanding and starting to look like a new city with its own police force and fire truck, George remained adamant that it would not become a separate municipality but instead what he called "the Keystone" of an enlarged Greater Miami. He predicted that Miami's city limits would soon expand to Red Road and include Coral Gables. To clarify his position, he wrote a full-page advertorial in *The Miami Herald Record* headlined "An OPEN LETTER Relative to the Proposed Greater Miami." At the time, Greater Miami had only three separate municipalities—Miami Beach, Coconut Grove, and Silver Bluff—with several areas like Lemon City, Allapattah, and Arch Creek agitating to incorporate. Mincing no words, he compared these small cities to "ticks fattening upon the involuntary generosity of a vigorous full-blooded dog."[26] He hoped that Miami would become more like Washington, D.C., or Greater Atlanta and shed its provincial small-town ways.

As 1922 came to an end, George, Dammers, and Burnes invited their one-hundred-member sales force to a banquet to celebrate their success. Because there was still no place to hold such a gathering in Coral Gables, the crowd drove to Fulford's Hotel Alabama (now North Miami Beach) for the event. Following pep talks by Dammers, Burnes, and several of the most outstanding salesmen and saleswomen, Jack Baldwin spoke. After helping George secure funding, he had become an investor and one of George's closest confidants. The highlight of the evening was George's eagerly awaited address. Although everyone knew George was the man behind Coral Gables, few really knew him. He preferred to work behind the scenes and was famous for not doing interviews. Still, his charisma was legendary and people clamored to meet him and hear him speak.

"I have seen most of the better developments of this country," George began, "and from the beginning it has been my aim and ideal to give Miami an all-year-round residential suburb that would be, first of all, distinctive in beautiful improvements and superior in all of the comforts and delights of home life."[27] By the time the evening ended, the salesmen and women were inspired and determined to help him achieve his dream.

As the new year began, the newspapers filled with a barrage of Coral Gables announcements. First came a story on the completion of what was called the Miami Entrance at Granada and Eighth Street. Until other entrances were built, it would be the principal gateway to Coral Gables. Writers praised its antique appearance and sense of age highlighted by full-grown trees, flowering shrubs and flowing fountains that surrounded its 240-foot façade.[28] With new landscaping also flourishing on Granada Boulevard, the new entrance and grand thoroughfare set the tone for what was to follow. In the distance, another wide plaza was under construction at Granada and Alhambra, from which visitors could see the almost-completed country club. The clubhouse overlooked the new nine-hole golf course designed by Langston and Moreau, which was receiving its first golfers at no charge while awaiting its grand opening. At the same time, Frank Button began work on three tennis courts just off the golf links. At last, a skeptical populace could see that Coral Gables had emerged from what George liked to call "A Land of Promise" to his much-quoted "Realization of the Ideal."

Of special interest to those following the Coral Gables story was a long interview with George Fink in *The Miami Metropolis*. For the first time, Fink explained Coral Gables' mandated architecture. He described it as a new style that was distinctly Miami's. "As California contributed the bungalow," he was quoted as saying, "and New England the Colonial house, so Miami is establishing the modified and Americanized Spanish with daring exterior development." He added that what he called Miami rock was another purely Miami development, even though he preferred not to build an entire rock house but instead to use it for foundations and decoration. He also mentioned the interior patio as one of Miami architecture's distinctive features, along with screened loggias and variegated antique tile roofs. Finally, he pointed out that the use of strong color was the most important Miami innovation. He admitted that not everyone liked the distinctive style that George Merrick required for all Coral Gables buildings and, as a result, some walked away when they learned they could not build whatever they wanted.[29] Most, however, returned converted.

Besides designing homes and business buildings, George Fink also focused on plans for five water towers that followed John Ruskin's vision of combining "beauty and utility." The first was on Indian Mound Trail. The sixty-foot-tall, fifteen-foot-square building, styled after a Spanish tower, included a balcony near the top where George Merrick planned to take people to see the vastness of his master suburb. At the same time, Fink completed drawings for the Alhambra Tower, which would hide the one-hundred-thousand-gallon iron water tank. The Alhambra Tower, which bore a striking resemblance to the one at Roland Park, Maryland, would rise from an island on Alhambra Circle and, in addition to a balcony, would have an illuminated glass beacon at its apex.[30]

Color—from tinted stucco to bright balustrades, doors, window frames, and awnings—became such an important element in Coral Gables that George Merrick hired a well-known artist/designer to be his color expert. His name was Phineas Paist and from the minute he arrived, in December 1922, he would become a key member of the team.

Paist came to Miami from Philadelphia in 1916 at the behest of James Deering's interior designer, Paul Chalfin. He had been trained as an artist and architect but did not have a Florida architectural license until 1923, so his Vizcaya work was under architect Burrell Hoffman. He designed Vizcaya's casino, Chinese bridge, and many of the farm buildings. Charles Deering, James' brother, chose him to design his new "stone house" in Cutler. His work for the Deerings garnered him the respect of Miami's leading architects.

Paist, first noted for his fine art, received classical art training and, later, architectural training, at the Pennsylvania Academy of Fine Arts. Next, he traveled to Europe on a Crisson Traveling Scholarship. After two years of study in England, France, Germany, and Italy, he worked with the Philadelphia firm of G. W. and W. D. Hewitt, eventually becoming a partner. As part of the firm, he participated in the design of Philadelphia's Belleview Strafford Hotel and the Willard Hotel in Washington, D.C.[31] Walter DeGarmo, who had worked with Paist and encouraged him to stay in Miami when he completed his work for the Deerings, introduced him to George, who valued his Miami work and realized he could be an important addition to his dream team.

In a lengthy article in *The Miami Metropolis*, George explained the unique role he expected Paist to play. "The attention we are paying and the expense to which we are going to work out all of the details which will gradually develop the completed plan," he began, "is something new, as you know, for any Miami development."[32] After explaining how he selected only architects who worked "sympathetically" with what he was trying to accomplish, he acknowledged that those same architects and artists had convinced him to change his original vision, in which all homes were to be built of "coral rock," to include homes built with stucco. Once stucco

Figure 36. Phineas Paist joined the Coral Gables team in December 1922 as the "color expert." In 1924, he completed his first architectural renderings for the Crafts Section. He would become one of Coral Gables' most important architects and leaders. Permission of HistoryMiami.

homes began to appear, George concluded, "It has become definitely apparent . . . that the matter of stucco texture and the coloring and tinting of these houses is a most important factor in the general scheme—probably the most important single factor."[33]

George praised the individual architects and their ability to work with the tinting and coloring of stucco but pointed out that a comprehensive color scheme was needed if the overall harmony he sought was to be achieved. Therefore, he concluded, "we have finally added the services of

Phineas E. Paist . . . as color expert and, from now on, he is to be in final charge of all stucco work and coloring and tinting."[34] Apparently, the architects and artists working in Coral Gables agreed with this new directive and had confidence in Paist's ability. In addition to drawing renderings of the color schemes for entire streets, Paist was given full authority to pass on all color plans suggested by the architects and "to vary or change same, at his discretion."[35]

Thus began a long and storied relationship among Phineas Paist, George Merrick, and Coral Gables. Within a year, he also began to design buildings and homes while still serving as color expert. Eventually, he would not only oversee all color but also have the final say on all architectural plans, as well. At this point, however, his role was as a color expert who had been given extraordinary authority over other professionals, who accepted his judgment.

January 22 brought the official opening and private sale of lots in the two-hundred-acre Coral Gables Business Section. Alhambra Plaza was almost completed, and the first buildings—the Coral Gables Garage and the much-anticipated Alcazar Tea Room—were open for business. (The first event in the Tea Room was a dinner for the entire sales force hosted by Dammers and Burnes.) In addition, a rendering of the first major Walter DeGarmo building, known as the Arcade Building, was published. Besides eight stores, it would house the new Ground Sales Office, giving George his first Coral Gables office.[36]

Walter DeGarmo also made the news after the Sisters of St. Joseph selected him to design a building for their proposed $250,000 Catholic girls' academy and college on two blocks near Anastasia and Indian Mound Trail. George had closed the deal with the Archdiocese following a quick trip to St. Augustine. It would include three three-story rock, stucco, and Cuban tile buildings in the best Spanish style.[37] The new college was an unexpected addition to Coral Gables, but George had not given up on the proposed University of Miami. He had convinced the Congregational Church group that operated Rollins College to come to Coral Gables to investigate the possibility of building the University of Miami under their auspices. Although impressed with the setting, they did not accept George's offer.

Even though George was thrilled with the possibility of two colleges, his first priority was to get the Dade County School Board to build a public grammar and high school in Coral Gables. At first, the board demurred, saying there were not enough students to warrant it. Just as his mother had done to get the board to open the Guavonia School two decades earlier, George sent Eunice out to canvass the surrounding area seeking signatures from the parents of potential students. Despite securing more than sixty signers, the School Board still refused to act. Determined to get his school one way or the other, George wrote an impassioned letter to Board members, reminding them how he was spending "tremendous funds" to build a unique community. To prove the point, he had hired the nationally known firm of Kiehnel & Elliott, which had designed the Bindley Estate in Coconut Grove (now Carrollton School), to design a $100,000 grammar school as part of a major civic area in the new Business Section. "These public buildings," he wrote, "will be the climax of what we are trying to realize at 'CORAL GABLES.'"[38] In his written proposal, he offered forty-eight lots valued at $76,475 for only $10,000, plus free water, lights, sidewalks, shrubbery, and paved streets. He also offered his own construction crew to build the school. Finally, to close the deal, he promised to temporarily finance the first $25,000 if the board would repay him as soon as possible because it was "a very heavy burden for us to assume this temporary school financing."[39] The rest could be paid off in two yearly payments as the school expanded. It was an offer like no other. With unanimous School Board support, the new Coral Gables Grammar School was soon under construction.

Sales continued briskly even though George decided to hold no more public auctions. He did, however, come up with several new sales gimmicks. First, he purchased a German biplane that took off from his flying field at the corner of LeJeune Road and Coral Way. For a five-dollar fee, prospects could go aloft and see the breadth of his plans. Next, he created what he called "State Days." Beginning in February, with full-page ads in *The Miami Herald* and *The Metropolis*, he invited Miami's state societies and visiting tourists from selected states to a series of special picnics at the country club. Beginning with Ohio and followed by Pennsylvania, New England, New York, New Jersey, and Indiana-Illinois, the events brought in thousands of people. Once again, William Fishbaugh was on hand to capture the crowd with his Cirkut photographs. In addition, Fishbaugh also shot every new Coral Gables home and business building. He then produced leather-bound albums stamped in gold with the logo "Coral Gables:

Figure 37. George hired Philadelphia architect Richard Kiehnel, of the firm of Kiehnel & Elliott, to design Coral Gables Grammar School. Kiehnel had received much acclaim after he designed El Jardin (now Carrollton School) for John Bindley. He would later design other notable Coral Gables landmarks including the Congregational Church. Permission of HistoryMiami.

Miami's Master Suburb, Miami, Florida." Each salesman received an album that bulged with more than fifty linen-backed photographs of structures either completed or under construction. Once again, the press singled George out for his creative marketing and for being the first to utilize photographic albums to promote sales.

In the midst of these popular events and promotional campaigns, the Coral Gables Country Club opened. Although the press called it "imposing" in its elegant Spanish style, it did not yet have a large meeting space. What it did have was men's and women's locker rooms and a tower that was quickly turned into an observation deck where salesmen could take prospective buyers to get a bird's-eye view of the new suburb. George immediately promised that the country club would double in size before the next season. The addition would include a dance hall, dining room, kitchen, and community center.[40]

Within weeks of the opening of the country club, work began to transform the old rock pit into a Denman Fink-designed swimming pool that did not yet have a name. Headlines claimed that at three hundred feet long and two hundred and fifty feet wide, it would be the largest swimming pool in the world. Although the original plan included an island with palm trees and a children's pool and pavilion, the final design was still percolating in Denman Fink's artistic mind, and it would undergo many stops and starts before opening.

Just as the 1922–23 season came to an end, George announced a $5 million building campaign. It promised five hundred new homes, educational facilities, a church, and additions to the business district, as well as new streets and sidewalks flanked with electric White Way lights. The first two months of the campaign focused on the smaller homes, which had risen to a starting price of $6,500 and were projected to soon increase by 20 percent. Of special interest were the thirty-four homes under construction on Obispo. With George Fink's architectural plans and Phineas Paist's and Denman Fink's artistic eyes, the entire street was planned to harmonize in every way, including the colors of the awnings.[41]

The small-homes program was followed with another promotion called "Homes of Distinction." These homes would be larger, mostly two-story, and on the golf course or streets like Granada and Desoto Boulevard. Prices would range from $10,000 to $25,000. To highlight the new luxury homes, George invited the Woman's Club of Miami to participate in a national program called "Better Homes of America Week," whereby the club would furnish one of the homes on Granada Boulevard and open it for public view. He would provide free transportation, refreshments, and lunch. During the one-week show, more than a thousand people came to see the beautiful home. It was soon purchased by Frank T. Budge, who owned the pioneer hardware store on Flagler Street where George once peddled his vegetables.[42]

One of the new homes of distinction was George's and Eunice's own home, which was still under construction on South Greenway Drive. During a quick trip to Cuba, George had purchased old tiles for their new home from a Cuban cathedral, with the leftovers being utilized by other builders. The boom in new houses had made it increasingly difficult to import enough antique Cuban roof tiles. So, with George's encouragement, and mimicking what Addison Mizner was doing in Palm Beach, contractors John and Giuseppe Stabile opened a tile company in the new Coral Gables Business Section. It would not produce ordinary tile but tiles made of Cuban clay whose production would be overseen by a foreman brought in from Italy. In addition, a concrete block company opened nearby and worked overtime to produce four thousand blocks a day to keep up with the demand.[43]

By this time, Coral Gables was taking on a national and even international perspective. In June, George and Eunice slipped away together to Asheville, North Carolina, for a few days before George traveled on to New York and Atlantic City to oversee the launching of Coral Gables sales offices there. That month, Harry Burnes prepared to open offices in Boston; Manchester, New Hampshire; and Detroit. Meanwhile, Martin Hampton had sailed for Europe, where he planned a trip through the British Isles, France, Italy, and Spain in order to study and sketch the ancient architecture he was adapting to South Florida.

George and Eunice returned to Coral Gables in time to inaugurate the Tea Garden at the Coral Gables Country Club, which instantly attracted many of Miami's young elite for the weekly subscription dances. Located east of the original clubhouse, the new Tea Garden also had an orchestra pavilion and terrazzo dance floor. As the new addition arose around the existing building and dance patio, the original open-air loggia became a popular venue for bridge parties, including many hosted by Eunice.

In the Business Section, workers rushed to complete the Coral Gables Grammar School in time for the opening of the school year. Richard Kiehnel's inspired architecture prompted George to give him a commission for forty homes, including ten on the new Country Club Prado that had replaced the St. Augustine Business District.

Just as Coral Gables architecture garnered constant attention, the landscape plan was equally noted. "Nothing at Coral Gables has attracted more attention," *The Miami Metropolis* reported, "than the planting of trees, shrubs and vines . . . set out in parks and parkways."[44] Frank Button, who was the genius behind the landscape plan, now had seventy-five men in his department who worked ten hours a day, six days a week. During the first year, Button had designed the plan and selected, purchased, and supervised the planting of more than twenty thousand trees, shrubs, and vines that cost George more than $50,000. In addition, he oversaw the propagation of more than forty-five thousand plants—including many rare tropical species—at the Columbus Boulevard nursery that he had recently expanded.

Even though Hampton, DeGarmo, and now Kiehnel had joined the Coral Gables architectural team, George Fink still held the record for home design with fifty new homes on his drawing board. Three of his notable larger homes on Coral Way were ready for occupancy. The first was a two-story rock home for Harry Burnes on the southwest corner of Columbus Plaza. Across the street, on the northeast corner, was Doc Dammers' imposing two-story, tinted-stucco home with "coral rock" features and a large, enclosed center courtyard. Finally, Fink moved his own family into a nearby rock home he dubbed "Casa Azul" because of its distinctive and singular blue-tile roof.

Fink was also active in the Business Section. His design for the new $90,000 Parker Art Printing Company's Spanish-style building on Salzedo received wide press coverage. It was only one of the new buildings that lived up to George Merrick's promise that the Business Section would be of the same style and as beautiful as the residential sections.

Walter DeGarmo was Fink's closest, albeit distant, competitor with more than thirty-five homes of distinction nearing completion. He also could claim the signature Arcade Building on LeJeune Road and Alhambra Circle, which officially opened during the first week of August. Described as a first-of-its-kind shopping center, stores included a grocery and delicatessen, a retail electrical store, and a soon-to-be-opened drug store and meat market.[45] The building also had a medical facility—the first one west of Coconut Grove. C. H. Benton, a well-known Coconut Grove physician, opened what a news article called a "complete and compacted mini-hospital." In addition to Dr. Benton's office, it had an emergency room, X-ray machine, operating room, and two wards.[46]

Not to be outdone by the other architects, Martin Hampton, who had recently returned from his trip to Europe, published his design for Coral Gables' first hotel, the Coral Gables Inn. The proposed fifty-room, $65,000 hotel would be patterned after the Palacio de Generalife—a notable building in Spain's Alhambra—and built around a patio. Those features would, according to a *Miami Herald* article, "set it apart from any other [hotel] in Florida."[47] A rendering of Hampton's hotel, his photographs, sketches, and watercolors, and samples of the tiles, books, and pottery he purchased in Spain were displayed in the window of Coral Gables' Flagler Street office. Hampton had the honor of being the first Coral Gables architect to travel to Spain and Italy for the specific purpose of studying building details to be incorporated into Coral Gables architecture.

The biggest story of the early fall, however, was George's purchase of the 180-acre Douglas Tract for $285,000. This purchase extended Coral Gables' borders to Douglas Road and the Tamiami Trail, where George planned to build another entrance. It was only part of a September buying spree that would total 480 acres. One of the new tracts expanded the northwest border to the Tamiami Trail, where George proposed another entrance designed by Denman Fink. George could now claim that his "Master Suburb" encompassed two square miles.[48]

At the same time, he opened the 450-acre Granada Section and began construction on thirty new homes designed by Fink, Hampton, and a new architect, Louis Brumm, who had come to Coral Gables from California, where he had previously worked in the Spanish-Colonial style. Although forty homes would be built at the same time, Fink promised repetition would be avoided and was "entirely confident that these homes will be entirely unique in Florida . . . and the results will be astonishing."[49]

Nothing pleased George more, however, than the October 8 opening of the new Coral Gables Grammar School. Like his mother, who spurred the opening of the old Guavonia School next to her home, George recognized the importance of having a school in Coral Gables and was relentless in its pursuit. He had personally pushed the contractors to complete the school in a record three months. On the first day, 39 students showed up, and within a week the number swelled to 150. Even though George and Eunice had no children, Eunice helped organize the PTA and became one of the school's most ardent supporters.[50]

Late summer newspaper articles announced an early fall opening of the new swimming pool. When Denman Fink arrived to oversee its completion, however, he delayed the opening again, preferring a new design. He also came up with a name for the former rock pit. "Pool at Coral Gables to be Venetian Lake,"[51] *The Miami Herald* headlined. His new design included a tall rock diving platform with a water cascade, a rock grotto, a colorful Venetian bridge and lampposts, and an expanded pavilion enhanced with two tall towers. Lavishly landscaped, the "lake" would be surrounded with a concrete and rock wall. Although the news article promised it would open soon, the complexity of the design and Denman Fink's determination to have it meet his artistic rendering caused the opening to be put off for more than a year.

Following the usual pattern, the so-called season was set to launch in November. Although George had relentlessly pursued buyers all summer, he realized the importance of beginning the new season with a series of ads that listed his accomplishments. As far as sales were concerned, the open-ing of the Ground Sales Office in the Arcade Building would give him a place in Coral Gables to bring in the winter visitors for the usual sales pitch. Like the Flagler Street office, the interior was decorated with Spanish-style furniture and the walls filled with Coral Gables photographs and drawings. It also had a large auditorium for sales meetings and lectures. Salesmen, under the leadership of Harry A. Burnes, were ready with their Fishbaugh photographic albums and a new promotional brochure that described all that had been accomplished in only two years. But before the new season was launched, George and the entire sales force faced the unexpected death of Burnes on October 21 after only a few days of what was described as a sore throat. As word spread throughout Coral Gables and to his hometown of Bridgeport, Connecticut, where his death was noted in a front-page ban-ner headline, accolades poured in describing his short but meaningful life. Few were more devastated than George. Burnes, who was only 43, had become one of his closest friends and advisors. Each admired the other's integrity, enthusiasm, and ability to lead. "In the owner of Coral Gables," the *Bridgeport Star* reported, "he [Burnes] found a man as enthusiastic, as-siduous and untiring as himself. And the remarkable vision and ambition of Geo. E. Merrick united to the notable energy and salesmanship of Harry A. Burnes made a combination that was ideal for results and which has pro-duced the Coral Gables of today."[52] Members of Burnes' Coral Gables sales team penned a tribute to their leader and promised George they would continue to follow his example.

~10

Expanding the Vision

> To employ poetic language about a highly materialistic
> subject, Coral Gables—so much in evidence today—is a
> romance—a dream—a vision. There is absolutely nothing
> like it in the American continent. The writer questions if
> there is anything like it on green earth. . . . Yesterday it was a
> dream—today it is a great fact and factor in land development
> and city planning.
>
> *Orlando Reporter-Star*, December 1923

As George and his team prepared to launch the new season, what began as a dream and a promise had been "made real," as George liked to say. In only two years, Coral Gables had lived up to its name as Miami's Master Suburb. The miracle of it all was that Coral Gables belonged to one man—George Merrick, owner and developer. There was no Coral Gables Corporation, and even though his staff was growing, he had no partners. Coral Gables was still mostly a one-man show—even more so after the death of Harry Burnes. Fortunately, in early January, Telfair Knight, a prominent Jacksonville attorney and realtor, accepted George's invitation to move to Coral Gables and become his personal representative. Knight quickly became George's closest confidant and most loyal supporter.

It had become easier for George to attract people from out of town. Coral Gables had already received state recognition and was starting to get noticed nationally. The money George spent on entrances, roads, sidewalks, parks, White Way lights, and landscaping was unprecedented in Florida history and even rivaled other nationally known planned communities. But studied through the lens of a two-year time frame, Coral Gables had no rival.

Carl Fisher's Miami Beach, incorporated as a city in 1915, was the largest South Florida development since Flagler's Miami but was not comparable to Coral Gables. Fisher created Miami Beach as a tourist destination and enclave for the rich, with little thought to planning middle-class neighborhoods. George frequently praised Fisher's work and the crowds he lured to Miami. In fact, just as the 1923–24 season opened, George took advantage of Fisher's draw and opened a Coral Gables office on Miami Beach's Fifth Street. Here, tourists could board a Coral Gables bus for a free sightseeing tour and lunch at the Alcazar Tea Room. The tours and bus service, according to a Coral Gables advertisement, would bind Miami's two dominating residential districts together.[1]

Meanwhile, the Tatum Brothers, who had once been George's greatest competitors, when he developed a series of Miami subdivisions prior to Coral Gables, were no longer a threat. George commented positively about many of their neighborhoods, especially Grove Park. None, however, were planned communities on the scale of Coral Gables. During late 1923 and into 1924, the Tatums advertised their latest subdivision—Altos Del Mar in Miami Beach—with a thinly veiled dig at Coral Gables' inland location.

On the surface, and if one believed their advertisements, Glenn Curtiss and James Bright's Hialeah might be like Coral Gables because of its size and community institutions such as schools, churches, residential neighborhoods, and shopping areas. Curtiss and Bright, however, had a different kind of vision. Hialeah's fame came not from its community building but from its racetracks, jai-alai fronton, and film studios—activities that did not appeal to George. In fact, he announced that he would never allow similar projects in Coral Gables.

M. C. Tebbets' 550-acre Fulford-By-The-Sea advertised as a Coral Gables–type subdivision with rock gates and wide boulevards. Tebbets completed many of the entry features and streets, but when it came to homes, Fulford did not live up to its promise. More like Hialeah, it became better known for its radio station and automobile racetrack.

Further north, Joseph Young's Hollywood-By-The-Sea completed some planning studies and made promises similar to those of Coral Gables, but construction lagged. Following George's lead, however, Young and Tebbets spent enormous amounts of money on newspaper advertising, and Young, in particular, was credited as the first to bring in out-of-town visitors by bus.

Although George continued to march to the beat of his own drum, he was not averse to adding new marketing techniques initiated by other developers. After Hialeah and Fulford inaugurated boat trips for prospective buyers, George brought Captain Clarence Starn and his sailboat *Favorite* to Miami from Atlantic City. The *Favorite*, with "Coral Gables: Miami's Master Suburb" emblazoned on its sail, departed each day from Elser's Pier in downtown Miami and sailed down Biscayne Bay to the Silver Bluff waterfront, where a Coral Gables bus awaited to transport prospects to Coral Gables.[2]

By late 1923, Coral Gables was more than a name, a plan, and some pretty drawings. Proof came via Fishbaugh's photographs, which had taken the place of many of the drawings so prevalent a year earlier. His images were also utilized in two photo-laden, thirty-page promotional brochures and an in-house biweekly newspaper called *The Coral Gables Bulletin*.

No one doubted that George was first and foremost a savvy developer, albeit an unusual one. Not content to simply sell land, he built and sold homes that seemed to pop up everywhere, like mushrooms after a rain. "Many Notable Things Beautify Coral Gables," a full-page advertisement proclaimed, "But its Greatest Glory is its Homes."[3]

George also pushed his Business District and acquired more land. But unlike most other developers, he had a broader vision that manifested itself in his fostering of community organizations, often with an offer of free land to spur their growth.

As 1924 dawned, Coral Gables had a new woman's club, a proposed garden club, an active Boy Scout troop, a volunteer fire department, and a newly incorporated community club. George even hired a full-time professional recreational director—Dr. Horace W. Taylor—to oversee community activities. Taylor, among other things, helped organize amateur sports teams that practiced on the flying field until modern facilities opened at the grammar school. "Mr. Merrick is leaving no stone unturned," *The Miami Metropolis* reported, "and his farsightedness was never more evident than in the inauguration of this department."[4]

His leaving no stone unturned included negotiating with Dr. Herbert L. Cox, of Tuxedo Park, New York, one of the planned suburbs he emulated,

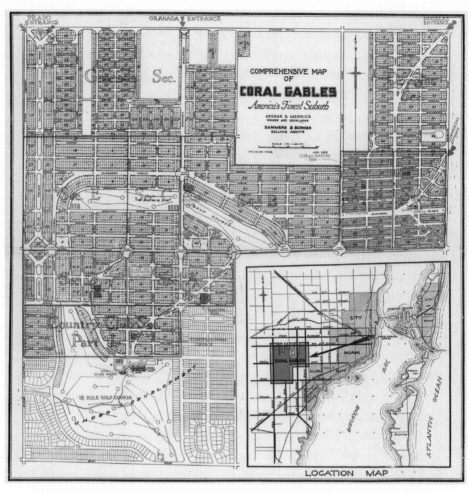

Figure 38. By 1924, Coral Gables had expanded in all directions. The new Business Section, east of LeJeune Road, sported many businesses, and new residential sections expanded west and south. Permission of HistoryMiami.

to open a riding academy in the Business District. In preparation for Cox's arrival, workmen laid out a bridle path on Alhambra Circle.

Although George envisioned these community-building organizations as part of his grand scheme for Coral Gables, he believed the most important institution besides the school was a church. To encourage its founding, he convinced the national office of the Congregational Church to send in a visiting minister to help organize a new congregation. As part of the arrangement, George built a George Fink–designed temporary parsonage, complete with bell tower, on Columbus Boulevard. Besides providing a home for the minister, it served as a launching pad for the church. Here, potential members, including members of the Merrick family, as well as most company employees, gathered to learn about the proposed new church, recruit members, and raise money.

Once the church was organized, the same group became its charter members and members of the board. (Not surprisingly, Althea Merrick was elected to lead the new Woman's Society and to be the first clerk—positions she held when her husband was a minister.)

More than one hundred people attended the first official service held at the parsonage on December 30. To ensure the church's success, George, now a board member, donated a triangular block of land and more than $5,000 in cash to spur the building campaign. Because his father had been a Congregational Church minister, he wanted Coral Gables' first church to be a monument to him. To ensure its prominence, he hired Kiehnel & Elliott, designers of the grammar school, to create a landmark building that would eclipse all others.

The holiday season kicked off with the opening of Coral Gables' first hotel, the Coral Gables Inn. Designed by Martin Luther Hampton following his European trip, it referenced the Palacio de Generalife in Spain's Alhambra. It had three floors and fifty outside rooms connected by a loggia that surrounded a distinctive tiled patio with a center fountain. *The Miami Metropolis* described it as "one of the most beautiful in Miami."[5] A full-page Coral Gables advertisement touted the new hotel, predicted more to come, and promoted other gathering places such as the Coral Gables Country Club and the Alcazar Tea Room. "But like the first born child in a happy family," it noted, "the opening of this first hotel is a red letter event and one in which we take great pride."[6]

To celebrate the holidays, George and his staff also launched Coral Gables' first community-wide event—the lighting of a huge Christmas tree in the center of Alhambra Plaza at LeJeune Road. Children from the Coral Gables Grammar School sang Christmas carols to a huge crowd. Following the formal program, everyone joined the chorus as it meandered through the streets singing.

On Christmas Eve, the entire sales force, now numbering more than one hundred men and women, gathered to celebrate the holidays and their success. George was on hand to thank them and pass out Christmas presents. To his surprise, the group presented him with an engraved, sterling silver loving cup to thank him for his vision and leadership. The engraving read:

> Presented to Geo. E. Merrick
> Owner and Developer of Coral Gables:
> "America's Finest Suburb"
> By the Coral Gables Sales Force
> In Appreciation of the Man and his Great Work.
> Christmas, 1923.

George, with tears in his eyes, was uncharacteristically speechless. A week later, he and Eunice hosted and served as judges at a community-wide New Year's Eve Mardi Gras costume party at the Ground Sales Office. Although well-known for avoiding social affairs, George reveled in being with new residents and witnessing the birth of what he called the "Coral Gables Spirit." After midnight, he and Eunice returned to their own new home on South Greenway Drive, which they had moved into on Christmas Eve. Designed by George Fink and surrounded by a wall of stucco and coral stone, its patios, vistas, arcades, and gardens became a showcase for Coral Gables' emerging architectural distinctiveness.

For George, the yearlong whirlwind ended with a flurry of successes. But new forces with an even stronger velocity gathered on the horizon. Soon, with George at the epicenter, what began as a roar would turn into a thunderous boom.

It is impossible to precisely document when the housing boom became "The Boom"—a national phenomenon and proper noun. Although unplanned by George, many historians named him among its primary instigators and 1924 the year it began.[7] At the time, however, George remained oblivious to his role in fueling Miami's historic real estate explosion.

One week into the new year, George announced the January 15 opening of the Douglas Section—named after the Douglas family groves that once occupied the site. It would expand Coral Gables' northeastern border to Eighth Street, soon to be known as the Tamiami Trail. As usual, purchasing additional acreage prompted him and his dream team to come up with new ideas. Unlike his previous sections, the Douglas Section would be primarily for apartments and hotels that catered to the increasing number of tourists pouring into Miami. Despite these more grandiose plans, George remained true to his original ideals. The new Douglas Section would also include medium-priced, single-family homes and a new cultural center.

Denman Fink was busy drawing another grand entrance for the intersection of Douglas Road and Eighth Street. It would be surrounded by apartment houses designed by Martin Hampton. This new entrance, the completed Granada Entrance, and the Country Club Prado Entrance under construction were Coral Gables place markers on the proposed Tamiami Trail that was inching its way across the Everglades from Tampa to Miami. It would bring in thousands of new visitors and spur further development west of Miami. For many newcomers, Coral Gables' Tamiami Trail entrances would be their first impression of Miami.

The announcement also included a rendering of a massive, $175,000 Richard Kiehnel–designed apartment complex and another large apartment/hotel designed by Lee Wade, a new architect to Coral Gables.[8] Of equal importance, especially to George, was his plan to build a grouping of public institutions heretofore unknown in Miami. The new cultural center would include a stadium designed by George Fink, an outdoor theater, a natural history museum, an art school along the lines of the Tiffany Foundation of New York, and a conservatory of music. The full-page advertisement also mentioned two blocks reserved for the proposed university and another for a children's hospital.[9] Of course, all the new buildings, from the smallest to the grandest, would reflect Coral Gables' distinctive architectural style, which, unlike the original plan, was evolving from "purely Spanish" to a still-unnamed style that incorporated Italian and other Mediterranean influences. A rendering of the U-shaped stadium, with its dual towers and encircling loggia, highlighted the fluid style while proving again that both beauty and utility mattered.

As hundreds of workmen laid out streets in the new Douglas Section and contractors broke ground for twelve homes and prepared the site for the new hotel, George had an additional crew preparing another new area he called Country Club Section Part One. Three days before its February 19 debut, *The Miami Metropolis* announced in a front-page headline that the new section would soon have a $1.25 million hotel designed by Martin Luther Hampton. Hampton, inspired by the legendary monuments in Spain

Expanding the Vision ～ 185

he had recently viewed firsthand, chose Seville's La Giralda as the defining feature of the proposed 350-room hotel. The article also noted that Denman Fink would create a series of murals depicting the life of Christopher Columbus that would rival anything found in New York. What Denman called "his life's work" would require six years to complete and cost more than one hundred thousand dollars.[10] Because of this long-term project, he decided to leave Haworth, New Jersey, and move his family into a new home on Alhambra Circle. In addition to the news story about the new hotel, a full-page Coral Gables advertisement highlighted the Country Club Section. Besides the hotel, it would also have an eighteen-hole golf course and country club, the $150,000 Congregational Church, and the previously announced College for Young Women.[11]

The following week, the local press covered an unprecedented amount of Coral Gables news stories and announcements. Additional renderings of the hotel, the first drawings of the proposed country club, the new church, and the girls' college appeared in separate full-page advertisements. The advertising blitz ended with a rendering of the latest Denman Fink-designed, three-hundred-foot-wide plaza called the Columbus Esplanade. Described as having the ambience of an Italian garden, including a water feature, it extended one thousand feet between the church and hotel. Readers could not help but notice that Coral Gables had also changed its logo from Coral Gables: "Miami's Master Suburb" to Coral Gables: "America's Finest Suburb."

Like the Douglas Section, the new Country Club Section, which George called his "crowning effort," was another departure from his original plan. For the first time, advertisements announced a "Millionaire's Circle" of homes on the golf course. The grandiosity of the advertisements relied on beautiful renderings. They, plus George's reputation for following through on his ambitious and unique plans, brought in a record number of buyers, with the first day of sales netting more than $225,000. It took less than a month to sell out the new section with more than a million dollars' worth of lots sold.[12] Before long, the Country Club Section expanded with three additions.

Even though Denman Fink focused on a plethora of new projects, he never lost sight of his favorite creation—Venetian Pool. The former rock-pit-turned-swimming-pool had been under construction for more than a year. During that time, it had undergone a series of name changes, from

Figure 39. Denman Fink's artistic rendering of what he called the "Venetian Lake" was completed in March 1923. It bore a striking resemblance to the finished product, which opened in December 1924. Fink later called it his most important work. Author's collection.

Grotto Park to Venetian Lake to Venetian Plunge. Newspaper articles routinely announced its opening only to quickly report another postponement. The main reason for the delay was that Denman continued to make changes and insisted he be present to oversee them. When he moved to Coral Gables in March, he brought a painting of the pool with him that included a new, two-tower pavilion, a dance patio, and a rock diving platform. The painting appeared in *The Miami Herald* and was prominently displayed in Coral Gables' Flagler Street office.[13] It was remarkable in detail and, when compared to the completed pool, demonstrated how accurately his nephew, George Fink, could transform his paintings into architectural drawings and then concrete. With Denman Fink in town, the pool would have its grand opening before year's end.

Announcements of new projects continued. George, however, never forgot that sales were the lifeblood that made everything else possible. With that in mind, he and his staff continued to come up with new and innovative sales promotions, including inaugurating a radio broadcast from the Flagler Street office. It featured live music and Doc Dammers promoting Florida and Coral Gables as the land of opportunity.

The most successful promotions continued to be the bus tours. Although George had inaugurated a statewide effort the previous October, the opening of the Coral Gables Inn and the Ground Sales Office spurred the tour's expansion with astonishing results. His statewide director, W. C. DeLong, organized the tours from his office in Daytona. By early 1924,

Figure 40. The Arcade Building, on the corner of LeJeune Road and Alhambra Circle, housed the Coral Gables Sales office, as well as other businesses. Buses brought in hundreds of prospects to the sales office to learn about Coral Gables. Courtesy of State Archives of Florida, Florida Memory.

more than two hundred visitors a week from towns all across Florida came to Coral Gables. The group usually included a member of the local press who returned home and penned a glowing report. One of the first was by A. D. Codrington of the *Deland Daily News*. His description was reprinted in *The Coral Gables Bulletin* and became a model for the future.

All the tours followed the same format. Each twenty-seat bus had the words "Coral Gables" emblazoned on its side in bright pink. The Deland group, with participants listed by name and hometown, included both visitors and residents. Traveling down Dixie Highway, they spent the first night in a quaint inn at Micco, a small community south of Melbourne. The following day, they lunched in Fort Pierce and had dinner in Palm Beach before continuing on to Miami and what the author described as "the Mecca of their pilgrimage—Coral Gables."[14] Inviting comparison and unafraid of competition, the buses often stopped at other advertised subdivisions along the way. When the tour left Coral Gables after a two-day sojourn, many of the participants had bought lots as an investment or decided to purchase a home and move to Coral Gables.

Because of the tours, newspaper accounts describing Coral Gables began to proliferate across Florida. The author of a story in the *Sanford Herald* was so impressed with Coral Gables' Spanish-style architecture that she wrote: "To appreciate it is to see it, in all its colorful glory. The second Old Madrid City delights the eye even at a casual glance. . . . The only thing lacking are the Spaniards themselves."

Of course George's advertising staff, now under the direction of E. C. Purcell, utilized all the tour descriptions in various promotional pieces, including a full-page ad in both Miami newspapers.

Not everyone liked the proliferation of Spanish-style architecture. In a scathing article published in *The Miami News and Metropolis*, Charles Torrey Simpson, a highly acclaimed naturalist, bemoaned "fake aging" and argued that architects needed to disregard the past and create what he called a "Miami-style."[15] In a similar article, architect E. L. Robertson called "Spanish-type" an abused term, adding that much of it was "merely a gaudy show of bad taste."[16] In the same series, a well-known Cuban architect added to the negative point of view when he wrote that what was being built in Miami was not a true Spanish style.

George paid little attention to his detractors because most of the reviews were positive. As early as February 1924, a magazine called *Travel* included an article by Ruth B. Jeffreys entitled "Creating a Spanish City in Florida." It highlighted Coral Gables' beauty, calling it "a suburb, a city in itself, whose history reads like a tale from the Arabian Nights."

Besides bus tours, boat rides, and radio shows, George and his team came up with other events to draw attention to Coral Gables and spur sales. One occurred after the owners of *The Miami News and Metropolis*, its pages bursting with Coral Gables advertisements, bought a lot on Navarre Avenue and announced they would build and display "The Ideal Home," designed by Martin Hampton.

For two months, the paper included a weekly update. After the home was completed, but before the public viewing, additional articles listed local businesses that provided furnishings and appliances, even groceries to fill the kitchen cabinets. A local automobile dealer placed a new Chevrolet in the garage. The Ideal Home turned out to be an unprecedented success. More than five thousand people toured the Ideal Home during its week-long open house. One day after closing, it sold.

George was known for multitasking, but most found it hard to comprehend how he could accomplish as much as he did. In another national magazine story, S. M. Shelton described him as "a tireless systematic worker capable of paying strict attention to a multitude of details and knowing to a minute fraction what is being done by his associates." Shelton concluded with the question: "What will George Merrick do next?"[17]

With the two new sections launched and sales increasing, George refocused on the Business District, where new businesses opened almost weekly. Mindful of the success of Addison Mizner's Industries that produced items for his Palm Beach–style homes, George encouraged Miami companies to create products specifically for Coral Gables. Contractor John M. Stabile led the way when he built what he called the Stabile Building on the corner of Aragon and Salzedo. Behind its impressive, two-story façade was a business office above a first-floor factory where artisans and stone cutters created concrete lawn furniture—benches, sun dials, stands, and bird baths.

Two blocks north, the Parker Art Printing Company built another Spanish-style building designed by George Fink. When it opened in March, the Coral Gables advertising department created a two-page spread in the local press that highlighted the company's architectural splendor, as well as five state-of-the-art printing presses. "It is one of the most beautiful and well equipped printing establishments in the country," *The Miami Metropolis* opined.[18] The minute the presses began to roll, Parker Art printed all the Coral Gables promotional material, including *The Coral Gables Bulletin*.

Another especially attractive building was the Moorish-inspired, George Fink–designed headquarters for the New York Decorating Company on Aragon west of Salzedo. Previously located in downtown Miami, company artists and artisans had already painted more than 250 Gables homes and businesses in what they called "Tiffany-style." Working with color expert Phineas Paist, they created a new, multilayered, and multicolored effect for both interior and exterior walls that gave new buildings a sense of antiquity. The firm also offered interior design services, sold Spanish antiques and reproductions, and employed artists who created murals and other decorative motifs.[19] By year's end New York Decoration also housed Ralph Wilkins' Granada Shops. Wilkins, who moved to Coral Gables from Fort Wayne, Indiana, brought in Adolfo Lobata from Havana as his partner. Together they designed and built high-end, hardwood reproductions of Spanish antiques.

Besides building for private interests, George's own Coral Gables Construction Company constructed several buildings for him. He believed that if he set an example, he could show that his favorite philosopher, John Ruskin, was correct when he preached that one could combine beauty and utility. Following the opening of his Arcade Building on the corner of LeJeune Road and Alhambra, the Utilities Building rose on the northwest corner of Salzedo and Alhambra Plaza. Diagonally across the street, he opened the Coral Gables Garage, later an automobile dealership, and behind it, another utility building. Next, he built the George Fink–designed Transportation Building on Aragon just west of Ponce de Leon Boulevard to store the growing fleet of Coral Gables buses and to house future trolleys.

In the midst of new construction, the Coral Gables Riding Academy opened on the northwest corner of Salzedo and Aragon, temporarily taking over the building that was formerly used to build concrete blocks. Dr. Cox brought in fourteen horses, two ponies, and several riding instructors. Three of the first students were Eunice and her sisters-in-law, Medie and Ethel.

Although George rarely took a break from business, occasionally he and Eunice escaped to Nassau for a quick respite, often with Denman and Betsy Fink. As the 1923–24 season came to a close, the foursome boarded the USS Miami for a week in their favorite Bahamian hideaway. Immediately upon their return, the news reported that George and Denman were off to New York on business.

Unbeknownst to most people, George was in New York to continue his negotiations with John McEntee Bowman, owner of the Bowman-Biltmore Hotel Corp. His dream was to convince Bowman to become his partner in the new hotel. Bowman's chain, arguably the nation's most prestigious, included the New York Biltmore, the Los Angeles Biltmore, the new Sevilla Biltmore in Havana, and New York's Westchester Country Club. Soon after George's return, he and Eunice, accompanied by Jack and Gladys Baldwin, traveled to Atlanta for the opening of the new Atlanta Biltmore—a clear sign negotiations were going well.

As George awaited Bowman's answer, he continued to announce a series of other large projects, including the new Coral Gables Bank and Post Office to be built at the intersection of Alhambra Plaza and the recently renamed Ponce de Leon Boulevard, originally called Alameda after the main street in St. Augustine. (At the same time he proudly announced that Coral Gables would be the only new Miami suburb to get direct mail.) Designed by Walter DeGarmo, with color work by Phineas Paist, it was described as "Spanish architecture with Mediterranean influences—especially Italian."[20]

In early June, George announced another new section he called the Coral Way District, which expanded the Business District two blocks south of Coral Way. This purchase gave him ownership of both sides of Coral Way and made it possible to begin planning another major thoroughfare. Days later, he announced that he would build a new Coral Gables Administration Building on the southwest corner of Coral Way and Ponce de Leon Boulevard. Designed by Walter DeGarmo and his new partner, Phineas Paist, who for the first time was listed as a building's architect, the new Coral Gables headquarters would house George's offices, the administrative staff, and the advertising department.[21]

That same month, ground was broken for the new Congregational Church, with George tossing the first shovel of dirt. It was a particularly meaningful ceremony for the members of the Merrick family. George spoke eloquently about his father, Solomon, giving him credit for choosing the right place, laying the foundation, and creating the dream that became Coral Gables.

After record sales from the bus tours, George convinced C. W. DeLong to move to Coral Gables from Daytona and take over the sales operation once overseen by the late Harry Burnes. DeLong initiated a series of incentives to encourage the salesmen to meet George's aspirational goals. At first they had celebratory dinners at the Coral Gables Inn and fish fries on Key Biscayne. George spoke to the sales force and set a new goal of $5 million for the year; they topped that goal by $2 million in only twenty-nine days, setting a new Florida sales record. George, who was on a business trip to New York, sent the team a congratulatory telegram that optimistically concluded, "I firmly believe that what appears to be a gigantic accomplishment this year, will fade in comparison with what will be done in the future."[22]

The future came sooner than expected. When July and August sales topped a million dollars—unheard of during the summer months—DeLong took the ebullient sales force and their families to Havana to celebrate. He personally celebrated by commissioning George Fink to design a $75,000 home on the Biltmore golf course for his family. The press described the five-bedroom, three-bath, two-car garage, "simple Spanish-style" home on Plaza San Domingo as the largest home ever built in Coral Gables.[23]

Although George Merrick named George Fink Coral Gables' official architect, having designed more homes than anyone else, he remained the only one of the four major architects—the others being Hampton, DeGarmo, and Kiehnel—who had never been to Europe. His knowledge of what was commonly called the Spanish style came from careful study of books and photographs. His only firsthand encounter was with Cuba's Spanish-Colonial buildings, which he viewed during his frequent trips to the island. But even though most of his homes and commercial buildings were described as Spanish style, he, like the others, incorporated Moorish details into his designs. This was a natural inclusion, considering southern Spain's strong Moorish architectural legacy, which Washington Irving made popular in his *Tales of the Alhambra*.

As the other architects, especially Kiehnel and DeGarmo, leaned more toward Italian than Spanish style, Fink, too, began to incorporate Italian details into his work. In fact, by 1924, most of the homes in Coral Gables could no longer be described as "pure Spanish," even though Coral Gables continued to be called a "Spanish city." Fink described the new, evolving, still nameless style as "Spanish design with features of Mediterranean architecture worked in to present a pleasing effect so noticeable in all Coral Gables homes."[24]

Shortly before he left for Europe, Fink announced that George had asked him to redesign the newly enlarged Flagler Street office, which now included the three-story building to the east. He planned to incorporate Moorish and Italian architectural elements into the addition, creating a new, composite style. He anticipated gaining new ideas and inspiration from his upcoming trip.[25]

In late July, George Fink and his wife, Josie, left for a two-month trip to Spain, Italy, and southern France. Upon his return in October, both *The Miami Herald* and *The Miami News and Metropolis* wrote lengthy articles about his new discoveries. Their coverage, however, was nothing compared to the stories in the new *Miami Tribune*. In full-page spreads with multiple photographs, the *Tribune* not only reported on his trip but also gave him a forum in which he declared a new name for what he described as a "composite of

European designs that were in reality, a style of architecture that should not be called Spanish, but 'Mediterranean.'"[26]

The following week, the *Tribune* printed another full-page article featuring seven homes designed by George Fink. It predicted that Miami, "now in its constructive infancy, will become a center of interest for those who desire to see what distinctive effects were produced from the composite of older designs in building motifs."[27]

George Fink did not invent the Mediterranean style; he simply gave it a name and argued that it was not a revival but a new style that came to life in Florida. Most architectural historians trace its beginnings to Henry Flagler's Ponce de Leon Hotel, built in St. Augustine in 1888. Designed by the New York firm of John Carrere and Thomas Hastings, it was said to reference Florida's Spanish past, even though few buildings remained from the Spanish era. Although the hotel was well received, the style did not immediately become popular. Instead, Florida architects leaned toward the more subdued Spanish-Mission style so popular in California and the Southwestern United States.

During the first two decades of the twentieth century, August Geiger, one of Miami's best-known and most respected architects, designed the Miami Beach Golf Club, the City Hospital, and the Redland School, all in the Spanish-Mission style. Both Martin Luther Hampton and George Fink worked in his office. Tastes began to change, however, after James Deering built an Italian-style home he called Vizcaya. Its beauty and ambience, which seemed to fit perfectly into South Florida's subtropical environment, caused architects, including Addison Mizner in Palm Beach and Walter De-Garmo in Miami, to look to the Mediterranean for inspiration. DeGarmo later wrote that Vizcaya had "the greatest single influence that has lifted Miami out of the commonplace."[28]

After Pittsburgh architects Kiehnel & Elliott designed El Jardin in Coconut Grove for John Bindley, other architects took notice of the new composite style that incorporated Spanish, Moorish, Venetian, Italian, and a touch of Spanish-Colonial into what seemed particularly appropriate for South Florida. Once the Bindley estate was completed, other members of Coconut Grove's wealthy elite hired Kiehnel to design their new homes as well.

George, determined that his master suburb would have strict architectural controls, adapted elements of the emerging new style for his planned subdivision. Although he called the first homes "Spanish," in reality his original insistence on rock homes reflected an Arts and Crafts ambience more than anything else. On the other hand, Denman Fink's entrances and plazas stamped Coral Gables with an indelible Spanish imprint.

In late 1922, after George accepted the advice of his personally selected architects to expand his vision, Coral Gables was on its way to developing a style of its own.

Thus, what George Fink called "Mediterranean" was born—slowly but not deliberately—when a talented group of mostly Florida architects modified the so-called Spanish style just as the invading Moors and the Italian Renaissance had done centuries before on the shores of old Spain.

George Fink returned from the Mediterranean with more than two thousand photographs, hundreds of ideas, and an autographed photograph and letter from Spanish King Alfonso XIII congratulating him for "his superb interpretation of Spanish art." In addition to the lengthy newspaper articles in which he explained the new style, he planned to use the remodeled Flagler Street office as a tangible testimonial to its correctness.

October also brought a twenty-one-page article on Coral Gables in *The National Builder*. It included a comprehensive map, photographs of plazas, entry features, and homes, and what was called the Venetian Lake. It also had an article on the Business District and floor plans of the country club, the Coral Gables Inn, the bank, the post office, and eight homes. Of special interest was a detailed article by Phineas Paist on how to color stucco. It was one of the first national articles focused on Coral Gables architecture and planning, and, unquestionably, the most detailed.[29] It also launched a series of articles in other national publications, making it clear that Coral Gables had become a national phenomenon.

Coral Gables' national publicity was responsible in part for the huge number of people flocking to South Florida. By late 1924, Coral Gables was not the only part of Greater Miami experiencing phenomenal growth. Not to be outdone, the City of Miami was rapidly becoming the drum major at the head of the parade as new building permits exceeded those in Coral Gables, which for most of the year held the local record. Flagler Street was beginning to look like a real estate mecca, with most major developers opening elaborate sales offices on every corner and real estate salesmen filling every available office.

In an effort to help "The Magic City" live up to its name, the reelected Banker's Commission signed a contract with Warren Manning, a respected national planner, to design a new waterfront park and grand boulevard to be created from pumped-up bay bottom. Almost weekly, newspapers announced building permit records as new hotels, apartments, and high-rise office buildings broke ground. The fact that the rest of the nation was talking about Miami as the epicenter of the Florida Boom caused the chamber of commerce and other business interests to increase their marketing budgets to help spread the word.

Kenneth Roberts, writing in *The Saturday Evening Post*, was one of the first national reporters to describe the scene as a "boom." "Everyone in South Florida," he wrote, "has just bought a piece of real estate or has just sold a piece of real estate or is on the verge of buying or selling a piece of real estate." He ended his story with a warning and reminded people that there were ten promoters for every legitimate developer, making the situation "as dangerous as any speculation of the stock market."[30] On the other hand, without mentioning Coral Gables by name, photographs of and positive references to Coral Gables stood out in contrast to some of the others.

No one accused George of being anything but a man of his word. But by this time, even George was catching boom fever, which seemed to spike after Bowman agreed to be his partner. Although the partnership was not publicly announced, the knowledgeable observer realized the deal had been consummated when a different rendering of the new country club appeared, listing Shultz & Weaver as the architects.[31] The New York firm had recently completed three hotels for the Bowman-Biltmore chain, as well as the Nautilus Hotel for Carl Fisher in Miami Beach. It must have been a blow to Hampton to be replaced in what he considered his most important project. As a consolation prize, he received the commission for a one-hundred-room hotel, the Casa Loma, to be built on the new golf course just west of the Biltmore Country Club. The owner was R. H. McLendon, the father-in-law of George's sister Medie.

At about the same time, George launched the one-hundred-acre Flagler Street Section—the first north of Eighth Street. The announcement included a drawing of the proposed Flagler Street Entrance, designed by Denman Fink.[32] Workmen began construction on a curving Ponce de Leon Boulevard extension to connect the proposed new rock entrance to the Business District and, more importantly, to create a pathway for future trolleys to enter Coral Gables.

The expansion continued with the addition of what George called the "Crafts Section." It incorporated the recently announced Coral Way Section into the forty-block section that extended from Coral Way south to San Sebastian between LeJeune and Douglas Roads. The Crafts Section, his most idealistic offering to date, allowed George to reconnect with John Ruskin and Ruskin's disciple, William Morris, and their veneration of artisans and craftsmen. On a practical side, it gave him a new way to compete with Mizner's Industries.

His new utopian village also referenced Elbert Hubbard and his "Roycrofters" in East Aurora, New York, who made handcrafted articles for sale. In addition, the Crafts Section would also include housing for the artisans—either above their shops or in nearby neighborhoods. "The Crafts Section," Merrick's advertisement proclaimed, "will attract wide-spread attention because of its appeal to the artistic sense."[33]

The centerpiece of the Crafts Section was the Permanent Exposition Hall, where artisans and craftsmen could display their wares. It would dominate an elliptical park that divided the north and southbound lanes of Ponce de Leon Boulevard between Sevilla and Palermo. Nearby, George also planned a community market reminiscent of the markets in Spain.

Phineas Paist, who had been working in Coral Gables as the color expert for a year, assumed a new role as the Crafts Section's key architect. His drawing of the proposed section appeared in newspaper advertisements and was prominently displayed in sales offices. His leadership in the Crafts Section and his new partnership with Walter DeGarmo thrust him into the pantheon of Coral Gables architects, and, for the most part, he replaced Martin Luther Hampton, who had become one of the most important architects in Joseph Young's Hollywood-By-The-Sea.

Before the year ended, George added the Coconut Grove Section, which extended south of the Crafts Section to Bird Road. With only a few missing blocks, Coral Gables now spread out between Douglas and Red Roads from Bird Road to Eighth Street, with a dogleg extending to Flagler.

Just a few days before George announced the Crafts Section, the new Bank of Coral Gables opened, followed by the post office. William Fishbaugh was on hand to photograph the officers and directors who participated in the historic event. With Telfair Knight as president and other familiar faces, including George Merrick, Doc Dammers, and Jack Baldwin, on the board of trustees, the new bank was another Coral Gables enterprise created under George Merrick.

Although everything appeared to be going perfectly for George and Coral Gables, his first real challenge came when Hugh Anderson, Roy C. Wright, J. B. Jeffries, and Ellen Spears Harris created the Shoreland Company and announced their twenty-eight-hundred-acre subdivision called Miami Shores. Anderson, well-known in Miami, had previously been involved in the building of the Venetian Causeway and the Venetian Isles. Beginning with a purchase of eight hundred acres from L. T. Cooper, who was developing the acreage as Bay View Estates, the Shoreland Company acquired other parcels, although some not contiguous, extending from Northeast Eighty-Seventh Street and Dixie Highway to Arch Creek (127 Street). It included miles of bayfront and even a group of offshore islands dubbed Miami Shores Islands (now Indian Creek and Bay Harbor Island). Ironically, the company's first advertisement began with "We Doff Our Hats to those who have worked so faithfully and are still working to build up Miami and its environs." After thanking all the important developers, including George, the promotion ended with a pledge to make Miami Shores "the greatest of all developments."[34] (A few days later, George responded in a full-page advertisement headlined "Greetings to Miami Shores—and Sincere Wishes for Success.")

Adding to what must have been George's concern was the fact that the Shoreland Company made Richard Kiehnel its most visible architect and John Livingston, who had drawn most of the renderings for Coral Gables, its illustrator.

Two days after Miami Shores' first flurry of advertisements, George dominated the headlines by hosting a dinner for two hundred dignitaries at the Coral Gables Country Club to officially announce the new Miami-Biltmore Hotel and to honor its president, John McEntee Bowman. Following George's flattering introduction, Bowman returned the compliment and promised the new hotel "would be the most pretentious in the world!"[35]

Bowman's announcement that he was bringing the finest hotel he had ever built to Coral Gables because he believed in George Merrick and wanted to be his partner made everyone take notice.

Miami Shores went on sale on December 4, the same day George announced Country Club Section Parts Three and Four, with the Biltmore Hotel at the center. For the first time, however, another subdivision eclipsed Coral Gables in one-day sales. Buyers purchased more than $2.5 million worth of Miami Shores lots, a new Florida record.

If George was worried about Miami Shores, it did not show. The next big Coral Gables event was the long-awaited opening of what was now being called the Venetian Casino. George hired superstar Jan Garber and his Victor Orchestra to play at a two-day series of events that also included the grand reopening of the enlarged Coral Gables Country Club. For the rest of the year, the press was filled with announcements of events at the two new venues, as well as reviews of their special ambience.

George topped off a truly remarkable year with the release of a large new brochure entitled "Coral Gables: Miami Riviera," authored by Marjory Stoneman Douglas. It was not a typical sales promotion but a romantic interpretation—more like a beautiful essay—by a gifted writer. Although it included full-page photographs, mostly unidentified, they were artistically blurred like an impressionist painting. "After the gateways and plazas," she wrote, "the houses and buildings grew. And literally, they seem to grow, because each house, each shop, each structure, has the sense of intimate belonging which only comes from loving foresight."

The new brochure demonstrated that even though George was a natural salesman and wanted Coral Gables to grow and prosper, he maintained the soul of a poet. He still dreamed of becoming a writer when he completed his master suburb. But, for the time being, Coral Gables was his masterpiece—his poem in stone.

1925

Building a City

> Building a city is as much a fine art, perhaps, as a painting, a
> portrait. The same human ingredients are needed for both—
> operations, training, a realization of beauty, genius [and]
> unbounded faith and confidence in one's ability to do the work.
> All of these qualities Coral Gables' master builder George
> Merrick has in profusion, coupled with the ability to command
> men. The year 1925 saw the fruition of many of his plans and
> dreams and the budding of many more, all to be welded into
> the next few years into a greater, more beautiful, city.
>
> "Coral Gables Reviews Year's Achievements," *The Miami News*,
> December 30, 1925

As 1925 dawned, no one, not even George, anticipated what was about to
happen in and to Miami. Although people talked about a boom, Miami's
leaders and major developers, including George, dismissed the idea. They
insisted that South Florida was thriving because people finally realized that
Miami, as well as all of Florida, was the nation's last frontier, the land of opportunity, and a place whose time had come. Even Addison Mizner, known
for his society connections, picked up the frontier theme in his Boca Raton
advertisements and included pioneers in covered wagons next to chauf-
feur-driven automobiles. Despite the denials, *The Miami News* summed up
the obvious in a cartoon showing a boy pounding a drum with a "Boom,
Boom, Boom." The caption read: "Pound Boy Pound, We Can Stand a Lot
of Noise."[1]

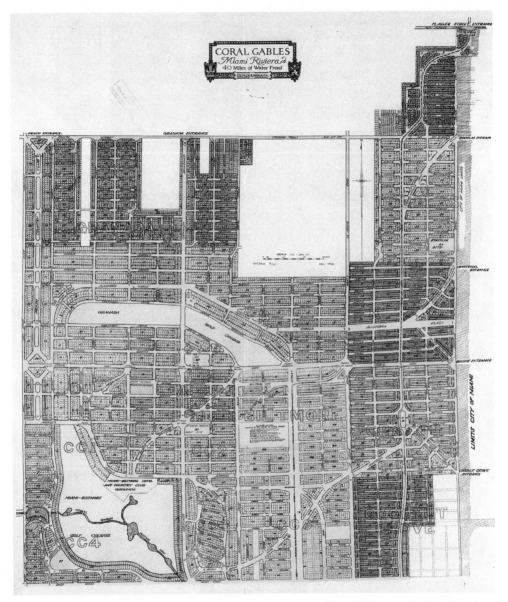

Figure 41. In December 1924, George issued a comprehensive map of Coral Gables north of Bird Road. Permission of HistoryMiami.

Miami was booming in large part because of George Merrick. He had opened the doors, set the stage, hired the actors, lifted the curtain, and written the reviews with his national advertising and marketing campaign. By 1925, what many called "boom fever" had spread throughout Florida and even infected the nation. Two eyewitnesses—Kenneth Ballinger, a reporter for *The Miami Herald*, and T. H. Weigall, a British journalist—later wrote books that chronicled the year like no other. Not surprisingly, both named George Merrick the protagonist.

"Miami never had a boom and is not having a boom now," George was quoted in an extensive March *New York Times* article that reported on national capital being drawn to Miami. It appeared during his trip to New York to cement the $10 million deal with John McEntee Bowman and his Biltmore Hotel chain. "To back up this statement of mine," George opined, "it is necessary to make further emphatic assertions which is that if no further person commonly designated as 'tourist' ever again visited Miami it still would steadily become a great city." He concluded with a pure George-style observation: "Miami is the minting in Americas in one fine, shining piece of the substantial compound of that very American dream of freedom, opportunity and achievement."[2]

No one questioned George's sincerity or that he believed every word he said. Little more than three years had passed since he launched Coral Gables. Its unprecedented success fueled his expanding vision. He became even more confident in his ability to transform Coral Gables into a community that would eclipse all local and even national developments.

Coral Gables' entrances, plazas, landscaping, and carefully planned neighborhoods with strict architectural controls certainly set it apart from other developments. In fact, no other subdivision matched the scale and speed of Coral Gables' achievements. Its marketing, sales, and advertising campaigns were equally singular and as important to its success. As Coral Gables grew, George brought in professionals from all over the country to help promote his ideal. In late 1924, he hired Walter W. Bruns as director of sales education to work with the sales staff, which now numbered more than two thousand. At the same time, the sales department initiated what they called *The Coral Gablesgram*—an in-house, almost-daily newsletter under the direction of Packard Lobeck. It included a list of lots and homes for sale, completed sales, and kudos to outstanding salesmen. Bruns also included sales hints. In one issue, he highlighted Jesus Christ as history's best salesman because he promoted a belief that eventually spread around the world. He suggested the sales force follow Jesus' example. He also ran salesmanship courses and, except for George, became Coral Gables' most vocal cheerleader.

"This is Coral Gables Year," Bruns wrote. "We enter this New Year with a hope brightened by past achievement and inspired by future possibilities."[3] In the same issue, George added his own challenge to the sales force he called the "Coral Gables Go-Getters." If they produced $10 million in sales between January 1 and April 30, he promised to place $100,000 in a bonus pot that, in addition to usual commissions, he would divide among salesmen and saleswomen who sold at least $50,000 in property during that period.[4]

Each day brought new ideas and unique promotional schemes. One that garnered the most press was the hiring of William Jennings Bryan to speak at the Venetian Casino. At the time, Bryan, the Democratic Party's three-time presidential candidate, was considered one of the nation's most admired statesmen and orators. In 1913, he and his wife, Mary, built a home on Brickell Avenue and, since 1917, had considered Miami home. Called Florida's and Miami's "First Citizen," he drew thousands of residents and visitors to his Sunday school class held each week at Royal Palm Park. Merrick paid him $100,000—part cash and part property—to bring similar crowds to Coral Gables.

Beginning promptly at twelve noon on January 2 and continuing every day except Sunday for the next three months, Bryan proved his worth. He rarely talked about Coral Gables directly but instead extolled Florida's and Miami's tropical lifestyle and unlimited opportunity. He also reminded the crowd how much money he had made buying Florida real estate. *The Miami News* frequently published his entire speech, adding to his promotional value.[5]

Other special events held at the Venetian Casino, coupled with free bus transportation, also enticed huge numbers of visitors to Coral Gables. From Miss America contests to alligator wrestling and water shows with Jackie Ott ("The Aqua Tot") and Olympic stars like future Tarzan Johnny Weissmuller, the wooden grandstands that surrounded the pool were always filled to capacity.

The Coral Gables Country Club also became a tourist draw, as well as a popular venue for local events. Each week, the social pages included photos and a who's who of Miami society and visiting dignitaries. Recently enlarged, the country club also hosted Broadway stars, Spanish dancers, and Jan Garber's orchestra.

Although Coral Gables had no real rival when it came to local suburban developments, Miami Shores was trying to change that perception. Coral Gables led with almost daily full-page and double-page newspaper ads, but Miami Shores was nipping at its heels. Its executives took pleasure in reminding readers that Miami Shores had miles of waterfront and more acreage than any other development. Sometimes Coral Gables' ads responded, albeit indirectly, to Miami Shores' challenge. In February, Coral Gables created a full-page ad headlined "Coral Gables Waterway Loop," which showed a proposed waterway that would begin at Biscayne Bay and snake north and west through Coral Gables, connecting with the Tamiami Canal, the Miami River, and the Port of Miami. Clearly, George was determined to have waterfront property, even if he had to create it. At the time, the Coral Gables workforce had already started digging the Coral Gables Waterway east of the Red Road terminus of the Tamiami Canal. The dredged material filled in lowland and created water features and hazards for the new Biltmore Golf Course.

Other developers joined the Coral Gables bandwagon, claiming that their subdivisions were lower-priced versions of Coral Gables. Fulford-By-The-Sea announced a planned, but never built, hotel with a full-page rendering resembling the Biltmore.[6] At the same time, Curtiss and Bright launched Country Club Estates (Miami Springs) in modified Spanish-Pueblo style. It gave Hialeah an upscale neighborhood surrounding a golf course complete with an elegant pueblo-style country club designed by noted New York architect Clinton McKenzie. Other smaller offerings like Sylvania Heights and Schenley Park advertised that they were near Coral Gables. Sometimes developers of new subdivisions with names like University Heights, University Park, and Riviera Gardens hoped buyers might be fooled into thinking they were new Coral Gables sections. None of these copycats bothered George. He found wannabe imitators flattering.

Doc Dammers, who had helped launch Coral Gables four years earlier, was busy promoting his own Central Miami while still lauding Coral

Gables. In fact, some of his ads suggested that prospective buyers visit Coral Gables first and then "walk across the street" to see Central Miami. He hired George Fink to design impressive entry features that mimicked Coral Gables. Many questioned Dammers' assertion that soon, Central Miami would be at the center of Greater Miami. Miami Chamber of Commerce leaders asked George to tell Dammers to stop what they considered false advertising. George demurred because he agreed with Dammers' prediction.

By this time, Miami's Flagler Street had become what author Fredrick Lewis Allen called "one frenzied real estate exchange."[7] The 1926 *Polk City Directory*, which included more than one hundred pages of real estate ads, documented the obvious. More than 150 real estate offices filled Flagler Street between Miami and Northeast Third Avenues, with hundreds more scattered throughout the rest of downtown.

T. H. Weigall wrote a colorful description of the scene:

> Everywhere there was building going forward at express speed; and mingled with the perpetual screeching of the motor-horns a thousand automatic riveters poured out their deafening music, a thousand drills and hammers and winches added to the insane chorus. Hatless, coatless men rushed about the blazing streets their arms full of papers, perspiration pouring from their foreheads. Every shop seemed to be combined with a real-estate market; at every doorway crowds of young men were shouting and speechmaking, thrusting forward papers and proclaiming to heaven the unsurpassed changes which they were offering to make a fortune.[8]

The salesmen he described were what the press dubbed "binder boys." Kenneth Ballinger described each as "an individual slightly under normal height, never very clean or neat, bending every effort to make a lot of money in a hurry without the slightest pretense of remaining in Florida once that was done. He was attired in golf knickers, because they didn't need pressing nor the addition of a coat, and the binder boy made the knicker at one time standard male daytime garb in almost any gather, even church."[9]

The binder boys hung out at the Ponce de Leon Hotel, located on Flagler Street just east of Northeast Second Avenue. Drawn by the lure of quick profits, most had never sold real estate before. At the time, the real estate trade had no regulations, so all the would-be realtors needed was an occupational license before they hit the streets. (Many didn't even bother with that formality.) By the first of July, the City of Miami had issued almost six thousand real estate broker licenses—sometimes as many as sixty a day.

The binder boys perfected a sales technique that spurred the boom. They would sell a piece of property with only a minimal down payment—never more than 10 percent, and often less. The deal would not be sealed or recorded for thirty days, until the title was cleared and the first regular payment became due. In the meantime, the buyer would receive a sheet of paper called a binder. What the binder boys figured out was that the binder was just as good as money. They would re-sell it—some said as often as eight times a day—at an ever-increasing price. "When closing time came," Ballinger wrote, "the buyers would group around the papers like hungry boys ready to take a slice out of the profits. Usually, by trading papers, it was possible for a deed to issue only to the last buyer, but it might have seven or eight mortgages clinging to it like ticks on a cow."[10] Of course the binder boy made a commission on every transfer.

Miami leaders, aware that the binder boys gave Miami a bad reputation, put an ad in *The Miami Herald* denouncing them and warning potential buyers to beware. "We no longer get a thrill out of the announcement that someone is coming to Miami to engage in the real estate business," *The Herald* editorialized. "We really feel that Miami has all the real estate dealers necessary."[11] In an effort to calm the mayhem, the city passed a law making it illegal to sell real estate on the sidewalk.

The Dade County Clerk's Office, which recorded deeds, could not keep up with the sales. In an attempt to ease the backlog, the county filled the hallways of the 1904 courthouse with secretaries and constructed a small addition to the existing building. At the same time, the mayor announced the county would build a $1.5 million, twenty-story courthouse around the old building.

By this time, all of downtown Miami was in the midst of a metamorphosis. Coral Gables' Flagler Street office was undergoing a major renovation and addition spearheaded by George Fink. The expanded showroom, which took over a three-story, nondescript, early-Miami building, had a new façade and a one-hundred-foot-long columned arcade with a ceiling matching the one in the Alhambra's Hall of the Ambassadors. An

Figure 42. After George Fink returned from his European trip, he designed an expanded Coral Gables downtown headquarters that he said illustrated the new Mediterranean style he named and promoted. Author's collection.

Italian Renaissance–style grand entrance topped with French windows and Venetian-style arches completed the new design. Authentic Spanish and Italian furnishings and decorative objects purchased by Fink during his travels completed the fantasy. Fink hoped that the Flagler Street office would prove Coral Gables had created a new style of architecture he insisted should be called "Mediterranean."[12]

The glamour of Coral Gables' existing showroom and planned expansion was not unique. Each of the other major developments had competing sales offices on the same block. Across the street, the Shoreland Company was building the highly decorated Miami Shores and Venetian Arcades between Flagler and Northeast First Street. They also planned a high-rise building to complete the ensemble. Next in grandeur was the Mizner Development Corporation's Boca Raton confection, followed by Fulford-By-The-Sea's main office. A short distance west of the Coral Gables office, Curtiss-Bright opened a Flagler Street presence for Hialeah and Country Club Estates. Each lured customers inside with evening concerts and other special events. The cacophony of competing orchestras and the exuberant voices of salesmen spilled out into the streets. When the music quieted, Flagler Street became a clogged parking lot as private limousines and buses arrived to whisk potential buyers to the promised land.

George had so much going on in Coral Gables and on the national scene that he left management of the downtown frenzy to his lieutenants. Coral Gables, unlike many of the others, stuck to George's carefully orchestrated, more subdued selling style. His national marketing campaign didn't need binders or aggressive salesmen accosting people on the sidewalk. In a speech to his sales team, he summed up Coral Gables' national reputation, comparing it to "Cadillac cars or Victrolas—for Coral Gables is a unique trade article—the only realty in the U.S. comparable with patent trade articles nationally sold."[13] Undoubtedly, his marketing campaign had a lot to do with Coral Gables' success, but Coral Gables itself provided the greatest sales pitch of all.

On February 22, George proved Coral Gables' singular position in the pecking order of developments when he announced he had purchased six thousand acres from James and Charles Deering for $6 million. He had fulfilled his longtime dream and, as the press reported, thrown a bombshell into his waterfront competitor's camp. Coral Gables not only reached Biscayne Bay but, in an instant, expanded to ten thousand acres. In addition, George proudly noted, the Deerings, famous for their estates, style, and artistry, would help him develop the property.

Although his plans were not yet fully formed, George predicted his proposed $100 million project would surpass any waterfront development in Florida and probably in the United States. It would have a six-mile-long boulevard, wide waterways, and a yacht basin. In addition, he would build waterfront homes in the Italian, French, Egyptian, and Algerian styles, as well as apartments and commercial buildings. It would also include a South Seas–themed beach, a string of South Seas islands connected by a causeway, and a Biltmore Company–developed casino and hotel, larger than the Coral Gables Biltmore then under construction.[14]

Few seemed to think George was expanding too rapidly. Biltmore architect Leonard Schultze summed up the prevailing view when he wrote: "George E. Merrick possesses greater vision and more courage to carry his ideals to completion than any man I have ever known. His objective

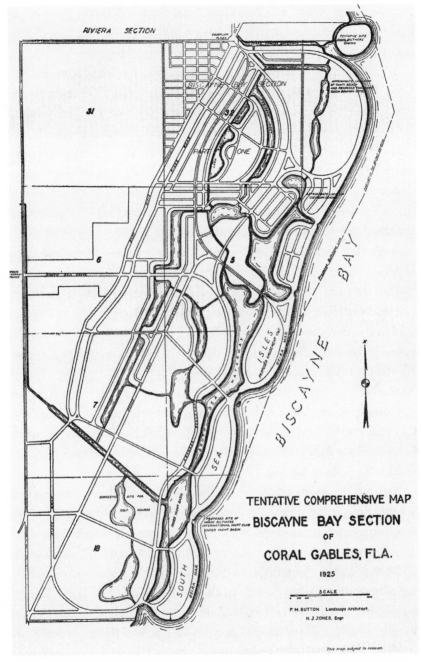

Figure 43. In early 1925, George announced the Biscayne Bay Section and published a
tentative map. It included what he called the "South Sea Isles" and a causeway named
"Bahia Mar" after Havana's grand esplanade. Author's collection.

became Biscayne Bay. His plans have been completed—the purchase of land has been consummated. The vision will be made an accomplished reality."[15]

To most, this was not simply hyperbole, even though it appeared in a Coral Gables advertisement, because at the same time, George reported that his $10 million sales goal set in January had been reached a month early—setting an all-time local sales record. In fact, people expected him to continue expanding. Charles Fox, in his 1925 book, *The Truth About Florida*, summed up the consensus view: "Merrick—he is a man of achievement whose goal will never be reached, for no sooner does it loom before him than he achieves some expansion for 'his' city, compelling him to begin all over the battle for its successful conclusion."[16]

Ironically, after the Deering purchase, George started calling the Coral Gables sections north of Bird Road the "older" part of Coral Gables, even though they were not yet four years old. One "older" section, the Coral Gables Business District, added new projects at a record pace. They included the first movie theater, designed by Hampton and Erdman; the large George Fink–designed Coral Gables Construction Building; a Spanish-style gas station complete with clock tower; and the one-story Louise Arcade, also designed by George Fink in a unique way that allowed future upward expansion. The new buildings and the beautiful Bank of Coral Gables were rapidly turning the intersection of Alhambra Circle and Ponce de Leon Boulevard into what advertisements predicted would become Coral Gables' own Times Square.

Nearby, the $300,000 Coral Gables Military Academy, designed by George Fink, opened near the Grammar School. One of its first students was George Fink Jr., known as Buddy. The Grammar School, already overcrowded, was preparing for a Richard Kiehnel–designed expansion and the addition of a large auditorium. After the bids came in higher than expected, the School Board asked George to change the plans. Once again, George refused to compromise and, instead, offered to pay half the additional cost in order to maintain the design's integrity. The School Board agreed.[17]

The speed of Coral Gables' unprecedented growth surprised even George. After the new Administration Building, which was only a few months old, could not accommodate his growing staff and sales force, he announced that a larger, even more impressive sales office would be constructed across the street. The Crafts Section also sported new buildings, including the Phineas Paist–designed Art Building under construction.

The most important event of the spring was the groundbreaking for the Biltmore Hotel, ominously, in retrospect, on Friday, March 13. Hundreds of dignitaries, including William Jennings Bryan, gathered to watch Biltmore Company Vice President Charles Flynn toss the first spade of dirt. The ceremony ended with Bryan boarding a steam shovel to start clearing the grounds. George was away that day, so Eunice represented him and stood front and center in the commemorative photograph.

Although Coral Gables had grown steadily since its inception, the boom accelerated its development. Almost every month, new sales records toppled old. George remained firmly in control, but the increased responsibility was taking its toll on his health and marriage. He worked late into the night and became even more reclusive. He was seldom seen in public and rarely gave a speech unless announcing a major new project. He spent more time out of town working out business deals. In his absence, Eunice entertained dignitaries and frequently attended social events without him. Occasionally, especially when she was away, he would hang out with some of his closest associates, who were known for paying little attention to prohibition laws. This upset Eunice who, as a devout Christian Scientist, avoided alcohol and kept her distance from those who imbibed. Adding to the growing difficulties was her annual three-month northern trip that George continued to dislike but, by this time, begrudgingly accepted.

In the midst of all the folderol, on Palm Sunday, members of the Merrick family and seven hundred attendees paused to dedicate the Congregational Church in memory of its "spiritual progenitor," Solomon Merrick. Its beauty and imposing presence in a section still filled with his father's grapefruit groves gave George more satisfaction than millions of dollars in sales. The new church was a meaningful and permanent memorial to his hard-to-please father and he had made it happen.

Across from the new church, workmen were laying the Biltmore Hotel's foundation. Nearby, the emerging Biltmore Country Club was starting to look like the beautiful renderings published just a few months earlier. The first eighteen holes of the thirty-six-hole golf course were almost completed and the first golfers were being introduced to the new championship course. Although the original plan was the work of Langford and Moreau, who designed the Granada course, Bowman brought Donald Ross to revise and expand the course.

While George continued to be the final arbiter on Coral Gables' development, major changes were about to occur that would dilute his absolute hegemony. The first was the creation of the Coral Gables Corporation in March. For the past four years, he had been the sole owner of all of Coral Gables. The new corporation, at least for the time being, was simply a legal document that named him president and his associates officers. The Corporation had the ability to sell shares, but George remained the supermajority stockholder and sole decision maker.

Within a month, it became apparent why he had created the corporation. Unbeknownst to most, he had changed his position on Coral Gables becoming a municipality. This occurred after he purchased the Deering property and realized that an individual owner or even a private corporation would not be able to complete his ambitious, $100-million plan for what he now called "Coral Gables: Miami Riviera." After Boca Raton and Miami Shores announced they would soon become cities, he felt the need to trump his competitors.

On April 27, without previous announcement, state senator John W. Watson introduced a fifty-page charter bill and sought and received unanimous consent from the Florida Senate to create the City of Coral Gables. Hardly more than a half-hour later, the Florida House of Representatives followed suit and sent the document on to Governor Martin for his signature. Thus, on April 29, 1925, the City of Coral Gables was born, with the same men who managed the Coral Gables Corporation named as its first commissioners. These were Edward L. Dammers, Telfair Knight, Charles F. Baldwin, F. Wingfield Webster, and George Merrick.

Most Miamians were surprised to read the front-page headlines announcing Coral Gables' incorporation, because George continued to insist that Coral Gables would not become a city but would be part of an expanded Greater Miami. Two days later, to avoid what he called "misunderstanding," he penned a lengthy statement in *The Miami Herald*. It read:

> Before asking that this charter be granted, I explained to the city commissioners of the City of Miami the necessity for the creation of a municipality in order that the plans we have made for the development

of Coral Gables might be properly carried out. . . . My chief thought is now to complete the work we have undertaken to do in making Coral Gables the most beautiful development in America and then to see it included in the one great municipality of the City of Miami.[18]

On the same day as his statement appeared, the first trolley arrived in Coral Gables, physically linking the two cities. The newly minted city fathers, along with featured speaker William Jennings Bryan and an army of other dignitaries, arrived by trolley to participate in the official inauguration ceremonies held on the corner of Ponce de Leon Boulevard and Coral Way. At the same time, George announced plans for extending the tracks southward and spoke of the creation of a new line he called the Coral Gables Rapid Transit. After speeches and congratulations, George invited the entire entourage to lunch at the Coral Gables Country Club.

Figure 44. The day after Coral Gables was incorporated as a city and its mayor and first commission named, the new municipal officers stood proudly to greet the first trolley into Coral Gables. *Left to right*: Commissioner F. W. Webster, Commissioner George E Merrick, Mayor Edward E. "Doc" Dammers, Commissioner Charles F. "Jack" Baldwin, and Commissioner Telfair Knight. Courtesy of State Archives of Florida, Florida Memory.

The following day, the new Coral Gables Commission met for the first time in the Coral Gables Corporation Administration Building, listed as the temporary city hall. With George as interim chairman, the first order of business was to accept the city charter, elect a mayor, and name the city officers. By unanimous consent, Edward "Doc" Dammers became mayor and Robert M. Davidson, city manager. The other officers were, for the most part, either connected to the Coral Gables Corporation or the Merrick family. Edwin Bishop, who was married to George's sister Ethel, became the city clerk and tax assessor, and R. B. McLendon, the father-in-law of George's sister Medie, the tax collector. Others were City Attorney Clifton Benson, Treasurer W. A. McFarlane, and Municipal Judge E. L. Semple. The commission also asked Denman Fink to design a city seal. Before the meeting ended, George convinced the newly elected mayor and commission to officially proclaim that they, too, supported the city's eventual annexation to the City of Miami.[19]

Amid the local news of incorporation, expansion, and record sales, another story was breaking in New York City that thrust Coral Gables' national reputation to a higher level. A week before the founding of the city, the American Institute of Architects opened its first International Exposition of Architecture and Allied Arts at Manhattan's Grand Central Palace. Its purpose was to encourage better city planning and architecture—a natural platform for Coral Gables. *The New York Times* covered the exposition, including sessions on city planning and reviews of the exhibits and the achievements of its architects.

George challenged his cousin George Fink to design an exhibit that would illuminate the Coral Gables story in a way that would attract national attention. With unlimited funds, Fink came up with an elaborate and original design and then traveled to New York to supervise its installation. The exhibit included some typical items like sepia and hand-colored photographs and a large painting of the Venetian Casino by Denman Fink, as well as plans and models of several of the larger homes. But its pièce de résistance was its full-scale decorated rooms. Each had authentic moldings, polychromed ceilings, hand-forged ironwork, antique lighting, and Spanish tile and furnishings. In addition, Spanish paintings and antique tapestries decorated the rough stucco walls. Described as one of the largest and most attractive exhibits in the show, it was viewed by more than 7,500 visitors on opening day. Adding to its popularity was Jan Garber's orchestra and a duo of Spanish dancers who performed every afternoon and evening in the midst of what one observer called "a piece of old Spain in Gotham." *The New York Times*, in a May 3 article, praised Fink as an eminent architect who had designed more than eight hundred homes in Coral Gables in a style he developed. Of course, the Miami papers picked up on the accolades and ran a series of articles on Fink and the exposition.

At the same time the exhibition was in progress, Fink was busy transforming a nondescript building just off Times Square into an elegant Coral Gables showroom. The plan was to incorporate parts of the exhibit into the new office. Fink postponed the showroom's opening until after Coral Gables had the opportunity to extend the exhibit into the Southern Exposition that opened at the Grand Central Palace just a few days after the Architecture and Allied Arts exposition closed. The Southern Exposition brought even more attention to Coral Gables and its most prolific architect.

On May 17, the Coral Gables office in Manhattan opened at 140 West Forty-Second Street. Fink and his team had completely removed the building's façade and created a new triple-arched entryway with twisted columns and a twenty-foot-deep tiled patio complete with a fourteenth-century stone well. The interior featured a large Coral Gables–style living room with tiled floors, Oriental carpets, antique tapestries, iron grilles, brass lanterns, and Spanish furnishings.[20] Its beauty and authenticity attracted considerable national attention. Even sophisticated New Yorkers had never seen anything like it and tried to figure out what it was when it was under construction near the Broadway theaters.

As the crowds gathered in New York, Fink was off to Atlanta, where he was creating another one-of-a-kind showroom at 185 Peachtree Street. "With the atmosphere of Old Spain brought to Atlanta," the *Atlanta Constitution* reported at its opening, "Jan Garber and his Coral Gables orchestra were presented to the throng that filled the offices and crowded the site."[21] The next night, George hosted a ball for one thousand people at the Atlanta Biltmore to celebrate the opening of the new office. The *Atlanta Constitution* described the elegant decorations and the group of prominent Atlantans in attendance. Eunice, who had already commenced her summer trip, was conspicuously absent.

Other developments had satellite sales offices, but none could compare to Coral Gables' extravagance and style, plus the offer of a free trip by bus or on the "Coral Gables Special" train. Before the year ended, every major city in America had a Coral Gables office.

As summer arrived, Miami unquestionably was in the midst of a boom. Sixteen downtown skyscraper hotels and office buildings neared completion and the steel girders of fourteen more filled the skyline. Flagler Street sidewalks had become impassable. For George, June marked the fulfillment of another dream—the launching of the University of Miami at Coral Gables.

The idea of a university had been in the works for many years. As early as 1916, William Jennings Bryan proposed that Miami build a great Pan American University. For a time, planning moved rapidly, with Bryan agreeing to be the chairman emeritus of the new institution. The committee disbanded after the United States entered World War I, but Bryan continued to promote the idea.

Although George had predicted Coral Gables would become a "university suburb" just weeks after he sold the first lots in late 1921, he was not involved in the next push, which began in 1923 under the leadership of Dr. John Dupuis, a local medical doctor, educator, and dairyman. The Dupuis Committee went as far as convincing James Bright to donate land in Hialeah for the new institution. But once again, the idea languished until another new committee surfaced in 1924.

The leaders of the 1924 effort were Judge William E. Walsh and retired banker Frederick Zeigen. Walsh favored the idea of a small outdoor university that would take advantage of Florida's unique climate and location. He and Zeigen, as the full-time pro bono secretary, pulled together a high-powered group of Miami leaders who molded the concept into what they called "The Pan American Outdoor University."[22]

George was not part of this group but kept abreast of its deliberations. On March 12, after word got out that they were about to seek a charter and select a site, George, away on one of his business trips to New York, sent Walsh a telegram. "Please delay any definite consideration of proposed university site until my return next week," he wrote. "I have a well formulated plan to submit that will put this over much larger than now contemplated and in much less time."[23]

It is hard to say for sure if George's concept was fully developed before the March telegram, but it probably was, because when he met with the committee a short time later, he presented them a carefully thought-out plan that included a gift of 160 acres of land in the new Riviera Section and an additional $5 million, if matched by the community. He also unrolled renderings of the proposed university drawn by Denman Fink and designed by Phineas Paist and Paul Chalfin. "The drawings staggered our imagination," Judge Walsh recalled in a 1950 interview. "We immediately passed a resolution to accept Mr. Merrick's offer." Within a month, the new University of Miami had its charter, with George as a member of the board of regents.

Clearly, George had expanded the group's vision. Instead of a small outdoor college, the University of Miami at Coral Gables, George predicted, would rival California's Leland Stanford University. The drawings depicted twenty-two Spanish Renaissance–style buildings surrounded by man-made lakes and canals. Besides the grand administration building named for his father, his proposal also included a president's house, library, chapel, and stadium. In addition, he envisioned separate buildings for literary activity; physical, chemical, and natural sciences; history; engineering; economics; law; medicine; mental science; music; and art.

On June 3, George financed a sixteen-page special section in Miami newspapers announcing the new university and launching a fundraising program to ensure its success. It included renderings of the proposed campus and photographs of and comments by President Walsh, Secretary Zeigen, and most of the regents, including Williams Jennings Bryan, his daughter, Ruth Bryan Owen, and the publishers of the three major Miami newspapers.

George also included a copy of his 1921 proposal and took the opportunity to explain his prophetic vision for the new university:

> It would not only be a university for Southern Florida and all of Florida as it grows into one of the most populous states of the union, but particularly a university of our own unique tropical America and a university equipped by reason of climate and architecture and our peculiar contact and kinship with Cuba and Central and South America, to supply that definite unfulfilled need of a cultural contact by a university facility with all of Latin America.

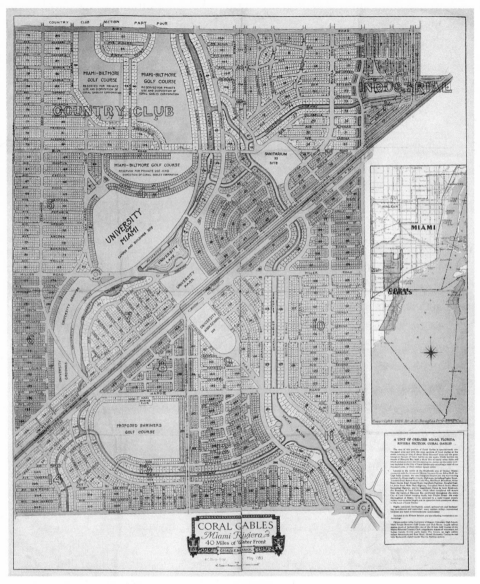

Figure 45. Although barely under way, in May 1925, the new Riviera Section map showed Coral Gables' expanded boundaries and proposed new development. It included the Cocoplum tract George had recently purchased from the Deerings. Permission of HistoryMiami.

In conclusion, President Walsh summed up the feelings of the board and thanked George "for his tremendous gift which has made this university possible."[24]

The special section was not only a boost for the fledgling university but also served as a preview of George's new Riviera Section. It included a detailed map with the university as its centerpiece. In addition to the university drawings, artistic renderings of other proposed developments added to the grandeur of the announcement.

Two days later, with Daniel Burnham's admonition "to make no little plans" ringing in his ears, George formally opened sales in the Riviera Section. He described it as "the greatest of all of Coral Gables' fine sections." In addition to the university, the two-page spread highlighted other proposed projects, including the fifteen-acre University High School, a golf course, clubhouse and temple of the Mahi Shrine, and the Riviera Sanitarium, modeled after the famous Battle Creek Sanitarium in Michigan. These new ventures would be linked by an extended Ponce de Leon Boulevard, a proposed rapid transit, and the largest and most beautiful Florida East Coast railroad station in the state. The Riviera Section would also have a new plaza—the largest yet built in Coral Gables. Called Garibaldi, after the Italian patriot, the circular roundabout, later known as Cocoplum Plaza, would connect LeJeune and Sunset Roads, Granada Boulevard, Main Highway, Riviera Drive, and a bridge across the Coral Gables Waterway. Buyers had the opportunity to reserve lots until June 15. When that date arrived, almost $7 million worth of down payments had poured in from investors all over the country.

At the same time, *The Coral Gables Bulletin* followed up with an issue devoted solely to the Riviera Section and university. It reported that George had asked Denman Fink, described as the "director of artistic growth," to design special light and trolley poles for the Riviera Section. The base, with the words "Coral Gables The Miami Riviera, Fla." in high relief, would also include two male and two female faces and the Spanish castle and lion that Fink featured in the Coral Gables city seal.[25] Despite Coral Gables' phenomenal growth, George still focused on the smallest details to set Coral Gables apart.

June also brought the completion of the Phineas Paist–designed Art Center. Located on a triangular lot across from the proposed Crafts Section

Exhibition Hall, now known as Fred Hartnett Park, the Art Center housed the Coral Gables Corporation artists, engineers, and architects. The company had recently named Phineas Paist its supervising architect, with Denman Fink and Paul Chalfin as artistic advisors. Until the new city had an organized architectural board, initially made up of the same three men, Paist had the authority to decide on the architectural appropriateness of all plans and held veto power over them.

The Art Center also housed an architectural library and the offices of consulting and landscape architect Frank Button, as well as a group of engineers. Although the Coral Gables Corporation no longer offered free plans, staff architects continued to provide advice to those wishing to build in Coral Gables.

Richard Merrick, who was home from New York's Art Students League, and Denman Fink's son, Bob, had studios at the Art Center. Each was a talented artist, and that summer they drew most of the beautiful line drawings found in Coral Gables advertisements. Richard rarely signed his drawings, so it is difficult to positively identify all of his work. Bob Fink, on the other hand, usually signed his, so it is possible to differentiate their renderings, which, in many ways, are quite similar in style. Richard's drawing of the Art Center building appeared in a Coral Gables advertisement in *The New York Times*. It was but one of the weekly advertisements appearing in *The Times*, as well as in other national newspapers.

After Coral Gables' longtime advertising and publicity director E. C. Purcell took over the national advertising campaign—purported to be the tenth-largest in the world—George separated the departments and hired another expert, P. J. Yoder, to take over publicity. Yoder had an extensive résumé that included work for President Theodore Roosevelt and the Federal Trade Commission, as well as serving as director of publicity for the Democratic National Convention. Yoder's acceptance acknowledged that Coral Gables had a national reputation that attracted the highest level of professionals.[26]

Advertising and Publicity was not the only Coral Gables department to undergo change. Before the great expansion of 1925, George had handpicked the small cadre of architects practicing in Coral Gables and named his cousin, George Fink, the supervising architect. Because of their work in Coral Gables, in early 1925, architects Fink, DeGarmo, Hampton, and

Kiehnel, who had designed most of the homes and buildings in Coral Gables, were drawn away by national clients and other developers. Following his New York exposure, Fink had been hired by Vincent Astor and L. B. Thayer to design summer homes for them in upstate New York. He also became the set designer for an Earl Carroll Broadway play called *Florida Girl*, which George had underwritten. Kiehnel became the most prolific Miami Shores architect and Hampton the chief Hollywood, Florida, designer. DeGarmo, who was still designing in Coral Gables, was also active in Miami Shores and Miami Beach. As a result, Phineas Paist, Paul Chalfin, and others, including Frank Wyatt Wood, Coulton Skinner, Harold Steward, and Robert Law Weed, received Coral Gables commissions. Adding to the list were nationally known architects brought in by northern investors who bought huge tracts of land in Coral Gables and announced their own building plans and project architects.

As Coral Gables boomed with new development, the new Coral Gables government barely let out a peep and, for a time, was almost irrelevant. At the second meeting, held a month after the first, commissioners set city boundaries that continued to expand at almost every meeting. The commission also accepted plats presented by the Coral Gables Corporation. Mayor Dammers was absent from the next four meetings, again indicating the small role the commission played in the big picture. George also missed three of the 1925 meetings, leaving most of the early votes to the other three members. Of course, George continued to make most of the decisions outside the formal gatherings. The most important commission votes concerned issuing a series of bonds for public improvements—including an administration building—and passing the first zoning and building codes. The governing body also set the date for the city's first referendum to authorize the new Coral Gables Rapid Transit system.

One of the additions to Coral Gables was a block of land south of Dixie Highway on the east side of LeJeune Road across from a half-completed "Colored School." Although George previously developed the MacFarlane Homestead and St. Alban's subdivisions solely to help Coconut Grove's black community expand, the new proposal was less altruistic. He wanted the property west of LeJeune to complete his Riviera Section, where, according to the School Board minutes, he planned to develop a high-class white residential neighborhood. But not forgetting his commitment and close connection to the Grove's black community, he promised the School Board and the community that he would build a new Walter DeGarmo–designed school at his expense in Coral Gables Mediterranean style and develop a new subdivision for blacks called Golden Gate.[27]

At the same time, George and his Coral Gables Corporation were lobbying the School Board to build what he first called University High School. Like the Grammar School, he offered an extended payment plan to convince the board to proceed with a group of Coral Gables–style Mediterranean buildings designed by George Fink. After they purchased fifteen acres across from the proposed University of Miami for $6,000 an acre, George made sure that the Coral Gables Construction Company submitted the lowest bid so he would have control over construction. In July, the board accepted his low bid for what he now called Ponce de Leon High School. Construction began immediately on the first three buildings—a classroom structure, home economics building, and gymnasium.[28]

Even though George had outdistanced all of his competitors, Addison Mizner's national reputation and his recently received Order of Isabella the Catholic by the king of Spain eclipsed George's and added to Boca Raton's cache. The Cloister, a new Mizner-designed Ritz-Carlton hotel in Boca Raton, gave the Biltmore its first competition, at least in the minds of Palm Beach society and rich Boca Raton investors such as the Vanderbilts and DuPonts.

Locally, Miami Shores, which now claimed twenty-eight hundred acres and a new business district, was way behind Coral Gables when it came to actual development. Still, in reading its ads and learning that its new Arch Creek section was oversubscribed by $11 million, a buyer could easily be lured into thinking it was comparable to Coral Gables.

As a growing myriad of developers filled Miami's newspapers with advertisements, *The Miami Herald* claimed it had set a world record in pages of advertising. By this time, the new *Miami Tribune*, *The Miami Herald*, *The Miami Daily News*, and a tabloid called *The Illustrated Daily Tab* were all in business. Each was crammed with real estate ads and announcements of new development.

In July, twenty thousand people attended the opening of the new Schultze and Weaver–designed Miami News Tower, which, like the Biltmore, referenced Spain's Giralda. In honor of its inauguration, the Cox Company published a 504-page edition with full-color section covers. The company claimed it was the largest newspaper ever printed. Of course, stories about Coral Gables as well as numerous advertisements helped fill the pages.

A few days earlier, Miamians and the nation were shocked to learn that on July 26, William Jennings Bryan had unexpectedly died in his sleep. He was still in Dayton, Tennessee, following his controversial role in the so-called Monkey Trial. He had just completed his testimony as a key witness in the eleven-day trial of John Thomas Scopes, who had been arrested for teaching evolution in a Dayton school. While the participants in a packed courtroom dealt with stifling heat, Clarence Darrow, a nationally famous defense attorney, grilled Bryan on his beliefs as an expert on the biblical story of creation. The heated exchange continued for hours as Bryan defended his position. Although Scopes was convicted and fined $100, the pressure, heat, and unprecedented ridicule took its toll on Bryan. Four days later, he was dead. George grieved not only for the death of a friend and supporter but for the greater loss to the University of Miami, which Bryan had championed for more than a decade and in whose future he had planned to have a key role.

The Florida Boom hit its peak in early fall after national capitalists increased their Miami investments. Several of the largest and most influential focused on Coral Gables. Atlanta's Builders Finance Company, headed by Coca-Cola investor Lindsey Hopkins and H. W. Nichols, developer of Atlanta's Druid Hills, was one of the first. In July, with fifty homes already under construction following an April investment, Hopkins and Nichols announced they would invest an additional $1.6 million for fifty more homes. At the same time, they promised to build four hundred more residences during the next eighteen months.[29]

A short time later, the American Building Corporation, made up of a group of millionaire industrialists from Cincinnati, announced plans to build a thousand Coral Gables homes at the cost of $75 million. They brought in developer and future Ohio Governor Myers Y. Cooper to oversee the operation from his new office in the Crafts Section. At George's and his architect's suggestion, the company agreed to introduce a new and unique element to Coral Gables. They would create a series of villages, or compounds, in new styles, including Venetian, Persian, Italian, Pioneer, Tangier, Mexican, French, African Bazaar, East Indian, and Dutch South

African. Each home would cost a minimum of $30,000. They would not only hire local architects but also bring in several others with national reputations in the proposed styles.[30]

Days later, George announced details for the 568-foot-wide new entrance, which would wrap around the corner of Douglas Road and Eighth Street. He promised it would be "the largest and most distinctive of all Coral Gables gateways." Designed by Denman Fink with Phineas Paist, it would become an authentic Spanish village filled with apartments, distinctive shops, and cafes. The central plaza, dubbed the Plaza Don Quixote, would have a monumental statue of Cervantes by New York sculptor Karl Illava. Capitalizing on Denman Fink's reputation as the designer of all the entrances and plazas and the Venetian Casino, George promised the new entrance would outshine all of Fink's previous work, as well as all other Coral Gables projects, except the Biltmore Hotel.[31]

Hardly a day went by without another major announcement. On August 24, George opened the new Biltmore Section and the Country Club Section Part Six. The Biltmore Section had been developed on the former LeJeune groves. After years of negotiation, George finally convinced pioneer Charles LeJeune to sell him his 160-acre homestead for $2.5 million.

The Biltmore Section included a high-end retail area on Biltmore Way west of LeJeune Road that ads proclaimed would soon become the "Fifth Avenue Business District." Newspapers reported that George was in New York negotiating with a major New York department store to locate on the street. The new section also would have luxury apartments and "probably" be the site of the new City of Coral Gables Civic Center. The two new sections would be linked by the proposed Coral Gables Rapid Transit, which traveled down Coral Way from Miami to Biltmore Way and then south on Segovia.[32] Two days after the first day of sales, Sales Director DeLong announced that the Coral Gables Corporation had sold almost $6 million worth of lots on the first day.

George had also announced another new million-dollar hotel called The Anastasia in the Country Club Section Part Six. Designed by George Fink in what he described as pure Mediterranean—a combination of Medieval, Spanish, early Italian, and Moorish styles—it was three stories tall with a six-story tower and had 310 rooms. Ads claimed it had the longest frontage of any hotel in the world. It also included an interior patio and elegant interior spaces with decorated pecky-cypress ceilings.[33] Workmen labored around the clock to have it open at the start of the next season. Ultimately, it would have an unexpected future use, but initially it was simply another luxury hotel being rushed to completion.

Although the new sections had more high-priced homes than the earlier ones, George continued to be concerned about those who now were priced out of the market. To mitigate the problem and help ease the housing shortage, he initiated cooperative apartments that, at the time, were rare and considered innovative. Under his plan, buyers would own their apartment as well as a percentage of the common rooms. The first was the elegant three-story San Juan Apartments on Avenue Menores, marking "a new ideal in development." Announcements of other co-op apartments in the Douglas Section soon followed. Owning an individual apartment was a new concept for most Miamians, but people arriving from the North eagerly purchased the new units, which sold as robustly as single-family homes.

Amid the heady growth, an event occurred that garnered only small notice in the press. On August 17, the Florida East Coast Railway declared a temporary freight embargo on Florida's east coast because all the railroad yards and warehouses were full of arriving freight—especially building material. Officials promised it would probably last no more than a week. Five days later, *The Miami News* editorialized for a "Decongestion Day" and asked residents to clear all the unclaimed freight to make room for the thousands of sidetracked cars that could not get into Miami. The situation was exacerbated by an acute labor shortage, making it difficult to find laborers to unload the freight and secure a truck to remove it. At first, no one paid much attention to the news and the selling frenzy continued unabated. No one realized that the freight embargo was destined to become the first nail in the coffin of the Florida Boom.

George and other Miami developers barely blinked because sales not only continued but exploded. Between August 25 and 31, George announced five new projects. The first was the San Sebastian Apartment Hotel, designed by Phineas Paist, in the Crafts Section. It would be built by the Coral Gables Corporation specifically for employees who were having difficulty finding housing. The following day, a drawing of the first home in the American Building Corporation's Italian Village appeared. Next came the announcement that the Miami Coliseum Corporation, under the leadership of J. K. Dorn, would build a million-dollar auditorium on Douglas Road acreage donated by George. Designed by A. Ten Eyck Brown, who was also designing the new Dade County Courthouse, it would be the first facility in the Miami area large enough to accommodate conventions, concerts, operas, and other cultural and athletic events. In addition, a beautiful rendering of the new Sales Headquarters, soon to rise on the corner of Coral Way and Ponce de Leon Boulevard, appeared in the press. Designed by Phineas Paist with Denman Fink and Paul Chalfin, it was reminiscent of the Palace of Charles V in Spain's Alhambra. Called the Colonnade, it, along with the others, showed that George's Coral Gables was growing into a more exclusive enclave than originally planned.

He ended the month with the announcement that Coral Gables residents had gone to the polls and voted to support the acquisition of the new Coral Gables Rapid Transit system already under construction. Capping that was the euphoric news that August sales of almost $13 million had exceeded the total sales for 1924. To tell this remarkable story, George paid well-known author Rex Beach $18,000 to write a history of Coral Gables, entitled *The Miracle of Coral Gables*. At this point, the title seemed especially appropriate. As soon as it was published, national advertisements included an order form to receive a free copy.

Feeling energized and happy following August's stellar achievements, George traveled to the Grove Park Inn in Asheville, North Carolina, to spend a few days with Eunice, who had been away all summer. Unfortunately, the brief sojourn did little to repair what George perceived as Eunice's indifference and lack of praise for his work. George was not blameless. In Eunice's absence, word got out that he had invited some visiting dignitaries to a drinking party with some showgirls at their South Greenway home. He also had been spending time with Helen Freeland, an old friend of his sister Ethel, whom he had known for many years. She was beautiful, well educated, and accomplished, having once been the principal of the Orange Glade School. They shared a love of books and history and became reacquainted during the time she and her husband, Judge William Freeland, were planning to build a large Italian-style golf course home on Santa Maria.

September began with voters going to the polls to decide whether the City of Miami could annex the towns of Coconut Grove, Silver Bluff, and Buena Vista and the neighborhoods of Lemon City, Little River, and Allapattah. Ironically, Coral Gables was not part of the deal, even though George had been promoting the creation of a larger, more inclusive Greater Miami for years. After the votes were tallied, Greater Miami was born despite the fact that the residents of Coconut Grove opposed it. Under the law, the total number of votes decided the outcome, so outnumbered residents of Coconut Grove became part of the City of Miami against their will. In one day, the City of Miami grew from thirteen to fifty square miles and touched the eastern and part of the northern borders of Coral Gables.

September also brought the sad news that James Deering had died aboard his yacht during a return trip from Europe. Miamians were saddened that one of their most famous residents would no longer be holding court in his beautiful Villa Vizcaya. He was a local icon and his Miami home had not only elevated South Florida's architectural tastes but also influenced George's selection of an architectural style for Coral Gables. George, however, had other reasons to grieve. Deering planned to help develop the land George had recently purchased from him and his brother. In many ways, Deering's death was also a deathblow for George's grandiose plans for his soon-to-be announced Biscayne Bay Section. Of course George would be the last to admit that possibility.

A short time later, the first section of the long-awaited St. Joseph Academy and College for Young Women opened on Indian Mound Trail and Palos. Designed in the Spanish style by Walter DeGarmo with Phineas Paist, the new school immediately reached capacity with two hundred girls enrolled in kindergarten through grade twelve. The following Sunday, the priest from Gesu Church in downtown Miami made history when he held Coral Gables' first Catholic Mass at the new school.

By this time, the iron skeleton of the Biltmore Hotel's impressive Giralda Tower had reached full height and workers were laboring day and night to finish the grand hotel for its announced January 15 opening. John Bowman arrived in late September to check on its progress. Miami newspapers were filled with stories about the new hotel and pictures of Bowman and George. In one story, Bowman described the planned opening events and promised they would be the "most brilliant of its kind in the history of Florida."[34] In another, he announced that architect Schultze had just returned from Venice, Italy, where he bought twenty-five authentic gondolas that were being shipped to Coral Gables. They, along with twenty-five singing Italian gondoliers, would ply the soon-to-be-completed Coral Gables Waterway, linking the hotel with Tahiti Beach, also under construction.[35]

Despite robust sales, storm clouds began to appear after seven Ohio bankers saw millions of dollars leaving their banks as depositors headed for Florida. In response, they launched a major advertising campaign, warning their customers to beware of Florida hucksters who promised huge profits. (Their outcry later caused the state of Ohio to pass what were called "blue sky laws" that forbade certain firms from selling Florida real estate in Ohio.)

Unfortunately, the Ohio story was only the beginning. The Scripps-Howard newspaper chain took up the cause and printed a series of articles claiming the Florida Boom was dead. As others joined the chorus, Florida leaders realized they needed to do more than cry sour grapes to counteract the growing negative publicity.

On October 9, Governor Martin, a who's who of Florida developers, including George, and some of the state's most influential investors arranged for a luncheon in a banquet room at New York's Waldorf Astoria Hotel to correct what they called the "misconception." They invited representatives of all the major national magazines and newspapers, with the exception of Scripps-Howard, to come and learn what they called "The Truth about Florida."

A myriad of pro-Florida speakers made convincing arguments while admitting some developers and out-of-state salesman had "overstated things." In a give-and-take session, Governor Martin asked for suggestions from the audience on how to curb these excesses. He also complained about what Floridians viewed as unjust criticism.[36] Like parrots repeating a well-learned phrase, the group argued that the bubble was not going to burst, because there was no bubble. Instead, it was simply Florida's time to get long-overdue attention. Once people discovered its natural attributes, rapid development was inevitable.

When the luncheon concluded, Kenneth Ballinger, *The Miami Herald* reporter on the scene, wrote: "Florida today made her appeal for truth in advertising in the very heart of the nation's publishing center, an appeal designed to still the propaganda that is being circulated to the detriment of the state."

Most of the Florida delegation felt better after the meeting, but as a precaution they promptly raised $20,000 to fight back if the anti-Florida propaganda continued.[37] Their promotional campaign had positive results. Several national magazines, including *The Saturday Evening Post*, published pro-Florida stories. In a follow-up article in *The New York Times*, an executive of the Florida Real Estate Board summed up their message: "The bubble would burst," he wrote, "when the sun decides not to shine any more, when the Gulf Stream ceases to flow, when the railroads lengthen their schedule and they stop making Fords. Then Florida will slow up."[38]

George returned from the New York meeting determined to prove the naysayers wrong. He increased his national advertising and promotional campaign. He penned an article in Joe Mitchell Chapple's *National Magazine* entitled "Is There a Florida Bubble?" in which he systematically refuted such an idea and later included the article in his advertisements. He focused on what he had achieved in only four years. Any visitor could see that Coral Gables was no huckster's illusion. It was real—a sixteen-square-mile planned city with elegant plazas and gateways, almost two thousand homes completed or under construction, a unique Venetian Casino, two golf courses, a viable business district, elegant apartment buildings, an operating trolley system, three schools enrolling more than one thousand students, and a half-dozen hotels completed or under construction. Add miles of landscaped boulevards, winding streets, tropical waterways, and the city's brightest new stars—the Biltmore Hotel and proposed University of Miami—and you had proof that, at least in Coral Gables, the only bubble came from celebratory champagne.

Many later said that if George had been content with what he had achieved by the end of 1925, he could have completed his dream city and avoided subsequent nightmares. But the lure of Biscayne Bay proved irresistible and his growing wealth removed all the fetters and allowed his dream to soar as high as his fertile imagination would take it.

On December 9, George announced the opening of the Biscayne Bay Section, predicting it would be "the greatest achievement ever undertaken in this country." Presales would begin the following day on the first section, with general sales beginning on December 15. In typical George fashion, Miami newspapers were inundated with news stories and daily double-page advertisements promoting the new section. The following advertisement in *The Miami News* on December 12 summed up the recurring sales pitch.

> Today—the same George E. Merrick visions another and far greater Coral Gables! A city with six miles of bayfront—with charming South Sea Isles rising from Biscayne Bay—with miles of broad boulevards and great waterways—with imposing Miami Biltmore Casino, International Yacht Club, imposing hotels, thousands of homes. A vastly glorified enlargement of the present Coral Gables. . . . Who will say today—with the actual evidence of the past four years before their eyes—that an American Riviera such as George Merrick plans is impossible?

Almost three thousand lots went on sale opening day, with 1,500 as low as $5,500–$7,500 with a predevelopment discount of 10 percent. A full-page "tentative comprehensive map" showed waterways and lakes, including one named Lago Eunice, dotting the landscape. Several major highways ran southwestward through the tract, plus the Havana Malecon–inspired "Biera Mar" causeway connecting a string of man-made "South Sea" islands.

Following the advertising blitz, George created a sixteen-page oversize brochure touting the Biscayne Bay Section. Unlike most of his other brochures, it contained no drawings or photographs, but only a full-page map of the new section. This brochure was more like a passionate closing argument to a jury of the public. It reminded scoffers of past successes and presented compelling arguments as to why George Merrick could still be counted on to turn his dreams into reality. "With the background and impetus of such an accomplishment," the text read, "a building goal of two hundred and fifty million in the finest of all Coral Gables property which extends along the shores of Biscayne Bay for a distance of more than six and a half miles will be easy of attainment." The text concluded by adding the new Coral Gables Corporation to the mix: "The vision of the builder of Coral Gables, George E. Merrick, so often in the past translated into accomplished facts, sees five thousand homes soon to be constructed in the Biscayne Bay Section, and as always heretofore, the Coral Gables

Corporation will back his vision with its dollars and will put full force of its earnings behind such a building objective."

The promotion worked. The first day of sales topped $7 million, another new record.

In the midst of all the hoopla around the opening of the Biscayne Bay Section, George's publicity men were busy cranking out other ways to promote Coral Gables. One of the most interesting was the plan to launch a midwinter event from New Year's Eve through the first two days of the new year. At first it was to be a strictly Coral Gables affair called "The Fiesta of the American Tropics." After the Miami Chamber of Commerce got involved, the concept expanded and included participation by the cities of Miami, Hialeah, and Miami Beach. Their joint proclamation even made super-promoter George sound bland.

"The Fiesta of the American Tropics—Our Season of Fiesta when Love, Good Fellowship, Merry Making and Good Sport," it read, "shall prevail throughout our domains." The proclamation added, "The most Richly Blessed Community of our most Bountifully Endowed State of the most Highly Enterprising People of the Universe."

In preparation for the festival, George constructed a stadium near the proposed Coliseum. It was not the grand structure that had been announced earlier but, instead, a large facility made up of wooden bleachers. Although the stadium wasn't finished, Coral Gables sponsored the first football game there on December 5 as a dress rehearsal for the planned Fiesta event. The games were between Rollins College, George's alma mater, and Oglethorpe University, followed by a high school matchup between Miami and Oglethorpe High. It was not an auspicious beginning. A week of heavy rains flooded the field, causing one reporter to quip that it was more like a swim meet than a football game. The railroad embargo, which was supposed to last a week, was now in its fourth month. Steamships, used to keep supplies coming, also called for an embargo after large numbers had to hover offshore, unable to come into the crowded harbor to unload. To deal with the crisis, developers hired anything that would float to bring in building supplies desperately needed to feed the boom. The Miami harbor filled with tall ships, their wooden masts looking strangely anachronistic against the iron skeletons of skyscrapers under construction.

Despite clear signs that the boom was starting to fizzle, George and the

Coral Gables Corporation presented a positive face. On December 27, George placed a full-page ad in the newspapers with the blaring headline: "When Coral Gables' Ships Come In." While acknowledging the problem, the ad blamed "the embargo which railroads and steamships raised because they were unable out of their wealth of resources to cope with the task which the building of a great city imposed on them. . . . The Spirit of Miami rose to the occasion and the men of the city accomplished as individuals what the big railroads and steamships could not perform." The pep talk concluded with the announcement that Coral Gables had brought in supplies on four three-hundred-ton vessels from New York, Baltimore, Charleston, Jacksonville, Havana, Mobile, and New Orleans. "They bring cargoes of needed materials far more precious in our work than Spanish galleons of old ever carried to Spain . . . [and] are symbols which represent the definite assurance of promise—fulfillment of continuation of performance which in the past has been the rock-bed upon which profitable investments in Coral Gables have been solidly built."

As the year ended, *The Miami News* included a five-column news story reviewing Coral Gables' accomplishments in 1925 month by month. It included a detailed description of more than forty major projects, most of which were completed or under way. The year officially closed with the announcement that Coral Gables sales had topped $100 million and the city had recorded $25 million in building permits.[39]

"Impossible things were happening under my very eyes," T. H. Weigall wrote, "and with everyone else, I was living now in a wild dream in which it seemed like every desire would be inevitably realized."[40]

~12

New Questions

> Who will question the power and resources of the man who
> created and built the present Coral Gables—to now carry
> on—on vastly larger lines—and with greater vision—
> the concept of the American Riviera?
>
> *The Miami News*, December 29, 1925

It was January 15, 1926. George, ensconced in his new office suite at the summit of the Biltmore Hotel's Giralda Tower, awaited the start of the hotel's inaugural dinner. The opening seemed like a miracle because five days earlier, the brigantine *Prinz Valdemar* ran aground in Government Cut as it was being towed to Miami Beach to become a floating hotel. The situation grew worse when it capsized, completely blocking the cut and entrance to the Miami harbor. Already overcrowded because of the railroad embargo, now in its fifth month, the harbor was critical to bringing in building materials. The latest problem completely stopped shipping and, as a result, most construction and new projects had to be postponed or abandoned. The Biltmore was the exception. Construction manager Charles Flynn had already figured out ways to bring in workers, food, furniture, and other items needed to open the hotel on schedule. In addition, John Bowman had arranged for two Biltmore Special trains to transport dignitaries and guests for opening night.

The *Prinz Valdemar* incident occurred just a week after the conclusion of the Fiesta of the American Tropics. Thousands packed partially completed Bayfront Park to cheer Miami City Manager Frank Wharton as he launched the events by presenting newly arrived "Ponce de Leon" and his entourage

Figure 46. George, joined by his secretary, sits at his desk in his fifteenth-floor suite in the Biltmore tower. University of Miami Special Collections. Courtesy of Mildred Merrick.

with a key to the city. The dignitaries joined the automobile parade as it looped the first section of Biscayne Boulevard, which, like the park, had recently been pumped up from bay bottom. That night, movie star Eugenie Selma was crowned Fiesta Queen during an elaborate theatrical production at the new Coral Gables Stadium—described as South Florida's largest outdoor venue.

Fiesta events continued on New Year's Day and added to the positive mood. As crowds grew, a second, larger parade with more than 350 entries snaked through downtown Miami and nearby neighborhoods. Besides bands, civic clubs, and state societies, the largest marching ensemble was the 1,200-member Coral Gables sales force.

Following the parade, more than 16,000 enthusiasts packed the Coral Gables Stadium to witness a football game between the Four Horsemen of Notre Dame and the Princeton All-Stars.

On the next and final day of the Fiesta, Coral Gables again became the center of attention when legendary golfers Bobby Jones and Tommy Armour beat Gene Sarazen and Lou Diegal in an exhibition golf tournament at the Biltmore. Although the golf course had been open a year, this event marked the "official" opening of the newly enhanced eighteen-hole course designed by Donald Ross.

George, in an introspective mood, was alone in the tower, except for his elderly valet, Fletcher. Sipping his favorite Bacardi Carta de Oro, he stood silently, looking north through the suite's twelve-foot-high, cathedral-like window. From what he described as his "High Olympus," he had a mountaintop view of what remained of the old Okra Sink, now home to the hotel and the Congregational Church he built to honor his father. He remembered how concerned his father had been about borrowing money to buy the sink and how he had barely slept until he had paid off the loan. What would he think if he knew his son had more than $40 million in debt?

In the distance George could see miles of wide boulevards, lush landscaping, artistic entrances and plazas, and streets filled with homes. He first fashioned all of this in his imagination as he harvested vegetables and planted grapefruit trees in the rocky pineland on his family's original, 160-acre homestead.

From the south window, he felt like he was seeing the future. Bathed in his favorite south wind, he imagined the new Riviera, Biltmore, and Biscayne Bay Sections filled with homes, apartments, hotels, business establishments, and a new university. He observed the armies of men who had been laboring around-the-clock to complete Tahiti Beach, slated to open within a few weeks. He also noted dredges carving the new Venetian canals, already snaking their way toward Biscayne Bay. Bowman's fleet of Italian gondolas and a group of authentic Italian gondoliers sat poised in the golf course lagoon ready to take hotel guests on a Venetian fantasy.

Gulping another Bacardi, he quietly inspected every detail of his private suite, touching its imported tile floors, hand-carved doors, and antique Spanish furniture. Bowman had recently given him an elaborate antique bed that once belonged to Italian tenor Enrico Caruso. He proudly placed it in his private bedroom, which he dubbed "the Caruso room."

He had come a long way from living with his family in "the shack" and peddling vegetables from a mule cart. He smiled at remembering how people smirked when, just four years earlier, he had come up with his original slogan: "Coral Gables: Where Your Castles in Spain are Made Real." "How all had derided that first romantically wishful slogan of his," he later wrote. "But he had done it. Despite Hell and high water, he had done it. This

Hotel, Club and its Giralda Tower—really was the climax of his whole great doing."[1] Although Heinz Schultz of Schultz & Weaver would get credit for the hotel's beauty and fidelity to Coral Gables ideals, George knew that it was he, with the support of his uncle Denman Fink, Phineas Paist, and Paul Chalfin, who told the world-famous architect his first design looked like a cotton mill. With Bowman's assent, George arranged for Fink, Paist, and Chalfin to take over the artistic work, including color, polychrome woodwork, and other architectural details.

Every time George celebrated another Coral Gables milestone, he thought about his beloved Grandfather Fink. He knew if he were here, he would proclaim in his booming preacher voice: "George, there's nothing like it in the whole length and breadth of Christendom." Finks, including his mother, were known for their lavish praise. His father, however, was different. Perhaps, he mused, if he could see what his son had accomplished tonight, he might give him the paternal praise he had so desperately craved.

"His father was always right," George wrote, and "he [George] was another edition of Grandfather Fink. A Fink like himself needed praise!" Eunice didn't seem to understand a temperament like his, either. "Praise does more for me than Bacardi," he thought. "Why couldn't she know it and sometimes, just sometimes, praise him?"[2] Helen Freeland did every time they were together, including that very afternoon.

Tonight's dinner was the second spectacular Biltmore celebration. The previous night, a thousand men had gathered at a private stag dinner to honor him and Bowman. The Country Club Ballroom was set up with long rows of tables filled with the formally dressed gentlemen, who stood and cheered as he and Bowman entered. Guests included senators, governors, mayors, and both local and national newspaper publishers. Many had come because of Bowman, yet George hoped they also came to see what he called "a City founded on what men usually, and of long custom, called intangibles. . . . And they were here to approve. To glorify. To hope for his city—this new kind of City, and even greater success."[3]

Keynote speakers included Bowman, Governor Cox, former presidential candidate and publisher of *The Miami News*, and Frank Shutts, attorney and publisher of *The Miami Herald*. Usually confident George was nervous about speaking to what he called the greatest assemblage he had ever encountered. "Still," he wrote, "something in him exulted in the

Figure 47. For George, the magnificent Biltmore Hotel with its Giralda tower would set the stage for other major projects he planned in collaboration with John McEntee Bowman. State Archives of Florida, Florida Memory.

opportunity . . . an opportunity to show them all, something of the soul which he knew was within him—of the ideas of Beauty and Romance, Poetry, yes and Music too that had impelled, yes and had driven him, into the building of this City."[4] When he rose to speak, he once again received a standing ovation. The following day, the local press published his speech, entitled "Towers of Inspiration," almost word for word.

George's spirits rose even more when he read the glowing reviews he, Bowman, and the hotel received. *The Miami Daily News* included a long article about him, his vision, and his unprecedented success. As in the past, George gave credit to others—his father for the original idea for Coral Gables and the black workers with whom he had worked side by side. "I do not believe any great body of men worked more wholeheartedly at a single job than the men who have been associated with me in building our city." The press, however, reserved their accolades for George and Bowman. "There is little space in the world today for dreamers," one article concluded, "but when dreamers of the type of John McEntee Bowman and George Merrick pool their dreams together and make them come true, then the entire world pays them homage."[5]

That afternoon, Bowman had personally taken his guests—many of whom had arrived that morning on the two Biltmore Special trains—on a tour of the hotel. From the tower suites and the grand ballrooms to the kitchen and laundry, he proudly displayed the Biltmore's modern innovations encased within a twelfth-century-style masterpiece. Even sophisticated New Yorkers, who were used to elegant Manhattan hostelries, could not believe the detail and artistry of the new hotel. Most concluded it was Bowman's masterpiece.

The jangle of the phone brought George back to the present. His wife was waiting for him in the lobby. When they met, Eunice, beautiful in a red cape with a fox collar, gave him a warm greeting. Despite their problems, George knew he could count on her to stand by him on such occasions. Maybe tonight, he silently hoped, she would realize that "the liquor, the women and all that she hated and hated him for, all that was nothing—less than nothing at all."[6] The only things that truly mattered to him were Eunice and his only child, whose name was Coral Gables.

When the handsome couple entered the ballroom, more than a thousand guests stood and applauded. Besides the ballroom, people sat in every available public space, including the lobbies, terraces, and even the grounds.

This event did not include formal speeches but the accolades continued to flow. Feeling both humble and proud, George, caught up in the spirit of the evening and relaxed by his Bacardi warm-up, did something he never did—he danced. He held Eunice especially close and thought maybe she was silently proud of him. He also danced with Helen who, as usual, exuded praise.

When the evening ended, and he and Eunice returned to their South Greenway Drive home, he hoped that tonight she would give him the praise he had long sought. Unfortunately, it was not to be.

"Was that the best you could do?" Eunice asked in an unusually angry voice. "You know what I mean! Get yourself sodden with Bacardi and make a holy show of yourself to all that room full of people all looking at you dancing, dancing all the night."[7] His attention to Helen Freeland had not gone unnoticed.

The heated encounter ended when George slammed the door and retreated to his room. Disappointed and angry, he considered moving into his Giralda Tower for good. But whenever he had thoughts like that, he recoiled with what he described as "the chill of loneliness away from her. . . . It was different when he got away from her by accident . . . but to cold bloodedly, deliberately, plan a life, a month or even a night away from her—it left him chilly, empty, lonely."[8]

The following day, *The New York Times* and other national newspapers covered the events. Locally, an editorial in *The Miami Daily News* thanked George and Bowman for counteracting the rampant negative publicity in the national press.

The people of Miami needed positive news because the *Prinz Valdemar* still blocked the harbor. Even the most optimistic had to admit that any comeback of the floundering boom was probably not going to happen. Publicly, however, their positive rhetoric continued. "Real estate men say a digestive period had set in," *The New York Times* reported. "'Florida,' they say, 'may suffer from a slight attack of colic due to swallowing more than she could really digest. But the attack won't be serious. Reverses can come,' they say, 'but Florida as a great vacation state is here to stay.'"[9]

If George was worried, he kept it to himself. Despite lagging land sales, he announced the opening of several additional Biscayne Bay sections and focused on completing Tahiti Beach. Nothing, however, could compete with his enthusiasm for the University of Miami.

On February 4, George joined other dignitaries and seven thousand supporters to lay the cornerstone of the university's first building, named for his father. The land he donated had been cleared but construction had not begun. In honor of the occasion, university administrators built a two-story wooden platform, covered with colorful bunting, as a stage for the dignitaries. Flag-waving children marched and sang and orchestras played, adding excitement and pomp to what the press described as one more "greatest" event in Miami's history. When it was George's turn to speak, the huge throng stood and cheered:

Some days ago at the opening of the Miami-Biltmore Hotel and Country Club I said that that was the biggest and proudest moment for me in the history of Coral Gables. This moment is far greater; and means vastly more. For today we are entering upon the realest thing that Miami can achieve. Hotels, Clubs, all the other great material things that Miami has accomplished, beautiful wonderful glorious though they be, are but of ephemeral insignificance beside this great enterprise of permanently real and vital influences upon the lives and hearts of the present and future Miami that we are here beginning.

When he read the cornerstone inscription he had written about his father, his eyes filled with tears and his voice cracked: "This building is dedicated to the memory of Solomon Greasley Merrick, 1858–1911. Minister, Scholar, Pioneer, Unselfish Builder of Material Achievements. Persevering founder of spiritual and intellectual foundations that underlie, also, this very stone."

Managing Regent Frederick Zeigen concluded the program with a tribute to Althea Merrick, who sat proudly on the grandstand. After Zeigen reviewed the ambitious plans for the new university, he invited several regents to come forward to place a piece of memorabilia in a copper box that would be embedded in the cornerstone. Items included the university

Figure 48. On February 4, 1926, just two weeks after the Biltmore opened, George spoke at the cornerstone laying of the University of Miami. For the rest of his life, he would say the University of Miami was his most important legacy. Courtesy of Gael Stanley.

Figure 49. The new South Seas Isles–themed Tahiti Beach opened in February 1926 to rave reviews. Guests marveled at the fantasy. Permission of HistoryMiami.

charter, a copy of the contract between George and the university, a current newspaper, copies of the architectural plans, and a picture of George Merrick. The final presentation came from George. Not surprisingly, he added a picture of his father.

Following the ceremony, George hosted a seven-course dinner at the Biltmore Country Club to honor the regents and almost a thousand supporters. The dinner also provided a boost for the university's fundraising campaign.

Just two days after the cornerstone laying, Tahiti Beach opened on schedule with an invitation-only preview hosted by the Coral Gables Corporation. Designer Paul Chalfin had adapted a similar, but never-built, South Seas–themed enclave he had originally planned for James Deering. The picturesque ensemble included hundreds of coconut palms, a whitesand beach, a South Seas atoll, a bandstand shaped like a seashell and a large dance floor. He also convinced a group of Seminoles to add their signature palmetto thatch to more than one hundred bath houses and pavilions.

Cornelius Vanderbilt Jr., who owned the *Illustrated Daily Tab*, wrote that Tahiti Beach, "as yet, is the most original idea we have seen in Miami. The newcomer will stand spellbound, enthralled by the sheer natural beauty and simple grandeur of the scene as it presents itself."[10]

The public agreed and, as one writer described, "stormed the place." A seemingly endless line of automobiles clogged Main Highway and Cocoplum Plaza, waiting to enter the mangrove forest that opened to reveal a one-thousand-space parking lot soon filled to capacity. Once again, George had created a unique public gathering place that some said rivaled the Venetian Pool and Casino. But what mattered most to him, and to Bowman, was that Coral Gables and the new Biltmore Hotel finally had a beach and a waterfront site for another Bowman hotel, casino, and yacht club.

A few weeks later, the northern and southern sections of the new waterway merged, providing direct access from the Biltmore to Tahiti Beach via gondola. "Although Rome was not built in a day," a writer for the *Miami Riviera* opined, in Coral Gables, "Venice is being built in a few weeks." When the city lit the authentically crafted Venetian waterway lampposts, it appeared that George's promotion of "Coral Gables: Miami Riviera: 40 Miles of Waterfront" was starting to ring true. Now all that was needed were homes to complete the picture.

Following the opening of Tahiti Beach, George and Eunice joined her parents in the Keys to celebrate their tenth wedding anniversary and, with Lillian Peacock's reinforcement, to focus on each other. Although neither wanted a divorce, for some time they had been leading separate lives, except when public duties brought them together. Eunice's annual four-month absence added to the strain. Only George's closest advisers knew of the growing problems and often tried to keep him away from his drinking buddies and other distractions.

Shortly after their return, Eunice cancelled her usual trip north and, for the first time since their marriage, remained in Coral Gables all summer. At about the same time, George purchased a fifteen-acre estate in Nassau, called "The Hermitage," as a gift for her.

Besides their Bahamian retreat, George also announced plans to build a new home on the Biltmore Golf Course, hoping others would follow his example. Designed by Denman Fink and Phineas Paist, who worked closely with George on the design, it encompassed two full blocks and on the street side was surrounded by a high wall. In the style of an Italian villa, newspaper accounts predicted it would be "one of the most beautiful residences in the entire South."

The mansion had two parts, one of which was described as George's private quarters. It had a separate entrance with an elevator and ten rooms, including a large library and study overlooking the swimming pool, two bedrooms, and a "huge" roof garden. The rest of the house had the usual living room, dining room, kitchen, sun parlor, another library, four more bedrooms (including one for Eunice), servants' quarters, and a six-car garage. The beautiful renderings that appeared in the local press and in Coral Gables advertisements showed two front elevations, one facing Ferdinand Court and the other facing the golf course waterway. The golf course entrance included a large outdoor porch and loggia. The city issued a building permit and workmen began digging the foundation, predicting it would be finished by fall. But for some reason, construction stopped soon after it began.

Amid continuing bad news on the economic front, South Florida's building spree slowed but, unlike in many other parts of Florida, did not stop. A short time after the Biltmore opened, South Florida welcomed two more Giralda Towers—the Roney Plaza on Miami Beach and the Everglades Hotel on Biscayne Boulevard. Advertisements for subdivisions continued to fill the pages of Miami newspapers. But despite the hype, the removal of the *Prinz Valdemar*, and the end of the railroad embargo, the damage had been done. George, however, refused to give in. Instead of scaling back like other developers did, he expanded. He enlarged the seating capacity in the Coral Gables Country Club from 1,500 to 3,000. Next, he paid a small fortune to bring in Paul Whiteman, arguably the most popular orchestra leader in America, to launch its grand reopening and lure people into Coral Gables. He moved Jan Garber to Tahiti Beach, where his orchestra played for nightly dances. Both Whiteman and Garber also entertained guests at special Venetian Casino events and hosted national radio broadcasts.

The Coral Gables Corporation welcomed its first residents into the partially finished San Sebastian apartments and resumed work on the nearby Anastasia Hotel, which had stopped when the Biltmore became the corporation's first priority. The new Douglas Entrance—Puerta del Sol—was also under construction. Newspaper accounts described the four-square-block enclave as "a town in old Spain."

The corporation's other major project was the Colonnade, rising on the corner of Coral Way and Ponce de Leon Boulevard. Slated to become the new sales office, it added a touch of grandeur to the Business District and Crafts Sections. Ponce de Leon Boulevard, which connected the two areas, showcased fifteen new buildings and proved that George had kept his promise to create an active downtown.

A private corporation broke ground in the Crafts Section for what was called a "Community Market." It was near the circle, whose future seemed to change almost weekly. The newest plan included a grand Seaboard Railroad Station with exhibition halls on the upper floors. George and his team continued to push for the Seaboard Railroad to come to Coral Gables with an electrical extension that would travel down Ponce and connect with the proposed Florida East Coast terminal across from the University of Miami.

George had become a public mass transportation enthusiast when he lived in New Jersey with his uncle Denman Fink while attending New York Law School. He witnessed Forest Hills Gardens coming to life after the Long Island Railroad connected it to Manhattan. Hoping for the same outcome he had seen in New York, and later in Shaker Heights, Ohio, he included a trolley in his original plan and later a railroad.

After the first trolley arrived in April 1925, he organized a company through the Coral Gables Corporation to build what he called the Coral Gables Rapid Transit from downtown Miami into Coral Gables and eventually points south. To create a route for the larger, faster cars, as well as another highway into Coral Gables, he pushed and helped finance the extension of Coral Way from Douglas Road to Southeast Third Avenue.

Like most of George's projects, the Rapid Transit was completed in record time. The line, which had its inaugural run on May 28, commenced in front of Burdines' Flagler Street store and ran south on Miami Avenue to Thirteenth Street and then west onto the median of newly completed Coral Way. After a twenty-minute run with a few stops along the way, the Rapid Transit arrived at the intersection of Coral Way and Ponce de Leon Boulevard. The *Miami Riviera* reported that spectators "looked with wonder" as passengers waved from what it described as "unusually attractive" pink,

Figure 50. George planned many high-rise buildings that were never built. One of the first was a major addition to the Tallman Hospital (now Coral Gables Hospital) (*foreground*) which opened in 1926. Author's collection.

fifty-two-passenger cars. Within a month, George added an electric loop down Coral Way from Ponce to Biltmore Way and then south on Segovia to Bird and back to Ponce. Before the year ended, he would extend the line to Sunset Drive.

Although George and the other executives of the Coral Gables Corporation focused on more than half a dozen major projects, they also courted private developers. The Tallman Hospital, Coral Gables' first major medical facility, opened in the Crafts Section on Douglas Road and Coconut Grove Drive, with plans to add a thirteen-story building. At the same time, George announced another ambitious project called "The Towers," formerly called the Riviera Sanitarium. Renderings of the proposed "rest resort," located near Blue Road and the waterway, showed five six-story buildings that included two imposing towers. George hoped the famous Kellogg Institute would operate the thousand-room co-operative "rest-recreation-and-health-hotel-home."[11] The Corporation also continued to promote the planned Mahi Temple, Sports Center, and Golf Course on the new Mahi Waterway that bordered South Alhambra Circle. Its expansive Arabian-style buildings were promoted as "the national Mecca of recreation." Another private corporation continued to seek investors for the new Coliseum, which, unlike the others, was actually under construction.

Each new project spurred George forward on his mission to build what he called "a complete community." Nothing fulfilled his dream more than new and expanded educational facilities. By early spring, work had begun on the University of Miami's Merrick Building—George's personal favorite. At the same time, the School Board broke ground at Coral Gables Elementary for a new classroom building, cafeteria, and auditorium, slated for a fall completion. Ponce de Leon High School, although not completed, prepared to admit its first students—525 transfers from Coconut Grove High School, soon to be closed. Private schools also flourished. The Coral Gables Military Academy's two new buildings neared completion. The Montmarte School opened south of Coral Way near Columbus Boulevard and announced plans for a three-story building. Finally, after a flurry of speculation, New York's Scudder School signed a $350,000 contract for a block of land near the University of Miami and announced that it would open a campus in Coral Gables with a building named in honor of Scudder alumna Ethel Merrick Bishop.

George also sought more religious institutions. As a preacher's son, he believed they were central to community well-being and would serve as architectural landmarks. To spur their development, he donated land to Catholic, Episcopal, Baptist, and Universalist congregations. Each announced plans to construct edifices valued at up to $500,000. One of the largest was St. Stephen's Episcopal. Church leaders voted to move from Coconut Grove to a large plot of donated land on Granada Boulevard and University Mall. They published renderings of an impressive Spanish Gothic–style sanctuary and parish house. With great ceremony, church leaders broke ground in March and announced the church would be completed by October.[12]

The Baptists also planned an impressive church called University Baptist on a donated block near the University of Miami at Miller Road and Fontana, which once ran through today's campus. Until they could raise the money for the new building, George loaned them a site on Coconut Grove

Drive, where they built a temporary wooden structure and began regular services. By summer they had almost two hundred members.

After George met with the Catholic bishop in St. Augustine and promised a $100,000 gift if the diocese would build a $500,000 church, the Church of the Little Flower was born, with plans to build on Indian Mound Trail next to St. Joseph's Academy.

The Southern Methodists and Presbyterians also began organizing, and the Jewish community met to discuss the possibility of building a synagogue. In the MacFarlane homestead, the Beulah Wesleyan Methodist Church, then known as the "Colored" Methodists, opened on Florida Avenue.

In addition to publicizing schools and churches, advertisements continued to proclaim that Coral Gables was first and foremost a "Home-City." Although the Coral Gables Corporation was no longer building homes, George and his team had succeeded in bringing in out-of-town builders who were. One of the earliest and most impressive was the R. W. Nichols Builders, Finance and Mortgage Company, which completed fifty-three homes in the Riviera Section despite the lumber embargo. With 550 men on his payroll, Nichols not only built homes but also gained fame when he opened a lumber mill and concrete block factory to manufacture material needed to complete his project.

Not to be outdone, Cincinnati's American Building Corporation (ABC) launched its first unique village—a group of French Country–style homes on Hardee Road designed by New York architect Phillip Goodwin. At the same time, they broke ground for a Normandy-style French Village on a five-acre tract between LeJeune Road and Riviera Drive. Local architects John and Coulton Skinner, who had recently returned from France, anticipated seventy-one homes that would faithfully replicate the feeling of an old Normandy village. The first home, completed before summer, set a Florida record for speed of construction.

The American Building Corporation also started construction on a group of Italian and Colonial-style homes on Santa Maria, some overlooking the Biltmore Golf Course. Designed by Skinner and Pierson, the Colonial homes took on the moniker of Florida Pioneer Village, the first non-Mediterranean-style homes in Coral Gables. A June article in the *Miami Riviera* reported that the American Building Corporation had constructed sixty-three houses since the fall of 1925, with many more on the drawing board. Earlier, the company had announced it would build a Chinese Village just south of Dixie Highway near Riviera Drive. They hired Henry Killiam Murphy, who was acknowledged as America's foremost authority on Chinese architecture, to design it. His drawings appeared in *The Miami News* in January 1926, but construction did not begin until the following year.

Indianapolis builder G. B. Clippinger focused on ten Italian-style homes in the vicinity of Granada Boulevard and Blue Road. Paist, who particularly liked the Italian style, praised his work, saying, "Your homes are unique, outstanding and individual . . . nothing like this has been attempted with such pleasing results."[13]

Nearby, George E. Batcheller was also building a group of Italian-style homes designed by A. L. Klingbeil and Frank Wyatt Woods. They set the style that was to become known as the Italian Village.

Construction also began in the new Golden Gate subdivision next to the Coconut Grove Colored School (later re-named George Washington Carver), which George had completed as promised. E.W.F. Stirrup, one of the most prominent leaders and builders in the West Grove, received permits to construct the first two homes.

In the midst of the new construction, Coral Gables had one neighborhood unlike any other. Known as the "Tent City," or "the little brown canvas settlement," this unlikely enclave sat on the corner of Bird and LeJeune Roads. Organized by William S. Hammon, fondly called "Mayor," it opened in October 1925. It would be a temporary home for Coral Gables Corporation employees until the completion of the San Sebastian Apartments. By early 1926, it had close to 500 residents living in 180 nine-by-twelve and twelve-by-twenty-four wood-floor tents set off the ground on concrete blocks. The "city" also had six alphabetically named streets, electric streetlights, and a Main Street that featured a public bath house, social hall, and market.[14]

The final component needed to fulfill George's dream for a perfect community was civic and cultural institutions. The Coral Gables Woman's Club led the way and by early 1926 claimed 111 members. In April, Eunice presented the club with a $10,000 check from the Coral Gables Corporation for its building fund. (George had already donated a building site.) The same month, she became the Garden Club's second president and entertained one hundred women at her home as she launched her regime. The local press covered the event and included a full-length picture of her standing by her garden gate. At the same time, the Cocoplum Woman's Club, formerly known as the Larkins Woman's Club, announced it would build an elegant Mediterranean-style clubhouse on Sunset Drive.

Not to be left out, a body of men created what they first called the Businessmen's Club, which met each week at the Coral Gables Country Club. (Members claimed that Coral Gables had a greater variety of businesses than any other American city its size.) In May, the club received a charter from Kiwanis International and became the first national service club in the city.

Another group launched the City Club. Telfair Knight described its founding as "the laying of the civic power house of Coral Gables." Impressed with the status of their seventy-five charter members and the fact that they named George their honorary president, the Coral Gables Corporation donated a site on the corner of Alhambra and Granada Boulevards, where the group planned to build a three-story edifice of Georgian-Spanish design.

A third committee of men chartered the Riviera Athletic Club. They, too, had grand plans, which included a $500,000, five-story clubhouse in the Biltmore Section near the Granada Golf Course and proposed Urmey Arms. It would include shops, a pool, and 1,500 locker rooms.

Although impressed by the elevated social status of the new clubs, George never abandoned his everyman values and gave Boy Scout Troop 7 a site on the Granada Golf Course for a clubhouse. Next, he enlisted Phineas Paist to design a picturesque log cabin that was soon under construction.

George never wavered in his commitment to Coral Gables residents, local businesses, and institutions, but he knew Coral Gables' future depended on his ability to sell property and attract new capital. With this in mind, he continued to focus on events, knowing that every time he initiated or sponsored a "first-time-in-Miami" extravaganza, people would come. Early in the year, Ruth Bryan Owen and Bertha Foster, head of the Music Conservatory and a University of Miami stalwart, respectively, came up with a novel idea. They would drain Venetian Pool and fill the basin with seated guests to view an opera performance held amid the pool's bridges, balconies, and towers. Its success inspired the women to reach higher for their next event.

First, they convinced the Chicago Grand Opera Company to give its first performance outside the regular playhouse. Next, they sought help from George and a stellar group of other Miami developers to sponsor it at a cost of almost $1 million. The group included Miami Shores and Venetian Isles mogul Hugh Anderson, Hollywood's J. W. Young, and Miami Beach's Thomas Pancoast. When the organizers realized the Coliseum would not be finished, they moved the venue to the nearby Coral Gables Stadium. Coral Gables Corporation Construction Company workers transformed the stadium into a tented, full-stage and back-of-the-house opera hall, complete with what ads described as "opera seats." The sponsors arranged for three trains to transport thirty chorus members, twenty-eight dancers, and their entourage. The scenery, costumes, curtains, and other accoutrements necessary to present what was billed as a production "exactly like seen in Chicago" filled eighteen baggage cars. The troupe performed nine popular operas, including *Aida*, *La Traviata*, *Madama Butterfly*, and *Carmen*. Each day, following the evening performances, Coral Gables made the news.

Three months after the opera ended, Coral Gables got its first "real" theater—the Martin Luther Hampton–designed Coral Gables Theater on Ponce de Leon Boulevard across from the Grammar School. Its gala opening included a vaudeville act, a movie, an *Our Gang* short, and a newsreel. Fifteen hundred people filled the theater to capacity, with an equal number turned away. The theater, operated by the same group that ran the Olympia in downtown Miami, had a "typhoon cooling system" that blew cool air into the main auditorium. Besides the movie theater, the three-story, Mediterranean-style building had nine storefronts and eight office suites.

While endless activities lured a variety of newcomers into Coral Gables, the Biltmore Hotel and Country Club remained the greatest magnet. Besides hotel guests, thousands of people came to see its architectural beauty, tour its public spaces, and gawk at what the hotel claimed was the world's largest freshwater swimming pool. Besides golf and swimming events, Bowman and his team continued to add new activities to entertain his patrons, tourists, and Coral Gables residents. Huge crowds came to witness the first Biltmore Art Show and enjoy the musical events every afternoon and evening in the hotel's patio. Bowman and George also launched the Biltmore Riding Club and announced what Bowman called the tropics' first and only foxhunt. He hired a director and brought in a number of horses and hounds and twenty-two "howling crates" of fox. Bowman also organized what he called the "First All American Horse Show" at the Coral Gables Stadium. Workmen dismantled the "opera house" and returned the site to its former use. Just as Bowman predicted, the horse show brought in a national audience who helped fill the 14,000 seats. This event, like the others, gave Bowman and the Biltmore national acclaim. Nothing, however, could top the accolades he received in Miami when he vowed to keep the hotel open all summer.

To celebrate the Coral Gables Corporation's first birthday, George, Telfair Knight, and Jack Baldwin hosted a party for its 1,200 employees at the Biltmore Country Club. When George, Eunice, and Althea arrived, the exuberant crowd cheered and burst into a lively rendition of "Hail, Hail, the Gang's All Here," followed by "When the Moon Shines in Coral Gables"— a song that always brought tears to George's eyes. Most of the corporation's executives spoke, each praising George for his iron will, perseverance, and refusal to give up. "George would not make any decision that wasn't good for all of us," Sales Director John Norman opined. "Neither would he make a decision that is not good for the good of Coral Gables. Let the year's slogan be George's decision is our decision." George, thanking everyone, reminded the crowd they must "never lose sight of the fact that every cloud has a silver lining and that no cloud is ever as dark as it first appears."[15]

Ten days later, the good feeling continued after 1,300 people showed up at the Spanish Garden of the Coral Gables Country Club for what was billed as the first annual community get-together. An impressive group of hosts and hostesses, including Althea and Eunice, planned the event, aimed to bolster community spirit. At the end of the evening, when George stood to speak, guests left their tables and circled around him.

"It is my proudest night since Coral Gables was founded," he began. "I have worked hard and am glad that I have been instrumental in bringing such a body of citizens together in such a short period." He went on to talk philosophically about how Tropical America needed people and towns with souls. He also spoke about the importance of a small-town spirit that he felt that evening. "[It] increases our concentration, our belief in ourselves and our power to do things. Let us make Coral Gables a city with a soul."[16]

These two positive events meant a great deal to George because for several months he and his dream child Coral Gables had been victims of particularly vicious personal attacks in the northern press. The situation became so bad that on March 24, *The Miami News* printed an unprecedented, thousand-word, front-page editorial that defended and praised him. It read:

> The lengths to which these scandal mongers have come is almost past belief. They have reported that the enterprise [Coral Gables] had failed, that a receiver had been appointed, that improvements had stopped, etc., etc., etc. Within the last fortnight, the editorial rooms of a mid-western newspaper called Mr. Merrick's residence at a late hour of the night. He chanced to be in his library reading. The inquiry was whether Mr. Merrick had committed suicide. He was in a very good position to deny it. . . . Mr. Merrick very willingly opened his books to Mr. Barron of the *Wall Street Journal*, concededly one of the country's foremost financial authorities. There was nothing to conceal. Solvency and stability were obvious to the practiced eye, and now the public has an exhibit of the strength of an enterprise that has long since passed the stage of uncertainty. . . . This community loves George E. Merrick. It would stay with him to the last ditch, but in his case there will be no last ditch. The affairs of Coral Gables are as solid as a rock, for the reason that America has a real appreciation of the standards Mr. Merrick has established and maintained, and which mean so much to the uplifting of community life.

By early summer, however, even George had to admit that his grand plans and dreams for Coral Gables were starting to unravel. Problems were particularly apparent at the University of Miami. The fundraising campaign had been impressive, and within weeks of the cornerstone laying its leaders claimed they had raised $7 million of the $10 million required to build the Merrick Building and open the university. Most of the amount, however, was in pledges, not cash. Even George could not pay his pledge in cash but instead gave what he called "proper securities" or equities in mortgages and land contracts payable quarterly with 8 percent interest. He further promised to take back and replace any that didn't pay. Frederick Zeigen traveled to New York to seek a loan based on $3 million in pledges and $1 million in George Merrick securities but was unsuccessful.

Despite increasing financial problems, university administrators continued to publish positive stories. They set tuition at $225 a year and announced an October 15 opening, when they predicted the Merrick Building would be completed. More than one thousand workers swarmed the campus and focused on clearing the pineland and raising the steel girders of what the *Miami Riviera* reported would "form the skeleton of the structure." (At the time no one realized this name "skeleton" would stick for the next twenty years.) The regents, however, were beginning to accept the fact that completing the Merrick Building by October was an impossible dream. Then, George came to the rescue.

At the board meeting on June 9, just two days after *The Miami Herald* ran a glowing story about the architectural beauty of the proposed campus, George offered the still-unfinished Anastasia Hotel as a temporary site until the Merrick Building could be completed. After the regents visited the hotel, they voted to accept his offer. George proposed a one-year, low-cost lease and promised he would reimburse the university once it moved out and the hotel opened.

However, an estimated $175,000 was needed to transform the Anastasia into an educational facility. Already short of cash, the regents stopped work on the Merrick Building in order to put all of their resources into getting the Anastasia ready for the fall opening. To help, George offered the services of Phineas Paist and Denman Fink to draw plans for the adaptive re-use of the original luxury hotel, designed by George Fink. They planned to construct temporary partitions that could be easily removed when the building was returned to hotel use. When the regents announced the change of venue, they added a positive spin, saying it was done "to avoid unnecessary haste in the interior finishing and to avoid study in the midst of noise and confusion."[17]

After workman shifted their efforts to the Anastasia, George also solved another of the university's problems. He offered the third floor of the nearby San Sebastian Apartment/Hotel for a girls' dormitory and provided space on the first floor for the school cafeteria. J. E. Hines, a private developer, also helped by starting construction near the main campus on what he described as a private dorm for 350 boys.

Despite the plethora of positive stories appearing in the press, a *Miami Riviera* editorial summed up the true situation. After a positive comment about the cornerstone laying as an "occasion for blind optimism," it reminded everyone that opening a new university was "an almost unbelievably arduous task." It added, "we hope they will have the stamina."[18]

If the public had known the growing problems George faced, they might have hoped the same for him. The one-year-old Coral Gables Corporation was facing serious financial difficulties. Most of the shortfall came from land buyers not following up on their mortgage payments. This made it difficult for the corporation to meet its own debt obligations. To lessen the overwhelming responsibility of a few, in March, the corporation spun off operation of the hotels and other public institutions into a new corporation called the Coral Gables Hotel Corporation. It would manage the corporation-owned Golf and Country Club, the Venetian Pool and Casino, Tahiti Beach, and the Antilla, San Sebastian, and new Don Quixote Apartment under construction at the Douglas Entrance. George would be president; Bowman, chairman of the board; and Charles Flynn, vice-president and managing director. More changes would soon follow.

The City of Coral Gables was also having difficulty meeting its obligations for much of the same reasons as George was. Many of the individuals and corporations that had purchased property during the boom were defaulting on their taxes. Despite having to borrow to keep municipal operations going, the city also sold municipal bonds to fund new projects. The first provided funds to purchase a warehouse, storage facility, and the stadium site (today's Phillips Park) from the Coral Gables Corporation. (George promised to clear the stadium site as part of the deal.) Although George had not attended a single 1926 commission meeting and was not present when the vote was taken, for the first time, people began to question the propriety of members of the commission also being officers in the Coral Gables Corporation.

George's first meeting of the year was on March 24, when he came to support the city's purchase of the site that would become Salvadore Park. For years, he had tried to acquire what he viewed as an unsightly hole-in-the-donut in his Country Club Section. Now, with Frank Button's design talent, it would become a beautiful city park.

In early summer, George, as president of the Coral Gables Corporation, sent the commissioners a letter requesting they float bonds to complete all the platted streets and sidewalks between Sunset Drive and Eighth Street. At first, a newly formed organization, called the Coral Gables Tax Payers League, questioned the expenditure. But after George spoke at the June 18 commission meeting and argued the improvements would raise property values, provide jobs, and spur development, the commission, with the agreement of the Tax Payers League, voted to proceed with almost $2 million in special improvement bonds and hired W. T Price to do the work.

The Coral Gables Corporation also faced challenges. In July, following months of discussion, the corporation became part of a new entity called Coral Gables Consolidated, Inc. George traveled to New York City to launch what he hoped would become a national effort. *The New York Times* covered the merger and quoted George as saying that the new corporation had been created "not only as a plan of national financing for the completion of a ten-year program of development and sales but also as a means of handling our properties more aggressively and more nationally."[19]

The Miami papers followed up with their own stories. "Coral Gables has become a national enterprise," *The Miami News* reported on July 13. "The announcement this week of the organization of Coral Gables Consolidated, Inc., a $100,000,000 holding company, places Coral Gables on a par with other great American financial organizations such as American Steel Corporation, and makes it in the value of properties owned and controlled, the largest corporation of its class in the world."

The *Miami Riviera*, in its July 16 edition, wrote a glowing editorial praising George for his "carrying Coral Gables to the rest of the country, and bringing the rest of the country to Coral Gables." With renewed optimism, everyone looked to George to bring not only Coral Gables but also all of South Florida out of their doldrums.

The new Coral Gables Consolidated, Inc., with George listed as president and chairman of the board, published a four-page prospectus entitled "CORAL GABLES enters the Second Phase of its AMAZING DEVELOPMENT." After listing the city's brief history and accomplishments, the text moved quickly to the future, reminding prospective investors: "Just as he has engaged the best brains of artists and architects for the creation of a City of Beauty, George E. Merrick has now gathered around him men of national prominence to serve as Directors in the future development of

Coral Gables now entering upon a ten-year program for the completion of the plans of its founder."

The prospectus listed the new corporation's seven subsidiary companies, beginning with the Coral Gables Corporation, which was involved in selling and development. Next came the Coral Gables Securities Company, chartered to take title to the land south of Sunset Road. The third entity was the Coral Gables Resale Company, a general brokerage business. The Coral Gables Construction and Supply Company, listed fourth, was built for both the Coral Gables Corporation and the public. The new Coral Gables Hotel Corporation was next, followed by the Coral Gables Rapid Transit Corporation, which operated both electric street railroads. Finally, Coral Gables Consolidated would also own the Miami Biltmore Hotel Corporation preferred stock with a par value of $3 million, plus one half of the common stock of the company operating the hotel.

The offering was further bolstered by an appraisal of the property of the new corporation at more than $100 million. It included buildings and income-producing properties; the Biltmore Hotel properties; buildings for sale; unplatted land in the Biscayne Bay and Biltmore Sections; and platted lots for sale.

The prospectus also enumerated the value of net balances owed the Coral Gables Corporation at $40 million. After adding equipment, machinery, and other tangible items, the final value of the subsidiaries being transferred to Coral Gables Consolidated would be in excess of $75 million.

"In order to accelerate the development and sale of Coral Gables properties," the prospectus concluded, "one hundred thousand shares of Preferred stock will be authorized at one hundred dollars a share with 8 percent cumulative dividends payable quarterly. In addition, five hundred thousand shares of common stock at no par value will be used to acquire the subsidiary companies from George Merrick."

The prospectus included an application for shares of preferred stock to be returned to Coral Gables Consolidated's office in the Coral Gables Corporation Administration Building.

As the economic problems increased, a minor but unexpected hurricane hit Miami—the first since 1906. Coconut Grove pioneer Ralph Munroe, who had gone through many hurricanes and tried to get newcomers to understand their destructive power, hoped the hurricane "would put the fear of the Lord into the scoffers." Unfortunately, it had the opposite effect. Because it caused little damage, people thought a hurricane was just a bad storm and a nuisance to be endured.

Despite continuing uncertainty, the University of Miami regents forged ahead. When their money ran short, George and the Coral Gables Corporation agreed to complete the work on the Anastasia, now called the University Building, at no cost. Thin cardboard partitions divided the northwest wing of the first floor into a large assembly hall, a lecture hall, freshman chemistry and physics labs, rest rooms, and a large lounge. The southwest wing housed a gymnasium and locker rooms. The second floor included an art studio, fifteen musical practice rooms, and a group of classrooms. For the time being, the third floor would remain unfinished.

Now that the university had a building, the regents and administration focused on hiring faculty. Keeping their promise to have a Pan-American focus, the regents made a prominent hire in Dr. Victor Andres Belaunde, a noted Peruvian scholar who would head the Latin American history department and work to promote mutual understanding between the hemispheres. The other big story came when the Miami Conservatory of Music merged with the university. It not only brought in a large number of students to the university but also gave it credibility.

One of the most publicized events of late summer was the two-day grand opening of George Fink's $100,000 studio on Ponce de Leon Boulevard. More than a thousand people came to see what architectural historians call one of the best examples of the Mediterranean style.

The *Miami Riviera* described his pastiche of architectural elements as an "astonishing paradox of harmonizing contrasts from all over the world." Besides Italian, Moorish, and Persian, which the article stated were "blended for the first time," he also combined a variety of other styles. The tower was Mexican-inspired and topped with an original weather vane he designed depicting an Arab on a camel heading toward a palm-fringed oasis. He imported the stone doorway and carved entry door from Cordova. It opened into a reception room with an Italian-style ceiling featuring a Tunisian frieze. It also had Spanish-tile floors with Algerian inserts and a stairway copied from El Greco's home in Toledo. Other antique elements included a Gothic church window and a Notre Dame–style gargoyle. A full-page Coral Gables Corporation advertisement in the September 6 *Miami News* summed up the public's approval: "Take the odd, the quaint, the chaste, the beautiful, the utilitarian from the best form of architecture in the Old World to stir this polyglot assemblage in the melting pot of the New World and out of the whole to pour into a new mold of Southern Florida a new distinctive and remarkably harmonious form of architecture in a process suggestive of some subtle alchemy."

Besides antiques, the furnishing included reproductions designed by George Fink and built by the Granada Shops. Ralph and Leland Wilkins' custom furniture had become so popular that the brothers built their own George Fink–designed, Spanish-style studio in the Crafts Section. It had a two-story, home-like interior that provided an elegant backdrop for their work.

Despite continuing problems, when compared to other developments, Coral Gables clearly was in a class by itself. While many developers, including Addison Mizner, had been forced out by irate creditors and suspended operation, Coral Gables continued to build—albeit at a slower pace. George's greatest problem was that he held almost $40 million in paper—the legacy of the boom. But ever mindful that Coral Gables itself was his best marketing tool, in early September he launched what he called a "Come and See" campaign in an effort to keep buyers from relinquishing their investments. He wrote personal letters to more than 20,000 individuals who had put money down but were not keeping up with their mortgage payments. He promised a homecoming party planned for mid-October, tickets to the first University of Miami football game, and discounted transportation. He believed that once out-of-town buyers saw Coral Gables, they would realize the soundness of their investment and resume payments. With the letters in the mail, George was feeling optimistic.

People reading the September 17 *Miami Riviera* might also have felt positive about Coral Gables' future. The new Ponce de Leon Junior-Senior High was set to open on September 19. Nearby, the fledging University of Miami began construction on its "temporary" stadium, designed by Phineas Paist. Capable of seating five thousand, it was located on a triangular plot at San Amaro and Levant. The university also proudly announced that it would add a law school to its list of offerings.

The *Riviera* carried a glowing story about the Coral Gables Commission voting to launch a major publicity campaign. George, believing his previous national advertising was a key element in Coral Gables' success, had convinced the commission to add two mills to the tax rate in order to fund it. Under the banner of the Coral Gables Chamber of Commerce, the city would hire a national firm to design full-page advertisements— many four-color—for the nation's most popular magazines. They included *The Saturday Evening Post*, the *Literary Digest*, *Cosmopolitan*, *Collier's*, and the *American Magazine*, which together had a circulation of fifty million people.

Ironically, no one realized that before the week ended, South Florida would receive more national publicity than at any other time in its history. Disaster loomed just off shore, but few paid attention to a four-inch story on page one of the September 17 *Miami Herald* headlined "Hurricane Reported." Unfortunately, the writer added the caveat that it was not expected to hit South Florida. As a result, Greater Miami's three hundred thousand residents, lulled into complacency by the mild July storm, went about their daily business unconcerned. When *The Miami News* came out that afternoon, its banner headline read: "Miami Warned of Tropical Storm." But, once again, the threat was minimized, except to shipping. Even weather bureau chief Richard W. Gray spoke of possible "destructive winds" but did not urge preparation.

Gables resident Leo Reardon later wrote a book about the storm that mirrored what most other Coral Gables residents experienced. After he spent the afternoon playing golf at the Coral Gables Country Club, his golfing partners joined him and his family for dinner at their Murcia Avenue home. When the guests departed at about 11 p.m., Reardon noticed the wind was rising but was not concerned and went to bed. Nonchalance turned to fear when at about 2 a.m., the first window shattered. The increasing gale had lifted one of his canvas awnings and turned its metal support pole into a battering ram. Unbeknownst to Reardon, this terrifying scenario was happening all over Coral Gables, where almost every window, including hundreds adorning the Biltmore Hotel, had the city's trademark striped canvas awnings. As the tumult increased, the sickening sound of breaking glass continued and, one-by-one, the awnings did their terrible deed.

Gathering his two young children from their beds, Reardon and his wife sought shelter in their car, parked in the garage. They remained huddled together until about 6 a.m., when the storm suddenly stopped. Believing it was over, the dutiful father got into his car to seek staples. He later described what he saw:

> The scene of wreckage brought tears to my eyes. Coral Gables' buildings with a few exceptions, had weathered the terrific blast, but the beautiful foliage was laid low. Light and telephone wires were strewn about in reckless abandon. The ground was covered with green grapefruit. A few weather-beaten policemen were standing around the ruins of destroyed buildings.[20]

He found an open grocery store on Ponce de Leon Boulevard and was able to buy a few staples, but as he returned to his car, winds picked up to almost forty miles per hour. "The storm was returning," he wrote.

Reardon, like most, did not realize that he had been in the eye of the hurricane, and what he called "the second storm" arrived with even greater strength. Barely making it home, he gathered his family together once again as the wind velocity increased from the opposite direction and began turning awnings into wrecking balls on the side of the house previously spared. He spent a harrowing morning holding doors against the wind and moving from room to room, seeking safety. He ended up in the laundry room, where he placed his two young children in a lead laundry tub covered with a wet mattress. "Will this cursed storm ever abate," he thought, "or is it determined to decimate us and our beautiful city?"

The winds did not die down until the early afternoon of September 18. The second half had been worse than the first and, coupled with those caught outside by the seduction of the lull, the death toll rose. "I have just come through Hell," Reardon wrote. "I'm not normal. I am not sure that I'm perfectly sane. My body feels as it would after ten rounds of fighting or three football games. Each foot weights a ton, and my head is splitting. . . . But we are all here."[21]

Reardon did not realize that, despite broken windows, shredded awnings, missing roof tiles, and fallen trees, Coral Gables, thanks to its strict building code, had fared better than any other part of Miami. For hours, winds of more than 135 miles per hour had whirled through Miami and its suburbs. Many buildings spared by the "first storm" succumbed to the second. A twelve-foot storm surge inundated Miami Beach and deposited six feet of sand into hotel lobbies. After sweeping across Miami Beach and into Biscayne Bay, the huge ocean tidal wave swept through downtown Miami and created a bore up the Miami River, causing flooding in many Miami neighborhoods. Biscayne Boulevard looked like a shipyard with hundreds of ships cast about like toys. Many of Miami's new subdivisions, which included hastily built wooden structures, were laid flat—especially Hialeah, where the death toll was the greatest. People wandered about, half naked, stunned next to their former homes, which had been turned into piles of rubble.

Downtown Miami's McAllister became the base hospital for the injured and a temporary morgue for the dead, whose numbers continued to rise. Miami City Manager Wharton declared martial law as the United States Marines arrived from Key West to keep order. With most roads impassable because of fallen trees, and telephone and electrical wires down, the only method of communication, albeit limited, was the wireless radio. The first messages to reach northern newspapers proclaimed: "Miami is Wiped Out."

Greater Miami was not the only area affected by the storm. It caused even more damage in Fort Lauderdale, Davie, and the small towns around Lake Okeechobee. Winds whipped up the lake's waters, causing massive flooding and the greatest loss of life.

At first, Coral Gables residents did not realize how their strict building codes had spared them the kind of destruction other areas experienced. It was true that Coral Gables suffered less damage and no loss of life, but the storm had still wreaked devastation there. The winds flattened several wooden, warehouse-type buildings in the downtown area, along with the temporary Baptist Church on Coconut Grove Drive. The winds also wrecked many garages in the residential neighborhoods that had less stringent building requirements. Tahiti Beach's palm trees toppled and the thatched pavilions disappeared, causing the beach to look more like a desert than a tropical isle. The winds destroyed the Indian Mound Trail water tower, but the other water towers survived and, unlike in the rest of Miami, safe water, although limited, continued to flow. The worst damage was to home and business interiors that had been destroyed by wind and rain that raged through broken windows.

Telfair Knight, George's second-in-command and closest confidant, barely escaped death when he ventured out during the lull to assess the damage. After being toppled head over heels by the returning 130 mph winds, he grabbed hold of the base of a tree and hung on for almost eight hours until the storm subsided.

George, realizing the horror of the situation, reached out to the stunned community. Just one day after the hurricane, he arranged for the *Miami Riviera* to publish a "Hurricane Extra." The one-page flyer, delivered door-to-door, continued publication for the next week, giving Coral Gables residents daily reassurance and a means of communication. George wrote the lead story in the first edition, making it clear that he and his organization were in charge. In his usual optimistic style, he called most of the damage "on the surface" and afflicting the landscaping that city workers were already busy replanting. He announced that the general reconstruction headquarters had been set up in the Coral Gables Construction Building on the corner of Ponce de Leon Boulevard and Aragon, with Rodney Miller in "supreme charge" of all rebuilding. In addition, all relief activities would be housed there and coordinated by Coral Gables Chamber of Commerce President F. J. O'Leary.

He encouraged homeowners to board up their broken windows, remove shredded awnings, and restore their own plantings. He ended on an encouraging note: "Remember that this is the time when we must stand together. I am not at all discouraged by the situation and all that we need is the cooperation of all Coral Gables people to repair such damage as has been done."

The *Extra* also had useful information about open bakeries and ice houses and how the Tallman Hospital was admitting the injured, most of whom came from other areas. The Biltmore Hotel was also noted for opening its doors to more than two thousand homeless. Other Coral Gables hotels were equally welcoming.

The final article, headlined "Mayor's Proclamation," reiterated what George had written and noted that the Coral Gables Police had recruited additional members to ensure safety. Police permits were needed to leave or reenter the city, but, unlike other municipalities, the city did not declare martial law.

The Tuesday edition of the *Hurricane Extra* repeated the practical information and told of expanding relief efforts. The thirty-bed Tallman Hospital had admitted more than six hundred people, turning no one away. Commissioner Don Peabody, who was out of town, opened his large Anastasia Avenue home to people in need. To raise community spirits and bring the community together, the Coral Gables Corporation even held a free dance at the San Sebastian Apartment/Hotel. "Our spirit knows no discouragement," writers of the *Extra* concluded. "The hurricane winds could shake steel frame buildings and tear huge trees up by the roots, but they could not lower the heads nor daunt the hearts of the builders of Coral Gables. . . . But that is really what everyone expects of the Coral Gables which George Merrick built."

Each day, the *Hurricane Extra* reported on the relief work being done by citizen-volunteers. Coordinated by the Congregational Church, women organized to help not only Coral Gables residents but also others throughout Greater Miami. They distributed food, provided support for the Tallman Hospital, and collected clothing. George turned the Country Club over to the Red Cross, which fed thousands of "hurricane refugees," as well as relief workers. Businessmen and bankers arranged for funds to be loaned to homeowners for repair work. Others worked to get the public schools opened.

George and Miami leaders cautioned residents against exaggerating the damage and, instead, encouraged them to talk about the remarkable rebuilding. "Coral Gables and Miami expect and will have many visitors within the next few months," George wrote in his "Official Statement." "So rapidly are repairs being made in the entire district that it is certain that Greater Miami, including the City of Coral Gables, will be ready to adequately care for all the visitors this winter." To prove his point, he invited reporters from the *Chicago Tribune* and Hearst newspapers to come to South Florida to see the work being done in Coral Gables and Miami. The reporters saw more than five hundred workers, under Frank Button's leadership, propping up thousands of fallen trees and shrubs. Others were busy hauling away debris and helping residents replace broken windows. The writers returned home and reported on the remarkable rebuilding going on in Miami and, especially, in Coral Gables, where George Merrick had promised all vestiges of the storm would be removed in sixty days. In fact the story was so positive about Coral Gables that some said the storm had missed Coral Gables—an untruth the city quickly refuted.

The real story was not that Coral Gables was spared but that its building code proved equal to the winds. The hurricane was unprecedented. It had a lower barometer reading (27.61) and caused more damage (more than $112 million) than any prior hurricane, including the infamous Galveston, Texas, disaster. The worse statistic, however, was loss of life. Different sources had different numbers but somewhere between two hundred and four hundred people perished, though none in Coral Gables. The hurricane's long-term effect, however, would cripple all of South Florida, including Coral Gables. It was "the final blow" to the already faltering boom that had transformed South Florida from a small town into a growing metropolis. For a period following the hurricane, new construction stopped and all efforts went toward rebuilding. Many newer residents and out-of-town developers departed, often leaving half-finished buildings bleaching in the sun. Three years before the Great Depression swept the nation, South Florida held a dress rehearsal for the big event.

George refused to admit that Coral Gables would not come back stronger than before. Mindful that now, more than ever, the Coral Gables story had to be told to the nation, he expanded his "Come and See" campaign, which had been postponed because of the storm. Following a mass meeting at the Biltmore Hotel, he and others organized "Progress Week," set for late November. It would be a celebration of Coral Gables' remarkable progress, not only in hurricane recovery but also in its five years of development. Special events would include parades, a circus performance, groundbreakings, grand openings, golf and tennis tournaments, and a University of Miami football game. The newly formed committee promptly named George, Mayor Dammers, and Ruth Bryan Owens honorary chairs.

George also focused on the continuing recovery. Aided by the Coral Gables Corporation and the Coral Gables Construction Company, all Coral Gables schools opened two weeks after the storm. At about the same time, the city strengthened what was already the area's strongest building code. From this time forward, garages had to be masonry, an architect had to oversee all construction, and awnings had to have pulleys operable from inside.

Spirits rose on October 15, when, despite the hurricane, the University of Miami opened on schedule. Even though the Anastasia Building had been damaged by rain pouring through broken windows, an army of workers had

Figure 51. Despite the devastating September hurricane, the University of Miami opened on schedule in the partially finished Anastasia Hotel offered by George. During the summer of 1925, Richard Merrick had drawn a romanticized rendering of the proposed luxury hotel that was later used to promote the university. The cupola was not completed until the 1940s. University of Miami Special Collections. Courtesy of Mildred Merrick.

removed the damaged walls and installed a new set of "temporary" interior partitions. Within days, the new university had almost seven hundred students—three hundred in arts and sciences and four hundred in the music school. Within weeks, the evening and the law schools added two hundred more.

Just four days after classes began, the new university held its first football game against Rollins College freshmen at the hastily completed college stadium on San Amaro Drive. The *Miami Riviera* described the forty-member, newly named "Miami Hurricanes" under Coach Cub Buck as "green but spunky." Fans cheered and waved orange and green ribbons, representing the school colors suggested by Denman Fink. George and Eunice did not attend.

At about the same time, the Dream Theater designed by John and Coulton Skinner opened on Ponce de Leon Boulevard, giving Coral Gables its second movie house. Described as resembling a Spanish bullring, it had 1,500 open-air seats, twenty-nine shops, and a café. But more than another beautiful downtown building, the Dream Theater proved that good dreams still came true.

In another burst of optimism, the Coral Gables Commission, with the support of a citizen's committee, voted to float $4.5 million in thirty-year bonds at 6 percent to acquire and build community facilities. The acquisitions included purchasing the Granada Golf Course and Coral Gables Country Club, Venetian Pool, and the trolley system from Coral Gables Consolidated. It would also fund three fire stations, a city hall, parks, an emergency hospital, and a sanitary sewer system. Finally, $300,000 would be appropriated to complete the Coliseum. The funding required a citizen referendum set for December.

The proposed bond program caused a great deal of controversy and, for the first time, George became the target of a local campaign to discredit him. A group of Coral Gables residents, led by "Dr. Sheehan and four others," sent out a circular opposing the bonds and asking residents to fight the Coral Gables Corporation and George Merrick because both had a financial interest in the outcome. In response, George, deeply hurt by the accusations, published a three-page, 1,800-word rebuttal entitled "A Personal Statement From Geo. E. Merrick," in which he stated:

> First and fundamentally, no citizen of the town should ever feel called upon to fight the Coral Gables Corporation, . . . for the Coral Gables Corporation, of which I am President and controlling and directing owner, is a corporation with a soul and that soul is Coral Gables. If our history and achievement of the past five years in Coral Gables do not absolve the corporation and myself from any possibility of being charged with selfish interest, there is nothing further that I can say or point to regarding the past.

He reiterated the fact that he had continued to put all of his profits back into Coral Gables and would continue to do so in the future. "I and the corporation are into Coral Gables 'for life,'" he added. He pointed out that because of current circumstances, he had been unable to raise capital by selling stock in the new corporation and came to the conclusion that the only way to get northern capital into Coral Gables was through municipal bonds. He reminded the public that the city would be buying logical municipal properties appraised by an independent agency that would enhance the city's future. "The great big thing behind this plan, (or that part coming to the corporation under the plan)," he added, "will be sacredly used by the Coral Gables Corporation for the stabilizing and enhancing of every piece of property in Coral Gables."

He concluded with a plea that "true permanent fundamental motives be felt, soberly appraised and realized . . . by carrying through and successful marketing of this $4,500,000 issue at this really crucial time in history. Yours sincerely, George E. Merrick."[22]

To avoid growing negative comments about a conflict of interest, corporation officers Telfair Knight and Jack Baldwin resigned from the Coral Gables Commission. For the first time since the city incorporated, the majority of the commission was non-Coral Gables Corporation officers. Only George and F. W. Webster remained and George rarely attended the meetings. The national publicity campaign, approved before the hurricane, proved to be an unexpected blessing. One of the first advertisements appeared in the October 23 issue of *Collier's* and proclaimed: "Coral Gables is anchored safely in the harbor of sound and normal business. . . . The building has never halted." Others followed almost weekly, most without any mention of the storm. The advertisements included beautiful line drawings by Denman Fink and Charles Chapman that set them apart from others.

Many of the advertisements touted the University of Miami, which was making rapid progress. After Bowman Ashe was named president on November 3, exuberant students and faculty celebrated with a cheering motorcade into downtown Miami, where Ashe spoke to a large crowd in Royal Palm Park. That night the celebration continued with a dance at the Coral Gables Country Club, which had become like a student club for the university.

Keeping the founders' promises, the university launched several events that brought a new level of artistic and cultural gravitas to South Florida. One of the first was a performance of the fledgling Civic Theater in the Anastasia Building's six-hundred-seat auditorium. The highly successful event prompted the theater and the university to continue collaboration, thus ensuring the theater's future. On another front, Professor Arnold Volpe announced the formation of a philharmonic orchestra, the first in South Florida. In addition, William Jennings Bryan's widow launched the university library—South Florida's first research library—with the gift of her husband's private collection.

Besides the constant publicity coming from the new university, the Coral Gables Corporation created another oversize brochure to assure everyone that Coral Gables was alive and well. Entitled "Coral Gables Today," the twenty-page, heavily illustrated tome touted the achievements of the past five years and highlighted the city's future plans. The text also included subtle references to the storm. Inserted in a section entitled "Building Progress" was the statement: "Coral Gables homes resist the worse assaults of elemental fury and meet any exigency of storm and stress."

At the same time, the brochure promoted the climate. It reminded readers that Coral Gables was part of what George called "The only American Tropics" and a year-round playground. The most important message—although mostly untrue—was that development had not slowed and the young city was still a unique place for investment. A concluding section, entitled "A City Without a Scar," provided one of the most enduring statements about George Merrick and his dream, and it continues to be quoted today.

> George E. Merrick had the vision of a dreamer, the soul of a poet, the imagination of the artist, the force of a zealot, the courage and determination of a warrior—and he dreamed: wrote the poems on the virgin page of the future; etched the picture against the sky-line of the actual; published his poems in brick and stone; framed his picture against the background of reality; drove home the message of a new, an ideal city, to the nation.[23]

Sadly, even the "courage and determination of the warrior" had been shattered by the onslaught of unrelenting disasters that threatened Coral Gables' future. As a result, George experienced a physical and mental breakdown. Few people knew of his condition until he wrote an article in the November 19 Progress Week Edition of the *Miami Riviera* explaining why he would not be able to participate in the events. In a statement signed Sincerely Yours, George E. Merrick, he wrote:

> The year 1926 has been a rather strenuous year. Many things have occurred that have required a great deal of time and thought and energy

on my part. My first idea is to always protect Coral Gables. After the hurricane, several weeks of very exacting labor were required of me. The result of this, in addition to the other work that I have been compelled to do this year, was that my physician insisted upon my taking a few weeks of absolute rest. This enforced inactivity comes at a time I would wish most to be in Coral Gables taking part in the wonderful celebration that has been arranged by its citizens, but I know that all my friends will agree that it is most important that I should try to safeguard my health.

He concluded with a personal appeal to the citizens of Coral Gables to vote yes in the upcoming bond referendum. "My message to the people of Coral Gables," he wrote, "is to go to the polls on December 7 and cast their vote for the success of the great ideal which you have all helped me to achieve, and that is the completion of our beautiful city."[24]

He wrote his statement from the Washington Sanitarium and Hospital in Takoma Park, Maryland, which he had entered several weeks earlier. Besides extreme fatigue, sleep deprivation, and problems from abscessed teeth, George's drinking had increased to an alarming level, causing even his most loyal partners to question his reliability.[25] Eunice suggested the facility because her father had been a patient there and experienced a positive outcome. The Seventh-Day Adventist Church, which operated the sanitarium, was similar to Christian Science and its healthy living philosophy.

George later wrote about the experience and "his depth of physical and earthly dregs." He felt "broken and defeated" and compared himself to "poor Humpty Dumpty," questioning whether anyone could put him back together again.[26] The one ray of hope came when his longtime friend and pastor, Reverend Kuykendahl, who knew of the seriousness of the situation, wrote a newspaper editorial commending George for what he had done with, as George remembered, "no mention of the bad to whose illusions the same one had yielded."[27]

Despite George's absence, Progress Week proceeded as planned. As part of the November 22 opening events, Mayor Dammers read a telegram from him:

On the occasion of the opening ceremonies of Progress Week to be conducted by you this morning, I wish to extend my greetings and best wishes to you and to all the citizens of Coral Gables and its visitors to the entire Greater Miami district. The enterprise of our people in perfecting this splendid demonstration of our progress is not only gratifying to me personally but is also further evidence of the Coral Gables spirit which knows no defeat and which carries our community forward in spite of every obstacle. May the entire week be one of success and happiness to our people.

Progress Week events outshone the highly successful Fiesta of the American Tropics, which George had helped launch a year earlier. Like the Fiesta, Coral Gables was the centerpiece, but organizers also brought the cities of Miami, Miami Beach, and Hialeah into the festivities. The 350-unit kickoff parade, described as a "brilliant spectacle," traversed from downtown Miami all the way into Coral Gables, concluding in front of the new Colonnade building covered in bunting. That same day, the Biltmore opened a radio, boat, and automobile show and during the following days held golf and tennis tournaments and evening fashion shows. The Coral Gables Theatre housed daily music events hosted by the University of Miami Music Conservatory. The university also held an open house just prior to a lively football game against the University of Havana.

Promising something for everyone, the Venetian Pool and Casino hosted a "Better Baby Show." Besides giving prizes to ninety of the most physically fit babies, Coral Gables pediatricians William McKibben and Warren Quillian gave free physicals. Schoolchildren also performed at a variety of community events, including song fests and a "Kiddie Kar" race.

For a week, every day and night was filled with a variety of events, from horse shows to a circus. Capitalizing on the desperately needed positive news, all Miami newspapers covered the events in great detail. One especially popular event occurred when Mayor Dammers drew more than two thousand people to the intersection of Ponce de Leon and Alhambra Circle to participate in one of his famous auctions. This time he was not selling land but Coral Gables and all the intangible attributes that made it unique. "Here we are in the midst of things of mighty proportions," he began, "our streets; our building, domestic, commercial, intellectual; our transportation and the broad spaces in which to make merry and be glad." With pure Doc Dammers hyperbole, he continued: "What is it, I ask you, that makes our citizens different; women more beautiful, men more dashing, enterprise more daring, while the song of the bird, the color of the flower, the smile of little children are all aglow and have to them a charm, a divine thrill unmatched the world around?"[28]

Not having lost his touch or his ability to entertain, the *Riviera* reported that he "sold" more than $12 million in values in two hours, including an imaginary bid for the weather, happiness and home, and children's smiles.

The following afternoon, hundreds of enthusiastic residents gathered at the Venetian Pool and Casino to honor George. Speaker after speaker lauded him and regretted his absence. Mayor Dammers, saying it was not easy to express "all that is in my heart," summed up the group's feelings when he described George as "one of the finest men who ever drew the breath of life." Following his introductory remarks, he presented a silver loving cup to his "dear wife," Eunice. The inscription read:

> Presented to George E. Merrick by the citizens of Coral Gables as a token of esteem, confidence and affectionate regard and in recognition of high achievement on the fifth anniversary of the founding of America's most beautiful and progressive city, Coral Gables, Florida. November 27, 1926.

He summed up the evening by saying that George "has done and given everything to make his dream come true and is now working a hundred times harder than ever." He reminded the audience that "men and women who stick to George E. Merrick and to Coral Gables will never regret it." In conclusion, he recited George's favorite maxim: "Nothing is as strong as the truth."[29]

Progress Week had achieved what everyone hoped it would. People felt confident that Coral Gables would not only survive but also serve as an example for all of Greater Miami. The residents of Coral Gables demonstrated their confidence and respect for George when they went to the polls on December 7 and voted positively for the $4.5 million bond issue.

Even though George was in the hospital, his lieutenants kept the telegraph wires humming in order to keep him abreast of Coral Gables activities and to seek his advice. In one telegram, Telfair Knight asked for his approval for a $150,000, three-month advertising blitz despite current economic problems. He also suggested that George stay as long as the doctor advised, adding, "I think nothing is so important as to complete what you are doing."[30]

Likewise, George's close confidant and attorney, Clifton Benson, sent a particularly warm and telling letter, indicating his concern about George's drinking and his hope that he was "still strictly observing the Volstead Act." "Be a good boy now," he concluded, "and get well and come home."[31]

On December 17, Eunice left for Washington to be with George and hopefully bring him home from the hospital for Christmas. Sadly, it was not to be. "Missing our loved ones," Eunice's mother and father wrote in a Christmas Day telegram. "Greatly hoping to spend next Christmas together in Matecumbe." Another from Biltmore Hotel Manager Charlie Flynn kept him up to date with happenings at the Biltmore and added encouragement from "All."

Despite the constant encouragement from his friends and associates in Coral Gables, at year's end George and Eunice remained in Washington. At least for a time, 1926 had taken its toll on George.

~13

Sustaining an Ideal

Coral Gables is what it is—and what it celebrates today—
because George E. Merrick is a man of selfless idealism. The
idealism sustains him and he sustains Coral Gables, through
a period which any man might—and many times—regard
as of black discouragement; and it exalts him to give freely of
himself and of all he has in even the brightest of days.

Editorial, *Miami Riviera*, November 8, 1927

More than a thousand merrymakers greeted 1927 at the Biltmore Hotel's
elaborate New Year's Eve celebration. *The Miami Herald* reported that Telfair Knight's party included most of the Coral Gables Corporation executives and out-of-town developers. George and Eunice were not there. Despite improvement, George's doctors wanted him to stay in the Washington
Sanitarium for another week. The good news was that Eunice was with him.
He had spent almost three months alone, so her presence and the prospect
of going home cheered him. A flurry of encouraging telegrams from Coral
Gables friends and business associates also gave him new hope. "It's a new
day and a new year," Telfair Knight wrote. "I have a very strong feeling that
it is going to be a good one for us." In another, Sales Director G. W. Hopkins
promised to "go into the New Year with a better fighting spirit than ever
before."

During his absence, George's loyal lieutenants had carried the torch as
best they could, covering for him and keeping his confidence. On January
6, when he and Eunice returned to Coral Gables, they greeted him like a

returning hero. A few days later, *The Miami Herald* ran a story about what he had learned on his so-called trip. "It has covered a period of weeks," he was quoted as saying, "and has given me time to learn through personal contact and conversation the public attitude toward Florida and our section in particular. . . . The interest in Florida today is vital and practical and not a mere guess or speculation. Capital in larger amounts will find its place in the development of our agricultural resources, our drainage and reclamation programs and in the building of our industrial activities."[1] He would soon translate this new "practical" outlook into concrete proposals.

Even though the pressure of deferred business was enormous, George's first priority was to tour the new University of Miami and address the student body. He felt encouraged by what he saw and the enthusiastic response he received. His former Anastasia Hotel, now the University Building, was still undergoing renovation, but students felt like pioneers and fondly called the half-finished building "their cardboard college." A few days later, students named him the official "Father of the University" and honored him at a dance at the Country Club.[2]

When George learned that the university had not been able to pay the faculty for two months and feared its first year would be its last, he arranged for the Coral Gables Corporation to pay for a fundraising event at the Biltmore. He also convinced his associates to contribute to the fund. Despite his personal financial problems, he pledged $1,000 to be paid in five monthly installments.

During the early months of 1927, the newspapers were filled with stories about the season's social events. One story told how the Biltmore, hoping to draw the northern "horsey" set, collaborated with the Coral Gables Corporation to open an expanded bridle path from the Coral Gables Riding Academy to Tahiti Beach. The hotel also held a second horse show and launched a series of foxhunts through the pinewoods. In addition, it held numerous balls and hosted an exhibition golf tournament between the legendary Walter Hagen and Gene Sarazen. *The Miami News* reported that it drew a "monster crowd."

The Biltmore also attracted national and international dignitaries. Owner John McEntee Bowman and his entourage arrived from New York to meet with George and then continued on to Cuba for the groundbreaking of the new Havana Biltmore Yacht and Country Club. Other notables included New York Mayor Jimmy Walker, Cuban President Geraldo Machado, and an assortment of socialites and entertainers.

For the most part, George and Eunice avoided the social scene except when his presence was needed to support the University of Miami, promote a new project, or refute increasingly negative comments. He also missed most Coral Gables Commission meetings. Trying to avoid a perceived conflict of interest, he stayed away from meetings at which commissioners discussed the recently passed bond issue. Most of the funds would be used to acquire the Granada Golf Course, the Venetian Pool and Casino, and the street railroad from the Coral Gables Corporation. He also skipped the February 10 meeting when, to everyone's surprise, the commission accepted the corporation's bid for the purchase of $4.5 million in bonds. Besides providing money to buy the three properties from the corporation, the proceeds would also fund a variety of other projects, including $300,000 to help construct the Coliseum and $250,000 for a new city hall. The *Miami Riviera*, in a front-page story, explained that the corporation purchased the bonds in order to ensure they were resold for par to a reliable syndicate.[3] This disclaimer did not quiet those who were becoming increasingly concerned about the close relationship between the commission and the corporation. In an attempt to address the problem, the Coral Gables Commission, with George in attendance, unanimously passed a resolution that memorialized the commission's desire to completely separate from the affairs of the Coral Gables Corporation. They asked the city manager and Commissioners Purcell and Peabody, who had no current connection with the corporation, to confer on any situation that might cause criticism and recommend ways to avoid a real or perceived conflict of interest.

In addition to missing most of the commission meetings, George also kept an uncharacteristically low profile and tried to avoid the limelight. Despite his absence, the accolades continued. Rollins College awarded him an honorary bachelor's degree and Spain's King Alfonso named him an honorary citizen—the first civilian to be so named. A few months later, the king presented him with the prestigious Order of Isabella the Catholic medal, the nation's highest honor. In each case, George sent others to accept the awards.

His stance changed on March 30, when a group of Coral Gables citizens announced a community event at the Coral Gables Country Club to honor him. More than two thousand people came to welcome him home and cheer as University of Miami President Ashe presented him with a silver loving cup in their name. *The Herald* reported that the response was "emblematic of the love and respect in which George Merrick, developer and creator of Coral Gables, is held by the citizens of that city."[4] Deeply moved by the outpouring of support, George spoke briefly, vowing to never give up. The following day, E. H. Schuyler, principal of Ponce de Leon High School, wrote him a letter that summed up the feeling of many in the crowd. "I wish to tell you," he began, "that your talk at the Country Club last night will go a long way toward the realization of your dream for this wonderful city. The hearts of most of the people here are with you. Even Jesus had his Judas, so we can hardly expect to escape without some disloyalty."[5]

Emboldened by the community's response, George began pushing new projects as if it were still 1925. In an address to the Kiwanis Club at a luncheon a week after the Country Club event, he fired up the crowd with a speech reminiscent of his old self. "We can do everything if we have sufficient inspiration," he began, "and the same inspirations that we have always had are still here. Let us use our imagination to look ahead—to see perhaps Coral Way when it is completed as a continuation of beautiful Biscayne Boulevard—of running past thriving stores, imposing city buildings and charming homes." He concluded with the promise that "what has been done in the past five years can be equaled in the next five years."[6] George seemed more determined than ever.

Coral Gables Corporation ads filled the papers, but due to fewer new projects became more inspirational and less specific. One proclaimed that the only thing that had come to an end was the "period of hectic and hysterical buying which marked such a passing phase." Illustrated with a Bob Fink rendering of an Everglades scene, it concluded with a reminder that the sun still shone and the resources that made South Florida famous were still there.[7]

At George's insistence, the corporation reinstituted the practice of bringing in visitors via bus from other Florida cities. Next, he launched "The Florida Forum" at the Coral Gables Flagler Street headquarters. Every Monday, Wednesday, and Friday nights, prominent individuals lectured on topics such as climate, Everglades draining, banking, development, industry, and agriculture. His goal was to convince people that South Florida continued to thrive and to debunk any notion that its glory days had passed. Truth, he was fond of saying, was the best marketing tool he possessed.

Development of the Biscayne Bay Section moved forward at a frenetic pace despite the death of Charles Deering, another blow to the section's future. Armies of workers cut canals, built streets, and laid sidewalks through the wilderness. Tahiti Beach, destroyed by the hurricane, reopened more beautiful than before. Striped tents replaced most of the thatched huts, giving the beach a more sophisticated image. The upgraded facility also offered docking for luxury yachts and a ferry service to Key Biscayne for those who wanted to swim in the ocean.

Next, George announced the Biltmore Addition, a new section bordering the recently completed trolley line down Segovia Street. It was zoned for both business and apartment development. Activity also picked up in the Industrial Section following the announcement that a spur railroad track and docking basin would be built to move materials in and products out. Several new businesses opened, including a roofing company, a concrete block manufacturer, and a fertilizer factory.

George also had other ideas to help Coral Gables. One was to annex Central Miami and other nearby subdivisions. Although he did not attend the City Commission meeting when it voted to ask the Florida Legislature to pass enabling legislation to allow a referendum on the subject, his support was well-known. Shortly before the vote, he published a full-page "Open Letter" in the *Miami Riviera*. He explained his position by listing ten reasons why annexation was the right thing to do. Among them was the importance of extending the city limits to include the new Seaboard Airline Railroad Station, which was about to open on today's Seventy-Second Avenue south of Bird Road. He predicted the area around the station would become another Industrial Section and help spur agricultural development in the "back country." He also noted how new residents would add to the tax base and help merchants. Not surprisingly, he argued that building artistic, but less expensive, homes in what he called the "extension" would benefit workers who could not afford to live in Coral Gables. "The Coral Gables Ideal of Beauty and Art," he opined, "can be wrought in homes of this nature just as well as in the more elaborate and costly buildings. . . .

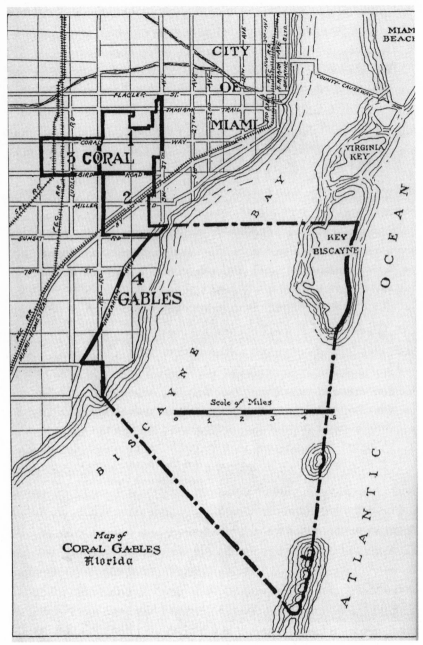

Figure 52. In 1928, Coral Gables extended its city limits west to Seventy-Second Avenue and included a large portion of Key Biscayne, as well as a slice of other nearby keys, as seen in the 1934 map. Permission of Aristides J. Millas. Image reproduced from Aristides J. Millas and Ellen Uguccioni, *Coral Gables Miami Riviera: An Architectural History* (Gainesville: University Press of Florida, 2004).

I always want to take the people of Coral Gables into my confidence. Our problems are the same. They are part and parcel of a city that is very dear to me. Our future progress must be based on mutual confidence."[8]

The enabling legislation flew through the Florida Legislature on its final day in session and the commission set June 28 for a special referendum on the extension. Despite low voter turnout, it passed and Coral Gables' boundaries were extended as far west as Seventy-Second Avenue. Besides Central Miami, the new area included the subdivisions of Schenley Park, Coral Way Villas, Coral Villas, McKeever Terrace, Coral Way Heights, Coral Way Center, and Central Manor.

Even though George promoted industrial development in the new extension and in the existing Industrial Section, his expanded "practical" vision did not trump his original dream of creating a perfect community based on beauty, harmony of design, and good planning. Realizing that fewer buyers were coming in from out of town, he focused on luring Miamians into Coral Gables with a series of ads entitled "Where Miami Leaders Live." He also persuaded the American Building Corporation to resume building a growing group of villages that one writer described as "a quaint colony of homes from all over the world."[9] They included a Marion Sims Wyeth–designed Dutch South African enclave on LeJeune Road and a group of Edgar Albright–designed Louie XIV–era country homes and Mott B. Schmidt French-style townhouses on Hardee. The French Normandy–inspired village on LeJeune, launched in 1926, now included two blocks of completed homes.

The press took special notice when the ABC Corporation completed the first homes in the Henry Killam Murphy–designed Chinese Compound off Riviera Drive. *Miami Herald* columnist Isabella Stone, who wrote about all the villages, provided a detailed description and explanation for the use of typical Chinese decorative elements such as colorful glazed roof tiles, gargoyle-like dogs, and fish-shaped drains. Highlighting its authenticity, she added that the compound had "thought built into every line."[10]

The George E. Batcheller Company added a group of A. L. Klingbell–designed, Italian-style homes south of Bird Road, east of Granada. Although more spread out and with larger lots than most of the other villages, the homes were distinctively Italian and followed a mandated Italian style.

Full-page newspaper advertisements promoted the villages, as well as

Figure 53. George convinced the American Building Corporation to create several new villages. One of the most talked about was the Henry Killam Murphy–designed Chinese Village that still stands south of Dixie Highway and east of Riviera Drive. Author's collection.

other homes under construction. Each included a statement that the current prices had been lowered to comply with the existing market and that buyers should seize the moment and buy before prices inevitably rose.

The downturn was caused by more than a slump in sales. A greater problem occurred after more than a thousand buyers, who, during the heady Boom days purchased property with a small down payment, defaulted on their mortgages. The situation became so critical that, for the first time, the Coral Gables Corporation filed suit against what they called "habitual delinquents." Citing how lenient the corporation had been, George continued to promise that if those who defaulted worked with him in repayment, the corporation would not foreclose.[11] Delinquent taxpayers also compromised the city's finances. In response, the city administration published a list of tax sales in the *Miami Riviera* that spread to more than four full pages. In an effort to set a good example, the Coral Gables Corporation paid more than half a million dollars in city taxes even though the company had to borrow money to do so.

Besides focusing on the Biscayne Bay Section, the Coral Gables Corporation also completed the Country Club Prado Entrance and the new million-dollar Tamiami Entrance, built and named in anticipation of the soon-to-be-completed Tamiami Trail. Designed by Phineas Paist, Walter

DeGarmo, and Denman Fink, the Tamiami Entrance dominated the corner of Southwest Eighth Street and Douglas Road. Its massive, arched automobile gateway included a tower, thirty apartments, and twelve stores, each with a separate and distinctive entrance. The façade, adorned with bas-relief sculptures, reflected Denman Fink's artistic style. The new entrance was the most elaborate of the gateways, but the downturn had forced George to abandon his original plan for a complete Spanish Village encircling a large plaza. Still, its beauty was unparalleled. In a full-page advertisement in the *Miami Riviera* announcing its May opening, George invited the public to "inspect the beauty of design; note the setting of its quaint old Spanish shops, the convenience of its apartments" and "witness its imposing stairways, its great rooms and halls." "Here," George continued, "you will recognize beauty, outstanding architecture, and consummate expressiveness in art, structural strength and militant challenging permanence."[12] Following the opening event—a dance in the grand ballroom sponsored by University of Miami students—George launched a contest to rename the

Figure 54. George also pushed for the completion of the long-promised Country Club Prado Entrance designed by Denman Fink. Author's collection.

Figure 55. Designed by Phineas Paist, Denman Fink, and Paul Chalfin, La Puerta del Sol (Douglas Entrance) opened in May 1927. It resembled Station Square at New York's Forest Hills Gardens. Courtesy of Frank Mackle.

new entrance. Entries included several suggesting it be named after him. He chose Ponce de Leon Entrance, which the city approved.

Work also resumed on the Miami Coliseum, thanks to the infusion of $300,000 from the City of Coral Gables bonds. The private Miami Coliseum Corporation transferred title to the city with the understanding that when the bonds were paid off, it would be returned to them. In the meantime, they would hold a thirty-year lease and manage the property.

In July, the city broke ground for the new city hall. At first, the commission planned to build on what is now Merrick Park, but when they realized they needed a larger site, George, through the Coral Gables Corporation, offered the city additional land across the street if they would pay off $16,000 in liens. (The property's value was estimated at more than $200,000.) The Corporation had previously sold the original site to the city at a reduced price and, even though it would no longer be the site of city hall, offered to give it to the city if it became a park. The commission agreed, named the new park after George, and announced the city would build a statue to honor him. For some reason, George Fink, the original city hall architect, had been replaced by Phineas Paist, Walter DeGarmo, and Denman Fink. (The Coral Gables Corporation agreed to pay half their fee.) Paist, following a trip to his former Philadelphia home, came up with a classical design that bore a striking resemblance to Philadelphia's Merchant Exchange.

As George struggled to keep his Coral Gables dream afloat, he also remained dedicated to his other dream-child—the University of Miami. Like the city and the Coral Gables Corporation, the university faced serious financial difficulties. Through Telfair Knight, George informed President Ashe that any money owed the Coral Gables Corporation for the use and restoration of the Anastasia Hotel could be deferred and used instead to complete the Solomon Merrick Administration Building. Supporters continued to proclaim that it would be completed by the fall, although most knew it was an impossible dream. The Corporation, under George's direction, also paid for a series of advertisements promoting and eliciting support for the university.

Some on the board of regents came up with the idea that they could raise operating funds by building an on-campus football stadium. They cited a similar effort at Stanford University whereby the university had not only

Figure 56. The last building completed under George Merrick's leadership was City Hall, designed by Phineas Paist, Walter DeGarmo, and Denman Fink. It bore a striking resemblance to Philadelphia's Merchant's Exchange. State Archives of Florida, Florida Memory.

raised money to build a stadium but also used the subsequent gate proceeds to fund other programs.

George was not a member of the blue-ribbon group that launched the $500,000 stadium campaign with a flurry of advertisements and public gatherings. The university planned to erect a Phineas Paist–designed, fifty-thousand-seat, horseshoe-shaped bowl west of San Amaro Drive and north of Ponce de Leon Boulevard, then known as University Concourse. In April, Senator Duncan Fletcher and Ruth Bryan Owen kicked off the campaign with a plan to secure funds through the advance sale of fifty thousand season tickets. Stadium committee members and students held rallies throughout Dade County. George did not attend any of the events, indicating it was not an idea he favored.

He and several other regents continued to seek more traditional ways to raise money. They convinced the Coral Gables Chamber of Commerce to donate $50,000 to the university from their publicity fund if other entities would do the same. They also sought funds from the City of Coral Gables, the City of Miami, and Dade County. At one point, the Florida Legislature even flirted with the idea of making the University of Miami a state university. President Ashe and the regents were amenable to the idea, but it died in committee.

Pushing forward despite the continuing financial crisis, the university held its first June commencement at the Coral Gables Theater. Its four graduates, and five others who would receive honorary degrees, gathered at the Grammar School and marched in a grand European-style procession into the theater.

No one was surprised when South Florida experienced its usual summer doldrums. An exhausted Telfair Knight, who had been carrying most of the Coral Gables Corporation burden, took a two-month vacation, even though he wrote that he had to borrow money to do so. George, however, did not slow down but instead increased his public presence. He attended five City of Coral Gables Commission meetings in a row, which was a personal record. Joining the majority, he voted positively for a series of revenue bonds to keep the city going. He was present when the anti–Coral Gables Corporation faction forced City Attorney Clifton Benson, who was both the corporation's and George's personal attorney, to resign.

George also attended University of Miami Board meetings and sadly reported that his fundraising efforts had failed. He spoke passionately about the need to keep the university going even if the budget had to be drastically reduced. The Board admitted that the stadium fundraising had not achieved its goal and soon abandoned the effort. It was clear the university would not be able to complete the abandoned administration building any time soon.

George also continued his role as Coral Gables' most visible cheerleader. In late July, he spoke on Coral Gables' future to the annual meeting of the Coral Gables Chamber of Commerce. Although not abandoning his optimistic outlook, he cautioned the group to have "less talk and more accomplishments this year. . . . Let's get practical and stop looking up in the clouds for something to do when there are lots of things right under our noses needing attention."[13]

Unbeknownst to most, George and Telfair Knight had been focused on trying to get the Coral Gables Corporation new financing. Despite George's best efforts to continue advertising and other promotional activities that had worked in the past, the corporation's growing debt forced him to face reality. Without new financing, the corporation would fail and, with it, his dreams for Coral Gables.

In early September, the social pages reported that George, Eunice, Denman, and Zillah traveled to North Carolina for a much-needed vacation. This absence, unlike the last, fueled those who blamed George and the Coral Gables Corporation for the city's and their own personal financial problems. Trying to quell the growing negative feelings, Telfair, in George's absence, addressed the League of Women Voters on the unique relationship between the corporation and the city:

In its inception and early growth, it [Coral Gables] was the idea and ideals of one man, George E. Merrick, who conceived it in his mind before it was born and who, by constant effort, has developed it into its present state of progress. . . . As it grew, Mr. Merrick has gathered around him a smaller family of aides to assist him and the larger family of the citizens. The smaller family of assistants forms the Coral Gables Corporation which is just another name for George E.

Merrick, because he still owns and controls all of its destinies and in the hearts of all of us, I am sure, is the hope that he will continue to do so through his life. . . . No city ever came into being as a municipality, with so much of its work already done.[14]

In early October, Telfair joined George in New York City in a last-ditch effort to seek funding. Ensconced in the New York Biltmore Hotel, the two men began a series of meetings and negotiations with New York, Southern, and Midwestern bankers and financiers.

By some miracle, the University of Miami opened for its second year on October 3. George missed the event. "We are confident that this year will see all our troubles ended," George and Telfair wired President Ashe from New York. Ashe responded with a telegram to Telfair saying that the University of Miami had a "smooth opening even though financial prospects were rotten." But realizing that the university's future was tied to the failure or success of their financial deliberations, he added: "Wish you and Merrick success of present mission." As the telegrams continued back and forth, Ashe occasionally sent a more positive note following the university's opening reception at the Biltmore. "Thought some of these things might be a bit encouraging to you and Mr. Merrick up there," he wrote Telfair. Although not mentioning specifics, George responded to Ashe and others that deliberations were going well.[15]

Things were not going well in Coral Gables. The Ponce de Leon Entrance had few tenants. To help fill the empty space and follow through on another of his promises, George agreed to give the Cathedral Room to the Coral Gables Woman's Club for two years if members would open and operate a public library there. He also offered the club temporary storage space in several of the empty storefronts. In addition, he convinced the Coral Gables Commission to give the club $1,000 to buy books. The Cathedral Room provided an elegant setting for a European-style library. It had thirty-foot-high decorative ceilings, paneled walls adorned with antique tapestries, and beautiful Spanish antique furnishings.

From New York, George also helped plan the second annual Progress Week set for November. If someone read the *Riviera*'s November 8 "Progress Edition" and was unaware of the true situation, he or she would have thought that Coral Gables was not only surviving but thriving. The *Riviera*'s lengthy editorial, headlined "The Founder," demonstrated that although critics waited in the wings, most of the citizens of Coral Gables stood by him.

> The *Miami Riviera*, at this time of celebration and rejoicing . . . invites its readers to pause for a moment—just to take thought for the man George E. Merrick.
>
> His was the genius that gave to Coral Gables its birth; his the soul that gave it character transcending any other city of our time; his the strength, fertility and resourcefulness of mind that sustained Coral Gables through periods of amazing strain; and that seized the highest moments of success to pour back into this city for its development, all—and more than all—of the substances that it yielded.
>
> George E. Merrick could have failed long ago—if he had that type of mind that knows or admits failure. George E. Merrick could have retired a multi-millionaire long ago—without a care in the world for the rest of his days if he had the grasping type of mind that would permit of stark selfishness at the expense of thousands who gave to him their confidence. . . .
>
> Let us make it known to him through the very enthusiasm of our rejoicing that Coral Gables—the whole community—is and will stay with him, behind him and for him to the limit of human capacity for loyalty. . . .
>
> We are with him to a man, in all his efforts on our behalf. We wish he were here. Since he can't be here, let us cheer him on with the knowledge that we are trying to further his ideals while we glory in his achievement. Let us take a moment to salute George E. Merrick— who works for us all.

Progress Week events included the official opening of the library, with F. Wingfield Webster presenting the ceremonial keys to the Coral Gables Woman's Club president in George's name. The next evening, eleven thousand people attended the grand opening of the Miami Coliseum. Touted as the greatest convention hall/coliseum in the South, promoters bragged that it was one-third larger than Atlanta's famous Armory. The following day, city fathers dedicated Merrick Park and laid the cornerstone of the new city hall, which was nearing completion.

The outpouring of community support emboldened George as he met with the bankers. He and Telfair continued to send telegrams to their Coral Gables associates stating how sorry they were to miss all the important events and keeping them abreast of their progress. In one, George predicted he would soon return "with some good news for you." In response, Ashe wrote, "all the sensible people in Miami are rooting for you."

George also missed the opening of two new churches—the First Christian on Avenue Menores and the Church of the Little Flower on San Domingo Plaza. The *Miami Riviera* noted that Little Flower was made possible "by the unstinted generosity of George Merrick and his associates and in every way the building will conform not only with the ideals of the founder of Coral Gables, but with the farseeing vision which from the beginning has planned and co-operated with the pastor in striving to make the group of Little Flower buildings one of the most notable architectural features in Coral Gables."[16]

George, still a preacher's son at heart, was especially proud of the new churches. To encourage them to build, he either gave land or sold it at a reduced price. After the 1926 hurricane blew away the Baptists' temporary church on Coconut Grove Drive, he helped them build another temporary building on Ponce de Leon and San Sebastian. The church published a rendering of a grand edifice on a waterfront lot George had given them near the University of Miami. The Baptists, however, like St. Stephen Episcopal, did not get their dreams past the drawing board. Before the year ended, however, both the Methodists and Presbyterians announced plans to build in Coral Gables. Although George would spend Christmas in New York, on December 24 he published a full-page Christmas greeting, complete with a Bob Fink drawing of a manger scene.

A huge crowd welcomed the new year at the Biltmore. The following day, a group of businessmen inaugurated what they called "The Palm Fete." One of its first events was a football game between the University of Miami and Furman. "It's Your University, They're Your Hurricanes," a full-page Coral Gables Corporation advertisement proclaimed in promoting the game and the university. Another event celebrated the opening of the new Coral Gables Seaboard Airline Railroad Depot on Seventy-Second Avenue. In Coral Gables style, it had a red-tile roof, a clock tower, a vine-covered loggia, and a patio with a Spanish fountain. The depot, designed by Phineas Paist, received glowing reviews as the most beautiful terminal in South Florida. Regular service between Coral Gables and points north began immediately.

Although Coral Gables was part of the celebration, most of the Palm Fete events focused on Miami. Highlights included the opening of Biscayne Boulevard, the expanded Port of Miami, Venetian Causeway, and the new Olympia Theater. (Within a few years, the Palm Fete would morph into the Orange Bowl Festival.) Coral Gables, however, was not left out of the festivities. Besides the football game, the Biltmore hosted a luncheon for a group of newspaper editors who held their national convention in Miami during the Fete. Hoping the editors would write positive stories about the area, the hotel also arranged for a tour of Coral Gables, including a stop at Tahiti Beach. The day before the editors' final dinner at the Coral Gables Country Club, the Coral Gables Corporation ran a full-page advertisement in both *The Miami Herald* and *The Miami Daily News* headlined: "Editors—A Word With You." It noted the corporation's accomplishments and its $150-million investment, and touted George's unyielding vision. "If you carry away but the conviction of sincerity of purpose in the heart of the Coral Gables founder," it concluded, "you carry the sole key to understanding Coral Gables."[17]

Even though George had been in New York for more than three months, community support continued. The Coral Gables Commission at its January 4 meeting voted to "excuse and exonerate" him for missing five consecutive meetings due to his being in New York to work out fiscal matters that would benefit the city. He and Telfair kept the telegram wires humming with updates about their negotiations. George also sent Eunice daily telegrams and expected her to do the same—sometimes complaining when she missed a day. Beginning with "My Sweetheart and My Dearest," George kept her informed of his meetings and often asked her to pass the news along. Some of his other close associates also became messengers. At a University of Miami Board of Regents meeting on January 16, Jack Baldwin told the regents that once the Coral Gables Corporation had its finances settled, "they will put the university on its feet financially and pay all current obligations." Clearly, George had not given up.

Just as he was completing his negotiations and preparing to return to Miami, a new crisis emerged. On Monday, February 6, Miami experienced an unexpected run on its banks. Fueled by an "anonymous letter" and "rampant gossip," people stormed Miami banks desperate to withdraw their money. Besides several smaller banks, the First National and Southern Bank and Trust—both of which had a long history and well-known presidents—also fell prey to the panic. J. E. Lummus, president of Southern Bank, called in State Comptroller Ernest Amos to help secure his bank and quell depositors' fears. *The Miami Daily News*, in a front-page editorial headlined "Let Us Be On Our Way," wrote that the event could be expected considering the problems South Florida had faced but reminded readers that calm had returned after a temporary flurry. "Deflation came and went," the editors declared. "The hurricane did its worse. The run on the banks, never severe, by the way, came in natural sequence and we have lived through it all, smiling, confident, with faith undiminished. So let's be on our way."[18]

For George, the timing could not have been worse. He later wrote: "Our morale has been shaken by two unfortunate financial developments. . . . A few more and we will be set back for many years."[19]

Fortunately, the run on the banks, although a harbinger of what was to come, was over before it caused irreparable damage. George was able to calm his potential investors and convince them it was but a blip in South Florida's ongoing recovery. A short time later, he consummated the deal and returned home triumphant.

It was mid-February and George and Telfair had been in New York for four and a half months. Now, with a signed agreement, George was eager to promote what he believed was the solution to his and the city's problems. His first public address came on February 15, when he spoke to a Miami Realty Board dinner meeting at the Biltmore. His speech, carried almost word for word in the *Miami Riviera*, explained the plan:

> You all know the history of the development of Coral Gables during the past six years, so I will not review it. Up to two years ago we went ahead at a tremendous speed developing our plans, possibly a little too fast, possibly with the fault of trying to get great things done too quickly and thoroughly. Possibly, we have thus created faults in our financial structure and we may perhaps grant that there may be grounds for criticism on that score.

Next, George explained how two years previously, unbeknownst to the public, the Coral Gables Corporation had hired Ford, Bacon & Davis, a nationally known industrial engineering firm, to study the situation. They sent twenty men to Coral Gables for five months to review the corporation's books and records and prepare a thorough report on their findings. With this report in hand, he and Telfair traveled to New York to meet with a group of bankers and financial institutions. They returned with a plan that not only proved George's skill as a salesman but also demonstrated that, like George, the consultants and financiers believed Coral Gables had a bright future. At the end of his speech, he invited the guests to come to his suite at the top of the Biltmore to see for themselves all that had been accomplished in only six years and to imagine what would be possible in the next decade.[20]

During the next week, George penned another of his "Personal Statements" and sent Telfair out to meet with creditors to explain the plan's complicated and multifaceted details. The key selling point was this: unlike what was happening to creditors in foreclosure proceedings, the corporation's "Comprehensive Refinancing Plan" would pay all creditors in full if they would agree to the proposed long-term payment schedule. To start, the bankers would immediately provide $6 million to $7 million to pay off 10 percent of the debt owed to twelve major companies. Fifty percent of the remaining debt would be secured in second mortgage income bonds and another 40 percent divided equally between preferred and common stock in a new corporation named "Coral Gables Incorporated." At the bankers' insistence, George and his associates would continue to own the majority stock and provide general management. The bankers would control the purse and handle all receipts and disbursements under tight budget controls. They would also receive a large share of stock. As a further inducement and an indication of their faith in the future, neither the bankers nor the corporation would receive any profit until all the debts were paid—a process estimated to take five to ten years.

Many of the corporation's largest creditors, including the American Building Corporation and several banks, agreed to the plan. Organized groups like the Miami Realty Board gave what was described as "warm approval and hearty support."[21]

The positive feeling continued with the grand opening of the City Hall. George attended the first commission meeting in the new chambers and can be seen sitting front and center in the photo commemorating the event. In fact, unlike the past year, he attended all the late February and March meetings and at one helped secure a $5,500 loan from the city to keep the University of Miami open.

He hoped his upbeat attitude and presence at the commission meetings and at other community events would help an increasingly doubting public accept the proposed financial restructuring. But other unexpected events occurred that undermined what he was trying to accomplish. The first blow came in early March, when a group of northern investors, many of whom were also involved in the financial plan, took over the Bank of Coral Gables. They replaced Telfair Knight as president, and other Coral Gables Corporation executives, including George, resigned from the board. A *Miami Riviera* editorial saw it as simply a sign of maturation and proof that Coral Gables was "no longer a one man town."

Despite the positive spin, the changes at the Bank of Coral Gables cast doubts on the proposed financial plan, which was still being debated. George, Telfair, and others were often quoted in the local press and spoke to a variety of audiences about the importance of its success.

In late March, more details emerged concerning changes, and what George called "improvements," to the original plan. Each new iteration, however, diminished his and the corporation's role. The first change was the creation of "Producing and Conserving Boards." The Producing Board would be made up of George, Telfair, and ten of his chief executives. It would handle development, promotion, and sales, the latter through the Coral Gables Corporation. The Conserving Board, headed by Miami businessman Pat Railey, would be made up of men representing several groups of creditors who would become partners in the business and oversee its finances. The Conserving Board would continue until all debts were paid.[22]

In another article, George told how, in concert with the Conserving Board, the Coral Gables Corporation had reduced its operational expenses to only $250,000 a year. This was in stark contrast to the boom years when the corporation had six hundred employees and expenses of more than $3 million. Following the collapse of the boom in January 1926, the corporation had been scaling back, but this final number was a radical departure from even the October 1927 budget of almost $1 million.

As a further inducement, George announced that once the financial plan was approved, five of America's largest life insurance companies had agreed to finance the construction of a thousand new homes. In a lengthy interview in the *Miami Riviera*, he reminded readers that Coral Gables had become well-known throughout the country because the corporation had invested $6 million in a national advertising campaign. As a result, northern bankers were well versed on Coral Gables' accomplishments. They were impressed with the more than $150 million in invested capital and the fact that twelve thousand people now called Coral Gables home. Of equal importance was the fact that since the end of the Florida Boom in January 1926, $42 million worth of construction had occurred in Coral Gables.

George ended the interview with a biblical reference to Jacob never giving up his quest to marry Rachel even if it required seven years of servitude. "Today," he told reporters, "I am prepared to serve another seven years for 'Rachel.' Today, I am fuller of faith in the future of Coral Gables and of greater Miami than I have ever been in the 30 years I have lived here." Reminding readers of what he accomplished, he concluded with a quote from a poem entitled "Father Squeers" by James Whitcomb Riley:

He said when he rounded his three score and ten
I have done it all once, I can do it again.[23]

George's positive comments about the ongoing negotiations continued into early April. For him, it was not just words but came from a deep belief that soon he would be able to complete his dream for Coral Gables.

He also continued to do everything he could to help the University of Miami. Despite the problems swirling around him, on March 30, he penned a letter to "Dear Friend" that explained the problems facing the university and gave an impassioned plea for help:

I am pausing in the midst of my successful Coral Gables re-financing work to appeal directly to you. . . . Through Miami's two hardest material years the University of Miami has steadfastly and bountifully provided inspiration. . . . The University is now in its Valley Forge period. . . . Their Lafayette, with fresh men, money and courage, must quickly come to their aid. *And it Must be you!* With you as their Lafayette; not only Yorktown will come, but also that great period of national and international recognition. . . . Therefore, once out of this crisis the upward growth of the "U" into its ultimate 20,000 yearly enrollment from the Americas is assured.[24]

Unbeknownst to George, he was about to face his own historical event that would be more akin to Waterloo than to Yorktown.

In a surprise move at the April 4 city commission meeting, the newly re-energized Citizens League demanded that the Coral Gables Commission hold a special election to vote on a new commission ahead of the 1929 regular election. League members argued that the city had never had an election and instead had allowed the Coral Gables Corporation to name its first commission. In a magnanimous gesture, and believing the citizens would reelect the present commission, George made the motion to call a special election for April 24. It was then agreed that any commissioner not reelected would resign. Most residents were shocked when they read the commission actions in a *Miami Riviera* "Extra" delivered to the door.

The timing, just when the financial plan was undergoing its final deliberations, could not have been worse for George. He tried to act like it was only a temporary setback. Putting on a positive front, two days after the commission vote, he spoke to the Coral Gables Woman's Club about his favorite poetry.

Adding to the turmoil, the opposition quickly launched an extremely negative campaign against all the commission members, but especially George. Led by Jack Kehoe, the Citizens League came up with a slate and a slogan that asked voters to "Clean House in City Hall."

George was one of the first commissioners to place an ad announcing his candidacy. The others, including Mayor Dammers, quickly followed suit. (In his ad, Mayor Dammers wrote that electing George was even more important than electing him.) The upcoming election energized residents to register to vote, setting a new record. As the day neared, fifteen candidates filed with the Citizens League backing their slate of five. The League held a mass rally at the Coral Gables Grammar School that the *Miami Riviera* described as a "bitter attack" on the present commission. For the first time,

George was attacked by name. "Merrick rode to the top on the crest of the boom," V. V. Wyman declared, "and ran his shoestring up to a $75,000,000 paper profit and left most of us the pleasure of riding down on the wave. Merrick built Coral Gables for businesses purposes only, and his advertising and sales methods have put a halo made of hokum about his head."[25] Even though the personal attack was shattering, the defection of E. T. Purcell, an original member of his Coral Gables team, to the opposition was especially upsetting to George.

The *Miami Riviera* responded with an editorial chastising the Citizens League for its "great injustice" and for selecting George Merrick as its "goat." It deplored the league's timing, just when the Coral Gables Corporation, as the chief Coral Gables property owner, was close to refinancing. "The *Riviera* feels," it continued, "that George E. Merrick stands in a class apart and ought to receive a terrific vote of confidence and encouragement in recognition of what he has done and can do in building the most beautiful city."[26]

In the same issue of the *Riviera*, George penned a full-page "Announcement by George E. Merrick" refuting some of the league's claims and reminding the public that the Coral Gables Corporation had given them streets, parkways, sidewalks, and beautiful entrances that normally would have been built by a municipality. He also noted that any negative circumstance that impacted the refinancing program would be catastrophic.

As the election neared, George retreated to Nassau for what he called "complete rest." He wrote a letter to his "Fellow Citizens" apologizing for not knowing everyone personally. "The demands of my time, during the past two years in which I have been engaged in working for the preservation and perpetuation of our city, has prevented this." Then, in a surprise announcement, he added, "Within the past week, I have been able to place the financial destinies of our various enterprises in the hands of men who have the ability and willingness to accomplish this purpose."[27]

The controversy at City Hall had taken its toll not only on George but also on the financial reorganization. In an attempt to keep the bankers involved and save his city, George reluctantly turned over all control of Coral Gables Consolidated to them, remaining only as a titular head. Telfair Knight, who had been George's right-hand man and closest confidant, resigned, along with most of the other officers. For all practical purposes,

George would no longer be the guiding force in the development of what he had created. It was a bitter blow.

George was still in Nassau when the city announced the election results. In the midst of his darkest night, one bright light appeared. The citizens of Coral Gables had not only voted to keep him on the commission but also honored him with the highest number of votes. The other commissioners and the mayor, however, were replaced by four of the five Citizens League candidates.

The day after the election, Dammers, Peabody, Purcell, and Webster resigned, but the issue was laid on the table until the April 30 meeting when George could attend. On that day, as George looked on, Mayor Dammers and each of the other commissioners resigned one by one, leaving him as the lone survivor. At the following meeting, the commission offered George, who had the most votes, the position of mayor. He declined because he believed other matters would cause him to miss meetings. The commission then elected P. E. Montanus, who had the next highest number of votes, mayor. George's importance to the citizens of Coral Gables had been validated, but he now stood alone in an increasingly hostile body. The commission's first order of business was to demand an audit of the city books. George seconded the motion.

As turmoil swirled around the city commission, Major Lynn Dinkins of New Orleans and Seneca D. Eldredge of New York, who, with George's acquiescence, had taken over Coral Gables Consolidated, addressed the more than four hundred creditors at a meeting held at the Ponce de Leon Entrance. They reminded the group that if it did not accept their proposal, bankruptcy was inevitable. George did not attend the meeting. He had already demonstrated that saving Coral Gables was his top priority, and if this new plan could achieve that goal, then he was willing to step aside.

Even though George received encouraging press and letters from those who refused to give up on him or his dream, he was about to experience another disaster that would send him deeper into despair. At the June 5 commission meeting, George, reeling from the recent setbacks, introduced a resolution asking that he be excused from commission meetings until his health was restored. "I can attend some meetings but not many," he said. "My being away does not impair my power to serve very much, for most of you know I keep in touch by telegraph and telephone. I can continue to keep in touch, given the proper cooperation by my fellow commissioners. I am putting as much brain power into Coral Gables every day as any of you, and my heart is in this city. Everything I have or hope is vested here."[28] The resolution failed, with his being the only affirmative vote. Next, Commissioner F. E. Kane moved that George's resignation from the commission be accepted. It received a positive vote, with only George voting "no." He then made it clear he would not resign.

In a shocking move, Commissioner Kane then proposed a prepared resolution entitled "Expelling Commissioner George E. Merrick." It stated that "whereas it appears upon the records of the Coral Gables City Commission that Commissioner George E. Merrick has attended only seventeen meetings during the past fifty-three meetings. . . . Be it resolved by the Commission of the City of Coral Gables that the said George E. Merrick has failed and neglected to discharge his duty as City Commissioner during the last five regular meetings and for such neglect of duty the said George E. Merrick be and is hereby expelled from office." The vote passed with only George voting no.

George refused to accept the ouster and vowed to seek legal counsel to fight it. It appeared to many that the new commissioners had carefully planned his expulsion. In a deliberate move, they had held unprecedented twice-weekly meetings in order to accelerate George's absences and reach the requisite five for removal. (Adding to the controversy, before the meeting adjourned, the commission canceled the twice-weekly meetings and returned to the regular schedule.)

At the next commission meeting, due to public outcry, some of the commissioners were having second thoughts about the expulsion. Adding to the controversy, Dilkins and Eldredge, who were leading the financial recovery, spoke angrily to several commissioners about the effect the ouster would have on their deliberations. Tensions soared as more than two hundred people filled the chambers and spilled out into the hallway. Feeling the pressure, Mayor Montanus stepped down from the chair and introduced a resolution, which read:

Whereas this commission at its last regular meeting adopted a resolution expelling Commissioner George E. Merrick; and whereas said resolution was adopted under provocative circumstances and without due deliberation; and whereas this commission does not desire to cause discord but to promote unity and harmony among its citizens, therefore be it resolved that the aforesaid resolution be, and is hereby, rescinded until further consideration postponed until the first regular meeting in August, 1928.

Following a second meeting, discussion began. George was not there to defend himself. Languishing in a hospital in Atlanta, he sent Clifton Benson to read his lengthy telegram into the record. It began with a statement that while he and his attorney believed the ouster was illegal, his physicians had advised him not to enter into any legal contest at the present time because he could not be in Coral Gables to fight it. "At such a time as my health is restored," he wrote, "I shall be prepared to take my proper place among those citizens who are willing to fight for the preservation of our city. Even if it should be found that the action of the city commission was legal, I would not under any circumstances be willing to accept any office whatever from any member of the present city commission of Coral Gables."[29]

Commissioner Kane, who had led the original expulsion crusade, reacted angrily to the telegram, attacking George. In response, Benson reminded the commission of George's years of loyal service and that he was "a very sick man."

The heated debate ended with a tie vote, leaving the question of expulsion in limbo. Within a month, however, the city attorney ruled that the tie vote did not alter the original resolution and at the July 17 meeting, the commission named A. H. Simmons to fill George's unexpired term.

George remained in Atlanta trying to work his way through what seemed like a bitter divorce. He had lost everything in the proceedings, including custody of his only child—Coral Gables.

~14

The Long Road Back

> George Merrick in the days of adversity proved over and over
> again that he had courage and character. Not the man who is a
> great dreamer but cannot survive the puncturing of his dream;
> not the man who is a great builder with blocks of stone but
> cannot fashion anything out of splintered chips; not the man
> who could win but could not lose and get up again and take
> the long road back.
>
> "George E. Merrick," *Miami Daily News*, March 26, 1942

Following his ouster, George later recalled how he spent many months
of "bitter brooding" after "his sea, sky and land—his world—caved in on
him."[1] He remained in Atlanta for several months, wrestling with his drinking and depression. Both were exacerbated by a vindictive city commission
that filed multiple lawsuits against him. They also forced Ted Bishop, who
was married to his sister Ethel, to resign as city clerk. Next, a group of creditors attempted, but failed, to force Coral Gables Consolidated and George
into involuntary bankruptcy.

Although the entire Merrick family had been impacted both financially
and emotionally by George's fall, they remained loyal and united. Eunice,
with head held high, continued to attend public events without him.

George was not only missing from public events but also, after years
of almost daily stories and advertisements, absent from the newspapers
as well. In September, when Coral Gables celebrated "Progress Week," an
event George had initiated three years earlier, he was not even mentioned.
In fact, a full-page City of Coral Gables advertisement in the *Miami Riviera*'s

September 28 "Progress Edition" touted the current mayor and commission as the fathers of "America's Most Beautiful Suburban City." During the celebration, the so-called city fathers invited people to celebrate the opening of a pony golf course located on the northwest corner of Coral Way and Ponce de Leon Boulevard and a hastily constructed band shell across the street. These new projects stood in stark contrast to those George had created.

George made his first public appearance in early October when he and Eunice slipped into the darkened Coral Gables Theater to attend the premier of *Glorious Days Neath Tropic Skies*, which had been filmed in Coral Gables when he was still the key player. To George's surprise, every time his name was mentioned or he appeared on screen, the packed house clapped and cheered. When fans realized he and Eunice were in the audience, Commissioner Simmons, who had replaced him on the city commission, stood and introduced him to a standing ovation that lasted several minutes. After George, with tears in his eyes, rose to express his appreciation, the crowd responded with another standing ovation. It was the first time in months George had smiled.

The following day, James Gilman, president of the Bank of Bay Biscayne, wrote George to express his pleasure after reading about the accolades he and Eunice had received. "It certainly is deserved," he added, "and am under the impression that something is going to be worked out in the very near future that will be satisfactory, profitable and acceptable to everyone."[2]

Despite what seemed like constant hammering and bad news, deep inside, George believed—just as Gilman predicted—that he would somehow be able to complete what he now called his "Coral Gables Ideal." He had already proved he was willing to give up everything to keep his dream alive. He had turned over control to out-of-town financiers who promised to raise funds to pay off the corporation's debt and then complete his plan. But as the new year began, the syndicate struggled after George's expulsion and the failure of Southern Bank and Trust. These events, plus constant lawsuits, caused others who had promised to provide funds to have second thoughts.

Apart from the corporation's failing refinancing plan, the city also struggled with its own inability to pay off its bonds. To no one's surprise, the public became confused because the corporation and the city had been and continued to be intertwined. In an effort to separate the two in the public's mind, the Coral Gables Commission passed a resolution condemning the media—including the *Miami Riviera*—for publishing misleading comments that combined the two entities. The commissioners passed a resolution requiring all media to check with the city before publishing anything on the subject. Of course, the resolution was ignored. In reality, Coral Gables' future depended on a positive resolution of both issues.

Huge debt and limited income also hampered the struggling University of Miami. Each semester, both the board of regents and the public questioned whether the school should or would reopen. Despite overwhelming financial problems of his own, George continued to view the university as one of his highest priorities. He was an unabashed supporter of President Bowman Ashe and frequently helped convince him not to resign.

The university also had close ties to the city. Realizing its importance to the city's future, the Coral Gables Commission, even during the worst of times, continued to give the university a $25,000 yearly stipend. The city also tried to help the university complete the Merrick Building and, on one occasion, commissioners pledged $100,000 if they could find a legal way to do it. (The university never got the money.)

Beginning in the fall of 1928, in contrast to his absences elsewhere, George attended every University of Miami board meeting. In early 1929, the board completely reorganized to include more national members who promised large donations. George was particularly outspoken at the meeting and was one of the few founding members asked to remain.

Besides the University of Miami, George also promoted another of his passions—South Florida's tropical landscape. In March 1929, he donated more than fifty thousand coconut trees from his defunct nursery to Dade County for street beautification. Dade County Commissioner Charles Crandon, a friend and fellow environmentalist, hailed George for his gift. "In the years to come," he predicted, "the citizens of South Florida will realize and appreciate the tremendous program of beautification that Mr. Merrick is responsible for in Coral Gables. It is my opinion, he has done more in the way of beautification than any other person or organization in South Florida."[3]

That same month, a new corporation called Coral Gables Inc. came on the scene after Coral Gables Consolidated failed to secure the promised refinancing. The new corporation required all of George's remaining executives—including his vice chair and closest confidant, Telfair Knight—to resign. This left only George as a powerless figurehead. To secure the deal, he had to relinquish all equity in the Coral Gables Corporation. This showed again that he was willing to make any sacrifice for a second chance.

Leaders of the new corporation announced that George, under a new entity called George E. Merrick Coral Gables Company, would handle sales and marketing from his office in the Administration Building. Seeing it as a comeback, *The Miami Herald* quoted him extensively in a front-page story. The thrust of the interview was that George believed the new corporation would make it possible for him to finally complete his plan. He promised that through aggressive national marketing he would, as he had done in the past, attract thousands of people to fill vacant lots with new homes. "I am bringing to the task a deeper knowledge, a wider experience, and a greater enthusiasm than when I embarked upon the starting of Coral Gables seven years ago."[4]

Imbued with a dose of his old spirit, George placed a full-page advertisement in Miami newspapers announcing the new development. Beneath his original Coral Gables logo, headlines proclaimed: "Today—A Greater Era Begins." Reminding readers of what he had accomplished in seven short years, he proclaimed that with the "refinancing becoming effective today the way has now been cleared for the final and complete fulfillment of its program." Citing South Florida's climatic benefits, which helped create what he described as the "City Unique in America," he promised that "the same spirit which gave it birth would round-out, enrich and bring it to full flower with even a shorter space of time in the future."[5]

George was not the only one excited by the promise of the new corporation. In a *Miami Riviera* article, A. C. Fry, selling agent for the American Building Corporation, one of the city's largest landowners and corporation creditors, chided George's critics and reminded them that nothing ever succeeds without a father or mother behind it. "That is why," he concluded, "everyone is so happy to see George Merrick, the father of Coral Gables, at the head of a newly announced organization." He added, "confidence in him by those who know him has never faltered."[6]

The new corporation caused George to feel more positive about the future, even though conditions continued to deteriorate. After the group who had leased the Coliseum defaulted, the city became responsible for its up-keep and operation. Struggling to find a solution for this "white elephant," the commission turned to George for the first time since his ouster, asking him to help convince the City of Miami and Dade County to utilize the Coliseum as a new armory. Despite George's impassioned speech before the Dade Commission, the effort failed. Nevertheless, the Coral Gables Commission formally thanked George for his help.

The Biltmore Hotel also remained on the financial rocks after Bowman failed to convince the Kellogg Foundation to take it over for a health spa. In October, it underwent a friendly foreclosure sale on the courthouse steps. A new group of bondholders paid $1.75 million for the faltering hotel—a far cry from its original $10 million price tag. The good news was that Bow-man, who helped arrange the sale, would continue to operate the hotel. The following month, he convinced a group of New York bankers and political leaders, including Al Smith, former New York governor and 1928 presiden-tial candidate, to purchase the hotel for $2 million. Even though George lost all financial interest in the hotel and had to vacate his tower suite, once a symbol of his success, he was overjoyed when he learned the hotel would reopen in January.

Despite continuing problems, George presented a positive front. He was drinking less, thanks to Eunice's influence. Although their marriage had been very shaky at the time of his fall from grace, Eunice stood by him and became his most important ally. A devout Christian Scientist, she also was able to interest him in her faith. It was not difficult, considering George had a strong spiritual side and was an eager learner, open to new ideas. After he read Mary Baker Eddy's books, he saw a new ray of hope and the possibility of a better way of living.

Surviving letters and telegrams document George and Eunice's renewed love and commitment as they struggled to put their lives back together. She became his most trusted confidant and an increasingly vital business partner.

George's mother and his brother Richard also played pivotal roles in his recovery. Althea, adoring and accepting, remained his greatest cheerleader. Richard, who once looked to him as a father figure after their father died when he was only eight years old, was now twenty-seven and had been liv-ing in New York trying to break into the art world. When George could no longer supplement his art and taxi-driver income, Richard came home and moved in with his mother. More than any other family member, Richard was the most like George and understood and shared his deep intellectual, spiritual, and creative being. Although considerably younger, he helped him deal with the earth-shaking changes in his life. During the late summer of 1930, as George waited for Coral Gables Inc. to complete its refinancing plan, Richard convinced him to join him on an automobile trek across the country to California. Eunice supported the idea, believing that George needed time to think things through. She promised to monitor their business interests until he returned.

George was away more than two months and during that time he and Eunice kept in touch by telegram. In a particularly warm one, Eunice wrote that she was glad he was getting so much out of the trip and hoped that "various things will be settled in your mind." She ended with "Love from Mr. Meow, BunBun, Mike, Stronger and Me."[7]

George responded to her tender note with a nine-page letter, which began: "Dearest Precious Sweetheart." He described his travels and travails and reminded her that Richard could not take her place and that he constantly wished she were with him. "I am missing you more than I ever did before," he added. Every time he saw a cat, he wrote, he thought of their "little family"—Mr. Meow the cat, BunBun the rabbit, and Macaws Mike and Stronger. Asking her to give them a kiss and pat for him, he ended with "Big gobs of love and kisses for you my sweetheart. Your George."[8]

George returned to Coral Gables rested and invigorated, and full of new ideas. During the trip, he and Richard had discussed the possibility of developing an upscale fishing camp on twenty acres of Lower Matecumbe Key, which he had purchased for Eunice's parents a decade earlier. Richard would design the buildings and the promotional material and George would train people to operate it. He began writing a plan that took on new meaning following R.A.S. Peacock's late-October death. With his mother-in-law's blessing, the fishing camp, which he called Caribbee Colony, was rapidly evolving into a much broader project.

On November 12, George sent out a five-page typed prospectus proposing not one but a string of eleven Caribbee Colonies in the United States, Cuba, and the Bahamas. In keeping with his realtor soul, he saw the Matecumbe project as more than a resort. It would become a training ground and "bait" for his broader real estate ideas. "I am convinced," he wrote, "that real estate can be sold in great quantities, at the right place by the right people who have the right vision and ability, this present winter."[9] In short, he believed that all he needed were people in order to sell his latest dream. He was convinced that an inexpensive vacation experience would bring in droves of individuals—especially during hard times. Following the same theory that gave birth to Coral Gables, he saw opportunity to sell a unique product to the middle class, those on salary with two weeks of paid vacation. He also saw a Florida future for the growing number of retirees. By charging 20 to 30 percent less than other tours did, he predicted that the Matecumbe project, spurred by offices throughout Florida, could draw two hundred people a day for one hundred days. The profits, he wrote, would not come from "the big tent" but the "side shows"—the most important being real estate.

Each colony would be designed by Richard Merrick, Denman Fink, or Phineas Paist and have a George Merrick–trained resident manager plus a local assistant. Only local food—Conch, Cracker, or regional—prepared by native cooks—would be served. Each colony would have a store and an in-house newspaper. George believed that the Matecumbe colony would set the stage and be the model for all that would follow—"wherever water and the sky and all the best of the out-of-doors meet."

Next, he listed additional locations he planned to open within a year. They included Tahiti Beach in Coral Gables, Mayport Beach in Jacksonville, Carrabelle on the Gulf of Mexico in Florida's Panhandle, and another on the Shark River in the Everglades. He also saw tremendous opportunity in Cuba, including a site on Matanzas Bay, the Santa Clara River, Camagüey Beach, and Santiago Bay. He planned to work closely with Cuban President Machado, General Hernando Herrera, and Bacardi Rum Company owner Fecundo Bacardi, whom he described as the "virtual king" of Santiago. He also proposed two more colonies in the Bahamas—one on Nassau Beach and the other at Tarpon Bay, Eleuthera. Later, he opined, the chain would spread throughout America and Caribbee Colonies would become "the greatest real estate vehicle America has ever seen."[10]

Additional handwritten notes expanded the concept even further. He predicted the Caribbee Colonies would provide the inspiration and opportunity to create a string of Caribbee chain stores. They could sell items

Figure 57. To promote Caribbee Colony, George created a series of advertisements that highlighted his latest venture. The ploy worked and huge crowds came to the opening. *The Miami News*, January 7, 1931.

that capitalized on the tropics and on what he described as the brains of artists, inventors, designers, and architects who would originate products that could be patented. They included everything from furniture, decorative objects, Richard Merrick watercolors and etchings, clothing, perfume, tropical foods, and even fertilizer. He also planned to launch a publication called *Outdoor Magazine*, which would have famous editors like Ruth Bryan Owen and Rex Beach.[11]

Although George was clearly dreaming again, he also realized that everything depended on the success of his pilot colony on Lower Matecumbe. With that in mind, in late December he placed a full-page advertisement for Caribbee Tours, Inc. in the local press. From a Samoan hut in downtown Miami's Royal Palm Park, the new company offered an unimaginable list of activities for only four dollars. Guests would board a special Florida East Coast excursion train at nine each morning for the one-hundred-fifty-mile round-trip to Caribbee Colony. Besides the train fare, the tour price also included a pass to the Colony's Beach Combers Club and special rates for huts, boats, fishing gear, and food. Free items included swimming at Matecumbe Beach, fishing from the pier, and dancing to a Cuban orchestra on the outdoor dance floor. In addition to activities at Matecumbe, participants received half-price green fees on what George called the "Caribbee Golf Course," the lower eighteen holes of the Biltmore that later became the Riviera Country Club. If these perks were not enough, tour-goers could also attend a free, ten-day Caribbee Chautauqua-style course at the University of Miami and five free concerts in Bayfront Park, plus enjoy a 5 percent discount at leading Miami stores in the Caribbee chain. Ironically, the ad also included a disclaimer promising no real estate solicitation.[12]

Figure 58. Richard Merrick designed the colorful brochure and Tiki-style huts and served as manager. University of Miami Special Collections. Courtesy of Mildred Merrick.

Richard Merrick moved to Lower Matecumbe to design and oversee the construction of the Samoan huts and help manage the entire enterprise. He also created a brochure to kick off the opening. His romantic, four-color cover, which highlighted the beautiful beach, coconut palms, and Samoan huts, was enhanced by George's equally colorful writing. Another brochure Richard designed offered tours of up to sixty days. Some even included a trip to Cuba or the Bahamas via boat or seaplane.

The official opening on January 6, 1931, was a huge success. Newspapers reported that many prominent people attended the gala event and, as a result, "Depression no longer depressed" as guests alighted into a "new Florida world of South Seas enchantment, Samoan huts [and] white Conch-type buildings with green trim."[13] Two days later, an equally glowing article in *The Miami Daily News* proclaimed that the opening proved "Florida is awake again—the psychology of success again walks her sun-lit beach, welcome reincarnate spirit." Each positive story added to the public perception that George Merrick had indeed made a comeback.

The euphoria was short-lived. Two months after it opened, a fire destroyed many of the huts and cabins and forced its closure. A few days later, George's friend J. H. Gilman wrote him to say how sorry he was to learn of the fire. "It just seems as if everything is falling in your lap at one time. Am sorry," he concluded, "there is nothing I can do for you except to tell you to keep your head up and your chin out, and let them take a crack at it if they want to."[14]

Although George rebuilt some of the huts and cabins and reopened the colony on a smaller scale, the wind had been sucked out of his sails and any plan for expanding the Caribbee Colony concept died aborning. Instead, he sought someone to lease the property so he would not have to spend time there and worry about its operation.

George experienced another humiliating blow that March when disgruntled buyers who had lost money had him arrested and charged with embezzlement and grand larceny. He had to go to the police station and post bond to avoid going to jail. (Of course, details of his arrest made the news.) The combination of events caused him to retreat again.

In the fall, he faced another loss when his former Administration Building was sold for a pittance and became a gas station. Even though George had been forced to vacate his private office following foreclosure proceedings,

Figure 59. After oil magnate Henry L. Doherty and his wife, Grace, purchased the Biltmore Hotel, George convinced him to buy the University of Miami out of bankruptcy. Doherty also indicated he might help George complete his Coral Gables dream. Doherty died in 1939, dashing George's final hopes. Grace Doherty continued to benefit the area, especially the University of Miami. Author's collection.

the thought of it becoming a gas station was another bitter pill to swallow. The hurt was slightly mitigated by the fact that the new owner, Sam Weissel, was a popular and active member of the community. He owned two other filling stations and was active in the chamber of commerce.

Continuing what seemed like a never-ending seesaw ride, the Biltmore also faced new problems. Following a lackluster 1930–31 season, the New York investment group pulled out, forcing Bowman to find new financing or lose the hotel. Fortunately, within a month he was able to convince his friend Col. Henry L. Doherty to take over and provide the cash to keep the hotel alive. Doherty, considered one of the richest men in America, was the founder of Cities Service Company, a huge oil conglomerate. Knowing that Doherty suffered from rheumatism and would appreciate South Florida's warm weather, Bowman invited him to spend some time in the Biltmore tower suite. At the same time, he introduced him to George, knowing they would connect because both were self-made men of vision. The ploy worked and in September, Doherty took over the hotel and kept Bowman in charge. One month later, however, tragedy struck again when Bowman died unexpectedly at age fifty-six.

The public viewed Doherty like a knight in shining armor coming to rescue the princess from the tower. The perception was not far off. Not only would he save the Biltmore, but also, for almost a decade, he would be one of the most important players in resuscitating South Florida's image.

Like George, Henry Doherty made no little plans. In fact, many saw a striking similarity between the two visionaries. Within a month after acquiring an option on the Biltmore, Doherty added Miami Beach's Roney Plaza Hotel to his portfolio. Next, he created the "Florida Year-Round Club" and purchased the Key Largo Angler's Club. He connected the properties with a fleet of twelve Glenn Curtiss–designed "Aerocars"—eighteen-seat trailers that also transported guests to nearby tourist attractions. He then launched a speedboat he called the "Sea Sled" that traveled between Coral Gables and the Key Largo Angler's Club. Finally, he purchased an "Autogyro"—an airplane with large rotor blades that allowed it to land almost vertically, like a helicopter. The Autogyro, a tourist attraction in itself, could make the trip between Miami Beach and the Biltmore in ten minutes.

To promote his new venture, Doherty hired nationally known publicist Carl Byoir, who put Coral Gables and all of South Florida back on the map. While the rest of the nation continued to languish in the depths of the Great Depression, Doherty and Byoir instituted a series of events at the Biltmore pool, including water follies, beauty contests, diving exhibitions, and alligator wrestling. He then built a grandstand to accommodate the crowd. They also created a series of nationally recognized golf tournaments that brought in superstars like Gene Sarazen and Walter Hagen. South Floridians hailed Doherty as a true hero who almost singlehandedly was leading the area out of the Great Depression.

Despite these positive developments, many continued to suffer. Both the City of Coral Gables and Coral Gables Inc. had failed to solve their debt problems, thus stalling new development. George and Eunice's circumstances also continued on a downward spiral. After creditors foreclosed, their South Greenway Drive home was sold on the courthouse steps. At first, they moved in with Althea and then to the former Flagler Street home of Eunice's parents, where she and George had been married fifteen years earlier. The only good news was that in April 1932, George was cleared of embezzlement and all other charges were dropped.

While struggling with his own problems, George continued to support the University of Miami. In December 1932, after the university filed a voluntary petition of bankruptcy, he sought help and advice from Doherty. Doherty, who had become a fan of the university and its president, had already helped it through the Greater Miami Athletic Association, founded to support the football team. In late 1932, the association, as part of the "Palm Fete," launched a New Year's Day football game between Manhattan College and the University of Miami. When funding failed to materialize, Doherty came to the rescue with a $5,000 donation and free rooms at the Biltmore for the visiting team.

Doherty also stepped in after some of the members of the University of Miami board sought President Ashe's resignation. George wrote him an impassioned, six-page letter explaining the controversy and asking him to intervene. Doherty responded with a terse telegram he said George could share with the board. "In my opinion," he wrote, "such an act would be most unfair and unwise and is so contrary to my ideas that if done, I pledge myself to neither contribute my moral or financial support to the Miami University regardless of my great interest in its future."[15]

Two days later, following a lengthy and heated board meeting at which George presented the telegram and forcefully stood up for Ashe, he sent a congratulatory telegram to Doherty. "Your wire did the job," he began. "I personally sincerely thank and congratulate you for this effort and right action."

George and Ashe kept Doherty informed of the continuing bankruptcy proceedings and pledged to keep his involvement confidential. After months of correspondence, in August 1934, Doherty came through with a $25,000 loan that Ashe used to buy the university out of bankruptcy. Doherty promised that if the university could raise five times the amount of the loan during the next two years, he would forgive it.

George also refused to give up on Coral Gables and continued to believe that once the bond refunding issues were resolved and thousands of Coral Gables lots were free from liens, he would be able to complete his Coral Gables dream. As the years slipped by, however, and a series of proposals failed, he realized he must find another way to make money. Recalling his enchantment with the works of Ruskin, Morris, and especially Ebenezer Howard's Garden City ideas, he came up with an unusual, almost utopian, plan he called "Biscayneland," America's first "Country City," which he presented to Doherty. The fourteen typed, legal-size pages included four sections. The first was about a land-buying syndicate he hoped Doherty would lead. It would purchase one hundred thousand acres of South Dade farmland near Peters and Perrine. Next, a group called the Biscayne Society would spread out across the nation to sell individual five-acre units for $500 each. George would run a third entity he called the Biscayne Land Company. It would operate the program and oversee a fourth called the Community Foundation. The Foundation would sell bonds to help build homes, fund what he called "little factories" of homegrown fruits and vegetables, and construct and operate larger factories to manufacture local products like jellies and jams. It would also fund community amenities like parks and civic centers. The plan, George predicted, would bring in two hundred thousand people within ten years.

The "Biscayneland" proposal had many other innovative, albeit impractical, components like free tuition for one family member to attend the University of Miami. It also included a separate, model Negro community and beachfront resort, plus a Tuskegee-type educational center.[16] Although Doherty showed some initial interest, the overly ambitious plan, like many of George's other ideas, collapsed under its own weight.

George, of course, was not one to quit. When Franklin Delano Roosevelt became president and initiated his New Deal, George revised the plan, added "Subsistence Homesteads" and "Country Coral Gables" to the title, and sent it to the Department of Interior, which had recently announced a program seeking proposals. He convinced developer and friend Vance Helm and attorney Clifton Benson to help push it forward. Together they wrote to their congressmen and senators, as well as other politically connected individuals.

The promotional campaign worked, at least initially. A series of letters between the Department of Interior and Benson indicated interest but cautioned that the plan was broader than other proposals. Following specific suggestions from Washington, George drastically reduced the plan's scope and Benson resubmitted it with the caveat that his team would make any sacrifice necessary to get it funded. The government ignored George's revision and chose other projects.

Despite another failure, George's spirits soared in May 1934 following a dinner at the Biltmore to honor "Old and New Gables Pioneers." The principal honorees were George, "the creating pioneer," and Doherty, "the pioneer of today." For the first time since 1928, the citizens of South Florida publicly and enthusiastically praised George for what he had accomplished. When asked if Coral Gables lived up to his expectations, George gave a stirring speech, proclaiming that, despite difficult times, Coral Gables did live up to his expectations and thanking the current city commission for following his plan. He also lauded the University of Miami and stressed its singular role in South Florida's future. He concluded with a nod to his latest passion—subsistence homesteads—predicting the present Coral Gables would become a gateway for thousands of people who, due to the Great Depression, would flock to his proposed Country Coral Gables.

As part of the celebration, the *Miami Riviera* published a special edition that included a two-page spread honoring George. "George Edgar Merrick today may look out on the city with justifiable pride," it began, "and know that he is responsible for all it represents—that here is beauty manifested to the nth degree, for here is 'such stuff as dreams are made of in the real.'"[17]

Following the dinner and newspaper stories, George increased pressure on Doherty to work with him on his plan to develop twelve thousand Coral Gables lots. He asked him to show his support by sending a letter to the bondholders committee stressing the importance of including George's plan as part of the City of Coral Gables bond settlement. In a letter to Doherty's assistant, M. M. Mallory, he reiterated the importance of the proposed letter and hoped it would be as unqualified as the one he had sent regarding President Ashe. "We have now arrived, I feel, at a sound financial rock to build on in regard to Colonel Doherty's backing of me which I have long been working for," he wrote. "I ask that you present this to Colonel Doherty as my very urgent, from-the-heart appeal *now* for his necessary action in my behalf—necessary if I am ever to get into timely, proper action, and with the very minimum of financial assistance from Colonel Doherty."[18]

When George did not hear back from Doherty, his lawyer and partner Clifton Benson followed up with another letter. It included a proposal for a new business that George hoped Doherty would help finance at $400 a month. The monthly stipend was to be a loan and would be paid back as soon as the two were able to launch Country Coral Gables or the Coral Gables lot plan. Once again, Doherty did not respond.

A month later, George wrote him a personal letter that included a startling announcement. "It may be somewhat foolhardy of me to 'burn my bridges' without hearing from you," he wrote, "but I am feeling very much that it is the right thing for me to now get my wheels moving if only slowly."[19] He followed up by registering his new corporation called Merrick, George E. Incorporated with the State of Florida. In reality, George didn't do anything slowly.

A short time before he wrote Doherty, George typed a long letter to Benson explaining why he was moving ahead so quickly. After Sam Weissel offered him space in his former Administration Building for $100 a month, he saw it as an opportunity he could not let pass. Even though the building was now a gas station topped with a huge red and green neon sign announcing "Sam's Place," the proposed office faced Ponce de Leon Boulevard, had two storefront windows, and was next door to the Coral Gables Post Office, which recently had moved in. Besides his emotional attachment to the building, he believed the public would view a new office there as tangible evidence that he was back in business. After consultation with Doherty's assistant, who supported the idea and believed Doherty would come through with the money, George and his new partner, Vance Helm, signed the lease.

As he awaited the bond settlement, he saw opportunity in selling lots and homes in lower-priced subdivisions outside of Coral Gables. Recalling his past success, he planned to reinstitute a series of auctions similar to the ones he did in his early real estate ventures. After predicting a bright future for his new business, he ended, almost apologetically, by asking Benson for a loan to tide him over until money came in from Doherty or from sales.[20]

George strongly believed that his new headquarters must resemble the old. With Eunice's approval, he emptied their home of antique rugs and Spanish furniture and furnished the new office in elegant style. The only change was that he filled the blank walls with original Richard Merrick paintings and etchings instead of what he considered outdated Coral Gables photographs.

George felt encouraged by positive comments celebrating his latest comeback. But despite predictions of future success, Doherty did not come through with the requested funding and the bonding resolution stalled. Undaunted and believing that if he did it once he could do it again, he opened other offices—one in downtown Miami's McAllister Hotel and another in the Roney Plaza. He launched a new advertising campaign, albeit on a much smaller scale. Instead of full-page advertisements, he placed weekly classified ads in such national papers as *The New York Times*, *The Philadelphia Inquirer*, and *The Boston Post*. In addition to small ads in local papers, he created several modest, black-and-white foldout brochures. Next, he inaugurated "informational trips" and transported prospective buyers from downtown Miami through Coconut Grove, Coral Gables, and then south to the area he continued to promote as Country Coral Gables.

Never one to overlook new opportunities, he invested $200 a week to sponsor "News of the World"—a nightly, ten o'clock radio broadcast on station WQAM. Besides opening with the tagline "George Merrick Presents," each program ended with "George Merrick Says"—a personally written promotion that covered specific offerings laced with history. As a ploy to gauge his audience, he ran a poetry contest asking listeners to submit original poems that celebrated South Florida. Hundreds responded.

Besides general real estate, George also promoted several new ideas, including one for Grand Bahama patterned after Biscayneland. With assistance from the Bahamian government, he hoped to build a self-sufficient town on a swath of waterfront. It would focus on middle-class individuals from Great Britain, Canada, and the United States. He succeeded in attracting some interest from Bahamian leaders and even made several trips to the Bahamas to push his ideas.

He also planned an experimental farm in South Dade to highlight Cuban products. He hired W. H. Morales Jr., head of the Cuban Chamber of Commerce in Miami, and sent out formal announcements in English and Spanish to inaugurate his bilingual Pan American (later Latin American) Department. Richard Merrick created individual letterheads with a thematic drawing for each department, which, besides Pan American, included "Island," "Country," and "Waterfront."[21]

But before any of his plans could be fully launched, much less carried out, another tragedy struck. On Labor Day 1935, the strongest hurricane ever to hit the United States struck the Florida Keys, making landfall near Lower Matecumbe. By this time, George had leased Caribbee Colony to H. Wayne and Nicky Dumas, who were having some success. They paid George and Eunice $120 a month rent—not a small amount for the time. Sadly, Dumas, his wife, and twenty-four guests perished as the ocean surge and winds, estimated at almost two hundred miles per hour, swept all of the buildings and their hapless inhabitants into the sea.

The hurricane also ravaged longtime Keys residents, most of whom had Bahamian roots. As true pioneers, they had survived many storms, but none like this. Almost everyone experienced personal loss. In some instances, entire families perished, including several who were Eunice's distant cousins.

Adding to the tragedy, more than two hundred and fifty out-of-work World War I veterans died when their camps were destroyed. The New Deal's Federal Relief Emergency Administration had hired and sent them to the Keys to construct the new Overseas Highway. If that were not enough, the powerful storm surge also overturned the rescue train.

Even though George also experienced another unexpected loss, he was more thankful than distraught. At the last minute, Eunice and her mother had changed their plans and decided not to spend the Labor Day weekend in the Keys.

When he arrived at Lower Matecumbe as part of the relief effort, George saw piles of dead bodies and helped load the ones that were not cremated in a huge funeral pyre onto a train for burial in Miami. Even though he wrote that his property had been "wiped as clean as a floor," he considered it a small matter compared to the more than four hundred people who lost their lives.

Just two weeks after the storm, George faced another blow when the federal Securities and Exchange Commission subpoenaed him to testify at a hearing in Washington, D.C. The commission called the hearing to investigate why so many cities had defaulted on their bonds. The City of Coral Gables was the first of several municipalities to be called, and George the first to testify.

Investigators began by questioning the propriety of the City of Coral Gables selling bonds to purchase and improve Coral Gables Corporation property when George and other members of the corporation served on the city commission. According to a September 17 *New York Herald Tribune* article, vice-chair and future Supreme Court Justice Abe Fortas took George "severely to task" for his dual roles as owner and commissioner. The article continued with quotes by Thurman Arnold, who accused George of being "a loan shark." In response, George reminded the commission that, unlike other cities, Coral Gables began with much of its infrastructure already built by him and his Corporation. In addition, he said at the time of the purchase, he was paying as much as 30 percent interest. This caused the price for community amenities like the Country Club and Venetian Pool to rise but, contrary to public opinion, the cost was not excessive. He explained that instead of creating huge profits, the cash infusion allowed the corporation to proceed with development that benefited the city. "I considered Coral Gables my town," George was quoted as saying. "I founded it, I was trying to do the best for everyone in it."[22] Once again, George made the national news. But this time, to his chagrin, the stories were predominately negative.

Embarrassed and humiliated, he returned home only to find a letter from his friend and associate Clifton Benson that sent him into deeper despair. After writing that he was sure George "acquitted himself nobly" at the hearing, Benson shifted to a philosophical rant, quoting the biblical admonition that "the Lord chasteneth those whom he loveth." "You must be greatly beloved from that standpoint, and Eunice, as well," he wrote, " . . . for you have certainly known the meaning of hardship in recent years. I greatly admire the noble way in which you both have borne it."

After more philosophical ramblings, he changed his tone and chastised George for not learning from his mistakes. He reminded him how, as a friend, he had constantly told him he was going too fast and forcing through his own ideas even when facts called for a slower pace. While saying that sometimes this approach accomplished wonders, at other times, he reminded him, it created disaster.

Benson wrote that going too fast was his undoing in Coral Gables, as well as at the Caribbee Colony: "I am wondering whether this last disaster for you is not to cause you pause as to whether you are again going too fast in your present enterprise. It grieves me at times to see you work so hard with no apparent results. You make life hard for yourself."

Benson ended by acknowledging that he realized George had done and would continue to do big things but wondered why he could not learn to do them more gradually. "This may be the lesson that you must learn," he wrote, or he would continue to have "disaster upon disaster until that lesson is learned."[23]

Deeply hurt by Benson's letter, George refused to speak to him for several months, until Benson reached out with an apology. In truth, Benson's advice was right on target and George needed Benson more than Benson needed him. They had been friends and partners since their Realty Securities days and Benson knew him better than most. He had been a silent partner in the Caribbee Colony project and a visible one in George Merrick Inc. He also provided legal counsel.

To no one's surprise, George ignored Benson's advice and instead of slowing down, he did just the opposite. He hired more salesmen, opened more branches, and increased his national advertising. His business, while not exactly prospering, was doing better. This prompted him to create a new brochure entitled "Merrick's Realty Service." It included the address for eight offices in Greater Miami, as well as others in Fort Lauderdale, Palm Beach, and Nassau, Bahamas. It also included a list of more than one hundred properties for sale, many including photographs. In another instance, he added his own personal touch to a "Visitors Guide of Miami and Miami Beach" by noting his office locations on a detailed map of the area.

George received a boost in the fall when Florida Governor Sholtz appointed him to Dade County's first planning board. It had been created by a legislative mandate following a New Deal requirement that all states had to have planning boards in order to qualify for federal grants. At the first meeting, the new board elected George chair. Clearly, he was in his element and had a new, very public forum for his ideas. The position did not require him to give up his business; instead, it helped it prosper.

George's new role was important because the federal government, through such agencies as the Federal Emergency Relief Administration (FERA), the Civilian Conservation Corps (CCC), Works Progress Administration (WPA), Public Works Administration (PWA), and the Federal Art Program, had launched many government-funded projects in South Florida. The planning board was asked to review the proposals and submit recommendations to the county commission and later the state board. George worked tirelessly to push the Dade County Commission to aggressively seek funding for a variety of projects, including schools, roads, sewage disposal plants, post offices, and projects to help the black community. He also promoted an airport on Virginia Key and an ambitious Pan American Exposition on the former Royal Palm Hotel site.

Many of the proposed projects were in Coral Gables. These included a community house, a police and fire station, an art center, improvements to Matheson Hammock Park, and paving and beautification of Coral Way between downtown Miami and Coral Gables. In addition, he tried but failed to get funding for the University of Miami to complete the Merrick Building.

His greatest effort, however, focused on convincing the Dade County Commission to provide part of the funding to create a comprehensive planning study of Dade County that would primarily be funded by the federal government. Through this document, he would be able to promote some of the ideas he had for South Dade, including agriculture (what he called "a show park"), Everglades National Park, and an overseas highway that connected the Keys and provided waterfront views for everyone. He, with the help of Charles Crandon, also pushed for the Florida East Coast railroad tracks to be moved west and the site turned into a beautiful parkway that would extend all the way to Homestead.

For George, 1937 began on a high note. On a personal level, with Eunice's support, he had completely stopped drinking and joined the Christian Science Church. As a result, he and Eunice became closer than ever before. Now a true partner, Eunice worked full time at George Merrick, Inc., and took on increasing responsibility after he became chairman of the planning board. His planning board leadership brought him new accolades and, for a time, it appeared that George had made a true comeback.

Adding to his renewed sense of confidence and accomplishment was the fact that, after two failed efforts, the Coral Gables bond issue was finally nearing settlement. He had aided the process by helping convince Henry Doherty to purchase a large group of bonds. The January 1 edition of the *Miami Riviera* listed George as a supporter of what it called "the history making refunding ordinance." After describing him as the founder of Coral Gables, the article continued with his prediction that if the plan was adopted, "Coral Gables will be the scene of unprecedented growth."[24]

Shortly after voters approved the refunding ordinance, George experienced his most primal loss. On February 27, Althea, his beloved mother, died at age seventy-seven after a long illness. Despite crippling and painful arthritis, as well as financial problems, she never lost her positive outlook. Fondly called "Mother Merrick" by Coral Gables residents, she held a special place in the city's heart. Besides being an unabashed supporter of her husband and family during their pioneer days, and her son in his plan for Coral Gables, she was a leader in her own right. She was the one who convinced the Dade County School Board to open the Guavonia School. She founded the women's societies at both Plymouth and Coral Gables Congregational Churches and served as clerk of both—an unusual position for a woman at that time. She even took on the role of preacher when her husband was ill. She also was a founder of the Coral Gables Woman's Club and the Garden Club and helped establish student support groups at the University of Miami. Besides her community activities, she was an acknowledged artist and poet.

George, along with her other children, received hundreds of telegrams and sympathy letters. Following her funeral at Plymouth Church, she was laid to rest at Woodlawn Park next to her husband.

In April, after the court validated the voter-approved bond refinancing, George saw a glimmer of sunshine amid the gloom and hoped that his, and his city's, roller-coaster ride had finally ended. He had other reasons for optimism. His new visibility and New Deal programs, like the Federal Housing Administration, helped his business. In one fortuitous example, Daino-Fine-Homes, the owner of a large number of Coral Gables lots, hired him as its exclusive agent. In addition, Daino also hired Phineas Paist and Harold Steward as its architects and began building homes around Cocoplum Plaza and on the Coral Gables Waterway. For the first time in years, George placed three-quarter-page advertisements for Daino-Fine-Homes in the local press. Next, he moved his Flagler Street office into larger, more visible quarters in the nearby Calumet Building.

Although George was pleased that construction had resumed, the miniboom also caused him concern. He worried that the city would abandon his original plan in the name of recovery. His fear increased following the death of Phineas Paist in May. Paist had served as the city's supervising architect since its founding and was the acknowledged watchdog. To counteract what appeared to be an emerging lax attitude, George and Denman spoke out on the importance of holding fast to his ideal.

His planning board role, plus signs that Coral Gables was making its own comeback, gave him clout and visibility as an expert planner. In May 1937, he made an important speech to the Miami Realty Board. It was so well received that the board asked him to repeat it at a large public gathering in Bayfront Park. Many of his strongest points were not only original but also prophetic. He spoke on the need for an interstate highway, a countywide transportation and water system, and more fairness for blacks. Quoting William Jennings Bryan's Pan American views, he, like Bryan, predicted that South Florida's destiny lay to the south. He promoted beautification by suggesting that all of Dade County should have tropical planting just like Coral Gables did. Continuing the tropical theme, he pushed for public support for what would later become Fairchild Tropical Botanic Garden. He included his usual prediction that the University of Miami would play the key role in helping launch South Florida's future and, as such, deserved community support.

George also spoke out against gambling. He reminded his listeners that there was growing support for legalizing what was already a pervasive, illicit industry. Instead of legalizing slot machines and back-room casinos, which he believed were detrimental to South Florida's future, he encouraged the government to stop all gambling and, instead, promote South Florida's natural advantages.

Following his speech, the Realty Board published his words in a twenty-page booklet entitled *Planning the Greater Miami for Tomorrow*. It received wide distribution and became a planning bible.

His stature increased more in July 1937, when Dade County created its first zoning commission following another legislative mandate. At its inaugural meeting, the new commission, many of whose members also served on the planning board, elected George president. One of his first orders of business was to appoint a committee to draft an emergency resolution against saloons and nightclubs in residential areas.

Even as he focused on immediate problems, he knew that planning and zoning needed a big-picture view to make a difference. His new role as president of the zoning commission gave him the opportunity to turn items on the 150-page planning document, already approved but not implemented by the county commission, into law. He convinced the board to complete a county survey that would identify specific districts and suggest appropriate zoning regulations. When the zoning plan was completed, he organized a series of public meetings to explain the proposed rules and to gain community support.

In August 1938, after more than a year of time-consuming study and deliberation, the Dade County Commission adopted the board's 101-page proposed zoning ordinance. George, who presented the document to the commission, was ecstatic and believed that what he had accomplished in Coral Gables could now be achieved throughout Dade County.

Unfortunately, it was not to be. Immediately following its passage, a group of opponents demanded that the Dade County Commission rescind its approval. Feeling the heat, Commission Chair J. Lamar Paxson called a special meeting to hear the public's concerns about putting any restraints on development. Besides property owners, opponents also included well-known attorneys, realtors, and developers, as well as celebrity-author Hervey Allen, who had a winter home just outside of Coral Gables. In a scathing letter, Allen called the zoning commission a "white ribbon hatchet brigade."[25]

After George accepted the fact that the commission would repeal the heart of the new code, he abruptly resigned, writing that "it was unwise to exert further personal effort." Included in his resignation letter was an angry formal statement to the public.

"Ignorance—plain unadulterated ignorance—is endeavoring to deprive all of Dade County of one of its greatest gains," he wrote. "Ignorance yes—not because they are saying ranting things about us, no, just plain ignorance of the body of zoning regulations itself, and of its spirit, aims, effect and various application." He accused the "ranters" of not even bothering to read the ordinance. "Is Dade County to lose through ignorance or petty politics?" he added. "That is the question."[26]

George felt like his two years of hard work had come to naught and it was a familiar feeling. During that time, his business had suffered and he was beginning to worry that because of Doherty's deteriorating health, he was not going to help him complete his dream for Coral Gables.

Adding to his despair was the tragic death of Frank Button, who had been one of the most important members of his original Coral Gables team. Sadly, Button had been killed in a freak accident while planting banyan trees on Bird Road. Despite his death, George continued to honor Button's singular role in the unprecedented landscaping plan that helped create Coral Gables.

Overcoming his pessimism, George saw renewed hope after the long-awaited bond settlement, plus an infusion of federal New Deal funding, began to bring Coral Gables back to life. In celebration, the city adopted a new moniker: "Coral Gables: The City Beautiful." A short time later the city erected a concrete sign at the Granada Entrance with the new title.

It seemed particularly fitting following the construction of two beautiful, new WPA-funded buildings. The first was the community center. Following a donation by the Coral Gables Woman's Club to help complete it, the city turned it over to the group with the caveat that they would operate a public library in part of the building.

The Woman's Club had been seeking a new home ever since George lost ownership of the Douglas Entrance and the club had to move out. The city offered them several city-owned lots, but the club had no money to build so the land reverted back to the city. In another instance, the club sought to take over the Coral Gables Country Club. The city, struggling to keep the Country Club afloat, agreed provided the public approved the transfer in a special referendum. To the club's dismay, voters said "no."

The community center was constructed on East Ponce de Leon Boulevard of "coral rock." Its beauty was enhanced by WPA art, including a striking fountain in front and a historic mural in the main meeting room by Dewing Woodward, who had once done illustrations for Coral Gables advertisements. Deeding the building to the Woman's Club caused a great deal of controversy because the club was a private organization and public money had been used to construct the building. Eventually, the issue was resolved and the Woman's Club received title.

Construction also began on the WPA-funded Municipal Building. In addition to being a police and fire station, it would house the city jail. Designed by Paist and Steward shortly before Paist's death, the new building (also built of "coral rock") would include distinctive sculptures created by Federal Art Program artists.

Thanks to the New Deal, Coral Gables was emerging as an art center. A

Figure 60. Although frustrated in his desire to complete Coral Gables, George continued to support the University of Miami and Fairchild Tropical Garden. He was a featured speaker at the Garden's opening, in 1938. *Left to right*: Colonel William Montgomery and his wife, Nell; Eunice and George Merrick; and Onie and Charles Fuchs. University of Miami Special Collections. Courtesy of Mildred Merrick.

WPA survey identified twenty-eight artists who lived permanently in the city. Because of the critical mass, the Federal Arts Project opened a studio on Alhambra Circle that focused on sculpture and ceramics. The studio gave local artists new visibility by sponsoring a series of art shows to highlight their work. Dewing Woodward, Denman Fink, and Richard Merrick, who had recently drawn illustrations for a WPA-funded Key West guide, were featured, along with Carmel Wilson, who had been hired to draw city landmarks. Art enthusiasts tried, but failed, to convince the federal government to build a permanent art facility in Coral Gables.

Fairchild Tropical Garden fared better. After the CCC constructed a rock wall down Old Cutler Road and developed Matheson Hammock Park, CCC workers built a two-story gatekeeper's lodge, as well as the overlook and amphitheater at Fairchild. George, who had supported the garden from its inception and served on its board, was a speaker at its March 1938 grand opening. In closing, he predicted that Fairchild "would be only second to the University of Miami as our most vital institution—the ever expanding expression of our true ideals."[27]

As Coral Gables continued its comeback, George saw his fade. He was besieged by creditors and had no money to pay them. He was no longer able to help members of his family. In August, he wrote a poignant letter to his sister Helen, telling her he could no longer help support her. "Not that I don't want to," he added. "I just have no means to do it. . . . The Merrick dynasty is ended. There ain't any more ability in *me*, at least to do anything for you."

He ended by asking her to understand and accept the fact that "the George Merrick who could once work miracles, who could and did help people and brothers and sisters (as well as harm them as they thought) that that George Merrick is no more."[28]

George's financial situation continued to deteriorate. In early 1939, he typed a similar letter to Clifton Benson, explaining the reasons for his latest crisis and why he was unable to pay him the money he owed. He wrote how he had closed all but two of his offices but, even with downsizing, he was having difficulty paying his telephone and electric bills. "If we don't get some breaks very soon," he wrote, "I am going to be forced to close these two offices and call it quits."

Even though some lots would be freed up following the bond settlement, he wrote that he lacked the funds to secure them and was fighting to pay the mortgage on the few he had. "You can see," he added, "there are today no released lots and only a desperate chance remaining of getting anything for my four years work in this matter."

After explaining how he had to borrow money from his mother-in-law for the most basic needs like food and gasoline, he ended on a humorous note. "I am wearing a pair of shoes with the bottom on the ground for the last few weeks," he wrote, "so you can tell your friends that George Merrick's feet are on the ground at last."[29]

George sent a similar letter to Telfair Knight, whom he considered to be his most loyal friend. Like George, Telfair suffered financial ruin following the failure of the Coral Gables Corporation. He had recently secured a job at the United States Maritime Commission in Washington but continued to stay in close touch. In response to George's letter, he wrote that he believed George could make a good living if he specialized in what he did best and did not try to carry so many people along with him. "Maybe I am just getting old," he concluded, "but somehow I cannot help but feel that fighting windmills is a rather futile undertaking."[30]

George answered with a confidential assessment of the Doherty situation, saying that for four years he had believed that he would "be in front of the whole picture," just as Doherty had promised. He had kept his business going because Doherty had assured him the time would come when he would help him finish what he had started. Now, he was afraid he had been "shunted aside" and others had taken over. He added that his only chance was to get a one-on-one meeting with Doherty and hoped to do so soon.[31]

But George was unable to meet with Doherty. In August, in one last attempt to gain his backing, he sent him a sixteen-page, typed proposal that included some new ways to proceed. It began with the idea that unless he were involved in the whole program, Coral Gables would become another "Tom, Dick, and Harry subdivision."

To keep Coral Gables' original standards in the forefront, George proposed a new idea that he called the "Build the University Plan." It would serve two purposes. First, it would help the University of Miami return to its main campus—a move he knew Doherty supported. The completion of the Merrick Building, in its originally designed splendor, would raise the property values of nearby lots. Here, under George's guidance and protection, only high-quality, individually designed homes by outstanding architects would be built. He concluded with the pledge that Doherty's full intent to be the greatest aid to Coral Gables would be faithfully carried out and that he would be part of all decisions.[32]

For several months, George, at least on the surface, believed Doherty would still come through. As he waited for a reply, he kept busy with a series of public events. He gave a highly publicized speech, "Intelligent Planning," at a statewide planning meeting at the Hollywood Beach Hotel. Along with his friend Gaines R. Wilson, he also created a new organization that would be called the Historical Association of Southern Florida and the Caribbean. (It was officially launched in January 1940 with George as the first president.)

He also resumed writing. He hoped to publish a new volume of poetry he titled *New Leaf on the Almond*. In addition to the poetry, he also wrote a series of short stories—the first since "Sponger's Delilah" was published during his law school days. Most used local themes that revolved around his experiences. He even hired an editor and agent, who sent him encouraging letters. He had always said he would resume writing when his Coral Gables development work was completed. Of course, he never dreamed it would end this way.

When Doherty died in late December, cold, hard reality hit George in the face. The time had come to accept the unthinkable. It was over. He would never have the chance to complete his dream.

Even before Doherty's death, George's financial situation became so precarious that he began to look for other ways to make a living. When he learned that the Miami postmaster position had become vacant and had been granted civil service status, he decided to apply. The job would provide security because it did not have a specific term and provided a lifetime pension upon retirement. The big draw, however, was the $7,000 a year salary—more than he had earned in a decade. A regular income would also allow him to gradually pay off debts—including his mother's burial expenses.

To qualify, he had to take the civil service exam. To no one's surprise, when the test results were published, George had the highest score of all sixty-six applicants. But even though he topped everyone, it was an appointed position. He needed the support of Congressman Pat Cannon and the Post Office Department in order to win the nomination. With that in mind, he asked his many friends and associates to write Cannon and other political leaders on his behalf.

Cannon's office was deluged with more than a thousand letters and on March 1, he approved George for postmaster.[33] One of George's first letters of congratulation came from his sister Medie, who now lived in upstate New York. "Again," she wrote, "it is you that is pulling the Merricks up from depths of well-nigh defeat that was about to submerge us as a family for by your abominable courage and perseverance thru years of hardship, battle and discouragement, we can't help but renew our courage thru your reflection and go on with greater strength each to our own individual struggle in life's game. So my hat's off to you once more, George, and once again tis true: You can't keep a Merrick down."[34]

Before George's nomination could go to the U.S. Senate and then to the White House for confirmation, he had to pass a physical exam.

Unfortunately, his weight and high blood pressure caused several Miami physicians to question his ability to do the job. Requesting a second opinion, he lost twenty-two pounds and flew to Washington, D.C., where, after several days of extensive testing, government doctors cleared him for the position.

George returned home just in time to help celebrate Coral Gables' fifteenth birthday and be honored at an April 29 event hosted by the chamber of commerce. That evening, when he stood to speak, more than 450 enthusiastic fans stood and cheered him. Tears flowing from his eyes, George needed several minutes to regain his composure. "If I keep on like this," he quipped, "you'll think those reports about my physical condition were right. It's a good thing those doctors are not here to see me now."[35]

When he spoke, it was not about Coral Gables' past but its future. He predicted that as long as the city followed his original plan, Coral Gables would continue to blossom. It would fill in to the bay. The business district would expand and experience enormous growth. Despite the accolades, the event was bittersweet. He knew he would not be the one in charge of Coral Gables' future. On the other hand, he realized, perhaps for the first time, that his dream had come true—at least that is what the myriad of newspaper articles claimed.

On June 1, following Senate and White House confirmation, George became the Miami postmaster. His office was in the downtown Federal Building, completed in 1933. It had been designed by Phineas Paist and Harold Steward in a modified Mediterranean style. Besides its oolitic limestone walls, it had a beautiful interior patio encircled by a columned loggia. George immediately felt at home. In addition, his uncle Denman Fink was hard at work completing a WPA-commissioned mural for the central courtroom.

When George arrived, he found his desk piled with congratulatory telegrams and letters, his office filled with baskets of flowers, and a pack of reporters waiting to interview him. He also found a handwritten note from Eunice that meant more to him than anything else.

His first item of business was to write to all postal workers telling them that in the upcoming weeks he planned to make a personal visit to all sections of the Main Office as well as the branches, in order to get to know each employee. He also pledged to be a fellow worker, not a figurehead.[36] A

Figure 61. After accepting the fact that he would be unable to complete his Coral Gables dream, George was named Miami postmaster in 1940. He remained in that position until his death, in 1942. University of Miami Special Collections. Courtesy of Mildred Merrick.

few days later, as Florida's newest and most visible postmaster, he traveled to Tallahassee for the state post office convention.

When he returned, he found a lengthy *Miami Herald* article that featured three pictures of him during his first days on the job. He told the *Herald* reporter that he was surprised to learn that the post office was a $25-million business and that he marveled at how many things he had to manage besides stamps, money orders, and pickup and mail delivery. He became the de facto manager of the Federal Building and oversaw signing people up for Social Security and veterans bonuses. He was also in charge of organizing and completing a new requirement for immigrant registration. He had to find space for an armed forces recruitment office—a new office created by the war raging in Europe. No one doubted his ability to do the job. Pledging to make his post office work his full-time job, he resigned as the head of George Merrick, Inc., and named Eunice president. At the same time, he announced he would continue his civic involvement as an advisor to the

Dade County Planning Board, as well as a board member of the University of Miami and Fairchild Tropical Garden.

The newspapers covered George's every move both inside and outside the post office. They even reported on a stag dinner organized by his original sales force and real estate friends at the Coral Gables Country Club. They gathered to congratulate him on his new job and honor him for creating Coral Gables. In another emotional thank you, George told the audience that he felt the "old Coral Gables Spirit" that had made the city possible. He hoped it would always be preserved.

On a more serious note, he was the keynote speaker at a Young Men's Hebrew Association gala on Miami Beach. For George, it was a personal statement that demonstrated his admiration and support of South Florida's Jewish community and those in Europe who were experiencing Hitler's wrath.

Despite constant objections from the nearby white community, he continued to stand up for a model black community patterned after Grant's Town in the Bahamas. Although it was never built, his advocacy was appreciated by black leaders who supported it.

George enjoyed all the recognition he was receiving for his favorite causes and past achievements, but his first priority was the post office. He was eager to use his creative skills to institute new ideas that would not only improve service but also raise public awareness of the post office's expanding role. One of his first ideas was to initiate a program to group and beautify unsightly rural mailboxes. He called on his friend Robert Fitch Smith, an outstanding architect who had replaced him as chairman of the planning board, to sketch some examples of how to do it. Next, he enlisted the garden clubs to help with a planting plan and convinced Dade County to provide some of the plants. The plan was well received and implemented with wide press coverage.

He also focused on a new law that required noncitizen immigrants to register. Estimating that there were more than 15,000 living in Miami, George opened several branch offices to help the effort. Because of his long relationship with the Bahamian community, which made up one of the largest groups, he opened a special branch that catered to them. Next, he went on the radio to allay fears, saying that all immigrant newcomers would be "treated as guests" and only the undesirables would be deported. Finally, he convinced an unlikely group—the Daughters of the American Revolution—to help with the registration. Although the effort had some difficult problems to solve, no one was surprised when the Miami Post Office was the first in the state to complete the job.

As the Christmas season neared and he knew the postal service would be inundated with packages and mail, he created what he called the "Post Office College." Here more than five hundred temporary and new employees would practice helping the public in a miniature post office that included dummy packages and stage money. He also took to the airwaves to encourage patrons to mail early.

Even though George was spending ten hours a day at the post office, he continued to speak out on the importance of planning and zoning. He made headlines in early 1941 when he spoke twice before the Dade County Commission in support of the zoning director. He blamed the commission for letting politics and factionalism overcome good government. "The county's future is at stake," he shouted, "and zoning must be above politics because there is nothing else in county affairs so important."[37] (The following day another newspaper article reported that calm had returned to the commission following the storm Merrick had created.)

George also kept a close eye on Coral Gables. A few months earlier, he, along with Denman Fink, had addressed the Coral Gables City Commission urging the board to guard against what he called a "deviation of ideals." He encouraged commissioners to take a stand against commercial pressure. Denman was particularly incensed by the "garish" blinking lights the city had installed on the De Soto Fountain. They both were dismayed that most of the new homes were not in the Mediterranean style, even though the law requiring it was still in place. "It is the atmosphere and then artistic appeal that has made Coral Gables famous," Denman concluded.[38]

Their talk had a positive effect on the commission. The city removed the lights from the De Soto Fountain and strengthened the power of the planning and zoning boards.

George and Denman made another joint appearance when Denman's mural—eleven feet high by twenty-six feet long—was unveiled in the central courtroom of the Federal Building. As postmaster and custodian of the building, George had an official role in the ceremony. His connection, of course, ran much deeper. Denman had been his closest collaborator in his original plan for Coral Gables.

The mural brought back fond memories of George's pioneer days. In the center was a young man carrying a box of grapefruit that family members believed represented George and the Coral Gables Plantation. The mural also included a drawing of Phineas Paist, who had a close connection to both Coral Gables and the Federal Building. Even Denman's granddaughter Enna was depicted. Although art critics were not kind, George and many South Floridians loved the mural because it told their story.[39]

As postmaster, George was called to speak at many public gatherings. His main concern, however, continued to be the postal workers. He lived up to his original promise to be a "fellow worker" and, as a result, had become extremely popular with the rank and file. With his encouragement, the Letter Carriers of Miami Central Labor Union launched a monthly newspaper they called *Tropical Letter Carrier*. The first issue was dedicated to "Our Postmaster" with the following statement:

> Mr. Merrick we salute you not only for your official capacity as our postmaster, but as a man. The letter carriers in Miami think a lot of that man; they appreciate his cooperation and altruism. We know that in the few months that you have been with us that a happier understanding now exists between the Miami Postal personnel than ever before.

It praised him for always being willing to meet with the postal employees and for reinstituting the seniority system, which had been ignored by the previous postmaster.[40]

Women postal workers were equally impressed with George's leadership. They sent him a letter complaining about a man who was in the post office every day making inappropriate remarks when they walked by. They reported that the previous postmaster had ignored their concerns and had done nothing to address the situation. The day after George received the letter, he had the man permanently removed from the premises unless he was there on official post office business.

After he learned that women were being discriminated against in hiring for post office positions, George made it clear he would select the best candidate, regardless of gender. Despite objection by some of the male workers, he refused to budge on his decision. It turned out to be a good one. An editorial in a post office publication called *Clerk's Mail* hailed him with the headline: "Mr. Merrick is Right Again."[41]

George and Eunice considered the regular salary a blessing. They were able to pay off the mortgage on their Matecumbe property, giving them at least one asset. They also began paying off their creditors—including Clifton Benson and Telfair Knight—with small monthly checks. In addition, George finally was able to pay off his mother's funeral and burial debt.

But all was not well. George complained that since he had gotten the job, everyone whom he had owed during the "hard times" was insisting on repayment. This forced him to work out a budget "for taking care of scores of old dead horses." He wrote that it would take him at least two years or more before he could emerge a free man.[42]

Despite continuing financial problems, George and Eunice, as well as Richard and Ethel, stepped up to help Helen's sons. George secured a University of Miami scholarship for Merrick, who was living with Ethel. Following her mother's death, Ethel had turned the family homestead, "Coral Gables," into "Merrick Manor" and operated it as a boarding house. (Although it violated the zoning code, no one objected.)

Due to Helen's inability to handle her teenage boys, the family had sent her second son, Donald, to live with Medie and her husband, Quint, in upstate New York. They had helped turn his life around. He became a good student and played in the high school band. Upon graduation, George got him a music scholarship at the University of Miami and promised to pay his fees and give him some money for food. In an especially strong letter to Ethel, who had driven to New York to drive Donald to Miami, George asked her to tell Donald that if he did not do well, he would "drop him like a hot potato." He wrote that his first duty was to creditors and Eunice, "who has had nothing but grief from life with me for many years." But always hopeful, he ended by saying: "If Donald applies himself right and gives promise to amounting to something I am willing to further burden myself to help him."[43]

At the end of November, George penned an especially moving Christmas letter to "Our Post Office Family" that he signed "your friend and co-worker." "Christmas should mean more to us this year," he began. "Our own

Country, our own Americas—are largely spared from the World Conflagration."[44] A week later, the Japanese bombed Pearl Harbor and the United States declared war on Japan.

George came to work early the next day because he knew he would have added responsibility. A year earlier, following a government mandate that required men between twenty-one and forty-five to register for the draft, he had set up the registration and recruitment offices on the second floor of the Federal Building. When he arrived, he discovered more than seventy-five young men crowded into the hall in front of the navy recruiting office waiting for it to open. The lines continued throughout the week and grew even longer after the United States declared war on Germany and Italy.

Post offices also became the favorite place to buy "defense bonds" (later called "war bonds"). George had the responsibility of overseeing and promoting their sale. He also became one of the chairmen of the Defense Council of Dade County, organized to help sell bonds.

As the new year began, George's ten-hour days were starting to take their toll. His blood pressure soared and he was having trouble sleeping. He felt so bad he even stayed home from work—something he had never done before. He asked Eunice to call in a Christian Science practitioner to counsel him. Unfortunately, he did not improve and on March 20, Eunice sent for a doctor, who immediately put him in Jackson Memorial Hospital. The prognosis was not good.

Only the immediate family was aware he was there until Sunday evening, March 21, when Walter Winchell, who had one of the most popular radio programs in America, informed the nation of his condition. Following the broadcast, Eunice was deluged with telegrams and telephone calls from people offering hope and support. The following day, *The Miami Herald* and *The Miami Daily News* carried front-page stories on his precarious condition.

Eunice rarely left George's side. She was the only one who could calm him—the only one he wanted near him. When it became clear that the end was near, she called in the rest of the family—brothers Richard and Charles, and sisters Ethel and Helen. (Medie was in New York.) Death came at two-thirty in the morning on March 26. Sadly, at age fifty-five, George succumbed to the same heart condition that, for generations, had doomed Merrick men to an early grave.

Just a few hours after his death, *The Miami Herald* reported the loss in a front-page banner headline. Although the press had been covering his illness, *The Herald* called his death a "profound shock to this community." The myriad of articles included a series of tributes by Miami leaders who mourned his loss and reminded people of his vision, integrity, and dedication to an ideal.

Richard Merrick took charge of the funeral arrangements, supported Eunice, and held the family together. The funeral was set for Saturday, March 28, at Plymouth Congregational Church, where the Merrick family's roots ran deep. Not only had George's father been the minister at the Union Congregational Church that became Plymouth, but George had served as chairman of the board of trustees and led the building campaign for the new complex. At the time of his death, however, he was a member of the Christian Science Church, though he still supported both Plymouth and the Coral Gables Congregational Church, built to honor his father. Understanding George's dual loyalties, Eunice reached out to Plymouth for permission to hold the Christian Science memorial service there. Former First Church of Christ Scientist reader Fred Yould would conduct the service and the Reverend J. D. Kuykendall, George's close friend and former Plymouth pastor, would give the eulogy.

George's innate sense of inclusivity did not stop there. Following his wishes, the active pallbearers would be postal employees whom he had championed in his brief career as postmaster. In addition, honorary pallbearers highlighted the institutions he had helped create and support. They included members of the Coral Gables City Commission, the Dade County Planning Board, and the University of Miami and Fairchild Tropical Garden Board of Trustees.

If there were ever any doubt of George Merrick's popularity, it was dispelled at his funeral. Thousands of people—black and white, rich and poor—filled the church and spilled out to the grounds. Loudspeakers had been erected outside so everyone could share in the service.

Knowing his love of beauty, the church and the surrounding grounds were filled with flowers. Newspaper accounts not only pointed out that it was the largest funeral ever held in Miami but also highlighted the diversity of the mourners. Kuykendall's eulogy, which *The Herald* printed word for word the following day, reminded the crowd of his singular attributes.

He was a man—is a man in the most ample sense. Strong physically, as he had to be to do the prodigious things he did. Strong in mind, poet, thinker, philosopher, planner of great undertakings. His strong mind drove his body relentlessly, to meet the developing tasks that the years brought. He was strong of spirit—amazing vision, amazing faith, amazing courage, amazing understanding of the spiritual values which to him were as real as the wood and stone with which many of his dreams were given material form.[45]

Following the eulogy, Christian Science reader Fred Yould conducted the Christian Science Memorial Service with reading from the Bible, as well as Mary Baker Eddy's *Science and Health*. At the same time, radio station WQAM broadcast a memorial that included music and George's own words. In addition, Mayor Whitley and the Coral Gables Commission asked that all Coral Gables businesses be closed during the funeral. All Dade County post offices followed suit.

Following the ceremony, the honorary pallbearers lined up as the post-men-pallbearers carried the casket to the waiting hearse. The funeral cortege passed slowly through Coral Gables on the way to Woodlawn Park for burial. All along the route, people lined the streets and stood silently in respect.

Amid throngs of mourners, George was laid to rest next to his parents in the cemetery he helped create almost four decades earlier. As a final gesture, following the internment, his friends gathered the thousands of blooms and delivered them to the sick.

Eunice received literally thousands of letters and telegrams, as friends and even strangers continued to express their esteem and appreciation for George as a creator and extraordinary human being. Besides local coverage, newspapers all across America carried his obituary.

An especially meaningful tribute that highlighted the measure of the man beyond Coral Gables came from the postal carriers. His photograph, with a black border, filled the front page of the April 1 *Tropical Letter Carrier* "Merrick Memorial." The lead editorial expressed their esteem and grief:

Not the dreaming poet, not the builder of a beautiful city, but we lost in the passing of George E. Merrick a man who has tasted life from the bitter cup of unhappiness and disappointment, a man who rose back to the heights of his fond dreams, nothing overwrought, nothing fantastic. His sincerity and simplicity of heart, his fairness and cooperation will live in the hearts of his co-workers as an everlasting monument.

As a final tribute, the Coral Gables City Commission passed a resolution that summed up both George's legacy and the commission's responsibility to the future:

Whereas George E. Merrick in whose mind and heart Coral Gables was conceived and through whose genius it was brought into being, has departed from among us, and we, who are left to carry on and protect the ideals he established should pay fitting tribute to his memory.

$\sim$15

An Enduring Legacy

Coral Gables is not a thing of the moment, of the year, or
even of the passing period, but a wonderful monument to the
achievement of worth-while perseverance in the creation of
beauty and the bringing true of dreams that will as solidly endure
and as beautifully and bountifully age as does the everlasting
coral upon which this master development is founded.

George Merrick, 1921

It was hard to accept the fact that George Merrick was gone. People wondered if his vision for Coral Gables would survive without him. Although
he suffered a series of failures in his attempts to keep Coral Gables alive,
Miamians followed his every move and applauded his vision and determination never to give up. He continued to hope that if Eunice kept the company going and the city settled its financial problems, he would resign as
postmaster and raise the money to complete his city. Ironically, after years
of failed negotiations, a month after his death the long-sought refinancing
of the city's debt was finally settled. At this time, however, the nation was
at war and Coral Gables' future remained on hold.

Eunice, who stood by him through good days and bad, was left in precarious financial straits. She moved in with her mother and fought to keep
George Merrick Inc. open. Sadly, the company did not stay open long because the war stopped private construction and slowed sales.

George was spared witnessing the war's impact on his beloved Biltmore
Hotel. He had attended a gala dinner there just months before his death. In
November 1942, the War Department filed a condemnation suit to take it

28th AAF Base Unit,
(AAF Regional Hospital)
Coral Gables, Florida.

Figure 62. In March 1943, the Biltmore Hotel opened as the Army Air Forces Regional Hospital. At war's end, it became a veterans hospital and continued in that role until a new VA hospital was built in 1964. Author's collection.

over and turn it into a military hospital. The owners accepted $895,000 for the entire 166 acres plus furnishings. The War Department also purchased the next-door Casa Loma Hotel and turned it into nurses' quarters.

The Army Air Forces (AAF) immediately began to transform the luxury hotel into a hospital. Workmen lowered ceilings, filled in windows and doors with concrete block, and turned one of the grand ballrooms into a cafeteria and the other into a movie theater. They painted the antiqued walls white or battleship grey and removed many custom features like iron grilles and decorative molding. They stacked all the hand-carved, Spanish-style furniture on the curb for pickup and disposal. Although most was lost, many Coral Gables residents raided the trash piles and took some of the discarded furniture home.

The new Army Air Forces Regional Hospital at Coral Gables officially opened on March 7, 1943. At its peak, it housed and treated more than a thousand patients.[1] Coral Gables residents stepped in as volunteer "grey ladies" and helped the wounded in a variety of ways, from writing letters to pushing them about in wheelchairs. The Army Air Forces also recruited teenage boys to climb into the tower and look for enemy aircraft.

Shortly after the hospital opened, newspapers, both locally and nationally, covered the final disposition of George's estate. What made it newsworthy was the fact that it was only three hundred dollars—quite a comedown from the heady boom-time days when he was one of the richest men in America. In late 1943, Eunice began dating Army Lieutenant Colonel Ralph H. Sartor, a family friend who was stationed in Panama. They married in early 1944 and for the next few years she spent only part of the year in Coral Gables.

In Eunice's absence, George's sister Ethel became the most visible member of the family. She continued to run Merrick Manor in the family's home and often was interviewed by the press. Soon after George's death, she launched a campaign to convince the City of Coral Gables to purchase the historic home as a shrine to her brother. Although the city showed no interest, in May 1944, George posthumously received an unexpected honor. At the suggestion of the Harvey Seeds American Legion Post 29, the navy built the *SS George E. Merrick*, a liberty ship, at St. John's Shipyard in Jacksonville. Ethel was on hand to christen it with a bottle of champagne.

By late 1944, the Allied Forces had gained an upper hand and Americans began to plan for war's end. One of Coral Gables' most meaningful ideas was to build a War Memorial Youth Center that would honor the 1,400 residents who served in the conflict while nurturing the next generation. In October 1944, the city condemned a large block of land facing LeJeune Road at Andalusia and began clearing it for the new facility. The first wing, designed by architect William Merriam in the Colonial style, opened on Pearl Harbor Day 1945.

The University of Miami also contemplated its future. The original campus, now covered in weeds, had only a few crumbling streets, one Mediterranean-style small apartment building, and the vine-covered "skeleton." For the past almost twenty years, the university had been buying property in the vicinity of the Anastasia Building. They added the San Sebastian Apartments, other smaller apartment buildings, and even the French Normandy Village and the Granada Shops to the mix. As the war came to a close, the university published a drawing of an expanded campus around what was still being called the "cardboard college." A far cry from George's original concept, the new proposal had more modest, Colonial-style buildings.

This was not the only idea under consideration. The Board of Regents also flirted with a plan to move the entire university to Vizcaya, Cocoplum Plaza, or Key Biscayne, where they hoped the Matheson and Deering families would donate land. In early 1945, however, the board decided to move back to the original campus and began clearing title and adding more acreage in order to move rapidly when the war concluded.[2] Henry Doherty's widow, Grace, aided the effort by donating forty-five acres to what now was being called the "Main Campus."[3]

The preponderance of so many new Colonial-style buildings, albeit with red-tile roofs, caused some Coral Gables residents to protest the loss of the mandated style the zoning code described as "Spanish, Italian or other harmonious styles." In response, the city commission spoke out against modern architecture, enlarged the planning and zoning board, gave it more power, and added Denman Fink as a member. This effort, however, failed to stem the tide of change. Thousands of GIs who had trained in Miami during the war returned to stay at war's end. The GI Bill, which provided for free college education, thrust the University of Miami into a period of unprecedented growth. Likewise, low-interest GI mortgages and a plethora of vacant land south of Bird Road spurred residential development.

The stalled Coral Gables Business District was particularly affected. In 1942, George Zain, a Lebanese-American businessman from New York, moved to Coral Gables and came up with the idea of transforming Coral Way between Douglas and LeJeune Roads into a fashionable, high-end retail district. At the time, Miami Beach's Lincoln Road was South Florida's most upscale shopping street. New York stores such as Saks Fifth Avenue and Bonwitt Teller anchored the numerous designer shops that gave the stylish street its cache.

In early 1944, Zain and his wife, Rebyl, began promoting a Lincoln Road–type shopping street for Coral Gables. Zain proposed that all buildings must be "modern, artistic and substantial."[4] He spoke out against what he called "old-looking" buildings from the 1920s and encouraged their demolition or remodeling. In an attempt to lure more Latin American shoppers, he came up with a plan to rename the side streets after different Latin American countries and then to highlight their culture with decorated terrazzo sidewalks.

The street renaming, except for Coral Way being rechristened "Miracle Mile," was never picked up but the new, modern shopping street took off.

Within a year, more than five hundred feet of new stores turned Miracle Mile into a modern-day phenomenon.

It did not come without controversy. In early 1946, Walter DeGarmo, one of Miami and Coral Gables' most respected architects, who had helped stamp the city with Mediterranean-style buildings, had his design for a new Mediterranean-style downtown building rejected by the architectural board because it did not match new buildings in the area. An angry DeGarmo took his case to the Coral Gables Commission, claiming that "recent trends threatened to destroy the City Beautiful's uniqueness."[5] The bitter fight continued for months, with longtime residents preferring the Mediterranean style and newcomers more streamlined, functional designs. Even the city's architectural board was divided. Marion Manley believed that "architectural styles could not be frozen." She was joined by Upton Ewing, who wanted to allow modern buildings in undeveloped and commercial areas. Denman Fink, upholding his and George's original vision, believed that the city had become world renowned because of its mandated architectural style and should not depart from the original plan. George Fink, who returned to Coral Gables a few years earlier and reopened his Coral Gables office, said the Mediterranean style, which he had named, was somewhat out of style but firmly opposed what he called "ultra-modern." William Merriam, who was in the process of designing the new Riviera Country Club in the Colonial style, believed property owners should be able to do what they wanted.[6] Although Merriam's point of view was gaining support, many still considered it heresy.

The commission's final compromise was to give an enlarged architectural board the ability to make decisions on style as it related to individual neighborhoods. As a result, the rampant new construction that occurred mostly in the underdeveloped sections ignored Coral Gables' historic style and embraced the new.[7]

Even though Miracle Mile set the tone for postwar construction, few, if any, buildings stood out as being outstanding examples of what today is called Mid-Century Modern. The reverse was true at the University of Miami. After making the decision to move back to the original campus, President Bowman Ashe came up with some unique ideas to launch the new era. First, he secured a series of wooden barracks and buildings from Army surplus and moved them to the new campus. These "temporary" buildings, fondly called "the shacks," made it possible for the university to begin classes there in the fall of 1946. At the same time, the university acquired the former Richmond Naval Air Base, where it housed male students and held classes. Bus service connected what they called the South Campus to the Main and the prewar North Campus. President Ashe also talked the Federal Housing Administration into building apartments on the Main Campus for married veterans. They also became the dormitories for single students.

Departing from Merrick's original plan, the regents hired Robert Law Weed and Marion Manley to design the new campus in a modern style. Their first work was to transform a group of cast-off wooden buildings into the new Administration Building, which became the university's front door. (It was restored and reopened as the College of Arts and Sciences in 2014.) They also designed the Memorial Classroom Building—the first new building on the Main Campus. Its Mid-Century Modern style set the tone for all future buildings, including the "skeleton." Utilizing its "bones," architect Robert Little turned it into a modern, award-winning multipurpose building. In April 1949, it was re-christened the "Merrick Building" after both George and his father, Solomon. George may have been disappointed that his elegant Spanish-style campus was not to be, but most believed the fact that the university was finally becoming what he envisioned would overcome any objections to style. In fact, for the first time in almost two decades, the new University of Miami's modern architecture gave Coral Gables national attention as the "World's Most Modern Campus."[8] In the November 19, 1949, issue, *The Saturday Evening Post* included a very positive article about the growing university. Its title—"They Love it at Sun-Tan U"—however, became a pejorative that the university was not able to shed for almost fifty years.[9]

When the 1950s began, Coral Gables was booming again. The city's population more than quadrupled, the new Coral Gables High School was under construction, and homes sprung up as if by magic. Eunice had returned to Coral Gables following her 1949 divorce from Col. Sartor and changed her name back to Mrs. George Merrick. She became the most visible reminder and proponent of George's legacy. When the city celebrated its silver anniversary in April, a *Miami Herald* reporter asked her what she thought George would say about what Coral Gables had become. She replied that she thought he would like it even though the new architecture was a little too modern to have pleased him.[10] By this time, however, most of the city's newcomers had little knowledge or appreciation of George or his original plan.

Even though the Coral Gables commissioners insisted they were maintaining the original style in many areas, an example of the favored style published in the newspapers showed current homes to be more Colonial than Mediterranean. The last vestige of the past had come down to requiring red-tile roofs. That, too, would soon disappear.

By the late 1950s, rampant new construction and development caused many to believe that George Merrick's Coral Gables was under siege. This view was exacerbated in August 1960, after developer Albert Sakolsky received commission approval to build a twelve-story hotel called the "David Williams" on Biltmore Way. Public pressure and the election of an anti-high-rise commissioner caused the commission to rescind approval. Sakolsky appealed their decision all the way to the Florida Supreme Court and won his case in February 1963.[11] Soon, the David Williams Apartment/Hotel vied with the Biltmore to dominate the skyline. Other modern high-rise buildings soon followed.

Although hardly a groundswell, some began to fear that Coral Gables was losing its historic identity. The home of the Merrick family, now called "Merrick Manor," was particularly threatened, despite Ethel Merrick's continued crusade to get the city to purchase it. In early 1954, the city finally began to negotiate with her. But after neighbors objected to its becoming a museum, the commission gave up and dropped the idea.[12] Ethel was furious and, a decade later, after several more attempts to change the city's position, she put it on the market. She found a buyer, but before the sale could be completed, she died, on March 16, 1966, and it passed to her nephews Merrick, Richard, and Donald Kuhn.

As the Merrick home continued to deteriorate, the following year a group of citizens launched Coral Gables' first preservation effort when word got out that the city was going to demolish the Alhambra Water Tower. After months of protest, the city relented and purchased the landmark from the Consumer Water Company. Although no one realized it at the time, the saving of the Alhambra Water Tower was the beginning of Coral Gables' pioneering preservation movement.

The future of the Merrick home, however, remained in doubt. After Don Kuhn bought out his brothers' interests, he attempted to operate it as a boarding house like his Aunt Ethel had done for almost twenty years. When he rented it to a group of Cuban refugee priests under Father Lorente, who had fled from Havana, neighbors rose up in protest and, citing the zoning code, forced the priests to vacate.[13] Kuhn tried to get the city to purchase it, but after continuing threats of litigation by neighbor Richard Maxwell, a five-man committee formed to investigate the possibility advised the city not to buy it.[14]

Then a true hero emerged. In January 1967, City Commissioner W. L. Philbrick founded the Merrick Manor Foundation and purchased the home for $35,000. With Charles, Helen, and Richard Merrick present at a press conference, he vowed to restore it.[15] Sadly, the neighbors continued to protest any change of zoning. Philbrick's aggressive leadership style added to the controversy.

The Biltmore Hotel also drew public attention. As early as 1947, the city had tried to acquire it from the army after rumors surfaced that what was then called "Pratt General Hospital" would close. Mayor Thomas Mayes, with unanimous commission support, worked to have the hospital declared surplus but backed off when the army announced it would become a veterans hospital. The new veterans hospital opened in July 1947, and for the next twenty years it continued to operate as a major medical facility that also housed the new University of Miami Medical School.

In 1963, after the Veterans Administration announced it would build a new veterans hospital in the Jackson Memorial Hospital Complex, the city again showed interest in acquiring the Biltmore. The commission appointed a citizen's board called the Biltmore Advisory Committee to study possible uses for the buildings. Deciding the aging hotel/hospital's fate was not an easy task.

As the committee struggled with the Biltmore's future, another landmark made headlines. In 1966, the Food Fair grocery chain purchased the decaying Douglas Entrance and announced it would tear it down and build a modern supermarket with a surface parking lot. In response, a group of design professionals, led by architect James Deen, banned together and raised the funds to purchase it for a design center. Many of the investors' wives also got involved and formed an auxiliary organization they called

"The Villagers." Its purpose was to raise funds and community support to restore the Douglas Entrance.

At about the same time, W. L. Philbrick, fresh from his purchase of the Merrick home, formed the Save the Biltmore Committee. In March 1968, the group held a highly successful tea dance in the courtyard of the former Biltmore Country Club to raise community interest. Eunice Merrick was the honored guest. Richard, Helen, and Charles Merrick joined her and other luminaries from the Doherty years, including impresario Alexander Ott and swimming stars Johnny Weissmuller and Pete Desjardins.

Deliberations moved slowly. Congressman Dante Fascell signed on to help and began trying to convince the General Services Administration (GSA) to turn over to the city the former Biltmore Country Club building and Casa Loma Hotel because their future use was clear. (The City of Coral Gables had purchased the Biltmore Golf Course from the federal government in 1966.) "My approach to the GSA," committee chair Michael Tobin said, "is that the country club buildings are inseparable as a pair of shoes. If the two properties are not reunited, both the Federal Government and the City of Coral Gables are left barefoot."[16]

In early 1970, before any deal with the GSA was finalized, more controversy erupted. The committee discovered that Tobin had approached a private developer about taking over the property and introduced him to the GSA. This not only bypassed the city's interest but also killed the attempt by President Charles Perry of the new Florida International University to acquire it for a campus. After the GSA announced it would swap the hotel site for property that developer Maston O'Neal owned in the Atlanta area, the city-appointed Biltmore committee demanded Tobin's resignation. He was succeeded by attorney Robert Koeppel, who lived nearby. Koeppel immediately began to pressure the city to fight Maston O'Neal and acquire the property for civic use.[17]

In the midst of the Biltmore fight, another hot topic emerged. In August 1968, the Atlanta-based Crow, Pope and Carter had purchased what was then called the Cocoplum tract from the Deering heirs. It had remained undeveloped ever since the Coral Gables Corporation failed and the Deerings reclaimed it. George's extensive plans, which included another Biltmore Hotel, a shopping center, and a Monte Carlo–style casino, were long forgotten and, except for Tahiti Beach, most of the 497 acres remained pineland and mangroves.

The developers announced they planned to build a group of high-rise apartments, townhouses, single-family homes, a golf and country club, a yacht club, a shopping center, and more. Their plan required a zoning change from single-family, which had been in place since the 1930s. Neighbors rose up in protest, with more than two hundred showing up for the zoning commission meeting. They organized under the banner of the Coral Gables Citizens League and, under the leadership of Dr. James Jude and Robert B. Knight, declared war on the developers and the city commission. The League proposed that the zoning remain single-family and that the city purchase Tahiti Beach and other lowland to turn into public recreational facilities.[18]

Despite the fact that the developers made several major changes to their plan, opposition continued. A year after the initial proposal, the zoning board denied the revised plan by a vote of three to two. Another year passed and the issue remained unresolved.

After the developers presented their fourth plan to the zoning board in late November 1970, it passed. On December 15, the city commission also voted in the affirmative on the first reading, with only Commissioner Bill Kerdyk Sr. voting against it.[19] The Citizens League, now under the leadership of Knight and attorney Charles George, refused to give up and promised to launch a referendum and recall the four commissioners who supported the plan. On March 23, 1971, following a series of delays and two years and eight months after the initial proposal, the Coral Gables Commission passed the controversial rezoning on the second reading. "We have just begun to fight," Citizens League Chair Knight said following the vote. "They don't know what real fighting is yet."[20]

The controversy continued to rage. The Citizens League collected more than 6,500 signatures to force a referendum, only to have the court deny the legality of the effort. Following an appeal that reversed that decision, and after the attorneys for the Citizens League won another appeal concerning the vote on the second reading, the Coral Gables Commission rescinded the ordinance's second reading and rolled back the zoning to single-family. The League's success not only held the zoning on the Cocoplum tract but also stopped an attempt by the Sheraton Hotel Group to rezone another bayside track off Old Cutler Road for a hotel and resort.[21]

In the midst of the Cocoplum controversy and after the O'Neal deal became public, what was now called the Biltmore Development Board, with broad community support, convinced the city commission to ask the citizens of Coral Gables to approve a $3-million bond issue to purchase the Biltmore. Shortly before the April 1971 vote, O'Neal held a press conference at which he unveiled a scale model of his $20 million proposal.[22] It included turning the hotel into an office building with a new three-story wing and adding two, ten-story condominiums, as well as a four-story, one-hundred-room hotel. With the reality of O'Neal's proposal clearly in front of them, voters flocked to the polls and voted for the $3 million bond to purchase the Biltmore.

Following the vote, which was viewed as a mandate, the commission joined the lawsuit against GSA filed by Gables residents M. Lewis Hall and C. B. Kniskern. Attorney Parker Thompson, another Biltmore neighbor, represented them. The growing opposition celebrated their success after U.S. District Judge C. Clyde Atkins ruled that the GSA had exceeded its authority and declared its contract with O'Neal illegal.[23]

Although O'Neal threatened to continue to fight the decision, along with W. L. Philbrick, who had become an O'Neal supporter, the die was cast. Mayor Keith Phillips Jr. launched a new effort to acquire the property for the city, although only three commissioners supported it. With a stroke of good luck, the city's proposal came at the same time President Richard Nixon's Historic Monuments Act and Legacy of Parks Program passed Congress. This made it possible for the federal government to give the city the property.

On April 23, 1973, the president's daughter, Julie Nixon Eisenhower, stood in front of the Biltmore and presented Mayor Robert B. Knight the deed for the twenty-acre parcel. Other dignitaries included Eunice Merrick, Congressmen Dante Fascell and Claude Pepper, and former Mayor Phillips, who had become the city's most visible preservationist. Unfortunately, the Biltmore controversy was far from over. Almost immediately, many questioned why the city would want such a "white elephant."

Although Eunice had stayed out of the Biltmore fray, she clearly supported the city's acquisition. Ever since her return to Coral Gables, she had

Figure 63. After years of controversy, the City of Coral Gables acquired the Biltmore Hotel from the federal government. Julie Nixon Eisenhower, daughter of the president, presented the deed to Mayor Robert B. Knight as others involved in the transfer looked on. *Left to right*: Congressman Claude Pepper, Mayor Robert Knight, Julie Nixon Eisenhower, former Mayor Keith Phillips Jr., Eunice Merrick, and Congressman Dante Fascell (speaker unidentified). Permission of HistoryMiami.

clipped every newspaper article on Coral Gables and, making her position clear, often underlined, circled, and wrote comments in the margins. She made public appearances when asked to participate in an event honoring her husband. These included the placing of a historical marker in Merrick Park and another at the north campus of the University of Miami. She also worked behind the scenes to encourage those trying to save other Coral Gables landmarks that were threatened.

In 1971, she aided the nascent preservation movement by sharing her scrapbooks and personal knowledge with Professor Woodrow W. Wilkins of the University of Miami School of Architecture. He and a group of students had launched the first survey of Coral Gables' historic structures. Their work, later housed in the Library of Congress, was part of a federally funded Historic American Building Survey. It received wide publicity and helped Coral Gables residents realize they had to become proactive or lose what had made the city famous.

The following year, the city passed South Florida's first historic preservation ordinance. It created what was called a "Historic Monument Board of Review" for the purpose of "preserving and protecting historic structures and neighborhoods that serve as visible reminders of the history of the City of Coral Gables."[24]

That same year, the Villagers became a broader preservation organization that focused on advocating and supporting preservation throughout Greater Miami. At the same time, another organization called Dade Heritage Trust came on the scene, led by some of the same people who had created the Villagers. Under the leadership of President Dolly MacIntyre, the new organization became involved in local preservation issues.

With no model to emulate, the original Coral Gables ordinance that had no criteria for designation was repealed in October 1973, and ordinance 2050 took its place. The new ordinance followed strict criteria developed by the U.S. Department of Interior and the National Trust for Historic Preservation. Don Lebrun, the city's administrative programs director, was named secretary of the board of review and became a strong advocate for its implementation.

The board was just getting started when its first chair, Dr. Anthony Amerise, died. The following year, the new board reorganized and, for the first time, gave the city a strong voice for historic preservation.

The new board's first order of business was to survey the downtown historic properties and designate as historic landmarks all the Merrick-era entrances, plazas, and sites, including Venetian Pool, the Desoto Fountain, and City Hall. They became the first listings under the new ordinance.

The board's first major victory came when it led the effort to save the Merrick House. Even though W. L. Philbrick had vowed to restore it, his efforts had failed and it continued to deteriorate. Not known for his diplomacy, he continued to take on both the neighbors and the city commission, often with highly controversial proposals. Members of the preservation board, with Philbrick's approval, walked the neighborhood and talked

Figure 64. After years of efforts to save the Merrick House, the new City of Coral Gables Preservation Board convinced the City Commission to purchase it. Several members of the Merrick family attended its opening in October 1978. Author's collection.

to the neighbors about a new plan to create what they called Coral Gables House. It would not be a museum, they argued, but a home patterned after the new Florida House in Washington, D.C. The ploy worked and the neighbors, including Richard Maxwell, who had been the most vocal opponent, agreed to support it. Although not stated publicly, the preservation board hoped that someday, after the city proved the home would not impact the single-family neighborhood, it would become a museum.

On January 27, 1976, the Coral Gables Commission, with a unanimous vote, acquired the historic home for $21,000 from the Merrick Manor Foundation and appointed the preservation board to oversee its restoration. As the meeting ended, Eunice, a strong supporter of city ownership, wiped tears from her eyes.

Eunice, Richard, Charles, and Helen Merrick were present when the restored home opened to the public in October 1978. It had been a true labor of love; in addition to benefiting from a community redevelopment grant, many organizations, including the Junior League, the Coral Gables Garden Club, the Daughters of the American Revolution, the Jaycees Auxiliary, and the Villagers helped bring the house back to its 1926 glory. Richard

Merrick, the only family member born in Coral Gables, spent many hours with the Junior League committee that funded the interior restoration. He described every room, every piece of furniture, and completed a drawing of the original curtains that the league reproduced. Everyone was pleased with the outcome. The board's greatest satisfaction came when Richard was quoted as saying it was just as he remembered it.[25]

As the Merrick house came back to life, the Biltmore remained dark and abandoned. The only positive development occurred in 1974, when members of the junior class of Coral Gables Senior High School received permission to hold its Junior-Senior Prom in the Country Club Ballroom. During the hospital era, the once-elegant ballroom had been partitioned into individual cubbyholes and laboratories complete with sinks and Bunsen burners. Unattractive lowered ceilings completely hid the painted and vaulted ones. Using crowbars and hammers, two hundred and fifty school volunteers demolished the partitions and hauled away the debris. They painted, refinished, and restored many of the room's original features. Their effort not only gave the Class of 1974 a prom like no other, but the refurbishing gave everyone in Coral Gables a glimpse of the ballroom's future possibilities.[26]

The following year, still struggling to figure out what to do with the site, the city commission leased the former Biltmore Country Club to the new Metropolitan Museum and Art Center for twenty years at ten dollars a year. It opened to the public in 1979 and two years later launched a special exhibit on the Biltmore's history. The exhibit, along with a forty-eight-page catalogue, helped educate the public on the importance and beauty of the entire site.

Despite growing community interest, a short time later, City Manager Martin Gainer proposed demolishing the hotel and turning the vacant land into tennis, handball, and volleyball courts. Residents, aided by the new, increasingly vocal preservation board, rose up to oppose such a suggestion. Gainer had already had a public run-in with the preservation board after he leased the Old Police and Fire Station and proposed removing the outside sculpture and filling in the bays with concrete block and aluminum windows. After an emotional hearing, the commission agreed with the preservation board and nixed Gainer's plan.

His Biltmore proposal suffered the same fate. After much debate, the commission voted against demolition and asked Gainer to come back with another idea. He then encouraged developers Joel and Elias Sussman to submit a new plan for the hotel. They proposed turning it into 175 luxury apartments and ten hotel suites. As the negotiations continued with little public input, the preservation board asked the city commission to create a new committee to prepare a national request for proposal (RFP)—something the city had never done. The commission, however, refused to consider the idea, instead relying on the Sussmans' promised proposal as a solution to the problem. After Commissioner Dorothy Thomson visited the Sussmans' Miami Beach projects, she, unimpressed with their work, changed her vote, making it possible for the Biltmore Advisory Committee to proceed with an RFP.

The new committee, made up of lawyers, architects, real estate mavens, and preservationists, convinced the commission to hire Ralph Warburton, a University of Miami architectural professor, to produce a formal document. Fortunately, at the same time the RFP was completed, Congress had passed the 1981 Economic Recovery Tax Act that allowed a 25-percent investment tax credit for the rehabilitation of historic buildings. After the city advertised the RFP in both the local and national press, it received more than four hundred inquiries—quieting even the most vociferous doubters. Emboldened by the unexpected response, the commission created the Biltmore Evaluation Panel to select the best proposal from the six formal submissions.

In February 1983, the commission accepted the Biltmore Evaluation Panel's selection and awarded a contract to the Coral Gables Biltmore Corporation, headed by the Worsham Brothers. They, along with local architect and investor Richard Rose, proposed returning the building to a luxury hotel. After four years of continuing struggle, the beautifully restored hotel reopened on January 3, 1987—sixty-one years and one day after its original inauguration. Sadly, Eunice, now ninety years old, could not attend.

With the Biltmore tower once again aglow, and the city committed to preserving other historic properties, residents realized that the strict, thirteen-story zoning regulations for high-rise buildings, plus the proliferation of poured concrete and glass-box-style new buildings, had robbed Coral Gables of its historic ambience. The issue came to a head after the Colonnade, the last structure George built, was threatened with demolition.

In 1983, under the leadership of Mayor Bill Chapman and Commissioner Ron Robison, the commission created a new committee to study ways to bring Mediterranean-style architecture back to Coral Gables. The committee discovered that most of the architectural characteristics that defined the Merrick years, including arcades, loggias, balconies, tile roofs, towers, and exterior ironwork, had become illegal under the zoning code. In an attempt to control building height, the city had enforced strict, thirteen-story limits that had made the skyline flat and monotonous. After studying what characteristics defined the historic style, the committee proposed what was called the "Coral Gables Mediterranean Ordinance." It awarded bonuses and special allowances for developers who either built or remodeled buildings in the Mediterranean style. They cited remaining examples such as the Biltmore, the Colonnade, and George Fink's office as references. After limiting the ordinance to the Central Business District, the commission passed the new law in June 1986.

The first project under the new ordinance was the Colonnade Hotel and office building. Intercap Investments, headed by David Weaver, hired Spillis, Candela and Partners to restore the original Colonnade and design a new high-rise building adjoining it. The new facility, complete with historic photographs and other references, opened to rave reviews, launching a new appreciation of both George Merrick and his legacy.

But all was not well with the Biltmore. The hotel, along with the Metropolitan Art Museum, struggled to stay alive. The museum, lacking any public funding, closed in January 1989, after donating its collection to the new Florida International Art Museum. Eighteen months later, the hotel group was forced into Chapter 7 bankruptcy. Despite the gloom, the good news was that the hotel had been restored and still belonged to the citizens of Coral Gables.

Barnett Bank, which had taken over the hotel, finally found a new lessee—the Seaway Group, led by Robert Kay and Gene Prescott—that would operate the hotel following a second failure. In June 1992, the city signed a long-term lease with what Kay and Prescott named the Biltmore Hotel Limited Partnership. Despite Hurricane Andrew—eerily reminiscent of the 1926 storm that delayed its original 1926 opening—the hotel reopened on schedule.

The Biltmore, listed as a National Historic Landmark in 1996, became

Figure 65. The Colonnade Hotel and Office Building launched the new Mediterranean Ordinance that gave developers bonuses for utilizing the Mediterranean style. The restored Colonnade opened to rave reviews in 1989. Other buildings soon followed. Author's collection.

the centerpiece of the Coral Gables renaissance. It welcomed the pope and presidents and hosted both international conferences and local affairs. Its glowing presence linked past to present and served as a living monument to the city's founder.

By the time Coral Gables celebrated its seventy-fifth birthday in 2000, the spirit of George Merrick's Coral Gables was alive and well. The Coral Gables Garden Club, founded even before the city was incorporated, solidified the feeling by erecting a larger-than-life statue of George in front of City Hall. It culminated their multi-year effort, led by President Betsy Adams, to complete three new entrances—Red Road, Ponce de Leon Boulevard and Eighth Street, and Coral Way (Miracle Mile), all of which George had planned but never built.

What was now called the Coral Gables Merrick House had undergone several restorations since its 1978 opening. Just as predicted, it had become a museum highlighting the Merrick family and its pivotal role in the creation of the city. In honor of the home's 100th birthday, the Coral Gables Garden Club erected a statue of Althea sitting in the garden she loved.

Figure 66. The new Coral Gables Museum opened on October 10, 2010. Dignitaries who helped make it possible joined the celebration. *Left to right*: Miami-Dade Commissioner Carlos Gimenez, Miami-Dade Commissioner Rebecca Sosa, Coral Gables Commissioner Ralph Cabrera, Congresswoman Ileana Ros-Lehtinen, Coral Gables Commissioner, William Kerdyk Jr., Museum Board Chair George Kakouris, Coral Gables Mayor Don Slesnick, Coral Gables Commissioner Marie Anderson, and Coral Gables Commissioner and museum founder Chip Withers. Permission of Jeannette B. Slesnick.

The Historic Preservation Board added to the revival by continuing to designate historic structures. By 2014, it had listed almost 1,500 properties and created twenty-two historic districts. The Coral Rock Thematic District, which protected George's original coral rock structures, was especially meaningful to those trying to preserve the Coral Gables story. Likewise, the MacFarlane Homestead Historic District honored the city's historic black neighborhood, which George had championed from the beginning.

Historic neighborhoods also got a boost from a new community organization called the Historic Homeowners Association. Founded in 1991, it later broadened its mission and became the Historic Preservation Association of Coral Gables. After forty years of effort by an enlightened public and the support of political leaders, Coral Gables' past had become a vital part of its future.

The Mediterranean Ordinance had the hoped-for effect on the central business district. After its passage, almost every new and restored building utilized the bonuses, thus reviving elements of the historic style. A multitude of towers seemed to puncture what George had called Florida's cloud mountains. They housed an abundance of businesses, Latin American headquarters, and foreign consulates that gave the city an international air, just as he had predicted. Owners of historic properties also began to use the Transfer of Development Rights, which allowed low-rise historic properties to transfer their development rights to others.

George's legacy received another boost in October 2010, when the new Coral Gables Museum opened. Commissioner Wayne "Chip" Withers had conceived the idea of a Coral Gables Museum in the mid-1990s. Following initial meetings with cultural leaders, the idea evolved, and in 1999, after the Coral Gables Community Foundation became the fiscal agent, serious planning began.

The museum took off in 2003 after philanthropist Kirk Landon donated $250,000 to the Coral Gables Community Foundation to help launch the dream. That same year, the 501.c.3 Coral Gables Museum Corp. was born. Its board created a public-private partnership with the City of Coral Gables to house the new museum in the 1939 Police and Fire Station. The building would also house the city's archives and historic preservation department.[27]

Work began in earnest in 2008 under the supervision of the city's historic resource department and architect Jorge Hernandez. The dream had expanded with the addition of a new $2 million gallery funded by Robert and Marian Fewell. As construction began, the board established a unique mission for the new museum. It would "celebrate, investigate and explore the civic arts of architecture and urban and environmental design, including fostering an appreciation for the history, vision and cultural landscape of Coral Gables."

After the new museum opened and received rave reviews, it became an award-winning community center and a place to celebrate all the reasons Coral Gables had not only survived but thrived. In combination with the new Coral Gables Art Cinema and the legendary Books & Books, one of the nation's most successful independent bookstores, Aragon Avenue became a cultural hub. Nearby, the Actors' Playhouse in the restored Miracle

Figure 67. The Biltmore Hotel, now a National Historic Landmark, serves as a "Tower of Inspiration" to remind current residents of George Merrick's legacy and the importance of historic preservation. Author's collection.

Theatre, plus the city's many art galleries, fulfilled George's prophesy that Coral Gables would become a major cultural center.

The University of Miami, which George called his most important legacy, also lived up to his expectations. It had become a major research university and international center. The Lowe Art Museum—Miami's first—continued to evolve and grow, along with the university's other unique offerings.

More than ninety years have passed since George launched his dream in the front yard of his and Eunice's Coral Way home. At the time, who would have predicted that in 2013 his carefully planned "Master Suburb" would receive the LivCom award in Beijing, China, as one of the most livable communities in the world?

"The Miracle of Coral Gables," as Rex Beach titled his 1926 book, is that George had only seven years to leave his imprimatur on the city he spawned. Despite the passage of time and an untold number of human and natural disasters, his legacy endures.

Figure 68. A view through the historic Alhambra Entrance documents the return of George Merrick's legacy. The Allen Morris Company's Alhambra Towers added another Giralda tower to the skyline. Permission of the Allen Morris Company.

Epilogue

From the groves of grapefruit and avocadoes to groves,
patios, plazas, entrances, cloisters, campuses, parks, gardens
of culture, beauty, harmony and realization of larger living
for the many now and for the many, many who will come to
know what has been planted here: the Coral Gables ideal will
spread, take root and flourish.

George E. Merrick, speech, November 20, 1937

Until recently, most historians have overlooked Coral Gables even though, according to the editors of the 2013 book, *Paradise Planned*, it "deserves consideration as one of the world's preeminent garden villages."[1] Anyone visiting the "City Beautiful" will marvel at its unique neighborhoods, entrances and plazas, tree-lined streets, open spaces, civic monuments, parks, public buildings, and cultural offerings. This is because today, ninety-four years after George Merrick sold the first lot, his plan for Coral Gables survives. His strict building and zoning regulations are mostly intact. An architectural board continues to approve all building plans including the color of the walls, windows, awnings, and shutters. It also monitors landscape plans with an eye to preserving the city's garden-like quality. Even mandated architectural styles—although lost for a generation—have experienced a renaissance. The Historic Preservation Board, through historic designation, educates the public on the importance of preserving the city's historic built environment. In addition to Coral Gables' many advisory boards, its citizens are watchdogs and never fail to speak out if they believe the city's core values are threatened.

Figure 69. The Coral Gables Congregational United Church of Christ is listed on the National Register of Historic Places. It was the first church in Coral Gables and remains today as a living monument to Solomon Merrick and what George called "higher spiritual values." Author's collection.

Coral Gables is not the only exemplary planned community, but few, if any, can match its size, scale, and economic, social, and cultural mix. It encompasses thirteen square miles, with forty-seven miles of waterways. It has forty-two public parks—from small plazas and parkways to fully developed recreational facilities. It boasts more than twenty schools, a major research university, and thirty-four churches. Its many civic clubs add another important dimension.

Just as George predicted, Coral Gables has become an international city and what he called a "Gateway to Latin America." It is headquarters for more than 120 international businesses and 20 consulates. Its vibrant downtown attracts both tourists and people from all over South Florida.

The University of Miami, which George called his most important legacy, flourishes. Its College of Architecture, until recently under the leadership of Dean Elizabeth Plater-Zyberk, one of the founders of New Urbanism, has helped document the singularity of George's original plan and how it should become a model for others. Renowned art historian Vince Scully, who was a visiting professor, has extolled Coral Gables and its influence on New Urbanism.[2]

The "Miracle of Coral Gables," as author Rex Beach proclaimed, is that it was created out of the genius of one man and his handpicked collaborators. Until it was incorporated as a city, and for several years after, George Merrick controlled everything and made all decisions regarding its development. He admitted he was an idealist, influenced by the writings of John Ruskin and Ebenezer Howard. He never lost his dedication to the belief that everyone deserved both beauty and utility. His farsighted comprehensive plan for a perfect suburb had the makings of what he would later call "a perfect city," even though he resisted its incorporation.

It is hard, if not impossible, to find another developer who created more public spaces at his own expense. His tropical landscape plan and planting program, led by Frank Button, stands alone. It created what he called "parked" roadways that today have become tunnels of green.

In an especially prophetic 1937 speech, George predicted that Coral Gables would someday have a population of 40,000—close to what it claims today—and would spread all the way to Biscayne Bay. He envisioned a vibrant business district that served all of Greater Miami and a university of between fifteen and twenty thousand students.

In 1926, Marjory Stoneman Douglas wrote a poetic description of George Merrick's Coral Gables that could have been written yesterday. "Any brief glimpse of Coral Gables," she wrote, "gives one this splendid stimulating sense of discovery, the exhilarating realization that here at last wisdom and art and craftsmanship have met the age-old problem of how best shall a man live."[3]

Arva Moore Parks (*left*) with Mildred Heath Merrick. Author's collection.

Acknowledgments

After more than fifty years of writing the history of Greater Miami, I am indebted to legions of people who have helped me along the way. I wish I could acknowledge them all.

I will always be grateful to the late Mildred Merrick for sharing the priceless Merrick collection and encouraging me to write this book. I also want to mention the late Professor Woodrow W. Wilkins of the University of Miami School of Architecture, who was the first to study George Merrick's legacy through the built environment. We worked together for many years interviewing people and sharing knowledge. Unfortunately, he died before he could finish his book, but he honored me with the gift of his research and architectural perspectives.

Besides studying original Merrick papers, I have combed libraries, read newspapers, and called on the expertise of a variety of people. Two institutions—HistoryMiami and the University of Miami—stand out. HistoryMiami librarians Becky Smith and Dawn Hugh and research assistant Ashley Trujillo went out of their way to help, making suggestions, opening collections, and providing support. Likewise, the University of Miami Libraries Special Collections opened other new avenues of research. I am particularly grateful to former dean William Walker; head of Special Collections, Cristina Favaretto; university archivist, Koichi Tasa; Marcia Heath; Maria Estorino; and Corey Czajkowski. Their interest and help made a difference. Other librarians, including Sam Boldrick and John Shipley of the Miami-Dade County Public Library Florida Collection, also provided assistance, along with Jody Norman and Adam Watson of the State of Florida Photographic Archives.

I was also enlightened by Helen "Betty" Seymour of Easton, Maryland; Kathy Trager of Newark, Ohio; Jerry Boscia of Pittsburgh, Pennsylvania; Maureen Bentz of Lebanon Valley College Archives; and the late Janice Thaine of Gaines, New York. They shared their local expertise and introduced me to the places the Merricks and Finks once called home.

Many people in the City of Coral Gables also deserve special mention. Don Lebrun, former administrative programs manager and city manager; Dona Spain, preservation officer; Kara Kautz, assistant preservation officer; and Amanda Gonzalez, archivist, answered questions and shared their expertise. Former administrators Ellen Uguccioni and Carol McGeehan also helped. City Clerk Walter Foeman, Deputy Clerk Billy Urquia, and operational service assistant Imelys Sansores opened city records for my perusal. Ramon Trias, Craig Leen, Cynthia Birdsell, and Jorge Casuso provided important insight into Coral Gables today.

Many individuals also shared their time, memories, historical material, and expertise. They include Betsy Adams, Robert Fewell, Ron Gabor, Nita Norman, Dolly MacIntyre, Marilyn Mayes Hicks, Gael Stanley, Joan Sanders Tarsa, Leona and Paul Sangster, Winnie Smith, Debbie Lang, Cathleen Cotchett, Michael Spring, Beth Dunlop, Robert Burr, Tom Graboski, Peter Zorn, Jerry Wilkerson, Elizabeth Plater-Zyberk, Joanna Lombard, Jose Gelabert-Navia, Leigh Marion, the late Sarah Anderson, Christine Rupp, Caroline Parker, Gene Prescott, Danielle Finnegan, and Charles Cobb. Past and present members of the City of Coral Gables Preservation Board, leaders of the Historic Preservation Association of Coral Gables, the Coral Gables Garden Club, and the Coral Gables Museum provided additional help. The late Ralph Sanchez's eagerness to learn George Merrick's legacy gave me the opportunity to write the book *George Merrick's Coral Gables* and curate the Coral Gables Museum's first exhibit, "Celebrate," in Merrick's restored Art Building. Sadly, like George, he was not able to complete his "Old Spanish Village."

I cannot end without thanking those who played a special role in the journey. Laura Pincus, Howard Kleinberg, Larry Wiggins, Jeanne Weinkle, and Carolyn Klepser provided their knowledge, research, and encouragement. Former assistants Regina Dodd and April Bolet also contributed, as did Andrew Camner and Dorothy Stein. Invaluable assistance on every front came from Nuria Santizo, with help from her daughters, Kimberly and Valerie.

Finally, I am particularly indebted to Patty Shillington, who not only edited the work but also suggested ways to improve it. I also benefited from the encouragement of my many friends and especially my late husband, Bob McCabe, who kept me going.

Drawing of the Merrick house by a WPA artist, 1937. Author's collection.

Notes

Abbreviations of Manuscript Collections

GMHM   George Merrick Collection, HistoryMiami.

MCCG   Merrick Collection, City of Coral Gables Archives.

MCUM   Merrick Collection, Special Collections, University of Miami.

Chapter 1. The Merricks of Maryland

1. Leonard, Talbot County Maryland Land Records, 3:09.
2. John Merrick, will, November 1, 1706, Edward F. Wright, *Maryland Calendar of Wills*, LJP70:215.
3. *Eastern Shore Whig and People's Advocate*, November 4, 1834.
4. "Deed of Trust to Kersey," Talbot County Land Records, 52:517.
5. Merrick Bible.
6. "Deed, Theodore R. Blake and Charlotte, his wife," 1851, Easton, Maryland: Talbot County Circuit Court, Talbot County Land Records, 64:54.
7. Merrick Bible.
8. Ibid.
9. *Baltimore American*, March 7, 1839.
10. Otterbein Church Records, Obituary, Jacob Greasley, Maryland Historical Society.
11. Weaver, *The Life of Rev. Philip William Otterbein*, 205–12.
12. 1860 United States Census, Talbot County, Maryland.
13. Otterbein Church Records, April 16, 1860, 54.
14. Otterbein Church Records, 27:3.
15. Phillip Rogers Hoffman to J. Greasley, Baltimore County Land Records, L49/499.
16. Jacob and Louisa Greasley to Lewis Turner, Baltimore County Land Records, L80/09.
17. *Baltimore County Land Records*, L87/100.
18. *Sixtieth Anniversary Salem Church United Brethren in Christ*, 7.
19. Ibid.

Chapter 2. The Fink Family

1. Strassburger, *Pennsylvania German Pioneers*, 172.
2. Knittle, *Early 18th Century Palatine Emigration*, 19–22.
3. Tracy and Dern, *Pioneers of Old Monocacy*, 276.
4. Schildknecht, *Monocacy and Catoctin*, 170.
5. Tracy and Dern, *Pioneers of Old Monocacy*, 277.
6. Cutright, *History of Upshur County, West Virginia*, 175–79.
7. Cutright, *History of Upshur County, West Virginia*, 200–201. The Finks were even featured in a 1927 romantic novel called *The Scout of the Buckhannon*, by J. C. McWhorter.
8. Bosworth, *History of Randolph County*, 106.
9. Cook and Cook, *Fayette County Records*, Vol. 2, 200–202, 130, 351.
10. Hardy County West Virginia Will Book 3:235.
11. Hunter, *Papermaking in Pioneer America*, 117.
12. *Roster of Ohio Soldiers in War of 1812*, 118.
13. United States Census, Hocking County, Ohio, 1830.
14. *Register of Asbury Methodist Church*, Wilmington, Delaware, 36:48.
15. *Methodist Quarterly Conference Minutes*, Pickaway Circuit, August 16, 1825.
16. Hocking County, Ohio Land Records.
17. United States Census, Hocking County, Ohio, 1850.
18. "Henry and Eliza Fink to Henry Eckert," deed, Hocking County Ohio, November 28, 1850.
19. "Henry Fink to New Salem Baptist Church," deed, Hocking County Ohio, February 26, 1858.
20. "H.G.G. Fink," *Yearbook of the Ohio Annual Conference Methodist Episcopal Church*, 1911.
21. George E. Merrick, "I Remember Gaines," Albion, New York: *Albion Advertiser*, July 12, 1941.
22. Licking County Ohio Land Records, 1/456.
23. *Ohio Methodist Conference Records: 1851–1866*.
24. United States Trademark: Registered December 9, 1871; received January 2, 1872, number 611.
25. U.S. Manufacturing Census. Third Ward. Pittsburgh, Allegheny County, Pennsylvania, June 1, 1870.

Chapter 3. Solomon and Allie

1. George E. Merrick, "Marco Polo in the 97 Blizzard," MCUM.
2. Ibid.
3. Wallace, *Lebanon Valley College: A Centennial History*, 4.
4. "D. D. DeLong Biography," President's Papers, Lebanon Valley College Archives.
5. *Fifteenth Annual Catalogue of the Officers and Students of Lebanon Valley College*, 1880–81.

6. Wallace, *Lebanon Valley College: A Centennial History*, 246.

7. *Lebanon Valley College Catalogue*, 1879–80, 1882–83.

8. Wallace, *Lebanon Valley College: A Centennial History*, 248.

9. Althea Corilla Fink, "Women," Merrick Collection City of Coral Gables, MCCG.

10. Althea Fink, "Fine Arts," MCCG.

11. Althea Fink, "Letter to Ma and Pa [H.G.G. and Almeda Fink]," January 26, 1881, MCUM.

12. "Lebanon Valley College News," Annville: *Annville Gazette*, May 17, 1882.

13. "Lebanon Valley College News," Annville: *Annville Gazette*, April 12, 1882.

14. Althea Fink, "Class Prophesy," Lebanon Valley College Class of 1883.

15. "Lebanon Valley College News," Annville: *Annville Gazette*, February 11, 1882.

16. "Lebanon Valley College News," Annville: *Annville Gazette*, September 28, 1882.

17. "Lebanon Valley College News," Annville: *Annville Gazette*, October, 14, 1882.

18. Althea Fink, "Class Prophesy," Lebanon Valley College Class of 1883.

19. Solomon Greasley Merrick to Althea Fink Merrick, 1907, MCUM.

20. Mrs. D. O. Jarvis to George E. Merrick, January 4, 1926, MCUM.

21. Minutes Gaines Congregational Church, Gaines, New York, August 13, 1886.

22. *Orleans Republican*, Albion: September 8, 1886.

23. *Orleans Republican*, Albion: November 24, 1886.

24. George E. Merrick. "I Remember Gaines," Albion: *Albion Advertiser*, July 12, 1941.

25. Ibid.

26. Ibid.

27. George E. Merrick, "My Mighty Century Lost," MCUM.

28. George E. Merrick, "Rainy Season," MCUM.

29. George E. Merrick, "My Mighty Century Lost," MCUM.

30. George E. Merrick, "I Remember Gaines."

31. George E. Merrick, "Rainy Season," MCUM.

32. *Orleans American*, Albion: April 4, 1895.

33. *Orleans Republican*, January 23, 1895.

34. *Orleans Republican*, October 9, 1895.

35. *Orleans American*, October 24, 1895.

36. Ibid.

37. *Orleans American*, October 31, 1895.

38. Winsor, *History of the Town of Duxbury*, 2–16.

39. Houghton and Houghton, eds., *The First 150 Years: Pilgrim Church*.

40. *Old Colony Memorial*, Duxbury: July 20, 1898; June 10, 1899.

41. George E. Merrick, "Marco Polo," MCUM.

42. George E. Merrick, "Africa and the Mission," MCUM.

43. Almeda Allison to George E. Merrick, October 16, 1898, MCUM.

44. George E. Merrick, "Marco Polo," MCUM.

45. George E. Merrick, "Story of Coral Gables," *The Miami Daily News-Metropolis*, November 26, 1921.

46. George E. Merrick, "Marco Polo," MCUM.

47. Ibid.

48. Ibid.

49. Ibid.

Chapter 4. "When the Groves Begin to Bear"

1. *The Miami Metropolis*, November 3, 1899.

2. *The Miami Metropolis*, October 8, 1898.

3. George E. Merrick, "Domes More Vast," MCUM.

4. "How the City of Coral Gables Received Its Colorful Name," *The Miami Herald*, April 25, 1950.

5. George E. Merrick, "Black Nat the Groceryman," MCUM.

6. "Notes From Our Neighbors,"
   The Tropical Sun, May 5, 1892.

7. W. H. Gregory, Homestead Proof, 1898.

8. George E. Merrick, "All Men Kill the Things They Love," MCUM.

9. George E. Merrick, "Domes More Vast," MCUM.

10. George E. Merrick, "Our Man Friday," MCUM.

11. George E. Merrick, "Bitter Myrtle," MCUM.

12. Ibid.

13. George E. Merrick, "The Flute and the Fiddle," MCUM.

14. George E. Merrick, "Our Man Friday," MCUM.

15. "Merrick's Furniture Hauled to Miami by Mules in 1899," *The Miami Daily News*, August 1, 1926

16. *The Miami Metropolis*, January 5, 1900.

17. Ibid.

18. "Twenty-Five Years Since Merrick's Arrival," *Miami Riviera*, November 12, 1926.

19. Peters, *Lemon City*, 245–56.

20. "Twenty-Five Years Since Merrick's Arrival," *Miami Riviera*, November 12, 1926.

21. "Life While Homesteading Gables Told by Mrs. Merrick," *Miami Riviera*, ca. 1930.

22. George E. Merrick, "Guava Ingersoll," MCUM.

23. *South East Florida Homeseeker*, September 1901.

24. George E. Merrick, "Guava Ingersoll," MCUM.

25. "Guavonia School Closes," *The Miami Metropolis*, July 12, 1901.

26. *The Miami Metropolis*, July 5, 1901.

27. *The Miami Metropolis*, March 22, 1901.

28. George E, Merrick, "Romantic Story," MCUM.

29. George E. Merrick, "Big Shots," MCUM.

30. George E. Merrick, "Gunjurs," MCUM.

31. George E. Merrick, "Local Planning Speech," MCUM.

32. George E. Merrick, "Don Juan of Poverty Ridge," MCUM.

33. George E. Merrick, "Men of the Magic Isles," MCUM.

34. Ibid.

35. George E. Merrick, "The Southwind and the Boy," MCUM.

36. Richard L. Merrick, interview, March 25, 1974.

37. *The Miami Metropolis*, July 6, 1901.

38. *The Miami Metropolis*, January 24, 1902.

39. "Plymouth Congregational Church Marks Its 25th Anniversary with Fine Banquet; Special Services Will Be Held Sunday," *The Miami Metropolis*, November 17, 1922.

40. George Merrick, "Althea Merrick," *Pioneer Women of Florida*, MCUM.

41. Mitchell and Ensign, *The Climate of Florida*.

42. George E. Merrick, "The South Wind," MCUM.

43. *Miami Weekly Metropolis*, March 28, 1902.

44. *Miami Weekly Metropolis*, April 4, 1902.

45. Donald C. Gaby, "The Early Years Upriver," *Tequesta* XLVIII (1988): 11–12.

46. *The Miami Metropolis*, April 4, 1902.

47. George E. Merrick, "Okra Sink," MCUM.

48. Ibid.

49. "Twenty-Five Years Since Merrick's Arrival," *Miami Riviera*, November 12, 1926.

50. Ibid.

51. Richard L. Merrick, interview, May 19, 1976.

52. George E. Merrick to Almeda and H.G.G. Fink, letter, ca. 1902, MCUM.

53. Ibid.

54. George E. Merrick, "And They Shall Hear Jezreel," MCUM.

55. Ibid.

56. "Dade County Fair," *The East Coast Florida Homeseeker*, March 1903.

57. George E. Merrick, speech, ca. 1939, MCUM.

58. George E. Merrick, speech, 1926, MCUM.

59. Richard L. Merrick, interview, March 25, 1974.

60. Richard L. Merrick, interview, ca. 1976.

61. George E. Merrick to George Anderson, July 18, 1907, MCUM.

62. George E. Merrick, "The Southwind," MCUM.

63. George E. Merrick, "Colored Counties," MCUM.

Chapter 5. Finding Self

1. George E. Merrick, "Silver Fleece," MCUM.

2. "President William Fremont Blackman and his Administration, 1902–1915," *Rollins College Bulletin* LIV, no. 4 (December 1959): 6–9.

3. Corra Harris, "The Town that Became a University," Reprinted from the *Florida Times Union*, March 15, 1930.

4. *Rollins College Bulletin*, 1907–8.

5. Ibid.

6. S. M. Shelton, "As a Boy He Dreamed of Castles in Spain," *Suniland Magazine*, November 1924, 46.

7. George E. Merrick, "Mother," November 24, 1907, MCUM.

8. George E. Merrick. "Silver Fleece," MCUM.

9. Ibid.

10. Ibid.

11. *The Sandspur*, Winter Park: Rollins College, 1908, 44.

12. George E. Merrick, "Silver Fleece," MCUM.

13. "George E. Merrick Won High Literature Honor," *The Miami Metropolis*, April 3, 1908.

14. Rev. S. G. Merrick to Althea Merrick, August 19, 1907, MCUM.

15. Walter's Park, brochure.

16. *The Miami Metropolis*, July 31, 1908; September 1, 1908; October 9, 1908.

17. George E. Merrick, "The Unattainable," *The Sandspur* XIV, no. 1 (1908): 20–22.

18. "Florida and the Sunny South," The Clyde Line, ca. 1905.

19. Schmidt and Schmidt, *The Haworth Story*, 34–44.

20. Malinda Lester Cleary, "Denman Fink, Dream Coordinator to George Merrick and the Development of Coral Gables, Florida," Master's Thesis: University of Miami, 1996, 3–5.

21. Catalogue New York Law School, 1909.

22. George E. Merrick "A Floridian in Manhattan On Christmas Eve," MCUM.

23. Cleary, "Denmam Fink," 35–36.

24. George E. Merrick, "The Sponger's Delilah," New York: *The Evening Telegram*, February 24, 1910.

25. George E. Merrick, "Big Shots," MCUM.

26. George E. Merrick to "Chaquita" [Zillah "Betsy" Fink], June 2, 1910, MCUM.

27. George E. Merrick, "South Wind and the Boy," MCUM.

28. Ibid.

29. Ibid.

30. Richard Merrick, interview, 1975.

31. "Merrick-Amsden Wedding," *The Miami Metropolis*, September 14, 1910.

32. "Beautiful Afternoon Among the Pines," *The Miami Metropolis*, October 6, 1910.

33. "Rev. S. G. Merrick Died Last Night in Pittsburgh, Pa.," *The Miami Metropolis*, June 17, 1911.

34. "More Grapefruit Ready for Market Going Immediately," *The Miami Metropolis*, October 6, 1911.

35. *The Miami Metropolis*, December 2, 1913.

36. "Merrick-McLendon Realty," *The Miami Metropolis*, October 27, 1913.

37. "150 Crates of Peppers Shipped to the North by the Coral Gables Plantation," *The Miami Metropolis*, January 15, 1913.

38. "Securities Corporation Capital Now $300,000," The *Miami Metropolis*, December 15, 1913.

Chapter 6. Eunice

1. Kent, *The Coconut Grove School in Pioneer Days, 1887–1894*.
2. Until 1919 the accepted spelling was Cocoanut Grove.
3. *The Miami Metropolis* May 15, 1896.
4. *The Miami Metropolis*, November 6, 1896.
5. Eunice Peacock to Flora McFarlane, with side note by Lillian Peacock, June 4, 1903, MCUM.
6. Alfred Peacock to Lillian Peacock, November 7, 1910, MCUM.
7. Letter to Eunice, n.d., no name, MCUM (Eunice saved many of these letters from her many young admirers).
8. John F. Simms to Eunice Peacock, October 8, 1912, MCUM.
9. Blackman, *Miami and Dade County, Florida* 151–52; 117–18; 156–57.
10. "Investments That Pay," *The Miami Herald*, January 7, 1914.
11. "Inviting Suburbs Sell Rapidly," *The Miami Herald*, January 15, 1914.
12. "Grand Auction Sale of Lots in Grapeland," *The Miami Metropolis*, January 8, 1915.
13. "Special Free Train to Coconut Grove," *The Miami Metropolis*, February 23, 1914.
14. "Heights of Riverside To Be Sold At Auction Monday, Next Week," *The Miami Metropolis*, March 21, 1914.
15. "Here's To Our Patrons," *The Miami Metropolis*, March 23, 1914.
16. "30,000 Boxes of Produce from Coral Gables," *The Miami Metropolis*, July 3, 1914.
17. George E. Merrick of S. G. Merrick and Son, "Statement As a Basis For Credit," THE MERCHANTILE AGENCY OF R G DUN & CO., October 1, 1914, MCUM.
18. Katie Miller McLendon to Eunice Peacock, February 2, 1914, MCUM.
19. George Merrick to Eunice Peacock, telegram, June 6, 1914, MCUM.
20. George Merrick to Eunice Peacock, telegram, June 6, 1914, MCUM.
21. George Merrick to Eunice Peacock, telegram, June 10, 1914, MCUM.
22. George Merrick to Eunice Peacock, summer 1914, MCUM.
23. Bazille Brossier to Eunice Peacock, August 2; September 19, 1914, MCUM.
24. George Merrick to Eunice Peacock, summer 1914, MCUM.
25. Ethel Merrick Amsten to Eunice Peacock, n.d., MCUM.
26. Mildred Rhodes to Eunice Peacock, March 10, 1915, MCUM.
27. Joe Ryan to Eunice Peacock, September 28, 1915, MCUM.
28. Zillah "Betsy" Fink to George Merrick, April 22, 1915, MCUM.
29. "Map of Railroad Shops Colored Addition," *The Miami Metropolis*, November 9, 1915.
30. "Fort Dallas Club Ready to Organize," *The Miami Herald*, July 25, 1915.
31. "Merrick Named Commissioner District No. 1," *The Miami Metropolis*, September 27, 1915.
32. "Hope Much From George Merrick," *The Miami Metropolis*, October 1, 1915.
33. "Miss Peacock and George E. Merrick Were Married On Saturday Evening," *The Miami Metropolis*, February 7, 1916.

34. "Central Floridians Building 'Another Coral Gables' on Sands of Cape," Orlando: *Sentinel Star*, April 3, 1949.

35. George Merrick to Eunice Merrick, telegram, July 14, 1916, MCUM.

36. George Merrick to Eunice Merrick, telegram, July 18, 20, 1916.

37. "Broke Ground for New Negro School," *The Miami Herald*, August 22, 1916; "Campaign On to Help Miami Negro School," *The Miami Herald*, March 15, 1916; "Immediate Construction of Negro Industrial School," *The Miami Herald*, March 26, 1916.

38. "Rev. James Bolton Shot Down in Cold Blood by Frantic Negro," *The Miami Herald*, December 12, 1916.

39. Dade County Florida Commission Minutes, October 4, 1915–December 24, 1916.

40. "$1200 Cash Is Offer Refused for First Car of Vegetables Grown in Dade," *The Miami Metropolis*, November 21, 1916.

41. "Great Year for the Realty Securities Corp," *The Miami Herald* December 31, 1916.

Chapter 7. The Dress Rehearsal

1. Walter DeGarmo, "The Deering Estate Influence on City Beauty," *Miami Daily News*, December 10, 1933.

2. George Merrick, "Plymouth Homecoming," May 26, 1941, MCUM.

3. Ibid.

4. "Happy Harwood Appeals to Many," *The Miami Herald*, January 21, 1917; "Swastika Park," *The Miami Metropolis* March 22, 1917.

5. Clifton Benson, "George E. Merrick Auto Party: May–June 1917," MCUM.

6. George Merrick to Eunice Merrick, telegram, June 6, 1917; July 27, 1917; August 4, 1917, MCUM.

7. Joe Ryan to Eunice Merrick, June 18, 1917.

8. Arva Moore Parks, "The History of Coconut Grove, Florida," Master's Thesis: University of Miami, 1971.

9. "War Camp Community Service Entertain Naval Air Station at Coral Gables Plantation," *The Miami Herald*, August 22, 1918.

10. George Merrick, "Valentine to an Island Love," February 14, 1918, MCUM.

11. H. H. Hamilton to George Edgar Merrick, August 1, 1918, MCUM.

12. "George E. Merrick Will Devote Most of Time to Grove," *The Miami Metropolis*, December 14, 1918.

13. "The Great Auction Sale at Riverside, The Beauty Spot," *The Miami Metropolis*, March 15, 1919.

14. George E. Merrick, "Wants It to Stay," *The Miami Herald* January 19, 1919.

15. F. M. Hudson, "The Dinner Key Station," *The Miami Metropolis*, January 20, 1919.

16. "Be a Man or a Mouse," *The Miami Herald*, January 20, 1919.

17. George Merrick to Eunice Merrick, August 3, 1919, MCUM.

18. George Merrick to Eunice Merrick, summer 1919, MCUM.

19. George Merrick to Eunice Merrick, summer 1919, MCUM.

20. George Merrick to Eunice Merrick, telegram, August 22, 1919, MCUM.

21. "South Bay Estates," *The Miami Herald*, February 25, 1920.

22. "North Miami Estates Lots Are In Demand," *The Miami Herald*, January 1, 1920.

23. "The Auction Sensation of the 1920 Season," *The Miami Herald* March 14, 1920.

24. "GEM," *The Miami Metropolis*, January 19, 1920.

25. "Illustrations Painted for Merrick's Poetry," *The Miami Metropolis*, May 29, 1920.

26. "Miami Rambles," *The Miami Metropolis* January 5, 1921.

27. Emma P. (Mrs. T. O.) Wilson to George Merrick, January 26, 1921, MCUM.

28. Florence P. Haden to George E. Merrick, January 27, 1921, MCUM.

29. George E. Merrick to Marjory S. Douglas, September 28, 1920, MCUM.

30. "Most Stupendous Auction," *The Miami Metropolis*, December 10, 1920.

31. "Investors in Real Estate Get Idea," *The Miami Herald*, February 11, 1921.

32. "Airplane Stunts Draw Crowds to Lot Auction," *The Miami Herald*, March 30, 1921; "Auto to Plane Change Made," *The Miami Herald*, April 1, 1921.

33. "George E. Merrick Views His Lots From Air," *The Miami Herald*, April 3, 1921.

Chapter 8. From Dream to Reality

1. "Quarter Million in Developing New Subdivision," *The Miami Metropolis*, April 16, 1921.

2. James Hay Jr. "The Biggest Builder in the World," unpublished manuscript, ca, 1925, MCUM.

3. "Quarter Million In Developing New Subdivision," *The Miami Metropolis*, April 16, 1921.

4. Samuel Howe, "Town Planning on a Large Scale," *House Beautiful*, October 1914, 129–36.

5. Stilgoe, *Borderland: Origins of the American Suburb, 1820–1939* 258–59.

6. "Merrick's Romantic Story," *MCUM*.

7. Bruce E. Lynch, "Shaker Heights: The Ambient Vision of the Suburb," Master's Thesis: University of Illinois, 1978.

8. Walter Chambers, "Merrick's Romantic Story of Great Coral Gables Development," *Florida Times Union* June 28, 1925.

9. "Prominent Artist Here Visiting Relatives," *The Miami Herald*, February 14, 1920.

10. Cleary, "Denmam Fink," 14–22.

11. Denman Fink, "Castles in Spain Made Real," *The Miami Herald*, November 19, 1921.

12. As quoted in Ashley, *George Merrick and Coral Gables, Florida*, 24.

13. "Personal Mention," *The Miami Herald*, February 29, 1920.

14. Mizner, *The Florida Architecture of Addison Mizner*, xii–xiii.

15. John Irwin Bright, "A Preliminary Report for Coconut Grove, Florida," Philadelphia, 1920.

16. Dade County Deed Book 35, 441–45.

17. Debbie Lang, "Button, Frank Morse," Birnbau and Foell, 40–41.

18. "The Best of All Answers to Pessimists," *The Miami Metropolis*, December 2, 1921.

19. Florence Button Coleman, interview, August 1976.

20. "Merrick to Occupy Macinac Building Early Next Month," *The Miami Metropolis* April 16, 1921.

21. Frank M. Button to George E. Merrick, April 18, 1921.

22. Frank M. Button, "Coral Gables," ca. April 1921.

23. Ibid.

24. "Fidelity Deal is Finally Closed," *The Miami Herald*, July 19, 1921.

25. George Merrick to Althea Merrick, July 27, 1921, MCUM.

26. H. George Fink, "Letter to the Editor," Miami: *The Village Post*, December 1967.

27. "Magnificent Building for Public School to be Built at Beach," *The Miami Metropolis*, July 28, 1919.

28. "Complete New Beach School," *The Miami Herald*, September 8, 1920.

29. "Coral Gables is Subdivision Deluxe Just West of the City"; "Coral Gables 'The Master Suburb' Goes on Sale Next November," *The Miami Metropolis*, October 24, 1921.

30. "Coral Gables Miami's Master Suburb," map, October 1921.

31. Ted Semple, interview by Helen Muir, Miami Public Library Oral History Project, February 3, 1966.

32. Frank M. Button, "The Suburb Beautiful," *The Miami Herald*, November 17, 1921.

33. Denman Fink, "Castles in Spain Made Real," *The Miami Herald*, November 19, 1921.

34. Edward E. Dammers, "Thanksgiving Proclamation," *The Miami Herald*, November 20, 1921.

35. H. George Fink, "A Coral Gables Home," *The Miami Herald*, November 22, 1921.

36. Edward E. Dammers, "An Invitation to Realtors," *The Miami Herald*, November 23, 1921.

37. "Pre-Sale Buyers at Coral Gables," *The Miami Herald*, November 26, 1921.

38. "Opening Auction Sales at Coral Gables," *The Miami Herald*, November 26, 1921.

39. "Trolley Project Is Explained by George E. Merrick," *The Miami Herald*, November 28, 1921.

Chapter 9. With Broad Vision and High Ideals

1. "H. George Fink, Sr., 84, Architect of Coral Gables," *The Miami Herald*, April 12, 1975.

2. Laurence Schwab, "Doc Dammers Dream Fulfilled," undated clipping.

3. "More than 5,000 Attend Opening of Coral Gables," *The Miami Metropolis*, November 29, 1921; "Coral Gables Draws Big Crowd on First Day of Opening Sale," *The Miami Herald*, November 30, 1921.

4. Dade County Deed Book 5/10, November 1921.

5. "Plan for Acquisition of Coconut Grove Golf Course Being Considered," clipping, ca. 1921.

6. Betty Burnes Saunders, "Coral Gables: I Remember When," ca. 1976.

7. "100,000 Dollars from Lot Sales for University Fund," *The Miami Herald*, December 18, 1921.

8. J. W. Kuykendall to George Merrick, December 8, 1921, MCUM.

9. "Spirit of Coral Gables is Brought to Flagler Street," clipping, George Fink Scrapbook.

10. "Business Section Planned for Coral Gables Subdivision," *The Miami Metropolis*, January 18, 1922.

11. "New Business Section in Spanish Style for Coral Gables," *The Miami Metropolis*, March 9, 1922.

12. "The Golden Galleon," *The Miami Herald* February 26, 1922.

13. Dade County Deed Book, 5/111.

14. William F. Fishbaugh, "Panorama View of Mabel Cody Circus at the Coral Gables Flying Field," February 12, 1922, Florida Memory.

15. "Flew to Nassau in Big Seaplane," *The Miami Herald*, March 30, 1922.

16. "The New Business Plaza at Coral Gables," *The Miami Herald*, July 23, 1922.

17. "The Coral Gables Home Offer," *The Miami Herald*, October 8, 1922.

18. "Start 50 Homes in Coral Gables: $5,000 Each," *The Miami Herald*, September 1, 1922.

19. Ashley, *George E. Merrick and Coral Gables Florida*, 30–31.

20. Ibid.

21. Margo Ammidown, "Walter DeGarmo: Fantasies in Concrete," *Update* II, no. 4 (February 1984): 3–9; Ellen Caroline Buckley. "Revisiting the Architecture of Walter DeGarmo," Master's Thesis: University of Miami, 2003.

22. "New Miami Beach Congregational Church to be Used for First Time at Sunday Services"; "One of State's Prettiest Churches," *The Miami Herald*, March 13, 1920.

23. "M. Luther Hampton is Leaving Miami for Washington," *The Miami Herald*, March 14, 1918.

24. "Bird's-Eye View of Miami for Advertising," *The Miami Herald*, July 26, 1916.

25. "Miami Country Club to be Opened to the Public First of December," *The Miami Herald*, October 16, 1920.

26. "AN OPEN LETTER Relative to the Proposed Greater Miami," *The Miami Herald*, November 9, 1922.

27. "Annual Banquet is Held by Coral Gables Force," *The Miami Herald*, December 8, 1922.

28. "Miami Entrance to Coral Gables," *The Miami Daily News—Metropolis*, January 1, 1923.

29. "Distinctive Miami Architecture Now a Reality with The *Miami Daily News-Metropolis* January 1, 1923.

30. "Water Tower Combines Beauty with Utility," *The Miami Daily News-Metropolis*, August 27, 1923.

31. Nicholas N. Patricios, PhD, "Phineas Paist and the Architecture of Coral Gables, Florida," *Tequesta* LSIV (1984): 6–13.

32. "Noted Expert to Help Carry Out the Vision of George Merrick," *The Miami Metropolis*, December 18, 1922.

33. Ibid.

34. Ibid.

35. Ibid.

36. "Opening of the Business Section is an Event of Much Importance," *The Miami Metropolis*, January 22, 1923.

37. "College Buildings at Coral Gables to Begin at Once," *The Miami Daily-News Metropolis*, February 12, 1923.

38. George E. Merrick, letter, Dade County School Board Minutes, June 5, 1923.

39. George E. Merrick, "Proposal," Dade County School Board Minutes, June 5, 1923.

40. "New Coral Gables Clubhouse Opens This Week," *The Miami Daily News-Metropolis*, March 12, 1923.

41. "Coral Gables Great 300—House Building Programs Interests Everyone," *The Miami Daily News-Metropolis*, April 6, 1923.

42. "Better Homes Week Proved Big Success at Coral Gables," *The Miami Daily News-Metropolis*, June 11, 1923.

43. "Roofing Tiles Will be Made in Coral Gables," *The Miami Metropolis*, December 18, 1922.

44. "Thousands of Plants Ready to Be Set Out Around Local Homes," *Miami Daily News-Metropolis*, January 15, 1923.

45. "Retail Store Building to Open This Month," *The Miami Daily News-Metropolis* August 6, 1923.

46. "Emergency Hospital Has Been Completed," *The Miami Daily News-Metropolis*, August 20, 1923.

47. "Fifty-room Hotel to Go up Immediately," *The Miami Herald*, September 3, 1923.

48. "Coral Gables Now a Half Mile Nearer Miami," *The Miami Daily News-Metropolis*, September 10, 1923.

49. "Start 40 Dwellings—15 Miles of Streets," *The Miami Herald*, September 24, 1923.

50. "School Registration to Reach 150 Mark," *The Miami Daily News-Metropolis*, October 15, 1923.

51. "Pool at Coral Gables to be Venetian Lake," *The Miami Herald*, September 24, 1923.

52. "Burnes Was Highly Esteemed by Associates in Miami, Florida," *Bridgeport Star*, November 20, 1923.

Chapter 10. Expanding the Vision

1. "Announced Opening of Miami Beach office on Fifth Street," *The Miami Daily News-Metropolis*, December 19, 1923.

2. "Come to Coral Gables by Bus or Boat," *The Miami Daily News*, January 26, 1924.

3. "Many Notable Things Beautify Coral Gables—But Its Greatest Glory Is its Homes," *The Miami Daily News*, June 17, 1924.

4. "Meeting Called to Plan Recreation Club for Coral Gables," *The Miami Daily News-Metropolis*, October 1, 1923.

5. "New Hotel to be Opened on December 10," *The Miami Daily News-Metropolis*, November 19, 1923.

6. "Opening of the Coral Gables Inn Marks Another Forward Stride in Beautiful Suburb's Development," *The Miami Daily News-Metropolis*, December 22, 1923.

7. Frank Bowman Sessa, "Real Estate Expansion and Boom in Miami and Its Environs During the 1920s," PhD Dissertation, Pittsburgh: University of Pittsburgh, 1950, 109.

8. "The Big Douglas Section Opens with Special Inducement for Investors," *The Miami Daily News*, January 6, 1924.

9. "Second Addition to Douglas Section," *The Miami Daily News*, January 13, 1924.

10. "Coral Gables Is to Have $125,000 Hotel," *The Miami Daily News*, February 16, 1924.

11. "Preparation Are Being Made for Gables Esplanade," *The Miami Daily News*, February 17, 1924.

12. "Country Club Sales Total $1,019,725," *The Miami Daily News*, February 16, 1924.

13. "Denman Fink's Venetian Pool," *The Miami Herald*, March 25, 1924.

14. "Deland News Official Praises Coral Gables After Visiting Suburbs," Reprint of article by A. B. Codrington in the *Deland Daily News* in *The Coral Gables Bulletin*, January 1, 1924.

15. Charles Torrey Simpson, "Making a Home in Lower Florida," *The Miami Daily News*, June 26, 1924.

16. "Spanish-Type is an Abused Term Says Patterson," *The Miami Daily News*, July 19, 1924.

17. Shelton, "As a Boy He Dreamed of Castles in Spain."

18. "Five Presses Installed at Parker Plant," *The Miami Daily News-Metropolis*, December 3, 1923.

19. "New Home of New York Decorating Company," *The Miami Daily News*, March 24, 1924.

20. "Construction of Bank and Post Office Is Progressing" *The Miami Daily News*, March 17, 1924.

21. "New Administration Building by DeGarmo and Paist," *The Miami Daily News*, June 4, 1924.

22. "Sales Reach Seven Million," *The Miami Daily News*, April 14, 1924.

23. "Largest Home at the Gables for DeLong," *The Miami Daily News*, August 28, 1924.

24. "Work Started Monday on Twelve New Residences," *The Miami Daily News*, January 21, 1924.

25. "Will Remodel Gables Office," *The Miami Daily News*, May 20, 1924.

26. Rhodes MacPhail, "Composite of European Designs Predominates in American Buildings," *Miami Tribune*, October 12, 1924.

27. MacPhail, "Miami Homes to Lure Future Artists," *Miami Tribune*, October 19, 1924.

28. Walter DeGarmo, "Deering Estate."

29. "The Story of Coral Gables," *The National Builder*, (October 1924): 36–57.

30. Kenneth Roberts, "Florida Loafing," *The Saturday Evening Post*, May 17, 1924.

31. "New Club House for Coral Gables Country Club," *The Miami Daily News*, July 30, 1924.

32. "Coral Gables Comes to Flagler Street," *The Miami Daily News*, August 8, 1924.

33. "The New Crafts Section Gives Double Assurance of Profit," *The Miami Daily News*, November 17, 1924.

34. "We Doff Our Hats," *The Miami Daily News*, November 14, 1924.

35. "Ten Million to be Expended on the Miami Hotel," *The Miami Daily News*, November 26, 1924.

Chapter 11. 1925: Building a City

1. "Boom, Boom, Boom," *The Miami Daily News*, January 15, 1925.

2. "Millions of Capital Drawn to Miami," *The New York Times*, March 15, 1925.

3. *The Coral Gablesgram*, December 1924.

4. Ibid.

5. "I Have Doubled My Money on Miami Real Estate Bryan Tells Audience," *The Miami Daily News*, January 11, 1925.

6. "The Glory of Italian Renaissance Blends with a Notable Achievement," *The Miami Daily News*, January 18, 1925.

7. Allen, *Only Yesterday*, 226.

8. Weigall, *Boom in Florida*, 34.

9. Ballinger, *Miami Millions*, 97.

10. Ballinger, *Miami Millions*, 98.

11. As quoted in Ballinger, *Miami Millions* 97.

12. "New Coral Gables Office to Embody Best in Architecture," *The Miami Daily News*, December 21, 1924.

13. George E, Merrick, speech, n.d., MCUM.

14. "Merrick to Spend $100,000,000," *The Miami Daily News*, March 3, 1925.

15. "Vision," *The Miami Daily News*, March 16, 1925.

16. Fox, *The Truth About Florida*, 220.

17. Dade County School Board Minutes, January 20, 1926.

18. "Official Signed Statement of George E. Merrick Regarding Coral Gables and Greater Miami," *The Miami Herald*, April 30, 1925.

19. City of Coral Gables, Minute Book One, May 1, 1925.

20. "Bit of Spain in Gotham," clipping, n.d., George Fink Scrapbook.

21. "Atlanta Offices of Coral Gables Officially Opened," *Atlanta Constitution*, May 31, 1925.

22. Tebeau, *The University of Miami: A Golden Anniversary History*, 1–10.

23. W. E. Walsh, "Founding the University of Miami," unpublished manuscript, University of Miami Archives.

24. "Special Section: University of Miami," *The Miami Daily News*, June 3, 1925.

25. "Dolled Up," *The Coral Gables Bulletin* III, no. 6 (June 1925).

26. "Widely Known Newspaper Man Heads Coral Gables Publicity," *The Miami Daily News*, August 16, 1925.

27. Dade County School Board Minutes, June 2, 1925.

28. Dade County School Board Minutes, May 27; July 14, 1925.

29. "Sixty Costly Homes Will be Erected at Coral Gables," *Atlanta Constitution*, July 23, 1925.

30. "Meyers Y. Cooper Company of Cincinnati $7,000,000 in Homes," *The Miami Daily News*, August 6, 1925.

31. "A Gateway to Old Spain," *The Miami Daily News*, August 9, 1925.

32. "Coral Gables Arranges for Shopping Area," *The Miami Daily News*, August 23, 1925.

33. "Gables Hotel to Open Doors About December 1," *The Miami Daily News*, August 30, 1925.

34. "Bowman Here on Visit," *The Miami Herald*, September 24, 1925.

35. "Coral Gables Hotel to Have Real Gondolas," *The Miami Daily News*, September 26, 1925.

36. "Governor Martin Sees Plot to Hit Florida," *The New York Times*, October 10, 1925.

37. Ballinger, *Miami Millions*, 127–29.

38. "Defends Florida's Boom," *The New York Times*, November 4, 1925.

39. "Coral Gables Reviews Year's Achievements," *The Miami Daily News*, December 30, 1925.

40. Weigall, *Boom in Florida*, 160.

Chapter 12. New Questions

1. George Merrick, "High Olympus," unpublished, hand-written ms. ca. 1926. This third-person recollection illuminates thoughts and feelings of George Merrick that are not found in any other of his writing.

2. Ibid.

3. Ibid.

4. Ibid.

5. *The Miami Daily News*, January 15, 1926.

6. Merrick, "High Olympus."

7. Ibid.

8. Ibid.

9. As quoted in Frank Sessa, "Miami in 1926," *Tequesta* XVI (1956): 27.

10. Cornelius Vanderbilt Jr., clipping, *Illustrated Daily Tab*, ca. June 1926.

11. "The Towers," *The Miami Herald*, April 14, 1926.

12. "Two Styles Blend in Church Edifice," *Miami Riviera*, January 22, 1926.

13. "Clippinger Building Italian Houses of Unusual Distinction of Design," *Miami Riviera*, May 7, 1926.

14. "Tent City Nearing 500 Population Mark Is Forced to Add Another Canvassed Street," *Miami Riviera*, January 30, 1926.

15. "Well Known Writer Gives Banquet Impression," *Miami Riviera*, May 7, 1926.

16. "Thirteen Hundred Boosters Pledge Loyalty to the City," *Miami Riviera*, May 21, 1926.

17. "Plans Advance at University," *Miami Riviera*, June 18, 1926.

18. "Time will Build the University," *Miami Riviera*, May 28, 1926.

19. "New Financing Deal for Coral Gables," *The New York Times*, July 13, 1926.

20. Reardon, *Florida Hurricane and Disaster*, 8.

21. Reardon, *Florida Hurricane and Disaster*, 4–11.

22. George E. Merrick. "A Personal Statement From Geo. E. Merrick," Coral Gables, privately printed, October 30, 1926.

23. George E. Merrick, "Coral Gables Today," The Coral Gables Corporation, November 15, 1926.

24. George E. Merrick, "Coral Gables: The Miami Riviera," The Coral Gables Corporation, November 19, 1926.

25. Packard Lobeck, interview, January 9, 1984.

26. George E. Merrick, "Twinkle, Twinkle Little Star," MCUM.

27. George E. Merrick, "Plymouth Homecoming," speech, December 6, 1936, MCUM.

28. "Progress Week," *The Miami Herald*, November 27, 1926.

29. "Progress Weeks Ends in Anniversary Ball," *The Miami Herald*, November 28, 1926.

30. Telfair Knight to George Merrick, telegram, December 20, 1926, MCUM.

31. Clifton Benson to George Merrick, December 5, 1926, MCUM.

Chapter 13. Sustaining an Ideal

1. "Merrick Cites Changed Ideas About Florida," *The Miami Herald*, January 9, 1927.

2. "University of Miami Dance Follows Game," *The Miami Herald*, January 15, 1927.

3. "City's Big Bond Issue Bought by Corporation," *Miami Riviera*, February 11, 1927.

4. "George Merrick to Get Community Cup," *The Miami Herald*, March 30, 1927.

5. E. H. Schuyler to George Merrick, April 1, 1927, MCUM.

6. "Club Hears Mr. Merrick," *Miami Riviera*, April 8, 1927.

7. "Faith in Florida Means Faith in Cora Gables," clipping, May 13, 1927.

8. "Merrick Suggests Extension of City Limits to Property On West; Says Time is Right for Annexation," *Miami Riviera*, April 22, 1927.

9. Isabelle Stone, "Dutch South Africa Moves to Coral Gables," *The Miami Herald*, May 1, 1927.

10. "Chinese Architecture Used Effectively Here," *The Miami Herald*, May 15, 1927.

11. "Coral Gables Starts Suits on Delinquents," *The Miami Herald*, April 9, 1927.

12. "The Key Note of Coral Gables," *Miami Riviera*, April 8, 1927.

13. "Merrick Suggests Everyone Get Practical," *Miami Riviera*, July 22, 1927.

14. "Knight Outlines Relationship Between City and Corporation to League of Women Voters," *Miami Riviera*, September 16, 1927.

15. Bowman F. Ashe, President's Papers, 1927, University of Miami Archives.

16. "Unit of Catholic Church Started This Week," *Miami Riviera*, August 5, 1927.

17. "Editors a Word with You," *The Miami Daily News*, January 6, 1928.

18. "Let's Be On Our Way," *The Miami Daily News*, February 7, 1928.

19. "Merrick Announces Refinancing Project," *Miami Riviera*, February 17, 1928.

20. Ibid.

21. "Support is Given Plan," *Miami Riviera*, February 24, 1928.

22. "Producing and Conserving Boards to Administer Business of Coral Gables Corporation Under Refinancing Plan," *Miami Riviera*, March 23, 1928.

23. "Vast Building Project Awaits Completion of Refinancing Program," *Miami Riviera*, March 23, 1928.

24. George E. Merrick to "Friend," March 30, 1928, MCUM.

25. "Bitter Attach on Present Administration Launched in Citizen League Talks," *Miami Riviera*, April 20, 1928.

26. "Editorial," *Miami Riviera*, April 20, 1928.

27. George E. Merrick to Fellow Citizens, April 21, 1928, MCUM.

28. "Merrick Fights Gables Fathers on Ouster Vote," *The Miami Daily News*, June 6, 1928.

29. "Gables Board Splits Evenly Upon Merrick," *The Miami Daily News*, June 13, 1928.

Chapter 14. The Long Road Back

1. George Merrick, "Why I Have Faith," speech to Advertising Club, February 27, 1938, MCUM.

2. James H. Gilman to George E. Merrick, October 8, 1928, MCUM.

3. "Tropic Trees for Roads: Merrick Gift a Boon," *Miami Riviera*, March 8, 1929.

4. "Coral Gables Refinanced by Bank Group," *The Miami Herald*, March 10, 1929.

5. "Today: A Greater Era Begins," *The Miami Daily News*, March 10, 1929.

6. A. C. Fry, "Says Gables Lacks Vision," *Miami Riviera*, March 15, 1929.

7. Eunice Merrick to George E. Merrick, telegram, August 25, 1930, MCUM.

8. George E. Merrick to Eunice Merrick, August 27, 1930, MCUM.

9. George Merrick, "Mr. Merrick—to Executives—November 12, 1930," MCUM.

10. Ibid.

11. George Merrick, "Caribbee Chain Store Distribution Plan," MCUM.

12. "Daily Excursion to Florida's South Seas," *The Miami Daily News*, December 30, 1930.

13. "Caribbee Tour Carries Many to New Colony," clipping, January 7, 1931.

14. J. H. Gilman to George M. Merrick, March 24, 1931, MCUM.

15. Henry L. Doherty to George E. Merrick, telegram, March 23, 1933, MCUM.

16. George E, Merrick, "Biscayne Society Plan," MCUM.

17. "Coral Gables Honors its Pioneers," *Miami Riviera*, May 4, 1934.

18. George E. Merrick to M. M. Mallory, May 28, 1934, MCUM.

19. George E. Merrick to Henry L. Doherty, November 5, 1934, MCUM.

20. George E. Merrick to Clifton Benson, October 8, 1934, MCUM.

21. George Merrick Collection, HistoryMiami Box-5, GMHM.

22. "Coral Gables Bond Activity Is Questioned," *Miami Riviera*, September 20, 1935.

23. Clifton D. Benson to George [Merrick], September 15, 1935, MCUM.

24. "Civic Groups and Leaders Heartily Join in Support of Bond Settlement Plan," *Miami Riviera*, January 1, 1937.

25. "Board Orders Zoning Parley," *The Miami Herald*, September 14, 1938.

26. "G. E. Merrick Quits County Zoning Groups," *The Miami Herald*, clipping, ca. September 1938, "Planning Scrapbook," MCUM.

27. George E. Merrick, "Address by George E. Merrick at the dedication of Fairchild Tropical Gardens," March 23, 1938, MCUM.

28. George E. Merrick to Helen Merrick Bond, August 6, 1938, MCUM.

29. George E. Merrick to Clifton D. Benson, January 16, 1939, MCUM.

30. Telfair Knight to George E. Merrick, January 31, 1938, MCUM.

31. George E. Merrick to Telfair Knight, February 18, 1939, MCUM.

32. George E, Merrick to Mr. Williams and Mr. Excelson, "Proposal," August 10, 1939, MCUM.

33. GMHM, Box 12.

34. Medie Lobeck to George Merrick, March 4, 1940, MCUM.

35. "Merrick Cries At Ovation He Is Given," *The Miami Herald*, April 30, 1940.

36. George E. Merrick to All Postal Workers, Box 12, MCHM.

37. "Citizens Row Over Zoning Director," *The Miami Daily News*, January 14, 1941.

38. "Merrick and Fink Urge City to Guard Against Deviation of Ideals," *Miami Riviera*, September 13, 1940.

39. "Unveiling of Federal Mural Scheduled for February 22," *The Miami Daily News*, February 16, 1941.

40. "First Issue Dedicated to our Postmaster," *Tropical Letter Carrier*, Miami: l:l, April, 1941, Box 15, No. 6, MCHM.

41. "Mr. Merrick Is Right Again," *Clerk's Mail*, clipping, Box 12. No. 7, MCHM.

42. George E. Merrick to Mrs. D. C. Maxden, January 23, 1941, MCUM.

43. George E. Merrick to Ethel Merrick Bishop, August 15, 1941, MCUM.

44. George E. Merrick to Our Post Office Family, November 29, 1941, MCHM.

45. J. D. Kuykendall, "Eulogy of G. E. Merrick," *The Miami Herald*, March 29, 1942.

Chapter 15. An Enduring Legacy

1. LaRoue and Uguccioni, *The Biltmore Hotel*, 86–90.

2. Tebeau, *The University of Miami*.

3. "Mrs. Doherty Makes Gift to University," *The Miami Herald*, May 5, 1945.

4. "Miracle Mile is Really a Miracle," *The Miami Daily News*, February 28, 1956.

5. "Gables Must Decide Quaint or Modern," *The Miami Herald*, March 1, 1946.

6. Special Meeting Coral Gables Commission, May 14, 1946; Coral Gables Commission Meeting, May 21, 1946, Scrapbook, Mayor Thomas Mayes, Collection of Marilyn Mayes Hicks.

7. City of Coral Gables, Ordinance No. 505 amending Ordinance 271, June 18, 1946.

8. "University of Miami Constructs World's Most Modern Campus," *The Miami Daily News*, December 10, 1950.

9. In the mid-1950s, the university began selling the City of Coral Gables the last six parcels of land they owned at what they called the North Campus. The city then moved the War Memorial Youth Center to its current site and built the new Coral Gables Library across the street. The city demolished the historic Anastasia Building and the site became part of an enlarged Youth Center.

10. "Merrick's Dream Castles Are Now Real But Their Lines Have Gone Modern," *The Miami Herald*, April 23, 1950.

11. A. H. Sakolsky v. City of Coral Gables, 151 So. 2d 433 (1963) No. 31842.

12. "Manor Misery: Everyone has a Proposition," *The Miami News*, June 8, 1960.

13. "Reprieve At Merrick Manor but Priests Still Must Go," *Coral Gables Times*, July 26, 1962.

14. "Don't Buy Manor, Gables Advised," *The Miami News*, December 16, 1964.

15. "Dade's Pioneer Manor Will Be Restored," *The Miami Herald*, January 13, 1967.

16. "Gables and Federal Officials to Parley Over Biltmore," *Coral Gables Times*, September 15, 1969.

17. "Gables Renews Biltmore Furor *The Miami Herald*, January 8, 1971.

18. Edwin Knight, "Commission Listens, Declines Action on Cocoplum Purchase," *Coral Gables Times*, August 29, 1968.

19. Raul Ramirez, "Cocoplum Wins Approval, but Foes Fight On," *The Miami Herald*, December 16, 1970.

20. Raul Ramirez, "Cocoplum Foes Vow Renewed Battle," *The Miami Herald*, March 25, 1971.

21. Sandra Bentley, "More Trouble at Cocoplum: Council Rescinds Zoning," *Coral Gables Times*, November 16, 1972.

22. Raul Ramirez, "$20-Million price Tag Put on Biltmore Plan," *The Miami Herald*, March 9, 1971.

23. Raul Ramirez, "Biltmore Hotel Sale Contract Ruled illegal by Judge Atkins," *The Miami Herald*, June 15, 1971.

24. City of Coral Gables Ordinance No. 1970, June 17, 1972.

25. "Best is Yet to Be for the Merrick House," *Miami Herald Neighbors*, October 22, 1978.

26. LaRoue and Uguccioni, *The Biltmore Hotel*, 116–17.

27. The Raul E. Valdes-Fauli Archives had been launched in the garage of the Coral Gables Merrick House in 2000 by a donation from Mayor Raul Valdes-Fauli in honor of his father. As a result, the city began to focus on important documents that illuminated its past.

Epilogue

1. Stern, Fishman, and Tilove, *Paradise Planned*, 337.

2. Behar and Culot, eds. *Coral Gables: An American Garden City.*

3. Marjory Stoneman Douglas, *Coral Gables Miami Riviera*, 8.

The first advertisement for Coral Gables, November 1921. Author's collection.

Bibliography

Allen, Frederick Lewis. *Only Yesterday*. New York: Harper & Brothers, 1931.

Apple, Lindsey, Frederick A. Johnston, and Ann Bolton Bevins. *Scott County Kentucky: A History*. Georgetown: Scott County Historical Society, 1993.

Ashley, Kathryne B. *George E. Merrick and Coral Gables Florida*. Coral Gables: Crystal Bay Publishers, 1985.

Ballinger, Kenneth. *Miami Millions*. Miami: Franklin Press, 1936.

Beach, Rex. *The Miracle of Coral Gables*. New York: Currier & Harford, 1926.

Behar, Robert M., and Maurice Culot, eds. *Coral Gables: An American Garden City*. Paris: Editions Norma, 1997.

Biribau, Charles A., and Stephanie S. Foell, eds. *Shaping the American Landscape*. Charlottesville: University of Virginia Press, 2009.

Bittinger, Emmert F. *Allegheny Passage: Churches and Families of Western Maryland and Virginia, Church of the Brethren 1752–1990*. 4th ed. Camden, Maine: Penobscot Press, 1990.

Blackman, E. V. *Miami and Dade County, Florida*. Miami: Victor Rainbolt, 1921.

Blassingame, Wyatt. *The Golden Geyser*. Garden City, N.Y.: Doubleday and Company, 1961.

Bosworth, Alfred Squire. *A History of Randolph County, West Virginia*. Baltimore: Clearfield Publishing Company, 2009.

Burns, Ric, James Sanders, and Lisa Ades. *New York: An Illustrated History*. New York: Alfred Knopf, 2005.

Byron, Gilbert Valliant. *St. Michaels: The Town that Fooled the British*. St. Michaels, Md.: St. Mary's Square Museum, 1963.

Clarke, Mary Helm. *Consider Coral Gables*. Coral Gables: Parker Art Printers, 1948.

Coleman, Stephen, and Paddy O'Sullivan. *William Morris and News from Nowhere*. Bideford, Devon: Green Books, 1990.

Cook, Michael L., and Bettie A. Cummings Cook. *Fayette County Kentucky Records 2*, Evansville, Ind.: Cook Publications, 1985.

Cutright, W. B. *History of Upshur County, West Virginia*. Buckhannon, W.Va.: Gilbert, 1907.

Drury, Reverend. A. W. *Life of Otterbein*. Ohio: United Brethren Press House, 1890.

Dykeman, Wilma, and James Stokely. *The Border States: Kentucky, North Carolina, Tennessee, Virginia, and West Virginia*. New York: Time-Life Books, 1968.

Fishman, Robert. *Urban Utopias in the Twentieth Century*. Cambridge: MIT Press, 1982.

Fox, Charles Donald. *The Truth About Florida*. New York: Charles Reward Corp, 1925.

Freeland, Helen C. "George Edgar Merrick." Tequesta II (1942): 1–7.

Geiger, Barbara. *Low Key Genius: O. C. Simonds*. Wilmette, Ill.: Ferme Ornée, 2011.

Hall, Robert W. *Early Landowners of Maryland*. Lewes, Del.: Colonial Roots, ca. 2003–2013.

Houghton, William H., and Celia Y. Houghton, eds. *The First 150 Years: Pilgrim Church, 1844–1944*. Duxbury, Mass.: Privately printed, 1994.

Hunter, Dard. *Papermaking in Pioneer America*. Philadelphia: University of Pennsylvania Press, 1952.

Ingraham, Prentiss. *Land of Legendary Lore*. Easton, Md.: Gazette Publication House, 1898.

Johnson, Charles Albert. *The Frontier Camp Meeting: Religion's Harvest Time*. Dallas: Southern Methodist University Press, 1955.

Kazin, Michael. *A Godly Hero: The Life of William Jennings Bryan*. New York: Alfred A. Knopf, 2006.

Kent, Gertrude. *The Coconut Grove School in Pioneer Days, 1887–1894*. Coral Gables: Privately printed, 1972.

Klaus, Susan L. *A Modern Arcadia: Frank Law Olmsted, Jr. and the Plan for Forest Hills Gardens*. Amherst: University of Massachusetts Press, 2002.

Knittle, Walter Allen, PhD. *Early 18th Century Palatine Emigration*. Baltimore: Genealogical Publishing Company, 1985.

Lang, Michael A. *Designing Utopia*. Montreal: Black Rose Books, 1999.

Laroue, Samuel D., and Ellen J. Uguccioni. *The Biltmore Hotel: An Enduring Legacy*. Miami: Centennial Press, 2002.

Leonard, R. B. *Bound to Serve: Indentured Children*. St. Michaels: R. B. Leonard, 1983.

Lombard, Joanna. "Lecture on The Legacy of Frank Button." Coral Gables: Coral Gables Museum, May 2, 2012.

Long, E. Waldo. *The Story of Duxbury*. Duxbury, Mass.: Duxbury Tercentary Committee, 1937.

Lorant, Stefan. *Pittsburgh: The Story of an American City*. Garden City, N.Y.: Doubleday, 1964.

Mangus, Becky, ed. *Druid Hill Park Revisited*. Baltimore: Friends of Druid Hill Park, 1995.

McIver, Stuart B. *The Greatest Sale on Earth*. Miami: E. A. Seeman, 1980.

McWhorter, Lucullus Virgil. *The Border Settlers of Northwestern Virginia from 1768–1795*. Hamilton, Ohio: Republican Publishing Company, 1915.

Millas, Aristides J., and Ellen J. Uguccioni. *Coral Gables, Miami Riviera: An Architectural Guide*. Miami: Dade Heritage Trust, 2003.

Mitchell, A. J., and M. R. Ensign. *The Climate of Florida*. Gainesville: Agricultural Experiment Station, 1928.

Mizner, Addison. 1928. *The Florida Architecture of Addison Mizner*. Republication of 1928 edition by William Hepburn, Inc. Mineola, N.Y.: Dover, 1992.

Moore, Mary T. *Coral Gables History*. Coral Gables: Chamber of Commerce, 1950.

Muir, Helen. *Miami, U.S.A.: Expanded Edition*. Gainesville: University Press of Florida, 2000.

———. *The Biltmore: Beacon for Miami*. Miami: Pickering Press, 1987.

New York an Illustrated History. New York: Alfred Knopf, 2005.

Nolan, David. *Fifty Feet in Paradise*. New York: Harcourt Brace Jovanovich, 1984.

Nolan, John. *New Towns for Old* [reprint of 1927 edition]. Amherst: University of Massachusetts Press, 2005.

Olson, Sherry H. *The Building of an American City*. Baltimore: Johns Hopkins University Press, 1980.

Parks, Arva Moore. *George Merrick's Coral Gables: "Where Your Castles in Spain are Made Real."* Miami: Centennial Press, 2006.

———. *Pathway to Greatness*. Coral Gables: University of Miami, 2001.

Patricios, Nicholas N. *Building Marvelous Miami*. Gainesville: University Press of Florida, 1994.

Perrine, William Henry. *History of Bourbon, Scott, Harrison and Nicholas Counties*. Chicago: O. L. Baskin and Company, 1892.

Peters, Thelma. *Lemon City*. Miami: Banyan Books, 1976.

Peterson, Jon A. *The Birth of City Planning in the United States, 1840–1917*. Baltimore: Johns Hopkins University Press, 2003.

Preston, Dickson J. *Talbot: A History*. Centreville, Md.: Tidewater Publisher, 1983.

Reardon, L. F. *Florida Hurricane and Disaster, 1926*. Miami: Miami Publishing Company, 1926.

Rosenberg, John D., ed. *The Genius of John Ruskin*. Charlottesville: University Press of Virginia, 2000.

Roster of Ohio Soldiers in the War of 1812. Ohio Adjutant General's Office, 1916.

Roy, Joaquin. *The Streets of Coral Gables: Their Names and Their Meanings*. Coral Gables: Ideas '92 Publications, University of Miami, 1989.

Schmidt, Rachel, and Frederick W. Schmidt. *The Haworth Story*. Haworth, N.J.: Privately printed, 1956.

Schnildknecht, C. E. *Monocacy and Catoctin*. Westminster, Md.: Family Line Publications, 1989.

Spencer, Jack T., and Edith Wooley Spencer. *The Spencers of the Great Migration*. Vol.1. Baltimore: Gateway Press, 1997.

Standiford, Les. *Coral Gables: The City Beautiful Story*. Coral Gables: Coral Gables Chamber of Commerce, 1998.

Stern, Robert A. M., David Fishman, and Jacob Tilove. *Paradise Planned: The Garden Suburb and the Modern City*. New York: Monacelli Press, 2013.

Stern, Robert A. M., and John Massengale. *The Anglo-American Suburb*. London: Architectural Design, 1981.

Stilgoe, John R. *Borderland: Origins of the American Suburb: 1820–1939*. New Haven: Yale University Press, 1988.

Strassburger, Ralph Beaver. *Pennsylvania German Pioneers*. Norristown: Pennsylvania German Society, 1934.

Stuart, John A., and John F. Stack Jr., eds. *The New Deal in South Florida*. Gainesville: University Press of Florida, 2008.

Tebeau, Charlton W. *The University of Miami: A Golden Anniversary History, 1926–1976*. Coral Gables: University of Miami Press, 1976.

Tilghman, Oswald. *History of Talbot County, Maryland, 1661–1861*. Baltimore: Williams & Wilkins, 1915.

Toomey, Daniel Carroll. *The Civil War in Maryland*. Baltimore: Toomey, 1983.

Tracy, Grace L., and John P. Dern. *Pioneers of Old Monocacy: Early Settlement of Frederick County, Maryland, 1721–1743*. Baltimore: Genealogical Publishing Company, 1987.

Uguccioni, Ellen J. *Mediterranean Architectural Style Guide: Illustrating the Principles of Design Associated with Coral Gables Mediterranean Architectural Style*. Coral Gables: City of Coral Gables Planning Department, 1987.

Wallace, Paul A. W. *Lebanon Valley College: A Centennial History*. Granville: Lebanon Valley College, 1966.

Weaver, Bishop J. *The Life of Rev. Philip William Otterbein*. Dayton, Ohio: United Brethren Publishing House, 1890.

Weigall, T. H. *Boom in Florida*. London: John Lane the Bodley Head, 1931.

Whitehorne, Joseph A. *The Battle for Baltimore, 1814*. Baltimore: Nautical and Aviation Publishing Company of America, 1997.

Wilkins, Woodrow W. "Coral Gables: 1920s New Town." *Historic Preservation* 30, no. 1 (January-March 1978): 6–9.

Wilson, William H. *The City Beautiful Movement*. Baltimore: Johns Hopkins University Press, 1989.

Winsor, Justin. *History of the Town of Duxbury*. Boston: Crosby & Nichols, 1849.

Withers, Alexander S. *Chronicles of Border Warfare*. Bowie, Md.: Heritage Books, 1993.

Wright, F. Edward, *Maryland Eastern Shore Vital Records*. Annapolis: Maryland State Archives, n.d.

———. *Maryland Eastern Shore Newspaper Abstracts*. Bowie, Md.: Heritage Books, 1981.

Coral Gables Promotional Booklets, 1922–1927

"Biscayne Bay Section." Coral Gables: Coral Gables Corporation, ca. 1925.

"Coral Gables: American's Finest Suburb." Coral Gables: Coral Gables Corporation, ca. 1925.

"Coral Gables: Its Advantages for Good Living, for Healthful Recreation, for the Enjoyment of Rest or Vacation, or for Profitable Business or Industry." Coral Gables: Coral Gables Chamber of Commerce, 1927.

"Coral Gables Facts." Coral Gables: Parker Art Printing, January 7, 1927.

"Coral Gables, Miami Riviera: 40 miles of Water Front." Coral Gables: Coral Gables Corporation, 1925.

"Coral Gables Today, The Miami Riviera." Coral Gables: Coral Gables Corporation, 1926.

"Coral Gables Homes." Miami: n.p., ca. 1925.

"Coral Gables: Miami's Master Suburb." Miami: Helfty Press, ca. 1923.

Dammers & Burnes. "The Story of Coral Gables." Miami: n.p., ca. 1922.

Douglas, Marjory Stoneman. "Coral Gables: America's Finest Suburb, Miami, Florida." Coral Gables: Parker Art Printers, ca. 1923.

"Italian and Spanish Homes in Coral Gables." Coral Gables: George E. Batcheller, ca. 1927.

Knowles, Vernon. "An Impression of George E. Merrick: Builder of the City of Coral Gables." Coral Gables: n.p., 1925.

Merrick, George E. "Announcing the Opening of the Country Club Section Part One." Coral Gables: George Merrick Company, 1924.

Merrick, George E. "Avenue Obispo, Coral Gables." Coral Gables: George Merrick Company, ca. 1924.

Merrick, George E. "Coral Gables: Florida's Most Beautiful and Finest Developed Suburb at Miami." Coral Gables: George Merrick Company, ca. 1924.

Merrick, George E. "Miami and the Story of its Remarkable Growth: An Interview with George E. Merrick Published by the New York Times." Miami: n.p., 1925.

Merrick, George E. "The Riviera Section and the University of Miami." Coral Gables: Parker Art Printing, 1926.

Merrick, G. E. "The Story of Coral Gables." Coral Gables: Coral Gables Corporation, 1926.

"Miami Home Seekers Guide: Special Coral Gables Supplement." Vol. 1/1. Miami: February 1926.

"Outdoor Fun at Coral Gables." Coral Gables: Parker Art Printing, ca. 1926.

"Progress, Coral Gables." Coral Gables: Coral Gables Corporation, 1926.

"Venetian Casino, Coral Gables." Coral Gables: George Merrick Company, ca. 1924.

Index

Page numbers in *italics* refer to illustrations.

Ashe, Bowman, 267, 286, 288, 301, 311, 342–43

Auctions, 155–58, *159*, 160–62, 314

Automobiles, 111, 123–25

Aviation, 135–36

Awards, 93. *See also* Honors

Backcountry: Coconut Grove, 56; education, 58–59, *64*, 64–65, 68, 69; society, 59–60

Bahamians, 75, 76–77

Baldwin, Charles S. "Jack," 163, 167, 212, 267

Baltimore, Maryland, family history in, 7–8, 11–15

Baltimore City College, 14–15

Banking: development and, 145–46; economy and, 145–46; financial difficulty in, 228; Miami and, 289–90

Batcheller, George E., 279

Bay View House, 103, 104

Beach, Rex, 363

Beauty, 122, 335

Benson, Clifton, 124–26, 130–31, 272, 284, 298, 313, 317–18, 325

Beulah Wesleyan Methodist Church, 247

Biltmore Addition, 277

Biltmore Country Club, 196, 239–40, 241, 346, 352; contstruction of, 211–12; tourism to, 250–51

Biltmore Hotel, 198–99, 237, 262; competition for, 222; construction of, 211–12, 227–28, 233; dignitaries at, 274–75; Doherty purchase of, *309*, 309–10; financial difficulty for, 303, 354; groundbreaking for, 211; home on golf course of, 242–43; office in, 233, 234; opening festivities of, 233–35, 236–37; Palm Fete at, 288–89; preservation of, xvi, 345, 346, 348–49, *349*, 352–53, 354–55, *358*; RFP for, xvi; tourism to, 250–51; World War II impact on, 338–39, *339*

Biltmore Section, Coral Gables, 224, 277

"Binder boys," 205–6, 208

Bindley, John, 122

Bird Road, 151, 277

Biscayne Bay Section, Coral Gables, 208, *209*, 210, 227; advertising for, 230–31;

construction of, 277; sales of, 230–31; vision for, 229–30

Biscayneland, 312–13

Blackman, E. V., 80–81

Blackman, William Freemont, 80–81, 85

Bolton, Eva, 55, 58, 69

Bolton, Rev. James, 69, 130; family history of, 55; home of, 55, 58; in marriage ceremony, 116–17; on Merrick, Solomon Greasley, 97; murder of, 119; in South Florida move, 48–49

"Boom fever," 196, 202

The Border States (Dykeman and Slokely), 16

Bowman, John McEntee, 191, 198–99, 202, 227–28, 236–37, 274, 309–10

Boy Scouts, 249

Bright, James, 180

Bright, John Irwin, 141–42

Brossier, Bazille, 112

Brown, A. Ten Eych, 226

Browning, Elizabeth Barrett, 84, 85

Brumm, Louis, 177

Bruns, Walter W., 202–3

Bryan, William Jennings, 203, 213, 216, 223

Builder's Finance Company, 223

Buildings: Administration Building in, 308–9; in Atlanta, 215; Coral Gables Construction Company, 191; Fink, Henry George's, 158, 206–7; Flagler Street, 206–7, 207; Mackinac Building in, 144; Merrick, 158; Miami, 121, 144, 216, 282, 283, 292; Municipal Building in, 323; New York City, 91, 215; planning and zoning of, 353–54; for sales, 207–8, 210–11, 215–16; uncompleted, 245; WPA, 323

Burdine, John, 144

Burnes, Harry A., 146, 148, 176, 178, 179

Burnham, Daniel, 138, 219

Business: Coral Gables and section for, 145, 161–62, 171, 176, 181, 190, 192, 210, 341–42; father and relationship in, 78; for Fink, Henry, Jr., 20–21; Greasley, Jacob, in, 11–12; illness and, 271–72, 273–74; Mediterranean Ordinance impact on, 357; religion and, 293, 317

Coral Gables City Hall, 214, 282–83, 287, 292

Coral Gables Commission: debt and, 266, 267, 275, 297–98–300–301; illness and expulsion from, 297–98; lawsuits from, 299; preservation and, 347–48, 351–53; recall election, 294–96

Coral Gables Consolidated, Inc., 255–56, 295–96, 301–2

Coral Gables Construction Company, 191

Coral Gables Corporation: advertising from, 231–32, 268; celebration of, 251; Coral Gables and, 266, 267, 275, 300–301, 316–17; debt of, 256, 286, 288, 289, 290–93, 316–17; development by, 230–31, 241–42, 243–44, 266–68, 276–77; financial difficulties for, 254–55, 256, 285, 288, 289, 290–93; public disapprobation for, 266–67, 284, 285–86, 294–95

Coral Gables Country Club, 173–74, 204, 243, 280–82, 323; advertising for, 186; construction of, 211–12, 243; development of, 183, 185–86, 195, 196, 199, 224–25; honors received at, 251, 275–76; hurricane relief efforts at, 263; tourism to, 204, 250–51

Coral Gables Garden Club, 355

Coral Gables Grammar School, 172, 177, 246

Coral Gables Historic Preservation Board, 350–53, 356, 361, 366

Coral Gables Hotel Corporation, 253

Coral Gables Inc., 301–2, 310–11

Coral Gables Inn, 183

Coral Gables Military Academy, 210

Coral Gables Municipal Building, 323

Coral Gables Museum, 356, 357

Coral Gables Plantation: development of, 101, 127, 137; labor force at, 98–99; makeup of, 94–95; management of, 115, 120, 127; naming of, 96

Coral Gables Rapid Transit, 213, 226, 244–45

Coral Gables Riding Academy, 191

Coral Gables Stadium, 234, 250, 251

Coral Gables Theater, 250, 265–66, 267–68, 300

Coral Gables Waterway, 228, 242

Coral Gables Woman's Club, 248–49, 323

Coral Way, 57, 151, 244, 341–42, 355

Coral Way District, 192, 197

Correspondence: of friends on poetry, 132; loneliness in, 117, 126, 130, 149; to wife, 111–12, 117, 126, 129–30, 149

Country Club District: Part One, 185–86; Part Six, 224–25; Part Three and Four, 199

Country Club Prado Entrance, 151, 185, 280

"Crackers," 58–59, 68, 76–77

Crafts Section, 197, 244

Cuba, 133, 139, 305

Cultural organizations. See Civic organizations

Curtiss, Glenn, 180

Cutright, W. R., 19–20

Dade County Commission, 116, 119, 318–19, 321–22

Dade County Planning and Zoning Board, 318–19, 321–22

Dammers, Edward W. "Doc," 110, 128, 128, 146; on advertising, 269–71; Central Miami development of, 204–5; in Coral Gables' auction, 156, 157, 158; in Coral Gables' government, 214, 221, 294–95, 296; in Coral Gables sales, 148, 153, 154, 156, 157, 158, 167, 271

Davis, Eliza, 22

Death: of Bolton, Eva, 69; of Bryan, 223; of Burnes, 179; of Button, 322–23; of Deering, James, 227; of Doherty, 327; family history of early, 6, 334; of father, 97–98; financial difficulty after, 338; of Fink, Henry, Sr., 20; of H.G.G., 95–96; honors after, 336–37, 340; of Kemp, 7; Merrick, Solomon Greasley, and sibling, 14; of Merrick, Daniel (2), 6–7; of mother, 319–20; of Paist, 320–21; of siblings, 46–47, 50–51

Debt: Coral Gables, 266–67, 269, 275, 300–302, 310–12, 319–20, 323, 338; Coral Gables Commission and, 266, 267, 275, 297–98, 300–301; Coral Gables Corporation, 256, 286, 288, 289, 290–93, 316–17; Coral Gables Inc. and, 301–2, 310–11; personal, 325, 333; World War II, 334

Family: Coral Gables' vision and, 235–36; in Duxbury, Massachusetts, 42–47, 50; father's death and responsibility in, 97–98; financial difficulty and, 46, 85–86, 145, 299, 325; Gaines, New York, and reception of, 38, 42; illness and, 2, 41, 70–71, 85–86, 97, 303–4; Merrick, Ethel, as leader of, 340, 344; perspective and background of, xviii; poverty of, 40–41; real estate, 47–49, 66, 72; religion for, 39–40, 44; social activities of, 44; South Florida move of, 46–51, 52–56, 60–61, 72; support for, 299, 333; values, 13–14; World War I and support of, 126

Family history, xvii–xviii; of Bolton, James, 55; during Civil War, 11; commerce in, 7–8; early death in, 6, 334; farming in, 9, 18, 22–23; financial hardship in, 8–9; Fink, 16–30, 17, 25, 28, 29; of Kemp, 7; in Maryland, 3–15, 12, 14; Merrick, John, in, 5–6; wife's, 107

Farming: experimental, 315; in family history, 9, 18, 22–23; financial success at, 77, 98, 99; fruit, 47, 48–49, 56, 63–64, 66, 72–73, 74–75, 96–97, 98, 99; at Gregory homestead, 63, 65–66, 72–73, 74–75; homesteading and, 56; work, 85–86

Federal government, 318–19, 323–24

Fernway Park, 127–29

Fewell, Robert and Marian, 357

Fidelity Bank and Trust Company, 145–46

"The Fiesta of the American Tropics" festival, 231, 233–35

Financial difficulty: Biltmore Hotel, 303, 354; Coral Gables, 228, 239, 252–53, 254–57, 266, 286, 295–96, 300–303, 323; Coral Gables Consolidated and, 255–56, 295–96, 301–2; for Coral Gables Corporation, 254–55, 256, 285, 288, 289, 290–93; after death, 338; family, 46, 85–86, 145, 299, 325; in family history, 8–9; illness and, 296–97; of Knight, 325–26; in Miami, 289–90; personal, 325, 327, 333; press on, 255; in sales, 279–80; for University of Miami, 252–54, 257, 283–85,

286, 293–94, 301, 311; weather and, 256–57, 264

Financial success: citrus growing, 77, 98, 99; Coral Gables, 167, 172–73, 183–84, 192–93, 202–3, 208, 210, 211, 225–26; of Coral Gables Plantation, 120; of Fink's Magic Oil, 27–28, 29; of Greasley, Jacob, 10; of H.G.G., 28–29

Financing. See Debt

Fink, Almeda "Medie" Wagy (maternal grandmother), 25; children of, 26; marriage of, 24–25; Pennsylvania for, 26–27; personality and physical attributes of, 25; South Florida arrival of, 71–72

Fink, Althea "Allie" Corilla (mother), 35; as artist, 27, 34–35, 37, 37–38; education of, 33, 34–35; H.G.G.'s visits to, 35; homesickness of, 35; honeymoon of, 37, 37–38; as leader, 34; marriage of, 37, 37–38; Merrick, Solomon Greasley, meeting, 30; Merrick, Solomon Greasley, relationship with, 31, 34, 36–37; in Pennsylvania, 27; personality and physical attributes of, 31; popularity of, 34; siblings and responsibility of, 30. See also Merrick, Althea (mother)

Fink, Denman (maternal uncle), 88, 89; as artist, 89–90, 141, 186, 331–32; in Coral Gables development, 140, 140–41, 146, 149–50, 152, 154, 177–78, 185, 186–87, 187; physical appearance of, 90; poetry illustrations by, 132; support from, 91–92

Fink, Henry (great-grandfather), 21; children of, 22; marriage of, 22; in Ohio, 21; in papermaking, 21–22; as physician, 26; religion for, 22

Fink, Henry, Jr., 19, 20–21

Fink, Henry, Sr., 19, 20

Fink, Henry George: buildings of, 158, 206–7; in Coral Gables' architecture, 146–48, 147, 162, 168–69, 176, 177, 182, 190, 210, 214–15, 220–21; European travel of, 193–94, 195; Mediterranean style of, 193–94, 258–59; Official architect, 193

Fink, Henry George Greatrake (maternal

Mediterranean architecture: Coral Gables, 341, 342; Flagler Street, 206–7, *207*; Ordinance, xvi, 354–55, 357; in South Florida, 194; for studio, 257–58; style of, 193–95, 258–59

Mediterranean Ordinance, xvi, 354–55, 357

Merrick, Althea (mother): in backcountry education, *64*, 64–65; death of, 319–20; depression and efforts of, 71; Gregory homestead for, 61–62; H.G.G.'s death for, 95–96; honors for, 355; marriage of, *37*, 37–38, 86; personality of, 31, 71, 86; preaching by, 41; in recovery from illness, 303–4; religious activities of, 41, 69; social activities of, 69; on South Florida move, 61; University of Miami dedication to, 240–41; work of, 38; writing encouraged by, 45. *See also* Fink, Althea "Allie" Corilla (mother)

Merrick, Charles (brother), 95

Merrick, Charles (paternal grandfather): children of, 10, 14; Civil War and, 11; hardship for, 9; marriage of, 9; religion for, 10, 11, 13–14. *See also* Fink, Henry George Greatrake (maternal grandfather)

Merrick, Daniel, 5

Merrick, Daniel (2), 6–7

Merrick, Ethel (sister), 81, 95, 114, 340, 344

Merrick, Eunice (wife), *118*; on Coral Gables' vision, 343–44; correspondence to, 117, 126, 129–30, 149; financial difficulty after death for, 338; marriage to, *116*, 116–17, 211, 226, 238–39, 242, 272, 273, 289, 299, 303, 304; northern travel of, 117, 124–25, 129, 149, 242; poetry inspired by, 126–27, 130; in preservation, 348–50, *349*, 351–52; religion for, 303; re-marriage of, 340, 343. *See also* Peacock, Eunice Isabella (wife)

Merrick, George. *See specific topics*

Merrick, George E. Incorporated, 314

Merrick, Helen (sister), 95, 325, 333

Merrick, Jane, 5–6

Merrick, John, 5–6

Merrick, Medie (sister), 81, 95, 99, 327

Merrick, Mildred, xvii, xviii

Merrick, Richard (brother), 73–74, 95, 315; as artist, 220, *307*; birth of, 62, *62*, 76; in Caribbee Colonies development, 308; funeral arranged by, 335; in Merrick House restoration, 351–52; in recovery from illness, 303–4

Merrick, Ruth (sister), 46–47, 50–51

Merrick, Solomon, 6–7, 8

Merrick, Solomon Greasley (father), 35, 211; adolescent relationship with, 52; Bolton, Rev. James, on, 97; business relationship with, 78; career desires from, 87; during Civil War, 11; death of, 97–98; depression of, 41, 46, 70–71, 85–86; education of, 14–15, 33, 36–37; family values of, 13–14; Fink, Althea, meeting, 30; Fink, Althea, relationship with, 31, 34, 36–37; on Gregory homestead, 56–58, *57*; H.G.G.'s relationship with, 73–74; honeymoon of, *37*, 37–38; illness of, 2, 70–71, 85–86, 97; marriage of, *37*, 37–38, 86; moral rectitude of, 15; personality of, 65; as preacher, 36, 37–39, 41–42, 69; sibling deaths for, 14; South Florida move for, 47–48; University of Miami dedication to, 240; on writing, 46, 94

Merrick, Susan (paternal grandmother), 9, 10, 11, 13–14. *See also* Fink, Almeda "Medie" Wagy (maternal grandmother)

Merrick House or Manor, 333, 340; preservation of, 344–45, 350–52, *351*, 355; restoration, xvi, 351–52, 355–56

Methodists, 23–24, 28, 29–30

Miami, Florida: architecture, 122–24, *123*, 148, 164–65; banking and, 289–90; buildings in, 121, 144, 216; development, 96–97, 121–24, 152, 195–96, 200, 202–8, 243; downtown, 121–22; early housing in, 53, *54*, 55; financial difficulty in, 289–90; fires in, 60; government in, 227, 282, *283*, 292; mansions, 122; Palm Fete in, 289;

from Doherty, 326; for Fairchild Tropical Garden, 324, *324*–25; for family, 299, 333; from Fink, Denman and Betsy, 91–92; for Jews, 330; for University of Miami, 311, 324; World War I and family, 126. *See also* Fundraising

Swimming pools, Coral Gables, 177–78, 186–87

Tahiti Beach, 241–42, 277
Talbot County, Maryland, 11
The Tallman Hospital, 245, *245*–46, 262–63
Tamiami Trail. *See* Eighth Street (Tamiami Trail)
Tatum brothers, 180
Taylor, Dr. Horace W., 181
Tebbets, M. C., 180–81
Tebeau, Charlton, xv–xvi
Tent City neighborhood, Coral Gables, 248
Time, 109, 317–18
Tobin, Michael, 346
Toledo Street, 57
Tourism: to Coconut Grove, 104; Coral Gables and, 172–73, 184–85, 203–4, 249–51; marketing and, 128, 131–32, 249–50, 276–77; Miami, 121–22, 184–85; to Tahiti Beach, 242
The Towers, 245
Transportation: Coral Gables, 154, 213, *213*, 224, 226, 244–45; Miami, 244–45; press on, 225; to Tahiti Beach, 242
Travel: automobile, 124–26; to Cuba, 133; family, 40; Fink, Henry George, European, 193–94, 195; wife's northern, 117, 124–25, 129, 149, 242
Trenton, New Jersey, 107–8
Tropical Letter Carrier, 336–37
Twelfth Street Manors, 131, 133, *134*, 135

UBC. *See* United Brethren in Christ
Union Congregational Church, 68–69, 122–23
United Brethren in Christ (UBC), 9, 10
University Baptist Church, 246–47
University of Miami: Anastasia Building,

253; architecture, 253, 340–41, 342–43, 349–50, 362–63; in Coral Gables, 171–72, 217, 239–40, 267; dedication of, 239–41, 240; financial difficulty for, 252–54, 257, 283–85, 286, 293–94, 301, 311; fundraising for, 217–18, 241, 252–53, 274, 283–85, 293–94; honors from, 274; involvement in, 301; opening of, 264–65, *265*; Pan-American focus of, 257; preservation involving, 349–50; support for, 311, 324; vision for, 216, 217, 219, 359; weather destruction and, 264–65; World War II impact on, 340–41
Urban parks, 12–13
U.S. Navy, 126, 129

Vacations, 191, 285–86, 295
Vanderbilt, Cornelius, Jr., 241–42
Venetian Pool and Casino, 186–87, 199, 203
Villagers, 350
Villages, 223–24; Chinese, 248, 279; Dutch South African, 279; Florida Pioneer (Santa Maria), 247; French City, 279; French Country, 279; French Normandy, 247; Italian, 225, 248, 279
Vision: of Coral Gables, 137–38, 142, 144–45, 155, 179–80, 229–30, 233, 235–36, 252–53, 276, 285, 302, 326, 338, 343–44, 355, 359, 361, 363; education, 217, 219; for Merrick groves, 91–92; press on, 237, 302; self-identification in, 137–38, 300; South Florida, 73–74, 235; for University of Miami, 217, 219, 359
Vizcaya, 122, 164, 194, 227

Walker, Jane, 5–6. *See also* Merrick, Jane
WCTU. *See* Women's Christian Temperance Union
Wealth, 111. *See also* Financial success
Weather: destruction from, 259–65, 315–17; financial difficulties and, 256–57, 264; hardships with, 69–70, 75, 259–63; relief efforts, 262–63, 264–65, 316; South Florida, 259–62
Weed, Robert Law, 343

ARVA MOORE PARKS—a native Miamian, historian, preservationist, and community leader—has authored, coauthored, edited, or contributed to more than thirty books and documentaries, including the City of Miami's official history: *Miami, The Magic City*. During her six-year tenure as chair of the Coral Gables Preservation Board, she helped preserved some of the city's most important landmarks and established relationships with members of the Merrick family. Widely honored for both her writing and her activism, she was awarded an honorary doctorate by Barry University and was named an Alumna of Outstanding Distinction by both the University of Florida and the University of Miami. She was inducted into the Florida and City of Coral Gables Women's Hall of Fame, and the Coral Gables Chamber of Commerce named her the Robert B. Knight Citizen of the Year and presented her with the first George Merrick Award of Excellence. The Florida Historical Society honored her as the Caroline B. Rossitter "Outstanding Woman in Florida History." She recently spent eighteen months as pro bono acting director and chief curator of the new Coral Gables Museum and two years as chair of the board.